Honolulu, Waikiki & O'ahu

Ned Friary
Glenda Bendure

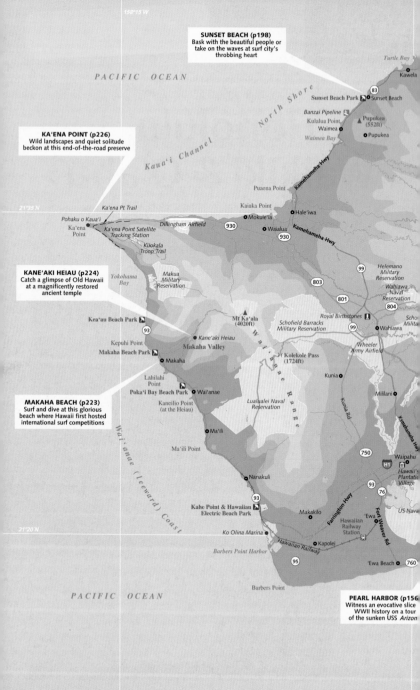

SUNSET BEACH (p198)
Bask with the beautiful people or take on the waves at surf city's throbbing heart

KA'ENA POINT (p226)
Wild landscapes and quiet solitude beckon at this end-of-the-road preserve

KANE'AKI HEIAU (p224)
Catch a glimpse of Old Hawaii at a magnificently restored ancient temple

MAKAHA BEACH (p223)
Surf and dive at this glorious beach where Hawaii first hosted international surf competitions

PEARL HARBOR (p156
Witness an evocative slice WWII history on a tour of the sunken USS *Arizon*

PACIFIC OCEAN

158°15 W

21°35 N

21°20 N

158°15 W

Turtle Bay

Kawela

North Shore

Sunset Beach Park · Sunset Beach

83

Banzai Pipeline
Kulalua Point
Waimea · Pupukea (552ft)

Waimea Bay · Pupukea

Kaua'i Channel

Puaena Point

Kaiaka Point

Mokule'ia · · Hale'iwa

930

Waialua

930

Kamehameha Hwy

Helemano Military Reservation

99

803

Wahiawa Naval Reservation

801

804

Royal Birthstones

Scho Milita

Pohaku o Kaua'i
Ka'ena Point

Ka'ena Pt Trail

Dillingham Airfield

Ka'ena Point Satellite Tracking Station

Kuokala Troop Trail

Yokohama Bay

Makua Military Reservation

Mt Ka'ala (4020ft) ▲

Schofield Barracks Military Reservation

99 · Wahiawa

Wheeler Army Airfield

Kea'au Beach Park

93

Kepuhi Point

Makaha Beach Park

· Kane'aki Heiau

Makaha Valley

· Makaha

Wai'anae Range

Kolekole Pass (1724ft)

Kunia ·

Lahilahi Point

Poka'i Bay Beach Park

· Wai'anae

Kaneilio Point (at the Heiau)

Lualualei Naval Reservation

· Ma'ili

Ma'ili Point

Mililani ·

750

H1

Waipahu

Hawaii's Plantatio Village

93

76

US Nava

· Nanakuli

Wai'anae (leeward) Coast

93

Kahe Point & Hawaiian Electric Beach Park

Ko Olina Marina

Barbers Point Harbor

Makakilo ·

Hawaiian Railway

Hawaiian Railway Station

'Ewa ·

95

Kapolei ·

'Ewa Beach · 760

Barbers Point

PACIFIC OCEAN

Farrington Hwy

Kunia Rd

Fort Weaver Rd

KUALOA REGIONAL PARK (p186)
Head off to this picture-perfect beach for crowd-free picnicking and swimming

BYODO-IN (p182)
Scalloped green mountains, exotic peacocks and red temple gates – a treat for the eyes and spirit

KAILUA BEACH PARK (p177)
Windsurf around the bay or kayak to uninhabited islands at Windward O'ahu's premier playground

NU'UANU PALI LOOKOUT (p174)
Don't miss the breathtaking view from this ridgetop perch

HANAUMA BAY (p166)
Snorkel eye to eye with brilliant fish at this beautiful beach park wrapped in a volcanic crater

'IOLANI PALACE (p74)
Explore the past at the only royal palace in the USA

WAIKIKI (p111)
Hula shows, surf lessons, waterfront dining and sizzling nightlife highlight Hawaii's prime destination

LEGEND

Freeway
Primary
Secondary
Tertiary
Unsealed

0 — 8 km
0 — 4 miles

ELEVATION

4000ft
3000ft
2000ft
1000ft
500ft
0

Destination Honolulu, Waikiki & O'ahu

Graced with sunny beaches and abundant attractions, O'ahu hosts more visitors than any other Hawaiian island. And its cultural center is Honolulu – the very name rolls off the tongue like a gentle wave lapping at the shore. Verdant mountains on one side, sparkling surf on the other, tropical Honolulu is like no other place in the USA. Its multiethnic complexion shines like a rainbow from every street corner – the Thai restaurant next to the sushi shop, the Taoist temple opposite the Christian church. Walk through any neighborhood and a spicy mélange of scents awakens your tastebuds to Honolulu's infinite ethnic cuisines: foodies, get ready to expand your horizons.

Action central is Waikiki, a tourist mecca of sun-drenched beaches and sizzling nightlife. Diners savoring a sunset meal, beachgoers watching seaside hula shows, kids riding outrigger canoes – a cornucopia of delights are all within a sandal-shuffle of each other.

A different world awaits outside the urban enclaves. O'ahu's leeward west coast, largely untouched by tourism, is quintessentially Hawaiian. The rural windward east coast boasts family farms and stellar beaches just waiting to be explored. And at the top of it all is the North Shore – the undisputed world capital of surfing.

O'ahu offers an endless palate of opportunities. Revel in the action at beachside resorts in Waikiki or skip to a cozy B&B in small-town Kailua. Snorkel in glassy waters or hike into a remote rain forest. Or just kick back and spend an afternoon talking story with the locals. The twang of a slack-key guitar, the friendly chatter of islanders – the aloha here is as radiant as the sunshine.

Flowers comprise the Hawaiian lei (p45); necklaces are traditionally made from mokihana berries and maile leaves.

The poignant USS *Arizona* Memorial (p156) at Pearl Harbor, which draws 1.5 million visitors annually.

Pro surfers come from around the globe to master the spectacular barrel waves at Banzai Pipeline (p199), reputed to be the most epic left in the world.

LEE FOSTER

JOHN BO:

Rent a board near beaches like Waikiki (p123), Hale'iwa (p205), Waimea (p202), Kailua (p178) and La'ie (p192).

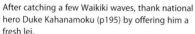

After catching a few Waikiki waves, thank national hero Duke Kahanamoku (p195) by offering him a fresh lei.

The remote and culture-rich Wai'anae Coast (p221) is home to the largest native Hawaiian population on O'ahu.

LINDI

JOHN BORTHWICK

O'ahu is the ultimate ocean-lovers paradise. Watery meccas and activities (p51) are in ample supply; pick a spot and a sport, and jump on in.

The history of surfing was written in Hawaii, and the wave-riding tradition still reigns on O'ahu. See p54 for an expert overview from *Surfer* magazine, replete with the lowdown on top spots.

ANN CECIL

ANN CECIL

The United States Golf Association rated the scenic Ko'olau Golf Course (p184) in Kane'ohe the toughest in the USA

Rural Waimanalo (p169), home to Magnum PI's favorite swimming hole, boasts O'ahu's longest stretch of beach (5.5 miles).

Contents

Regional Map Contents

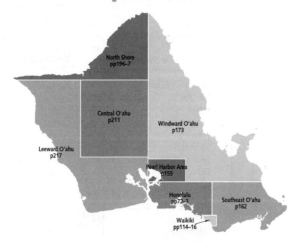

North Shore
pp196–7

Central O'ahu
p211

Windward O'ahu
p173

Leeward O'ahu
p217

Pearl Harbor Area
p155

Honolulu
pp72–3

Southeast O'ahu
p162

Waikiki
pp114–16

The Authors

NED FRIARY & GLENDA BENDURE

Ned and Glenda first set eyes on O'ahu after a stint of teaching English in Japan. Like so many others who come to Hawaii, it was love at first sight. What was intended as a short stopover turned into a year-long stay, exploring each of the Hawaiian Islands, driving the back roads, hiking remote trails and snorkeling hidden coves. Over the years they returned to Hawaii again and again, writing the first five editions of Lonely Planet's *Hawaii*, as well as a *Honolulu* city guide that has morphed into this current *Honolulu, Waikiki & O'ahu* guidebook. Honolulu is their favorite city in the USA – a place they know better than their own hometown. When they're not on the road, Ned and Glenda live on Cape Cod in Massachusetts.

Our O'ahu

As soon as we arrive on O'ahu, we drop off our bags and head to Ala Moana Beach Park (p82) for a long swim, letting the jet lag seep away. Then it's time for one of those inspiring sunsets at nearby Magic Island (p82). Ahh, that's better! Now that we feel at home again, it's off to the surf mecca of the North Shore, where poking around laid-back Hale'iwa (p203) unwinds the clock. Kailua Beach Park (p177) is always high on the itinerary, and a paddle around the bay is de rigueur. A tour of southeast O'ahu reminds us of how wonderfully varied the O'ahu coast is, and small-town Waimanalo (p169) with its unspoiled beaches rekindles our belief that there are indeed corners of 'old Hawaii' left on O'ahu. Our favorite end-of-the-road destination is windswept Ka'ena Point (p226), a place where we've watched dolphins frolic, whales pass and monk seals bask – without seeing another soul in sight.

LONELY PLANET AUTHORS

Why is our travel information the best in the world? It's simple: our authors are independent, dedicated travellers. They don't research using just the Internet or phone, and they don't take freebies in exchange for positive coverage. They travel widely, to all the popular spots and off the beaten track. They personally visit thousands of hotels, restaurants, cafés, bars, galleries, palaces, museums and more – and they take pride in getting all the details right, and telling it how it is. For more, see the authors section on www.lonelyplanet.com.

CONTRIBUTING AUTHORS

Jake Howard wrote the Outdoors chapter's boxed text on surfing (p54). Jake spent his formative years surfing the wild, cold Northern California coast. While going to college and playing water polo at the University of Massachusetts, he spent summers working as an ocean lifeguard in Southern California (where the water is considerably warmer and less sharky). He is currently the associate editor of *Surfer* magazine. Jake resides in San Clemente, California, and surfs as much as he possibly can.

Dr David Goldberg wrote the material from which the Health chapter (p253) was adapted. He completed his training at Columbia-Presbyterian Medical Center in New York City. He is an infectious disease specialist and the editor-in-chief of www.mdtravelhealth.com.

Getting Started

Oʻahu is a tourism-friendly island and most activities don't require reservations before you go. Hotel and car rentals typically work out better with advance planning, but unless you're traveling during the peak season (winter) you can usually get by if you're booking things at the last minute. Oʻahu offers something for every budget, from backpackers to luxury-seekers.

WHEN TO GO

Oʻahu is a great place to visit any time of the year. Although the busiest tourist season is in winter, from mid-December through March, that has more to do with weather *elsewhere,* as many visitors are snowbirds escaping cold winters back home. The weather in Hawaii is agreeable year-round. It's a bit rainier in winter and a bit hotter in summer (June to August), but there are no extremes as cooling trade winds modify the heat throughout the year.

See the Climate Charts (p231) for more information.

Unless you must, it's best to avoid the two-week period surrounding Christmas and New Year's Day as that's the busiest time on the island, with the highest room rates and the most crowded tourist sights. The rest of the year should pose few problems, though it's wise to book your accommodations well in advance if you're arriving in winter. In terms of cost, spring and fall are the slowest times, so you're more likely to find better deals on accommodations and airfares during this period.

Naturally, for certain activities there are peak seasons. For instance, if you are a board surfer, you will find the most awesome waves in winter, whereas if you are a windsurfer, you will find the very best wind conditions in summer. But one advantage with vacationing on Oʻahu is that just about everything, including those activities, can be enjoyed year-round.

COSTS & MONEY

The amount of money you need for your trip to Oʻahu depends on your traveling style. You can get by cheaply by eating plate lunches and staying in hostels. Or you can dine on haute Pacific Rim cuisine, sleep at plush

DON'T LEAVE HOME WITHOUT...

- Your coolest swimsuit.
- Good-quality sunglasses.
- Sunscreen to protect you from that hot tropical sun.
- A snorkel, mask and fins if you plan to spend a lot of time in the water.
- Dive certification cards and logbooks if you're going to take the plunge.
- Driver's license, a passport if necessary and a copy of your hotel reservations.
- A light jacket or sweater for those wind-whipped mountaintops.
- Binoculars for watching dolphins, whales and birds.
- Footwear with good traction for hitting wet trails.
- A flashlight for late-day hikes.
- A good appetite and a sense of adventure.

resorts and rack up huge balances on your American Express card. Most people, however, will opt for the Buddha's 'middle way.'

The airfare to Hawaii is usually one of the heftier parts of the budget – if you're coming from the US, fares can range anywhere from $400 to $800 depending on your departure point and travel dates.

O'ahu boasts a good, inexpensive bus system (p248), so it's possible to get around without a car, but if you want to thoroughly explore you should plan on renting one for at least a few days. Set aside about $65 a day for the car-rental fee, gas and parking.

The Waikiki/Honolulu area has a wide range of accommodations. Other than youth hostels, which have dorm beds for around $20, decent budget accommodations hover around $75. Opt for a cozier middle-class hotel or B&B and you'll be looking at $100 to $200. Luxury beachfront hotels typically begin around $250 but the finest can easily double that. Another option is a condo; they average about $200 a night and have kitchens, so you can cook and save a bundle on food costs.

Because much of Hawaii's food is shipped in, grocery prices are about 25% higher than on the US mainland. Waikiki restaurants typically reflect

HOW MUCH?

Public bus fare $2

Hawaiian plate lunch $5

Haute cuisine dinner for two $125

Local phone call 50¢

Surfing lesson $75

TOP FIVES

O'ahu's Best Beaches
O'ahu has scores of beaches, each with its own personality. Here are five standouts.

- Kailua Beach Park (p177); this beauty is tops for windsurfing and kayaking
- Ala Moana Beach Park (p82); Honolulu's favorite swim
- Sunset Beach (p198); monster surf and bathing beauties
- Malaekahana Beach (p192); ideal for families, bodysurfers and campers
- Hanauma Bay Nature Preserve (p166); O'ahu's year-round snorkeling mecca

Favorite Festivals & Events
O'ahuans love to come out for a good celebration, and there are numerous festivals large and small. For more, see the Festivals & Events sections throughout the book.

- Taste of Honolulu (p96); the city's big foodie event, on the last weekend in June
- Triple Crown of Surfing (p198); the world's top surfing event held on the North Shore in November–December
- King Kamehameha Day (p96); parades, hula shows and music in early June, in honor of Hawaii's first king
- Talk Story Festival (p97); Hawaii's long history of folklore lives on at this festival, in mid-October
- Honolulu Marathon (p97); this megamarathon, on the second Sunday in December, is one of the world's largest

Activities Around the Island
O'ahu has so much to choose from, you could spend a long vacation doing something fun and different every day.

- Surfing; in winter at Waimea Bay (p201), in summer at Waikiki (p123)
- Hiking through the rain forest to Manoa Falls (p91)
- Windsurfing around the bay at Kailua Beach Park (p177)
- Golfing like a PGA pro at Turtle Bay (p197)
- Playing *paniolo* (cowpoke) on a horseback ride (p203)

these higher prices, but food in neighborhood restaurants beyond Waikiki
is good value, with prices comparable to what you'll find on the mainland.
Families can save money by dining at kid-friendly restaurants and by taking advantage of discount coupons in the free tourist magazines, which cut
costs on all sorts of activities.

TRAVEL LITERATURE
Use the long flight to Hawaii to do some illuminating background
reading and bone up on island culture. Forget the clichéd *Hawaii* by
James Michener and instead pick up a copy of *Shoal of Time* by Gavan
Daws – the real authoritative history of the islands and the one used by
Hawaii students.

Part-time O'ahu resident Paul Theroux' *Hotel Honolulu* is a curious
read about a washed-up writer, an aging prostitute and a handful of
semiliterates who call a run-down hotel home. *Paradise News* by David
Lodge tells the humorous story of a former priest who, while paying a
visit to his dying relative in Hawaii, has an affair with a taxi driver, and
discovers the pluses and minuses of this exotic paradise.

For a rare glimpse into the year before the United States annexed Hawaii,
turn the pages of *Hawaii's Story by Hawaii's Queen;* Queen Lili'uokalani's
graceful autobiography was written during the last year of her monarchy
and like the lady herself couldn't be more eloquent. The first book to
recount the plight of Hawaiians from the native Hawaiian perspective, *A
Call for Hawaiian Sovereignty* by Michael Kioni Dudley and Keoni Kealoha
Agard, has been rightly dubbed the 'handbook on Hawaiian sovereignty.'

INTERNET RESOURCES
Alternative Hawaii (www.alternative-hawaii.com) An ecotourism website that promotes,
preserves and perpetuates Hawaiian culture.
City & County of Honolulu (www.co.honolulu.hi.us) Island government website includes
information for travelers.
Hawaii State Vacation Planner (www.hshawaii.com) Everything you need for planning an
aloha vacation.
Hawaii Visitors & Convention Bureau (www.gohawaii.com) The state's official tourism website.
Honolulu Advertiser (www.honoluluadvertiser.com) The state's main daily newspaper.
LonelyPlanet.com (www.lonelyplanet.com) Succinct summaries on traveling to Hawaii and
links to useful web resources.
O'ahu Visitors Bureau (www.visit-oahu.com) Tourist information specific to O'ahu.

Itineraries

CLASSIC ROUTES

HITTING THE HIGHLIGHTS
A Long Weekend

In one long weekend, you can sun on Waikiki Beach, hit the surfing epicenter on the North Shore and sail across Kailua Bay. You'll catch some of the island's finest views along the way. The whole drive is about 90 miles.

Start in **Waikiki** (p111), with a stroll along the beach and a breakfast at one of the oceanfront restaurants. Then join the crowds at Waikiki's Kuhio Beach Park to surf, swim, people-watch and enjoy the sunset hula show.

On day two, head out of town for the **North Shore** (p194). If it's winter, check out the world-class surfing at **Waimea Bay** (p201) and **Sunset Beach** (p198), where waves frequently reach 20ft to 30ft. If it's summer, snorkel with tropical fish over peaceful coral reefs at **Pupukea Beach Park** (p201). In **Hale'iwa** (p203), enjoy a fresh grilled-fish sandwich and pop in to the North Shore Surf & Cultural Museum to see some cool surf memorabilia. Hike to a waterfall at **Waimea Valley Audubon Center** (p202) and visit an ancient Hawaiian temple at **Pu'u O Mahuka Heiau State Monument** (p202).

The next day, take the scenic **Pali Hwy** (p174) drive, stopping at the **Nu'uanu Pali Lookout** (p174). Have lunch in **Kailua** (p180) before continuing on to **Kailua Beach Park** (p177); you can windsurf around the bay or rent a kayak and paddle out to a pristine island. Then continue your loop via southeast O'ahu, poking around the local shops in **Waimanalo** (p169). Make roadside stops to catch the views at **Makapu'u Point** (p168) and the **Halona Blowhole** (p168) before heading back to Waikiki, arriving in time for dinner and drinks on the beach to top off your long weekend.

North Shore
Sunset Beach
Pupukea Beach Park
Pu'u O Mahuka Heiau State Monument
Waimea Bay
Waimea Valley Audubon Center
Hale'iwa
Kailua
Kailua Beach Park
Pali Hwy
Nu'uanu Pali Lookout
Waimanalo
Makapu'u Point
Waikiki
Halona Blowhole

O'AHU TOP TO BOTTOM   Nine Days

Spend your first day exploring **Waikiki** (p111), have fun in the sun, rent a surfboard, catch a hula show and enjoy the night scene. On day two, stroll through **Chinatown** (p80), poke around the markets, slurp noodles with the locals and visit O'ahu's finest botanical garden. The next day head to **downtown Honolulu** (p74), tour history-laden 'Iolani Palace, enjoy the contemporary works at the Hawai'i State Art Museum, then mosey over to Aloha Tower for a fine view and a rockin' night at Kapono's.

On day four, tour southeast O'ahu, stopping to snorkel at **Hanauma Bay** (p166) and windsurf or kayak at **Kailua Beach** (p177). On day five, visit the **USS Arizona Memorial** (p156) at Pearl Harbor – get there early in the morning to beat the crowds – and follow it with a drive along the **Wai'anae Coast** (p221), ending with a swim at **Ko Olina Lagoons** (p218).

Venture up to the North Shore on day six, catching some of the world's top surf action at **Sunset Beach** (p198) and cooling down with a shave ice at **Hale'iwa** (p205). On day seven, make a tour of the Windward Coast, starting with the scenic **Pali Hwy** (p174), dropping by **Byodo-In** (p182) temple and doing a little bodysurfing at **Malaekahana Beach** (p192).

The next day, take your explorations out on the water, perhaps with a boat dive from **Hawai'i Kai** (p165) or a whale-watch cruise from **Kewalo Basin** (p93). Wrap up your last day with a hike to the summit of **Diamond Head** (p163) for a good workout and sweeping city views, then reward yourself with dinner and mai tais on the beach at sunset.

O'ahu is easy to explore on day trips from a single base, heading out in different directions, since no place is more than a 1½-hour drive from Waikiki. This nine-day tour covers about 400 miles and takes in the main island sights.

TAILORED TRIPS

KEIKI HOLIDAY

Keiki (children) love a day at the beach, so what better way to start your trip? At **Kuhio Beach Park** (p118) toddlers can play in the shallows, older kids can take a surfing lesson and the whole family can catch a wave in an outrigger canoe. Wee ones will enjoy getting hands-on friendly with the furry creatures in the petting section of the **Honolulu Zoo** (p122). And who wouldn't want to ogle meandering sharks through a towering window at the **Waikiki Aquarium** (p121)? At **Hanauma Bay** (p166), kids will delight in donning a mask and snorkeling among schools of colorful tropical fish in calm, shallow waters. For a little eye candy on land, stroll the grounds of **Hilton Hawaiian Village** (p132) with its penguin pools – and don't miss the Friday-night fireworks.

Waimea Valley
Audubon Center • Happy Trails
Hawaii
Dillingham Airfield
Dole
Pineapple • Kualoa
Pavilion Ranch • Kualoa Regional
Park
Hilton Hawaiian Village;
Hawaiian Railway Atlantis Submarine;
Society Royal Hawaiian
Hawaiian Waters Bishop Shopping Center
Adventure Park Museum
Sea Life Park
Hawaii Children's Hanauma Bay
Discovery Center; Kuhio Beach Park;
Kewalo Basin; Kapi'olani Park Honolulu Zoo;
Pagoda Restaurant Waikiki Aquarium

The picnic possibilities are endless – if shady green lawns sound good, pick up some burgers and head over to lovely **Kapi'olani Park** (p121). Or take the show on the road to **Kualoa Regional Park** (p186), where the beach, views and picnic facilities are spiced with exploring possibilities. The jeep tour at nearby **Kualoa Ranch** (p186) is great fun – snap a photo of your kids as they peer over the *Jurassic Park* sign used in the movie. The **Waimea Valley Audubon Center** (p202) is ideal for little boots, with short hikes past old Hawaiian homesites and wild peacocks to a cool waterfall with a pool. For a walk with a challenge, set the troops loose in the 'world's largest maze' at the **Dole Pineapple Pavilion** (p213).

OK, even in paradise it sometimes rains, but there's never a reason to get bored. Young kids will find tons of fun at the **Hawaii Children's Discovery Center** (p95) and kids of all ages (yep, that includes you, Dad) will be dazzled by the walk-through volcano at the **Bishop Museum** (p88). Or how about taking home a little aloha? Kids can try their hands at lei making and hula dancing at the **Royal Hawaiian Shopping Center** (p125). For something different on a Sunday afternoon, choo-choo along in an antique train at the **Hawaiian Railway Society** (p218).

If you're in Hawaii during the winter humpback whale season, seeing these awesome creatures on a **Kewalo Basin** (p93) makes for one memorable experience. Of course you won't get so close you'll touch the whales, but in southeast O'ahu kids can jump into a pool and join an Atlantic bottlenosed dolphin at the dolphin encounter program at **Sea Life Park** (p169). And then there's the world of the deep – peer through a porthole on the **Atlantis Submarine** (p124) to see all sorts of cool sights usually reserved for divers.

Water thrills don't stop in the ocean. **Hawaiian Waters Adventure Park** (p219) offers wild rides on all sorts of chutes and slides – some geared for younger kids, others for speed riders. For a fun family breakfast, head for the open-air **Pagoda Restaurant** (p101), which is encircled by a carp pond. Ready to play cowboy and cowgirl? **Happy Trails Hawaii** (p203) offers horseback rides through pastures where *paniolo* (cowpokes) once roamed. And the sky really is the limit with glider rides at **Dillingham Airfield** (p208).

O'AHU OUTDOORS

Welcome to surfer's heaven. Hawaii's the very place surfing got its start
centuries ago and it still attracts the world's best surfers. If you've already
mastered the board, head up to **Sunset Beach** (p198), where the big boys
and girls play. But if you're ready for step one, **Waikiki** (p123) is a fine
place to start, with pros hanging out at the beach kiosks eager to show
you the ropes. Good intermediate surfing can be found at the beaches
in **Hale'iwa** (p203).

Windsurfers flock to **Kailua Beach Park** (p177), where the winds are
consistent and strong, and there are great conditions for all levels from
beginners to pros. If you want to catch a breeze around Waikiki, **Fort
DeRussy Beach** (p123) offers the best action and, like Kailua, rentals are
available right on the beach. And at both beaches novices can readily
take lessons.

Bodysurfers who really know their stuff and want to try the island's
top shorebreaks should head for **Sandy Beach Park** (p168) in southeast
O'ahu and **Makaha Beach** (p223) on the Wai'anae

Coast. If you're not up for such a punishing
break, **Waimanalo Beach Park** (p170) has gentle
shorebreaks that feel more like a massage than
a pounding.

If it's winter, have your snorkeling adventure at **Hanauma Bay** (p166), but if it's summer
the pristine North Shore is the top underwater playground, with **Three Tables** (p201) offering splendid underwater scenery, including
arches, reefs and lots of colorful tropical fish.
To snorkel year-round with sea turtles, head
to **Kuilima Cove** (p196) near the aptly named
Turtle Bay.

Divers, start your engines. If you're into
wrecks, the **Mahi** (p224) off the Wai'anae Coast
is a terrific dive – this 165ft naval vessel was purposely sunk to create an
artificial reef and it's teeming with all sorts of corals, sponges and fish.
For a spectacular shore dive with reefs, lava tubes and ledges, head to
Shark's Cove (p201) on the North Shore.

Kailua Beach Park is the perfect place for kayakers to dip a paddle
into the water. Pack a picnic and make your way over to the bird sanctuary of **Popoi'a Island** (p177), where it will be just you, the birds and a
turquoise sea.

Bird-watchers will want to keep their life lists and binoculars handy.
Native Hawaiian ducks and stilts can be readily spotted at any time
at the **Hamakua Marsh Wildlife Sanctuary** (p178). Or join other birders on
a naturalist-led tour of native waterfowl at the **James Campbell National
Wildlife Refuge** (p193).

Got your boots laced up? For a real jungle experience just outside the
city, hike through lush vegetation and lofty trees to a cascading waterfall
along the **Manoa Falls Trail** (p91). For a quiet, windswept coastal walk past
tidepools, rare shorebirds and basking monk seals, hit the **Ka'ena Point
Trail** (p227) on the remote northwestern tip of the island. Or see gorgeous
ridge-top views and get a glimpse of rare forest birds along the **Wa'ahila
Ridge Trail** (p90).

And finally, for the wildest view of all, head on over to the **Dillingham
Airfield** (p208), where the hottest thing going is the tandem skydive jump
that is on offer.

INDULGENT O'AHU

Start by booking a room overlooking Sans Souci Beach at the elegant **W Honolulu Diamond Head** (p131), Waikiki's most sophisticated boutique hotel. When hunger strikes, let Hawaii's top chef – **Alan Wong's** (p102) – whip you up a gourmet dinner. After dessert, head over to the **Formaggio Wine Bar** (p105) to uncork a bottle of bubbly.

Set one of your evenings aside to enjoy the beachside luau at the historic **Royal Hawaiian Hotel** (p147). For some fun in the sun, how about a round of golf at the championship **Ko Olina Golf Club** (p219). Top that with a visit to the island's top-rated spa, **Ihilani Resort & Spa**

(p220), for a Hawaiian-style ti-leaf wrap or a vigorous *lomilomi* massage that'll soothe both body and soul.

Arrange for a private **chauffeur tour** (p252) to take you on an island circuit ride, enjoying the North Shore's sights and stopping for a horseback ride along the beach at **Turtle Bay Resort** (p197).

Come Sunday, make a reservation for the classiest brunch in Hawaii at **Orchids** (p136), complete with a harp duo and the most indulgent dessert bar you'll ever find. And don't forget to stop by for a drink at **House Without a Key** (p147), where you can watch the former Miss Hawaii hula dance to one of Waikiki's beautiful sunsets.

ARTY O'AHU

The **Hawai'i State Art Museum** (p75) combines a stellar setting with one of the finest collections of any regional museum located in the US – and all of the art has a connection with the islands. The **Gallery Walk** (p96) held on the first Friday of each month brings together artists and art lovers for a self-guided stroll through Honolulu and Chinatown's abundant galleries.

Swing by here to enjoy wine and lunch in the courtyard of the **Honolulu Academy of Arts** (p83) before taking the afternoon to browse the museum's extensive collections. Learn a few words of pidgin at the **Kumu Kahua Theatre** (p106), which is a little gem that showcases works by Hawaiian playwrights. Some of the best contemporary musicians and dancers perform at the **Banyan Veranda** (p146), in the courtyard of the

historic Sheraton Moana Surfrider, and also at the renovated **Hawaii Theatre** (p106), which is located on the edge of downtown Honolulu and Chinatown.

And then there are the festivals. If you happen to be visiting here in July, be sure to treat your tastebuds to the city's finest flavors at the **Taste of Honolulu** (p96), a delicious three-day food event. Should September be your month, check out the **Aloha Festivals Downtown Mele** (p97), when the streets of downtown Honolulu turn into one huge dance scene in honor of King David Kalakaua, who loved a party and revived the hula after decades of missionary suppression.

JOURNEY THROUGH THE PAST

You don't have to be a history buff to be awestruck by the wealth of extraordinary historical sites O'ahu harbors. In fact, the most visited sight in all of the Hawaiian Islands is the **USS Arizona Memorial** (p156), honoring those who died in the Japanese attack on Pearl Harbor.

The fascinating **Bishop Museum** (p88) traces Hawaiians from their origins in Tahiti to the 19th-century monarchy on O'ahu with precious, one-of-a-kind artifacts. And don't miss a tour of regal **'Iolani Palace** (p74), where Hawaiian kings and queens held court from 1882 until the monarchy's overthrow in 1893. For a glimpse at the plantation era that gave Hawaii its multicultural face, plan to visit **Hawaii's Plantation Village** (p218).

The **Hawai'i Maritime Center** (p80) evocatively covers all things seaworthy, from the discovery of Hawaii by the Polynesians and later Captain Cook, to the advent of tourism when travel was by steamship. The nearby **Aloha Tower** (p79) is a delightful Art Deco relic of that period.

Ancient Hawaiian sites that belong on your itinerary include the **Royal Birthstones** (p213), where many of Hawaii's kings were born, and the **Kane'aki Heiau** (p224), where Kamehameha the Great last worshipped. Other impressive temple ruins include the **Ulopu Heiau** (p177) in Kailua and the **Pu'u O Mahuka Heiau** (p202) overlooking Waimea.

HIP O'AHU

Hip-hop is hip in Honolulu and the most happening club scene is at the **Pipeline Cafe** (p105). **Duke's Canoe Club** (p146) is the focal point of the beachside music and social bar scene in Waikiki, especially on weekends when Hawaiian rocker Henry Kapono plays. The swankiest crowds line up at the door of the chic **Wonder Lounge** (p146). Jazz on your mind? Don black and join other like-minded improvisationists at **Jazz Minds Art & Cafe** (p106).

Chinatown is evolving into one of the hippest places in Honolulu, especially the bars, galleries and clubs on the edge of downtown. One of the most notable venues is the **ARTS at Marks Garage** (p107), where you can find everything from art exhibitions and poetry slams to dance performances and innovative music. The nearby **Opium Den & Champagne Bar** (p105) mixes up the coolest martinis in the tropics, and serves them to the tune of tribal rhythms.

In the windsurfing mecca of Kailua head to **Boardriders Bar & Grill** (p181), where an international mix of boardriders take to the dance floor. On the North Shore, **Sunset Beach Park** (p198) is the place for beautiful people to see and be seen, either taming the waves or strutting about in the latest swimwear fashions.

Snapshot

Although Oʻahu is indeed a paradise, it's not always an easy one to live in. People do love their island home and *aloha ʻaina* (love of the land) is one of the prevailing forces on Oʻahu. But for some people it's a real struggle just to stay afloat.

Oʻahuans like to say that mainland cities have a housing squeeze, while they've got a housing *vise*. Honolulu is the priciest city in the USA when it comes to putting a roof over your head. Since 2002 housing prices on the island have nearly doubled, pushing the median price for a single-family home to $650,000. And local economists expect the values to increase another 10% as we go to press! Condo prices, while lower, are also skyrocketing.

So how is that affecting people? It took 30% of the median family income to buy a house four years ago – now it takes 50%. Add to that Hawaii's other steep living expenses, such as the highest electricity rates in the US, and budgets often become impossibly tight. The situation has proved insurmountable for most people trying to enter the housing market for the first time. Although Hawaii's unemployment rate is the nation's lowest, new jobs are primarily opening up in tourism-related fields and they don't pay a living wage. Jobs in professional fields are few and far between. Consequently, Oʻahu is experiencing a brain drain as young people, drawn by higher pay and lower living costs, leave Hawaii for the US mainland.

Although the population of Oʻahu has been leveling off, that belies the true exodus as an influx of wealthy mainlanders have been arriving at a steady pace. Not only has their growing presence helped push up prices in a hot housing market, but it's contributed to a political shift in this once solidly Democratic state. Hawaii's current governor, Linda Lingle, is a Republican and a mainland expatriate. She is also pro-development.

Development issues are always a hot topic on Oʻahu. One development that Honolulu residents are rallying to stop is a proposal to turn the un-developed Kakaʻako waterfront, just beyond Ala Moana Beach Park, into a skyscraping 'urban village' of condominiums, offices and shops.

Still, the biggest current struggle in terms of development-vs-preservation has been over the fate of sacred Waimea Valley. This remote 1875-acre wilderness above the surfing mecca of Waimea Bay is an archaeological treasure loaded with historical sites. After the cash-strapped city failed in its attempts to take the valley from its would-be developer through legal proceedings, the mayor made a deal in which the city would accept 300 acres in return for letting the developer keep the rest. Public outcry was so loud, so vocal – so impassioned – that the mayor was forced to reverse his decision and in 2006 the winner-take-all battle turned into a victory for preservationists. As it stands, a broad coalition that includes the native Hawaiian group the Office of Hawaiian Affairs (OHA), the Audubon Society, and city, state and federal government agencies, is in the process of buying the land. The Audubon Society will administer the property, and the OHA will hold it in trust for a future native Hawaiian government.

That brings up the topic of native Hawaiians and sovereignty. A long-stalled Native Hawaiian Government Reorganization Act, sponsored by Hawaii's US Senator Daniel Akaka, aims to formally recognize native Hawaiians as an indigenous people along the lines of Native Americans

FAST FACTS

Population: 884,000

Unemployment rate: 2.5%

Median household income: $48,300

Income considered a living wage: $46,000

Percentage of new jobs that pay a living wage: 35%

Total purse for Triple Crown of Surfing: $670,000

Average visitors per day: 84,000

Cost of living: 20% higher than on the US mainland

Miles of sandy beaches: 50.3

Distance from Los Angeles: 2557 miles

on the mainland. The act would establish a native Hawaiian governing body with the power to negotiate with federal and state governments over the disposition of native Hawaiian lands and assets. The legislation, which is currently being considered by the US Senate, is supported by the Office of Hawaiian Affairs and most of Hawaii's state politicians. However, there are many splinter Hawaiian sovereignty groups and some of these are vehemently opposed to the bill, charging that it cedes too much authority to the US government. The conflict illustrates the diversity of opinion on sovereignty that native Hawaiians have, and it seems that it will be many years before any consensus emerges on what form sovereignty will take.

Despite their diversity, O'ahuans do come together on some things. In 2005 the entire island watched as a team of scruffy kids from the relatively modest 'Ewa Beach area took on well-funded teams from around the world and won the World Little League Championship title (see p36). Other sports also instill a sense of local pride. The University of Hawaii's Rainbow Wahine volleyball team is among the country's finest women's volleyball team and consistently packs the UH stadium with fans, as do the somewhat less successful but equally followed Rainbow Warriors, the men's basketball team.

The Honolulu-based Polynesian Voyaging Society is once again readying the double-hulled canoe *Hokule'a* to sail from O'ahu to Tahiti, following the migration routes of Hawaii's early Polynesian settlers. The *Hokule'a's* milestone maiden voyage in 1976 proved that the ancient Hawaiians had the ability to travel repeatedly across the vast Pacific to and from Tahiti using only traditional navigational techniques. This 30th-anniversary voyage not only celebrates the resurgence of native Hawaiian pride that the original 1976 voyage sparked, but it's also becoming a focal point for a new generation of Hawaiian students rediscovering their seafaring past.

And, of course, for more than a few people in O'ahu, the burning issue on their minds when they wake up in the morning is this: how high's the surf? Indeed, when the monstrous winter surf brings the pros to the North Shore, all eyes on O'ahu look northward.

24

History

ANCIENT HAWAII

In 1976 the double-hulled canoe *Hokule'a* pushed off from O'ahu on a history-making voyage to retrace the journeys of the ancient Polynesians. Under the guidance of the Honolulu-based Polynesian Voyaging Society, and after years of research and boat construction, the *Hokule'a* made the 4800-mile return trip to Tahiti and back using only traditional Polynesian navigational aids, observing stars, wave patterns, seabirds and clouds. Upon their triumphant return, academic skeptics who had long questioned whether Hawaii's early settlers really were capable of journeying back and forth across such vast, empty ocean came to see it indeed was possible.

In large part, the early history of Hawaii is also the history of O'ahu. The first boat of settlers to Hawaii washed ashore around AD 500. Not a lot is known about them, but artifacts left behind indicate they were from the Marquesas. The next wave of settlers were from Tahiti and arrived around AD 1000. Unlike the Marquesans, who sparsely settled the tiny islands northwest of O'ahu, the Tahitians arrived in great numbers and settled each of the major islands in the Hawaiian chain. Although no one knows what set them on course for Hawaii, when they arrived in their great double-hulled canoes they were prepared to colonize a new land, bringing with them pigs, dogs, taro roots and other crop plants.

Although their discovery of Hawaii may have been by accident, subsequent journeys were not. These Tahitians were highly skilled seafarers, memorizing their route over 2400 miles of open Pacific, and repeating the journeys between Hawaii and the islands to the south for centuries.

And what a story they must have brought back with them, because vast waves of Tahitians followed to pursue a new life in Hawaii. So great were the Tahitian migrations that Hawaii's population probably reached a peak of approximately 250,000 by the year 1450. The voyages back and forth continued until around 1500, when all contact between Tahiti and Hawaii appears to have stopped.

THE FIRST WESTERNERS

Hawaii was the last of the Polynesian islands to be 'discovered' by the West. This was in large part due to the fact that early European explorers who entered the Pacific around the tips of either Africa or South America centered their explorations in the Southern Hemisphere. Indeed, the great British explorer Captain James Cook spent the better part of a decade charting most of the South Pacific before chancing upon Hawaii as he sailed north from Tahiti in search of a northwest passage to the Atlantic.

On January 18, 1778, Captain Cook sighted the islands of O'ahu, Kaua'i and Ni'ihau. The winds favored approaching Kaua'i, and on January 19 Cook's ships, the *Discovery* and the *Resolution*, sailed into Kaua'i's Waimea Bay. The captain was surprised to find that the islanders had a strong Tahitian connection in their appearance, language and culture.

The *Honolulu Star-Bulletin's* Millennium Series (http://starbulletin.com/specials/millennium/index.html) colorfully covers the history of Hawaii in text and graphics, from the birth of the islands to current times.

For a quick read about traditional Hawaiian culture and community life, pick up *Ancient Hawaii*, written – and colorfully illustrated – by acclaimed artist Herb Kawainui Kane.

TIMELINE	10 MILLION BC	AD 500
	Lava from an underwater volcano breaks the surface and O'ahu first emerges as an island	The first human settlers – a small group of Polynesians from the Marquesas – arrive in the Hawaiian Islands

GODS & TEMPLES

Religion was center stage in ancient Hawaii and there was a hierarchy of gods. At the top were four main gods: Ku, Lono, Kane and Kanaloa.

Ku was the ancestor god for all generations of humankind, past, present and future. He presided over all male gods, while his wife, Hina, reigned over the female gods. When the sun rose in the morning, it was said to be Ku; when it set in the evening it was Hina. Like yin and yang, they were responsible for heaven and earth.

Ku had many manifestations, one as the benevolent god of fishing, others as the god of forests and farming. One of the most fearful of Ku's manifestations was Kukailimoku (Ku, the snatcher of land), the war god worshipped by the first ruler of the Hawaiian Islands, Kamehameha the Great. The temples built for the worship of Kukailimoku were offered sacrifices not only of food, pigs and chickens but also at times of human beings.

Lono was the god in charge of the elements that brought rain and an abundant harvest. He was also the god of fertility and peace.

Kane created the first man out of the dust of the earth and breathed life into him (the Hawaiian word for man is *kane*), and it was from Kane that the Hawaiian chiefs were said to have descended.

Kanaloa was often pitted in struggles against the other three gods. When heaven and earth separated, it was Kanaloa who was placed in charge of the spirits on earth. Forbidden from drinking the intoxicating beverage kava, these spirits revolted and, along with Kanaloa, were driven to the underworld, where Kanaloa became the ruler of the dead.

Below the four main gods, there were 40 lesser gods. Among those who are still revered today are Pele, goddess of volcanoes; Laka, goddess of the hula; and Hina, goddess of the moon. The Hawaiians had gods for all occupations and natural phenomena. There was a god for the tapa (pounded bark cloth) maker and a god for the canoe builder, as well as shark gods and mountain gods.

To praise the major gods the Hawaiians built stone temples, called heiau. There were two types, one a simple rectangular enclosure of stone walls built directly on the ground, the other a more substantial structure built of rocks piled high to form raised terraced platforms.

Inside the heiau were prayer towers, *kapu* (taboo) houses and drum houses. These structures were made of ohia wood and thatched with *pili* grass. Carved wooden *ki'i* (tiki, or god images) were placed around the prayer towers. Today one of the best examples of such a temple is Kane'aki Heiau (p224).

Heiau were built in auspicious sites, often perched on cliffs above the coast or in other places thought to have mana, or 'spiritual power.' A heiau's significance focused on the mana of the site rather than the structure itself. When a heiau's mana was gone, it was abandoned.

Cook named the Hawaiian archipelago the Sandwich Islands in honor of his patron, the Earl of Sandwich.

Cook, whose arrival in Hawaii happened to coincide with the *makahiki*, an annual harvest festival in honor of the god Lono, was seen as an earthly manifestation of the god, and he and his crew were given a warm reception. After two weeks of stocking provisions, the expedition continued its journey north.

Failing to find the fabled passage through the Arctic, Cook set sail back to Hawaii, where his arrival date virtually coincided with that of his initial visit to the islands one year earlier. Tragically, Cook, along with some of his crew and many Hawaiians, was killed in a battle spawned by

1000	1778
The first wave of settlers from Tahiti arrive and begin to establish sizable settlements throughout Hawaii	Arrival of Captain James Cook, the first Westerner to 'discover' Hawaii

HAWAII'S ALI'I

Hawaii is the only state in the USA to have been ruled by a monarchy. Beginning with Kamehameha the Great's 1795 unification of the islands, the reign of Hawaii's *ali'i* (royalty) continued until the overthrow of Queen Lili'uokalani by American businessmen in 1893.

Following are the dates that each of Hawaii's monarchs lived:

Kamehameha the Great c 1758–1819: Unified Hawaii as a single kingdom.

Kamehameha II (Liholiho) 1797–1824: Ended the old religion.

Kamehameha III (Kauikeauoli) 1813–54: Established the permanent capital of Hawaii in Honolulu.

Kamehameha IV (Alexander Liholiho) 1834–63: Established a Hawaiian branch of the Anglican Church.

Kamehameha V (Lot Kamehameha) 1830–72: Passed a constitution, strengthening the crown's power.

Lunalilo (William Lunalilo) 1832–74: Established trade relations with the USA and ceded Pearl Harbor to America.

Kalakaua (David Kalakaua) 1836–91: Revived the hula and the prominence of Hawaiian culture.

Lili'uokalani (Lydia Lili'uokalani) 1838–1917: Challenged foreign powers and tried to re-establish Hawaiian rights.

growing tensions between the two groups. A week after Cook's death, the expedition's ships set sail, landing briefly on O'ahu's North Shore before finally leaving Hawaiian waters on March 15, 1779.

After Cook's ships returned to Great Britain, news of his discovery quickly spread throughout Europe and America, opening the floodgates to a foreign invasion of other explorers, traders, missionaries and fortune seekers.

KAMEHAMEHA THE GREAT

At the time of the first European contact with Hawaii, the Hawaiian Islands were under the control of a handful of chiefs, and a power struggle for dominance over the entire island chain was underway. The main rivals were Kamehameha the Great, chief of the island of Hawai'i, and Kahekili, the aging king of Maui, who in the 1780s had defeated his stepson to take control of O'ahu.

After Kahekili died at Waikiki in 1794, his lands were divided between two quarreling relatives. His son Kalanikupule got O'ahu, while his half-brother King Kaeokulani of Kaua'i gained control of Maui. The two ambitious heirs immediately went to battle with each other, creating a rift that Kamehameha swiftly set out to exploit.

In 1795 Kamehameha swept through Maui and Moloka'i, conquering those islands before crossing the channel to O'ahu. The bloody O'ahu campaign started on the shores of Waikiki, where the invading canoes were so great in number that they covered the entire 2-mile stretch of beach. A brilliant general, Kamehameha employed a combination of storm and surprise, catching his opposition off guard as he led his warriors up Nu'uanu Valley to meet the entrenched O'auhuan defenders.

The first heavy fighting took place around Puowaina (present-day Punchbowl), where Kamehameha's men quickly circled the fortress-like crater and drove out the O'ahuan warriors. Scattered fighting continued up Nu'uanu Valley, with the last big battle taking place near the current site of Queen Emma's summer palace.

The O'ahuans, who were prepared for the usual spear-and-stone warfare, panicked when they realized Kamehameha had brought in a handful of Western sharpshooters with modern firearms. Under Kamehameha's

1795

Kamehameha the Great conquers O'ahu, completing the unification of the Hawaiian Island

1819

Kamehameha the Great dies and the ancient *kapu* (taboo) system is abolished command, the foreigners picked off the Oʻahuan generals and blasted into their ridge-top defenses.

What should have been the advantage of high ground turned into a death trap for the Oʻahuans when they found themselves wedged up into the valley, unable to redeploy. Fleeing up the cliffsides in retreat, they were forced to make their last stand at the narrow, precipitous ledge along the current-day Nuʻuanu Pali Lookout (p174). Hundreds of Oʻahuans were pushed off the top of the *pali* (cliff) to their deaths.

Some Oʻahuan warriors, including King Kalanikupule, escaped into the upland forests. When Kalanikupule surfaced a few months later, Kamehameha offered the fallen king as a human sacrifice to his war god Ku. Kamehameha's victory marked the end of an era. The Oʻahu invasion was the last battle ever fought between Hawaiian troops, and saw the beginning of Hawaii's emergence as a united kingdom. It also set the stage for the center of power to shift to Oʻahu.

THE FOUNDING OF HONOLULU

In 1793 the English frigate *Butterworth* became the first foreign ship to sail into what is now called Honolulu Harbor. Its captain, William Brown, named the protected harbor Fair Haven. Ships that followed called it Brown's Harbor. Over time the name Honolulu, which means 'Sheltered Bay,' came to be used for both the harbor and the seaside district that the Hawaiians had called Kou.

As more and more foreign ships found their way to Honolulu, a harborside village of thatched houses sprang up. Shops selling food and other simple provisions to the sailors opened along the waterfront. The port soon became a focal point for the lucrative trade conducted by Yankee clippers, those merchant ships that plied the seas between the US and China. The wealth of manufactured goods the ships carried – from iron cannons to ornate furniture – was unlike anything the Hawaiians had ever seen.

In 1809 Kamehameha the Great, who had been living in his royal court in Waikiki, decided to move to the Honolulu Harbor area, which by then had grown into a village of almost 1800 people. The king wanted to maintain control over the growing foreign presence and make sure Hawaiians

Get the skinny on how Honolulu sprang up from its harbor at www.hawaii.gov/dot/harbors/oahu/history.htm.

THE ROYAL-ENGLISH CONNECTION

The shipwrecked British sailor John Young washed ashore in Hawaii in 1790. Impressed by his soldiering skills and knowledge of firearms, Kamehameha the Great gave Young a leading role in his invasion of Oʻahu. Not only did the Englishman become Kamehameha's top general but he went on to become a trusted friend and adviser of the king. Young married into Hawaiian royalty and served as the governor of Hawaii's Big Island.

Young also had a home at the northern side of Honolulu, which he named Hanaiakamalama. The Englishman bequeathed the house to his granddaughter, Queen Emma, who was three-quarters royal Hawaiian and one-quarter English. You can visit the home today as the Queen Emma Summer Palace (p90).

So respected was Young that even in his death he is honored with a place alongside Hawaiian kings and queens at the Royal Mausoleum State Monument (Map pp72–3) in Honolulu, not far from his former home.

1820	1823
First Christian missionaries arrive from New England, as do the first whalers	Kamehameha II (Liholiho) becomes the first Hawaiian king to go abroad, but dies of measles in London

'To this day Honolulu Harbour remains the most important commercial harbor in the state.'

got a fair deal in any trade. To keep an eye on all the commercial action flowing in and out of the harbor, he set up a residence near the waterfront on what today is the corner of Bethel and Queen Sts.

Kamehameha traded Hawaii's highly prized sandalwood, which was shipped to China, mostly for weapons and luxury goods. As the trade grew, the king built harborside warehouses to store his acquisitions and he introduced wharfage fees to build up his treasury. New England Yankees, who dominated the sandalwood trade, quickly became the main foreign presence in Honolulu.

By the time of Kamehameha the Great's death in 1819, nearly 3500 people lived in Honolulu and it continued to boom as more foreigners arrived. Honolulu, the city that built up around the harbor, was firmly established as the center of Hawaii's commerce. To this day Honolulu Harbor remains the most important commercial harbor in the state.

Missionaries & Sinners

By 1820 whaling ships sailing the Pacific began to pull into Honolulu for supplies, liquor and women. To meet their needs, shops, taverns and brothels sprang up around the harbor.

To the ire of the whalers, the Christian missionaries came ashore in their wake. Hawaii's first missionary ship sailed into Honolulu on April 14, 1820, carrying staunch Calvinists who were set on saving the Hawaiians from their 'heathen ways.'

Although both the missionaries and the whalers hailed from New England, they had little else in common and were soon at odds. The missionaries were intent on saving souls and the whalers were intent, after months at sea, on satisfying more earthly desires. To most sailors, there was 'no God west of the Horn.'

In time the missionaries gained enough influence with Hawaiian royalty to have laws enacted against drunkenness and prostitution. In response, by the peak whaling years of the mid-1800s, most whaling boats had abandoned Honolulu, preferring to land in Lahaina on Maui, where whalers had gained the upper hand over the missionaries.

Interestingly, both groups left their marks on Honolulu. To this day the headquarters of the Protestant mission sits placidly in downtown Honolulu, while only minutes away Honolulu's red-light district continues to attract sea-weary sailors and wayward souls. Kawaiaha'o Church (p79), built by those first missionaries, sits opposite the royal palace and still holds services in the Hawaiian language today.

Downtown Honolulu also became the headquarters for the emerging corporations that eventually gained control of Hawaii's commerce. It's no coincidence that their lists of corporate board members – Alexander, Baldwin, Cooke and Dole – read like a roster from the first mission ships, for indeed it was the sons of missionaries who became the power brokers in the new Hawaii.

IMMIGRATION

Ko (sugarcane) arrived in Hawaii with the early Polynesian settlers. Although the Hawaiians enjoyed chewing the cane for its juices, they never refined it into sugar.

1835	1845
An American establishes Hawaii's commercial sugarcane industry, introducing the plantation economy	Kamehameha III establishes the capital of Hawaii in Honolulu

In 1835 a Bostonian, William Hooper, saw a bigger opportunity in sugar and set out to establish Hawaii's first sugar plantation. Hooper convinced Honolulu investors to put up the money for his venture and then worked out a deal with Kamehameha III to lease 980 acres of land for $300. His next step was to negotiate with the *ali'i* for the right to use Hawaiian laborers, as Hawaii was still a feudal society.

The new plantation system, which introduced the concept of growing crops for profit rather than subsistence, marked the advent of capitalism and the introduction of wage labor in Hawaii. The sugar industry emerged at the same time that whalers began arriving in force, and together they became the foundation of Hawaii's economy.

While the sugar industry boomed, Hawaii's native population declined, largely as the result of diseases introduced by foreigners. To expand their operations, the plantation owners looked overseas for a labor supply. They needed immigrants accustomed to working long days in hot weather, and for whom the low wages would seem like an opportunity.

In 1852 the plantation owners began recruiting laborers from China. In 1868 they went to Japan and in the 1870s they brought in Portuguese from the Azores. After Hawaii's 1898 annexation to the USA resulted in restrictions on Chinese immigration, plantation owners turned to Puerto Ricans and Koreans. Filipinos were the last group of immigrants brought to Hawaii to work the fields; the first wave came in 1906, the last in 1946.

In all, approximately 350,000 immigrants came to Hawaii to work on the sugar plantations. A continuous flow of immigrant workers was required to replace those who invariably found better options elsewhere. Although some workers came for a set period to save money and return home, others fulfilled their contracts and then moved off the plantations to start their own businesses.

Plantation towns, such as Waipahu (p217) and Waialua (p207), grew up around the mills, with barber shops, beer halls and bathhouses catering to the workers. Even today a drive through these sleepy O'ahuan towns, with their now-defunct mills (both closed in the 1990s), offers a glimpse of plantation history. To get an in-depth look at what plantation life on O'ahu was like, be sure to visit Hawaii's Plantation Village (p218).

Each of the major immigrant populations – Japanese, Chinese, Filipino and European – came to outnumber the native Hawaiians. Together they created the unique blend of cultures that would continue to characterize Hawaii for generations to come.

WWII's 442nd Second Regimental Combat Team, comprised of Japanese-Americans, was the most decorated unit in US history. Hawaii's Senator Daniel Inouye lost an arm in the fighting.

HONOLULU AS CAPITAL

In 1845 Kamehameha III, the last son of Kamehameha the Great, moved the capital of the Hawaiian kingdom from Maui to Honolulu. Kamehameha III, who ruled from 1825 to 1854, established Hawaii's first national legislature, provided for a supreme court and passed the Great Mahele Land Act, which established religious freedom and gave all male citizens the right to vote.

Hawaii's only 'invasion' by a foreign power occurred in 1843 when George Paulet, an upstart British commander upset about a petty land deal involving a British national, sailed into Honolulu commanding

1874	1893
King David Kakakaua begins his reign and challenges missionary repression of Hawaiian culture	Queen Lili'uokalani overthrown; the son of an American missionary declares himself the new leader of a provisional government

the British ship *Carysfort* and seized Oʻahu for six months. In that short period, he anglicized street names, seized property and began to collect taxes.

To avoid bloodshed, Kamehameha III stood aside as the British flag was raised and the ship's band played 'God Save the Queen.' Queen Victoria herself wasn't flattered. After catching wind of the incident, she dispatched Admiral Richard Thomas to restore Hawaiian independence. Admiral Thomas raised the Hawaiian flag in Honolulu again at the site of what is today Thomas Sq.

As the flag was raised, Kamehameha III uttered the words '*Ua mau ke ea o ka aina i ka pono,*' meaning 'The life of the land is perpetuated in righteousness,' which remains Hawaii's official motto.

In an 1853 census Honolulu registered 11,450 residents, a full 15% of the Hawaiian kingdom's population. Though still a frontier town with dusty streets and simple wooden buildings, Honolulu was both the commercial and political center of the kingdom.

In the decades that followed Honolulu took on a modern appearance as the monarchy erected a number of stately buildings in the city center, including St Andrew's Cathedral (p77), ʻIolani Palace (p74) and the supreme court building Aliʻiolani Hale (p77).

> Kamehameha IV passed a law in the 1860s mandating all children be given a Christian name along with their Hawaiian name. The statute stayed on the books until 1967.

THE LAND GRAB

In 1848 influential foreign missionaries convinced King Kamehameha III to pass a land reform act called the Great Mahele. This act permanently altered the Hawaiian concept of land rights. For the first time land became a commodity that could be bought and sold.

Through the provisions of the Great Mahele, the king, who previously owned all land, gave up title to the majority of it. Island chiefs were allowed to buy some of the lands that they had controlled as fiefdoms for the king. Other lands, divided into 3-acre farm plots called *kuleana*, were made available to all Hawaiians. In order to retain title, chiefs and commoners alike had to pay a tax and register the land.

The chiefs had the option of paying the tax in property and many did so. Commoners had no choice but to pay the taxes in cash. Although the act was intended to turn Hawaii into a country of small farms, in the end only a few thousand Hawaiians carried through with the paperwork and received *kuleana*.

In 1850 land purchases were opened to foreigners. Unlike the Hawaiians, the Westerners jumped at the opportunity, and before the native islanders could clearly grasp the concept of private land ownership, there was little land left to own. Within a few decades the Westerners, who were more adept at wheeling and dealing in real estate, owned 80% of all privately held lands. Even many of the Hawaiians who went through the process of getting their own *kuleana* eventually ended up selling it off for a fraction of its real value.

Contrary to the bright picture the missionaries had painted for Kamehameha III, the Hawaiians suddenly became a landless people, drifting into ghettos in the larger towns. In a bitter twist, many of the missionaries ended up with sizable tracts of land and more than a few of them left the church to devote themselves to their new estates.

Although Hawaiian commoners had no rights to the land prior to the Great Mahele, they were free to move around and work the property of any chief. In return for their personal use of the land, they paid the chief in labor or with a percentage of their crops. In this way they lived off the land. After the Great Mahele, they were simply *off* the land.

1898	1901
Hawaii is annexed to the USA and becomes a US territory two years later	The Moana Hotel, the first hotel in Waikiki, opens to guests

By the mid-19th century Honolulu had a prominent foreign community composed largely of American and British expats. These foreigners were not only active in missionary endeavors but were also opening schools and starting newspapers and, more importantly, landing powerful government positions as ministry officials and consuls to the king. As the city continued to grow and Westerners wrested increasing control over island affairs from the Hawaiians, the powers of Kamehameha the Great's successors eroded.

THE MERRIE MONARCH

King David Kalakaua reigned from 1874 to 1891. Although known as the 'Merrie Monarch,' he ruled in troubled times.

Kalakaua was an impassioned Hawaiian revivalist. He brought back the hula, reversing decades of missionary repression against the 'heathen dance,' and he composed the national anthem 'Hawaii Ponoi,' which is now the state song. Kalakaua also tried to ensure a degree of self-rule for native Hawaiians, who had become a minority in their own land.

Although he was unwaveringly loyal to the interest of native Hawaiians, Kalakaua was realistic about the current-day realities he faced. The king proved himself a successful diplomat by traveling to Washington, DC, and persuading President Ulysses Grant to accept a treaty giving Hawaiian sugar growers tariff-free access to US markets, which the US Congress had been resisting. In so doing, Kalakaua gained, at least temporarily, the support of the sugar plantation owners, who controlled most of Hawaii's agricultural land.

The king became a world traveler, visiting India, Europe and Southeast Asia. Kalakaua was well aware that Hawaii's days as an independent Polynesian kingdom were numbered. To counter the Western powers that were gaining hold of Hawaii, he made a futile attempt to establish a Polynesian-Pacific empire. On a visit with the emperor of Japan, he even proposed a royal marriage between his niece Princess Kaiulani and a Japanese prince.

Visits with other foreign monarchs gave Kalakaua a taste for royal pageantry. He returned to build 'Iolani Palace for what the business community thought was an extravagant $360,000. To many influential whites, the king was perceived as a lavish spender who was fond of partying and throwing public luaus.

As Kalakaua incurred debts, he became increasingly less popular with the sugar barons. In 1887 they formed the Hawaiian League and developed their own armies, which stood ready to overthrow Kalakaua. The league presented Kalakaua with a list of demands and forced him to accept a new constitution strictly limiting his powers. It also limited voting rights to property owners, which at that time meant the exclusion of the vast majority of Hawaiians.

On July 30, 1889, a group of 150 Hawaiians attempted to overthrow the new constitution by occupying 'Iolani Palace. Called the Wilcox Rebellion after its part-Hawaiian leader, it was a confused attempt, and the rebels were forced to surrender. Kalakaua died in San Francisco in 1891.

'Kalakaua was well aware that Hawaii's days as an independent Polynesian kingdom were numbered.'

1912	1936
Champion surfer Duke Kahanamoku wins his first gold medal in the 100m swim at the Olympic Games in Sweden	Pan American airlines flies the first passenger flights from the US mainland to Hawaii

THE END OF THE KINGDOM

Kalakaua was succeeded by his sister, Lydia Paki Kamekeha Lili'uokalani, wife of O'ahu's governor John O Dominis. Queen Lili'uokalani was even more determined than her brother to strengthen the power of the monarchy. She charged that the 1887 constitution, which she referred to as the 'bayonet constitution,' was illegally forced upon King Kalakaua. In a pivotal decision, the Hawaii Supreme Court upheld her contention.

In January 1893 Queen Lili'uokalani was preparing to proclaim a new constitution to restore royal powers when a group of armed US businessmen occupied the Supreme Court and declared the monarchy overthrown. They announced a provisional government, led by Sanford Dole, son of a pioneer missionary family.

A contingent of US sailors came ashore, ostensibly to protect the property of US citizens, but instead of going to neighborhoods where Americans lived, they marched on the palace and positioned their guns at the queen's residence. Opting to avoid bloodshed, the queen stepped down.

The provisional government immediately appealed to Washington for annexation, while the queen appealed to restore the monarchy. To the dismay of Dole's representatives, the timing was to the queen's advantage.

Democratic President Grover Cleveland had just replaced a Republican administration and his sentiments favored Lili'uokalani. Cleveland sent an envoy to investigate the situation, and also received Lili'uokalani's niece Princess Kaiulani who, at the time of the coup, was living in London and being prepared for the throne. In Washington, DC, the beautiful 18-year-old princess eloquently pleaded the monarchy's case to Cleveland and other American politicians. She also made a favorable impression on the American press, which largely caricatured those involved in the overthrow as dour, greedy buffoons.

Cleveland ordered that the US flag be taken down and the queen restored to her throne. However, the provisional government, now firmly in power, turned a deaf ear, declaring that Cleveland was meddling in 'Hawaiian' affairs.

On July 4, 1894, Dole stood on the steps of 'Iolani Palace and announced that Hawaii was now a republic and he was its president. A disapproving Cleveland initially favored reversing the situation, but he realized the US public's sense of justice was limited and that ousting a government of white Americans and replacing them with native Hawaiians could backlash on his own political future. Consequently, his actions were limited to rhetoric.

Weary of waiting for outside intervention, in early 1895 a group of Hawaiian royalists attempted a counter-revolution that was easily squashed. Although there was no evidence that she was aware of the royalists' attempt to restore her, Lili'uokalani was accused of being a conspirator and placed under arrest.

To humiliate her, the queen was tried in her own palace and referred to only as Mrs John O Dominis. She was fined $5000 and sentenced to five years of hard labor, later reduced to nine months of house arrest at the palace.

Lili'uokalani spent the rest of her life in her husband's residence, Washington Place (p77), one block from the palace. During this time

The Betrayal of Lili'uokalani: Last Queen of Hawaii, by Helena G Allen, is an insightful account not only of the queen's life but also of the missionary activity and foreign encroachment leading to her overthrow.

1941	1959
Japanese forces stage the surprise attack on Pearl Harbor that catapults the USA into WWII	Hawaii becomes the 50th state of the USA

she composed several songs, including the popular *Aloha 'Oe*, her parting song to the people of Hawaii:

> Farewell to you, farewell to you (Aloha 'oe, aloha 'oe); O fragrance of one who dwells in the blue; One fond embrace; Until I return; Until we meet again.

When Lili'uokalani died of a stroke in November 1917, all of Honolulu came out for the funeral procession. To most islanders, Lili'uokalani was still their queen.

US STATEHOOD

The Spanish-American War of 1898 gave Americans a taste for expansionism. Hawaii suddenly took on a new strategic importance being midway between the USA and its newly acquired possession, the Philippines. The annexation of Hawaii was approved by the US Congress on July 7, 1898. Hawaii entered the 20th century as a territory of the USA.

In just over a century of Western contact, the native Hawaiian population had been decimated by foreign diseases to which it had no immunities. It began with the venereal disease introduced by Captain Cook's crew in 1778. The whalers followed with cholera and smallpox, and Chinese immigrants brought leprosy. By the end of the 19th century the native Hawaiian population had been reduced from an estimated 300,000 to fewer than 50,000. Descendants of the early missionaries had taken over first the land, then the government. Without ever fighting a single battle against a foreign power, Hawaiians had lost their islands to ambitious foreigners. All in all, as far as the native Hawaiians were concerned, the annexation wasn't anything to celebrate.

The Chinese and Japanese were also uneasy. One of the reasons for the initial reluctance of the US Congress to annex Hawaii was the racial mix of the islands' population. There were already restrictions on Chinese immigration to the USA, and restrictions on Japanese immigration were expected to follow. In a rush to avoid a labor shortage, the sugar plantation owners quickly brought 70,000 Japanese immigrants into Hawaii. By the time the immigration wave was over, the Japanese accounted for more than 40% of Hawaii's population.

In 1935 Amelia Earhart became the first person to fly solo from Honolulu to California, spanning the distance in 13 hours.

To the chagrin of the Hawaiian people, President McKinley appointed Sanford Dole the first territorial governor. The US Navy quickly established a Pacific headquarters at Pearl Harbor and built Schofield Barracks, the largest US army base in the world. The military soon became the leading sector of O'ahu's economy.

Pan American airlines flew the first passenger flights from the US mainland to Hawaii in 1936, an aviation milestone that ushered in the transpacific air age. Waikiki was now only hours away from the US West Coast and was on the verge of becoming a major tourism destination. Everything was put on hold when on December 7, 1941, a wave of Japanese bombers attacked Pearl Harbor (p156), jolting the USA into WWII.

Read all about Pearl Harbor's 'Day of Infamy' and see photos of the attack at www.nps.gov /usar/home.htm.

The war brought Hawaii closer to the center stage of American culture and politics. The prospect of statehood had long been the central topic

1967	1971
Tourism reaches a milestone with one million visitors arriving in a single year	The first Rip Curl Pro Pipeline Masters, precursor of the Triple Crown of Surfing, is held at Sunset Beach

in Hawaiian political circles. Three decades had passed since Prince Jonah Kuhio Kalaniana'ole, Hawaii's first delegate to the US Congress, introduced the first statehood bill in 1919. It received a cool reception in Washington at that time, and there were mixed feelings in Hawaii as well. However, by the time the war was over, opinion polls showed that two out of three Hawaiian residents favored statehood.

Streetcar Days in Honolulu: Breezing Through Paradise, by McKinnon Simpson and John Brizdle, is a fun nostalgia book covering the years 1889 to 1941 from the perspective of a trolley rider.

Still, Hawaii was too much of a melting pot for many politicians to support statehood, particularly those from the rigidly segregated southern states. To the overwhelmingly white and largely conservative Congress, Hawaii's multiethnic community was too exotic and foreign to be thought of as 'American.'

In March 1959 the US Congress finally passed legislation to make Hawaii a state. On June 27 a plebiscite was held in Hawaii, with more than 90% of the islanders voting for statehood. On August 21, 1959, after 61 years of territorial status, Hawaii became the 50th state of the USA.

O'AHU TODAY

In the early 1970s O'ahu began to experience a resurgence of cultural pride not seen since the reign of King Kalakaua. It is difficult to pinpoint one event or activity that caused this resurgence, but the retracing of the Hawaii migration routes by the *Hokule'a* was certainly a catalyst. This project required the learning of ancient navigational skills and sailing techniques that had been nearly forgotten.

Learn more about Polynesian migration and the famous voyage of the double-hulled canoe *Hokule'a*, which retraced those routes in 1976, at www.pvs-hawaii.com.

Greater interest in the hula also began to be seen in the 1970s, especially among young men. New hula *halau* (hula schools) began to open, many of which revived interest in ancient hula techniques and dances that had been subjugated in favor of more modern, Western-style hula dances.

Revival of the Hawaiian language has also been a focal point of the Hawaiian renaissance. By the 1970s the pool of native Hawaiian speakers had dropped to under 1000 individuals statewide. In an effort to reverse this trend, Hawaiian-language immersion schools began to emerge and the University of Hawai'i began offering Hawaiian-language classes.

Music has also been affected by the ongoing Hawaiian renaissance and leading contemporary musicians, such as Hapa and Keali'i Reichel, sing in the Hawaiian language. Many people have also become interested in re-learning nearly lost arts, such as the making of *kapa* (bark cloth), drums, feather lei, wooden bowls and other traditional items. Many people feel that if this renaissance hadn't occurred, Hawaiian language and culture would be nearly extinct by now.

A heightened consciousness created by the 1993 centennial anniversary of Queen Lili'uokalani's overthrow served as a rallying point for a Hawaiian sovereignty movement, intent on righting some of the wrongs of the past century. Plenty of discussion has taken place in the past decade, but a consensus on exactly what form sovereignty should take has yet to emerge.

1976	1993
The voyaging canoe *Hokule'a* departs from O'ahu, retracing the Polynesian migration paths from Tahiti	President Clinton signs 'Apology Resolution,' recognizing the illegal overthrow of the Kingdom of Hawaii in 1893

The Culture

REGIONAL IDENTITY

O'ahu has many sides, and the place where someone lives on the island has a great deal to say about their regional identity.

Certainly Honolulu is the one 'big city,' not only to those who live on O'ahu but for all of Hawaii. Sure, it has a decidedly slower pace than its mainland counterparts, but it is no less cosmopolitan. As a crossroads between East and West, it is in some ways more worldly. Honolulu residents see themselves at the center of it all. They are the happening folks, on the cutting edge. They deal with the traffic and the high-rises because with it comes the better-paying jobs, the faster life, the excitement, the hip shops and nightlife.

On the other hand, the farming communities along the windward and leeward coasts are quintessential rural Hawaii. If it weren't for the occasional ride to the city to sell produce and pick up supplies, the lifestyle of rural O'ahuans is as 'small town' as you'll find anywhere else in Hawaii. And to O'ahu's rural people, 'the city' just bustles with activity. They take solace and no small measure of pride in their rural roots – at being from Waimanalo, from Waiahole, from Makaha.

And while many O'ahu residents see themselves as having a broader regional identity – the North Shore, the Wai'anae Coast, Windward O'ahu – their closest connection is their hometown. Indeed, when the late Israel 'Bruddah Iz' Kamakawiwo'ole, leader of the Ni'ihau Sons of Makaha band, sang about the home he loved, he described scenes of Makaha.

And, of course, when O'ahuans are on the mainland or out of the country and people ask where they're from, the answer almost invariably, and with a knowing smile, is 'Hawaii.'

Perhaps it's all that sunshine, but people in Hawaii really do tend to have sunny dispositions. They're more laid-back than their mainland cousins, they certainly dress more casually and they spend a lot more time outside. On weekends even those Honolulu city slickers can be found hanging on the beach stripped down to T-shirts and bikinis, and wearing those ubiquitous flip-flops known in Hawaii as *slippahs*.

People on O'ahu never walk by anybody they know without stopping to ask how they're doing and looking like they really want to know the

For an insightful look at Hawaiian culture, read *The Legends and Myths of Hawaii*, a collection of legends as told by the great Hawaiian revivalist King David Kalakaua.

GOT LUCKY?

When locals go on vacation, they go to…Las Vegas. Perhaps blasé about tropical scenery, a surprising number enjoy the man-made glitz, theme-park casinos, nearby golf courses, all-you-can-eat buffets and chance to win big (gambling is illegal only in two states: Hawaii and Utah).

Mostly, however, Hawaii people go to Vegas to hang out with other locals. On any given trip, locals are bound to spot folks they recognize from home. While the Vegas habit crosses ethnic and age lines, seniors are particularly frequent returnees.

The Honolulu–Vegas circuit has become a well-oiled machine, and companies such as Sam Boyd's Vacations-Hawaii offer discounted packages that keep locals coming back – often multiple times a year. Most stay downtown at the California Hotel and Casino, rather than at the upscale resorts on the Strip.

A sizable community of Hawaii expatriates lives in Vegas, largely due to the low cost of living. But most locals shake their heads in disbelief. Vegas is fun, but there's no place like Hawaii.

answer. People prefer to avoid heated arguments and they generally don't jump into a controversial topic just to argue the point with someone.

No matter what else they may or may not have in common, Hawaii people really band together to support each other when something local vaults to a national level. Take the summer of 2005, when the West O'ahu Little League baseball team started to make it big. This team made up of kids from rural 'Ewa beat one team after the other to reach the final play-offs. By that time everybody on O'ahu was watching; the mayor set up a giant screen on the beach at Waikiki and tens of thousands of people gathered there to watch the games and cheer the team on. Against all odds, they outperformed much bigger players, becoming the first team from Hawaii ever to win the Little League World Series Championships. Now *that* was a big-news day on O'ahu.

LIFESTYLE

In O'ahu, the family *('ohana)* is central to island lifestyles. *'Ohana* includes all relatives, as well as close family friends. Growing up, the words 'auntie' and 'uncle' are used a lot to refer to those who are dear to you, whether by the bond of blood or friendship. Weekends are typically set aside for family outings – expect to see lots of cookouts on the beach on Sunday afternoons. It's not uncommon for as many as 50 people to be together as a family group on one of these picnics. People in Hawaii are early risers, often taking a run along the beach or hitting the waves before heading to the office. Most people work a 40-hour week – overtime and the workaholic routine common elsewhere in the US is the exception here.

In many ways, contemporary culture in Hawaii resembles contemporary culture in the rest of the USA. People in Hawaii listen to the same pop music and watch the same TV shows as Americans on the mainland. Honolulu has hip-hop bands and classical orchestras, junk food and nouvelle cuisine. The wonderful thing about Hawaii, however, is that the mainland influences largely stand beside, rather than engulf, the culture of the islands.

Not only is traditional Hawaiian culture an integral part of the social fabric of Hawaii, but so too are the customs of the ethnically diverse immigrants who have made the islands their home. Honolulu is more than just a meeting place of East and West; it's a place where the cultures merge, typically in a manner that brings out the best of both worlds.

Recent decades have seen a refreshing cultural renaissance in all things Hawaiian. Native Hawaiian–language classes are thriving, local artists and craftspeople are returning to traditional mediums and themes, and hula classes are concentrating more on the nuances behind hand movements and facial expressions than on the dramatic hip-shaking that sells tickets to dance shows.

Traditional hula instruments still used today include gourd rattles, stone castanets and sharkskin-topped drums.

Certainly visitors will still encounter a measure of packaged Hawaiiana that seems almost a parody of island culture, from plastic lei to theme-park luaus. But fortunately for the visitor, the growing interest in traditional Hawaiian culture is having a positive impact on the tourist industry, and authentic performances by hula students and Hawaiian musicians are increasingly easier to find.

Folks on O'ahu are quite accepting of other people, which helps explain the harmonious hodgepodge of races and cultures that make up the society. Traditionally, sexual orientation is not an issue and gays tend to be accepted, though in reality acceptance is more widespread in the city than in tight-knit local communities.

Not all is sunny in paradise. A federal government crackdown on the growing of *pakalolo* (marijuana) in the 1980s successfully pushed growers underground, forcing them to abandon fields. Some literally opened subterranean greenhouses using artificial light, but the police eventually rooted them out by monitoring electricity bills. With the loss of the marijuana crop on the streets, crystal meth (ice) became rampant in the 1990s and it has wreaked havoc on an ever-increasing number of families – so many that nearly everyone on O'ahu can tell a story of a friend or family member that's been affected.

POPULATION
Honolulu accounts for nearly half of O'ahu's population of 884,000. But the official population and the number of people who are actually on the island at any one time are two different realities. Among the uncounted on a typical day are some 75,000 tourists – so many that in the tourist mecca of Waikiki there are more than two tourists for every local resident. And another largely transient group, members of the US military and their dependents, add approximately 120,000 more to the uncounted total. Add a couple of thousand more people for overlaying flight crews, and you get a more accurate glimpse of O'ahu's real population.

Locals do sometimes feel inundated by 'unofficial residents,' and there are mixed feelings about both tourism and the military. Since most tourism is concentrated in Waikiki, it is the military presence, which covers vast tracts of the island, that tends to be the larger issue. And it's an issue that's likely to grow as the US military seems poised to use O'ahu as an even greater staging ground for missions in Asia and the Middle East.

SPORTS
As in the days of old in Hawaii, no sport brings out the crowds like surfing. Locals and visitors alike flock to the North Shore when major surf competitions take place. By far the hottest of these is the Triple Crown (p198), the world's top surfing event, which takes place at Sunset Beach, Banzai Pipeline and Hale'iwa beginning in late November (see p51 for more on this popular sport).

Hawaii's Sports Hall of Fame at www.alohafame.org honors the state's champion athletes.

Another traditional sport, outrigger canoe racing, is also big on Hawaii. You can watch high-school teams rowing in the Ala Wai Canal nearly every afternoon and a couple of international races run from the island of Moloka'i to O'ahu in the fall. Windsurfing, a sport that has propelled to fame more recently in Hawaii, brings out scores of onlookers at hotspots like Kailua Beach and Sunset Beach.

Then there are the land sports. King of the road races is the Honolulu Marathon, which is held in mid-December and is one of the largest marathons in the entire USA.

Due to its isolation and relatively small population, Hawaii doesn't have any major-league sports teams. But it does play host to the National Football League's Pro Bowl in February and to the collegiate Aloha Bowl at Christmas, both nationally televised from O'ahu's Aloha Stadium. For ticket information on the bowl games, contact the **Aloha Stadium ticket office** (☎ 486-9300) as far in advance as possible.

They may lack pro teams, but O'ahuans don't lack interest in major sports. They rally around the **University of Hawai'i** (UH; ☎ 956-4481) teams; of particular note is the UH women's volleyball team, a longstanding powerhouse with several National Collegiate Athletic Association (NCAA) championship titles. The UH basketball and football teams also have a strong local following and can play to sellout crowds.

And then there's golf. O'ahu hosts several PGA events that attract top golfing pros, including the Sony Open in Hawaii at the Waialae Country Club in Kahala in early January; the Hawaiian Ladies Open at Kapolei Golf Course in mid-February; and, on the Senior PGA Tour, the Turtle Bay Championship at the Turtle Bay Resort in late September. And Honolulu residents are proud of their native daughter Michelle Wie, who has broken gender barriers on the golf scene (see p61).

MULTICULTURALISM

As the most ethnically diverse city in America, Honolulu enjoys a degree of racial and social harmony that has few parallels on the US mainland. Since no one ethnic group comprises more than 20% of the population, everyone in Hawaii belongs to a minority.

The face of Hawaii is literally the face of diversity. On average, islanders have a 50/50 chance of marrying someone of a race different than their own, and the majority of children born in Hawaii are *hapa* (of mixed blood). Any family gathering is likely to see a mixture of ethnicities, with grandchildren in a rainbow of colors.

Hawaii's history of acceptance dates back to the arrival of the first Westerners. When whaling ships began stopping in O'ahu in the early 19th century, freed or runaway slaves were well represented among the crew. Some of these black men, recognizing paradise when they saw it, jumped ship. Those that stayed on typically married into Hawaiian families and were assimilated into the culture.

In the mid-19th century sugar plantation owners began recruiting laborers from China, then from Japan, and later from Portugal, Puerto Rico, Korea and the Philippines. Although these six ethnic groups made up the bulk of the field hands, South Sea islanders, Scots, Scandinavians and other Europeans came in turn as well. Each group brought its own culture, food and religion. Chinese clothing styles mixed with Japanese kimonos and European bonnets. A dozen languages filled the air and a unique pidgin English developed as a means for the various groups to communicate with one another.

Hawaii's everyday culture borrows richly from its multicultural heritage. Pidgin is alive and well to this day. Rice is the main staple in most island meals. And taking your shoes off before you enter a house is as important a ritual here as it is in Japan.

And the immigration hasn't stopped. South Americans are among the most recent to make O'ahu their home, with a vital community of Brazilians adding the latest splash of color, most notably around Waikiki and on the North Shore.

RELIGION

Religion permeated every aspect of daily life in ancient Hawaiian society, and people's activities were dictated by strict religious regulations known as the *kapu* (taboo) system. The *kapu* forbade commoners from eating the same food or even walking the same ground as the *ali'i* (royalty), who were thought to be representatives of the gods.

Minor infractions – such as stealing – could result in banishment for a brief period of time. But for the breaking of a major *kapu*, such as murder or temple desecration, the punishment could be death.

Kamehameha the Great was the last king to live by the old religion. When his son King Liholiho broke the *kapu* in 1820 by dining with Queen Ka'ahumanu yet suffered no divine punishment, many Hawaiians rejected the entire tradition and became willing converts

Filmed on O'ahu, *Picture Bride*, starring Yuki Kudoh and Toshiro Mifune, depicts the blunt realities of 19th-century Hawaiian plantation life for a Japanese mail-order bride.

You'll laugh till you hurt reading the illustrated pidgin dictionary, *Pidgin to da Max*, by Douglas Simonson – a local classic available at www.bess press.com.

NO TALK LI' DAT

The Hawaii educational system has traditionally pushed local kids to use standard English and not pidgin in the classroom. State department of education leaders (and many parents) often blame low scores on standardized tests on local kids' speaking, thinking and writing in pidgin. But a movement to legitimize pidgin as a language is afoot. Da Pidgin Coup, a group of University of Hawai'i faculty and graduate students, asserts that pidgin can coexist with standard English and should not be forbidden if its use facilitates the learning process. As the argument goes, *what* you say is more important than *how* you say it.

The most well-known champion for pidgin use is Lee Tonouchi, a lecturer at Kapiolani Community College's English Department, who was hired with an application written entirely in pidgin. A prolific writer and playwright, he makes an intriguing, subversive argument for legitimizing pidgin. His books include *Da Word* and *Living Pidgin: Contemplations on Pidgin Culture*.

This debate parallels the 1996 debate over Ebonics (black English) in Oakland, California, where the local school board recognized Ebonics, a term derived from ebony and phonics, as a separate language. The board concluded that most African American children come to school fluent in their vernacular, and to condemn it would be counterproductive.

Granted, pidgin use is not universal among locals and is determined by socioeconomic class. At the top schools, such as Punahou and Iolani on O'ahu, you'll hear little, if any, pidgin. But all locals clearly understand it – and they regard pidgin as social glue, bonding one another to a shared identity and sense of humor. Most locals straddle the two languages, using either pidgin or standard English when it's most appropriate.

For more on pidgin, see the Language chapter (p257).

---

to Christianity. But others took the Hawaiian religion underground. While the traditional beliefs never regained their former command, the philosophy endured, often expressed as *aloha 'aina* (reverence for the land's sanctity). In part, the Hawaiian sovereignty movement is rooted in *aloha 'aina,* to reclaim the land regarded as abused by outsiders.

Almost all of the ancient historical sites in the islands, such as *pu'uhonua* (places of refuge) and heiau (temples), are religious sites, chosen for the mana of the land. At some sites traditionalists perform rituals and leave offerings – a ti leaf wrapped around a stone and placed on a heiau wall is such an offering. The spirituality of old Hawaii also lives in the arts, most notably in the hula, where the intricacies of many dances revere the age-old spirits of the islands.

Today most people in Hawaii remain devoted Christians, with Roman Catholics being by far the largest denomination. Mainstream Protestant Christianity is struggling with declining membership, while evangelical churches and the Mormon church are burgeoning. Hawaii has the highest statewide percentage of Buddhists in the USA, but the number of younger adherents is dwindling.

ARTS
Literature
Contemporary local fiction and poetry is published in a biannual journal by **Bamboo Ridge Press** (www.bambooridge.com); the journal has launched many local writers' careers. Some have hit the national scene, such as Nora Okja Keller, whose first novel, *Comfort Woman,* won the 1998 American Book Award, and Lois-Ann Yamanaka, author of critically acclaimed novels, including *Heads by Harry*. Another interesting read is Sylvia Watanabe's *Talking to the Dead,* about the challenges of growing up as a second-generation Japanese-American in postwar Honolulu. You can readily pick up these books at bookstores in Honolulu (p70).

TV & Cinema

Small Honolulu-based company, **Talk Story Productions** (www.talk-story.com) is producing TV programs shot on O'ahu. It just made its big break with the series *Beyond the Break,* broadcast nationwide on the teen-oriented N network. Shot on O'ahu's North Shore, the drama series builds around the challenges facing five island girls working to become pro surfers.

Not everything shot on O'ahu is small-scale. The biggest smash on the network TV scene currently, *Lost,* is also filmed on the island, and two other high-profile TV shows, the classics *Magnum PI* and *Hawaii Five-0,* were produced here. Then there's the big screen – scores of movie hits (p182), such as *Jurassic Park* and *Blue Crush,* have captured the beauty of O'ahu on celluloid.

Music

Contemporary Hawaiian music gives center stage to the guitar, which was first introduced to the islands by Spanish cowboys in the 1830s. The Hawaiians made it uniquely their own, however. In 1889 Joseph Kekuku, a native Hawaiian, designed the steel guitar, one of only two major musical instruments invented in what is now the USA. (The other is the banjo.) The Hawaiian steel guitar is usually played with slack-key tunings. For the slack-key method (*ki ho'alu,* which means 'loosen the key'), the six strings are slacked from their standard tuning to facilitate a full sound on a single guitar – the thumb plays the bass and rhythm chords, while the fingers play the melody and improvisations, in a picked style.

Slack-key guitar aficionados can find out all about the genre and upcoming concerts by logging on to www.dancingcat.com.

The most influential slack-key artist was Gabby Pahinui (1921–80), who launched the modern slack-key era with his first recording in 1946. Over the years, he played with the legendary Sons of Hawaii and later formed the Gabby Pahinui Hawaiian Band with four of his sons; his home in Waimanalo was a mecca for backyard jam sessions. Other pioneering slack-key masters were Sonny Chillingworth and Atta Isaacs. Today the tradition lives on in Dennis Kamakahi, Keola Beamer, Led Ka'apana and Cyril Pahinui, among others.

New Age piano whiz George Winston calls Queen Lili'uokalani one of the top five composers of all time.

The instrument most commonly associated with Hawaii is the ukulele, though it's derived from the *braguinha,* a Portuguese instrument introduced to Hawaii in the late 19th century. Ukulele means 'jumping flea' in Hawaiian, referring to the way players' deft fingers swiftly 'jump' around the strings. Hawaii's ukulele masters include Eddie Kamae, Herb Ohta and contemporary uke whirlwind Jake Shimabukuro.

Both the ukulele and the steel guitar were essential to the lighthearted, romantic music popularized in Hawaii from the 1930s to the 1950s, of which *My Little Grass Shack* and *Lovely Hula Hands* are classic examples. Due in part to the 'Hawaii Calls' radio show, which for more than 30 years was broadcast worldwide from the Moana Hotel in Waikiki, this music became instantly recognizable as Hawaiian, conjuring up images of hula dancers swaying under palm trees in a tropical paradise.

You can listen to live Hawaiian music by logging on to http://home.hawaii.rr.com.

In the 1970s Hawaiian music enjoyed a rebirth, and artists such as Cecilio & Kapono and the Beamer Brothers remain icons in Hawaii. Over the years the Hawaiian sound has spurred offshoots, like reggae-inspired 'Jawaiian,' but the traditional style lives on in gifted contemporary voices, such as Keali'i Reichel, also a hula master, and Raiatea Helm, who has been scooping up Hawaii's top music awards. Still, the most famous island musician is the late Israel Kamakawiwo'ole, whose *Facing Future* is Hawaii's all-time bestselling album. The genre is now breaking out of the niche market, with on-line sales mounting and a new Grammy Award for Best Hawaiian Music Album established in 2005. The Grammy-winning

---

A STITCH IN TIME

Hawaiian quilts are a unique art form, borne of unique circumstances. The concept of patchwork quilting was introduced by the early Christian missionaries, but the Hawaiians, who had only recently taken to cotton clothing, didn't have a surplus of cloth scraps to use – and the idea of cutting up new lengths of fabric simply to sew them back together again in small squares seemed absurd.

Instead, Hawaiian women created designs using larger cloth pieces, typically with stylized tropical flora on a contrasting background. As far as the patterns, the story goes that when the first group of Hawaiian quilters spread their white cloth on the ground, a breadfruit leaf cast its shadow onto the cloth and the outline of the leaf was traced to produced the first native design.

CD for 2006, *Masters of Hawaiian Slack Key Guitar, Vol 1,* features the work of such greats as George Kahumoku Jr and Led Ka'apana.

Top venues for live Hawaiian music are the Banyan Veranda (p146) and Duke's Canoe Club (p146).

Hula

In ancient Hawaii, hula was a type of spiritual expression. Dancers used hand gestures, facial expression and rhythmic movement to illustrate historical events, legendary tales and the accomplishments of the great *ali'i* (royalty). These were performed to rhythmic chants and drum beatings, serving to connect with the world of spirits. Eye movement was important; if the story was about the sun, the dancer's eyes would gaze upward, and if about the netherworld, they would gaze downward.

Hula dancers wore *kapa* (bark cloth), never the stereotypical grass skirts that are sometimes seen at tacky luau. When the Christian missionaries arrived, they viewed hula dancing as too licentious and suppressed it. The hula might have been lost forever if not for King Kalakaua, the 'Merrie Monarch (p31),' who revived it in the latter half of the 19th century.

Hula *halau* (schools) have seen an influx of new students in recent years. Some practice in public places, such as school grounds and parks, where visitors are welcome to watch. Although many of the *halau* rely on tuition fees, others receive sponsorship from hotels or shopping centers and give weekly public performances in return. And the county sponsors a nightly hula show (p148) at Kuhio Beach Park in Waikiki.

There were many schools of hula, including one called hula 'ohelo, which was very sensual, its movements expressing the act of procreation.

Arts & Crafts

All ancient crafts have an aesthetic component that reflect the simple stone and shell tools Hawaiians used to create everything from surfboards to clothing. Today the artistry lives in the handcrafted koa bowls that woodworkers still create in traditional styles. The age-old craft of carving canoes from giant logs is also making a comeback.

Lei making is a more transitory art form. Although the lei most visitors wear are made of fragrant flowers, such as plumeria and tuberose, traditional lei of *mokihana* berries and maile leaves were more commonly worn in old Hawaii. Both types are still made today, and can be readily purchased from lei-makers in Chinatown and elsewhere around the island.

Many artists draw inspiration from Hawaii's rich cultural heritage. Worth going out of your way to see is Herb Kawainui Kane's dynamic oil painting *The Discovery of Hawai'i,* which depicts the canoe landing of early Polynesian settlers; it's showcased along with the works of other leading island artists at the Hawai'i State Art Museum (p75). A score of galleries selling quality artwork can be found in nearby Chinatown (p108).

Environment

Hawaii's environment is like no other. The Hawaiian Island chain, 2500 miles from the nearest continental land mass, is *the* most geographically isolated group of islands in the world.

Since these volcanic islands were born beneath the sea as clumps of lava, they started with no surface land and hence no land life. All living things that reached Hawaii's shores were carried across the ocean on the wind or the waves – seeds clinging to a bird's feather, for instance. Fern and moss spores, able to drift thousands of miles in the air, were probably the first plant life to arrive on the newly emerged islands.

The City & County of Honolulu includes the Northwestern Hawaiian Islands, a couple of dozen unpopulated islands stretching 1300 miles across the Pacific.

Before human contact, a new species managed to take hold in Hawaii only once every 100,000 years. New arrivals found specialized habitats ranging from desert to rain forest and elevations climbing from sea level to mountain tops. Each species evolved to fit a specific niche in its new environment.

Today more than 90% of Hawaii's native flora and fauna is found nowhere else on earth, and some species have evolved so thoroughly that it's not possible to trace them to any continental ancestor.

THE LAND

Hawaii is the southernmost state in the USA. The equator is 1470 miles south of Honolulu, putting O'ahu in the Tropic of Cancer and on the same latitude as Hong Kong, Mumbai and Mexico City. At 594 sq miles, O'ahu is the third-largest Hawaiian island, comprising roughly 10% of Hawaii's total land mass. The island's extreme length is 44 miles, and its width is 30 miles. O'ahu's highest point, Mt Ka'ala at 4020ft, is in the central Wai'anae Range.

Hawaii is the northern-most point of the triangle of Pacific islands known as Polynesia ('many islands'). The other points are New Zealand and Easter Island.

The Hawaiian Islands are actually the tips of massive mountains created by a crack in the earth's mantle that has been spewing out molten rock for more than 25 million years. The hot spot is stationary, but the ocean floor is part of the Pacific Plate, which is moving northwest at the rate of about 3in a year. (The eastern edge of this plate is California's San Andreas fault.)

As weak spots in the earth's crust pass over the hot spot, molten lava bursts through as volcanoes, creating underwater mountains. Some of these build up enough to finally emerge above the water as islands.

Each new volcano eventually creeps northward past the hot spot that created it. The further from the source the volcano is, the lower the volcanic activity, until it is eventually cut off completely. Then the forces of erosion – wind, rain and waves – add geologic character to the newly emerged islands, cutting valleys, creating beaches and turning a mound of lava into paradise.

On O'ahu, two separate volcanoes arose about two million years ago to form the island's two mountain ranges, Wai'anae and Ko'olau, which slice the island from the northwest to the southeast. O'ahu's last gasp of volcanic activity occurred about 10,000 years ago, creating the tuff cone of Diamond Head (p163), O'ahu's most famous geographical landmark.

WILDLIFE

It's often said that if Darwin had arrived in Hawaii he would have developed his theory of evolution in a period of weeks instead of years. Almost all the species carried by wind and waves across the vast Pacific adapted so uniquely to these remote islands that they evolved into new species endemic only to Hawaii. And the adaptations are amazing – many of Hawaii's birds evolved from a single species, as is thought to have been the case with more than 30 species of native honeycreeper.

Having evolved with limited competition and few predators, Hawaii's native species generally fare poorly among more aggressive introduced flora and fauna. They are also highly sensitive to habitat destruction. When Westerners first came to Hawaii, the islands had 70 native bird species. Of those, 24 are now extinct and an additional 36 are threatened with extinction.

The first Polynesian settlers to arrive weren't traveling light. They brought food and medicinal plants, chickens, dogs and pigs. The pace of introducing exotic species escalated with the arrival of Europeans, starting with Captain Cook, who dropped off goats and left melon and pumpkin seeds.

The introduction of pigs, cattle and goats, which grazed and foraged at will, devastated Hawaii's fragile ecosystems and spelled extinction for many plants. Released songbirds and game birds spread avian diseases to the native Hawaiian birds, which did not have the immunities to fight off foreign pathogens.

Practical Folk Medicine of Hawaii, by LR McBride, has descriptions of many native medicinal plants and their uses.

The invasion of exotic species continues today. One of the latest aliens to surface is the giant day gecko, a native of Madagascar that is thought to have arrived on O'ahu as part of the illegal pet trade. And most environmentalists feel the biggest threat on O'ahu is from the brown tree snake, which has lead to the extinction of all native birds on the Pacific island of Guam. This tree-climbing snake has been found several times in arriving planes at Honolulu International Airport, though it's not known if any have yet made it past inspection and escaped into the wild.

Animals

Hawaii's creatures come in small bundles on land – mostly birds and nonthreatening insects. In the water they range wildly from tiny reef fish to 45-ton whales.

LAND ANIMALS

Prior to human contact, Hawaii had no land mammals, save for monk seals (see the boxed text From the Brink of Extinction, p44) and hoary bats (*'ope'ape'a*).

Most interesting of the introduced species is the brush-tailed rock wallaby, which was accidentally released in 1916 and is now residing in the Kalihi Valley, north of Honolulu. Although rarely seen, the wallabies are of keen interest to zoologists because they may be the last members of a subspecies that's now extinct in their native Australia.

O'ahu has an endemic genus of tree snail, the *Achatinella*. In former days the forests were loaded with these colorful snails, which clung like gems to the leaves of trees. They were too attractive for their own good, however, and up until the early 20th century hikers were collecting them by the handful. The deforestation of forest habitat and the introduction of a cannibal snail and predatory rodents, like the mongoose, have been even more devastating. Of 41 *Achatinella* species, only 19 remain and all are endangered.

MARINE ANIMALS

Hawaii excels in its rich and varied marine life. Almost 700 fish species live in Hawaiian waters, with nearly one-third of those found nowhere else in the world. O'ahu's nearshore waters harbor large rainbow-colored parrotfish, moray eels and ballooning pufferfish, just to name a few. The waters also abound in green sea turtles, manta rays and a variety of sharks.

Of all the whales that frequent Hawaiian waters, it is the migratory North Pacific humpback, which entertains with acrobatic breaches and tail flips, that everyone wants to see. Humpbacks, the fifth largest of the great whales, reach lengths of 45ft and weigh up to 45 tons. Luckily for whale watchers, humpback whales are coast-huggers, preferring waters with depths of less than 600ft. They can sometimes be seen in winter from the beaches along O'ahu's west and southwest coasts. Whale-watching boats (p93) take visitors straight out to the most likely viewing spots.

For all the skinny on humpback whales, go to the Hawaiian Islands National Marine Sanctuary website at www.hihwnms.nos .noaa.gov.

Numerous dolphins are found in the waters around O'ahu. The ones you're most likely to see are spinner dolphins, nocturnal feeders that come into calm bays during the day to rest. Although it may seem tempting to swim out and join them, because they are very sensitive it's illegal to approach them. However, you can easily watch them from the shore.

BIRDS

Native waterfowl include the graceful Hawaiian stilt *(ae'o)*, a black-necked wading bird with a white underbelly and long orange legs, which feeds along the marshy edges of ponds; the Hawaiian coot *('alae ke'oke'o)*, which is gray and black except for its white bill; and the Hawaiian moorhen *('alae 'ula)*, slate gray with a red bill. All three, which are endangered and endemic to Hawaii, can readily be seen in the Hamakua Marsh Wildlife Sanctuary (p178) in Kailua.

Hikers who take to the inland trails can expect to see some of Hawaii's forest birds. The *'elepaio*, a brownish bird with a white rump, and the *'amakihi*, a small yellow-green bird, are the most common endemic forest birds on O'ahu. The *'apapane*, a vivid red honeycreeper, and the *'i'iwi*, a bright vermilion bird, are less common but also sometimes spotted.

Hawaii's Birds, by the Hawaii Audubon Society, is the best pocket-sized guide to the native and endangered birds of Hawaii.

Most of the islets off O'ahu's windward coast are sanctuaries for seabirds, including terns, noddies, shearwaters, Laysan albatrosses and boobies. Moku Manu ('Bird Island'), off Mokapu Peninsula in Kane'ohe, has the greatest variety of species, including a large number of sooty terns that lay their eggs directly on the ground. Because the nesting birds are sensitive to human disturbance, visitors are not allowed at all on Moku Manu and are restricted on the other islands.

FROM THE BRINK OF EXTINCTION

One of the Pacific's rarest marine creatures is the Hawaiian monk seal *(Monachus schauinslandi)*, so named for the cowl-like fold of skin at its neck and for its solitary habits. The Hawaiian name for the animal is *'ilio holo kai*, meaning 'the dog that runs in the sea.'

The species has remained nearly unchanged for 15 million years, though in the past century it has been in danger of dying out completely. The annual birth rate for Hawaiian monk seal pups is around 175 a year, but due to shark attacks and other predators, the majority of pups don't reach maturity.

Fortunately, conservation efforts, including the relocation of some seals to create a better male-female ratio, appear to be bringing the seals back from the edge of extinction. The total Hawaiian monk seal population is estimated at approximately 1400 seals.

Although their prime habitat is the uninhabited Northwestern Hawaiian Islands, monk seals do occasionally haul up on O'ahu's more remote northwest beaches, near Ka'ena Point.

LEI'D IN HAWAII?

Don't assume that lovely lei draped around your neck is purely Hawaiian. Island flower growers have had such a problem keeping up with the demand for the blossoms used in lei that they now import flowers from Southeast Asia. A spurt in tourism and a decline in nursery farming has forced Hawaii lei makers to go further afield to get at least some of their flowers. Dendrobium orchids imported from Thailand, for example, are now commonly found in lei, especially during the winter months when they become particularly scarce in Hawaii.

If you have a pair of binoculars you can enjoy bird-watching right from the coast, however. Great frigate birds, aerial pirates that snatch food from other birds in midair, are commonly seen circling above Waimanalo Bay; graceful in flight, they are easily identifiable by their 7ft wingspan and distinctively forked tail. Another bird that can be spotted soaring along the cliffs of the windward coast is the red-tailed tropicbird, pure white except for its trailing red tail.

Plants

O'ahu is abloom year-round with colorful tropical flowers and plants. Two special places to visit are Foster Botanical Garden (p82) in the Chinatown area and the Lyon Arboretum (p87) on the northern side of Honolulu, both of which have excellent collections.

FLOWERS

Native coastal plants include *pohuehue*, a beach morning glory with pink flowers that's found just above the wrack line along the coast throughout O'ahu; beach *naupaka*, a shrub with oval leaves and a small white five-petal flower that looks as if it's been torn in half; and the low-growing *'ilima*, which has delicate yellow-orange blossoms and is O'ahu's official flower.

You'll find brilliant photos of Hawaiian plants at www.hear.org/starr/hiplants/images/index.html.

For travelers, perhaps no flower is more closely identified with Hawaii than the hibiscus, whose generous blossoms are worn by women, tucked behind their ears. Thousands of varieties of hibiscus bushes grow in Hawaii; on most, the flowers bloom early in the day and drop before sunset. The variety most frequently seen is the red *Hibiscus rosa-sinensis*, which is used as a landscape hedge throughout O'ahu.

Other tropical flowers commonly seen in gardens include blood-red anthurium, brilliant orange bird-of-paradise, colorful bougainvillea, red ginger, fragrant jasmine, and various heliconias with bright orange and red bracts.

TREES

The most revered of the native Hawaiian forest trees is koa (a timber tree), found at higher elevations in O'ahu. Koa grows up to 100ft high and is unusual in that the young saplings have fernlike compound leaves, while mature trees have flat crescent-shaped phyllodes. Koa's rich hardwood, traditionally used to make canoes, is still favored today by woodworkers to make smaller items, like bowls and ukuleles.

Another interesting native tree, the ohia lehua, has bright red pompom flowers and grows in barren areas as a shrub, and on more fertile land as a tree.

Brought by early Polynesian settlers, the *kukui* tree has chestnut-like oily nuts the Hawaiians used for candles, hence its common name, candlenut tree; it's recognizable in the forest by its light silver-tinged foliage.

Two trees found along the coast that were well utilized in old Hawaii are *hala*, also called pandanus or screw pine, whose spiny leaves were used for thatching and weaving; and the coconut palm *(niu)*, which thrives in coral sands and produces about 75 coconuts a year.

Expect to see kiawe, a non-native tree, in dry coastal areas. A member of the mesquite family, kiawe is useful for making charcoal but is a nuisance for beachgoers, as its sharp thorns easily pierce soft sandals. Also plentiful along the beach are stands of ironwood, a conifer with drooping needles that act as natural windbreaks and prevent beach erosion. The pesky and intrusive mangrove has a twisted root system that has choked natural ponds and has done a nasty job on O'ahu's ancient fishponds, winding its roots into the stone walls.

Noteworthy among O'ahu's flowering trees are monkeypod, a common shade tree with puffy pink flowers and longish seed pods, and plumeria, a favored landscaping tree whose fragrant pink and white blossoms are used in lei making.

NATIONAL, STATE & COUNTY PARKS

There are no national parks with forests and trails on O'ahu, but the Hawaiian Islands Humpback Whale National Marine Sanctuary encompasses the ocean waters around the north and south shores of O'ahu. The federal government also has jurisdiction over the coastal wetlands in the James Campbell National Wildlife Refuge (p193), a prime birdwatching venue.

But if you really want to take to the trails, it's the state forest reserves that will beckon. From Ka'ena Point (p226) on the remote western tip of the island to Diamond Head (p163) near the touristy Waikiki area, there's a rich system of state-run properties loaded with diverse hiking opportunities.

And then there are the abundant beach parks, which offer every water activity imaginable. Highlights include gorgeous Kailua Beach (p177), where windsurfing and kayaking reign supreme; Sunset Beach (p198), where banzai (pipeline) surfers ride monster waves; and Ala Moana Beach Park (p82), with stellar swimming conditions.

The **Department of Land & Natural Resources** (Map pp76-7; DLNR; ☎ 587-0320; www.state.hi.us/dlnr; State Office Tower, 1151 Punchbowl St, Honolulu) issues backcountry camping permits, and has many useful publications and on-line information about safe hiking, conservation and aquatic safety. The DLNR oversees all of the following divisions and programs, which have their own offices in the same building:

Division of Forestry & Wildlife (DOFAW; www.dofaw.net) Supervises public land management of Hawaii's forests and natural area reserves. Public outreach focuses on outdoor recreation, conservation and watershed protection.

Division of State Parks (☎ 587-0300; www.hawaii.gov/dlnr/dsp) Administers state parks, provides a free downloadable brochure and handles permits for camping at state parks.

Na Ala Hele Trail & Access Program (☎ 587-0062; www.hawaiitrails.org) Na Ala Hele ('Trails to Go On') coordinates public access to hiking trails, as well as historical trail preservation and maintenance. Its excellent website contains useful maps, guidelines for safe hiking and announcements of recently developed or reopened trails.

ENVIRONMENTAL ISSUES

Hawaii's ecosystem is a fragile one – so fragile that 25% of all the endangered species in the USA are native plants and animals in Hawaii. These native species are highly sensitive to habitat degradation and over the past century many species have become extinct, including more than a third

O'AHU'S TOP 20 NATURAL AREAS

Natural area	Features	Activities	Best time to visit	Page
Diamond Head State Monument	remnants of a volcanic crater	hiking	year-round	p163
Foster Botanical Garden	botanical garden featuring native and rare plants	garden walks	year-round	p82
Hamakua Marsh Wildlife Sanctuary	marshland preserve for endangered Hawaiian waterbirds	bird-watching	year-round	p178
Hanauma Bay Nature Preserve	Hawaii's only underwater park	snorkeling, diving	year-round	p166
Ho'omaluhia Botanical Gardens	400 acres of tropical trees and shrubs	hiking	year-round	p184
James Campbell National Wildlife Refuge	wetland habitat	bird-watching	Aug–mid-Feb	p193
Ka'ena Point State Park	O'ahu's westernmost tip, accessible only by foot	hiking, surfing, solitude-seeking	year-round	p226
Kailua Beach Park	sandy beach, calm waters, offshore islands	kayaking, windsurfing, swimming	year-round	p177
Keaiwa Heiau State Recreation Area	ancient heiau, forest	hiking, mountain biking, camping	year-round	p159
Koko Crater Botanical Garden	dryland plants, including cacti and plumeria	hiking	year-round	p168
Kualoa Regional Park	remote beach backed by scalloped cliffs	swimming	year-round	p186
Makaha Beach Park	stunning beach favored by surfers	surfing, swimming, snorkeling, diving	seasons vary	p223
Makapu'u Point	fascinating geological formations; cliffside beach	bodysurfing, hike to lighthouse	year-round	p168
Malaekahana State Recreation Area	sandy beach, Moku'auia (Goat Island) bird sanctuary	swimming, snorkeling, camping	year-round	p192
Manoa Falls	cascading waterfall in forest reserve	hiking	year-round	p91
Pupukea Beach Park	underwater caves and lava ledges	snorkeling, diving	May-Oct	p201
Tantalus Forest Reserve	forest reserve crisscrossed with trails	hiking	year-round	p88
Wahiawa Botanical Garden	arboretum of grand old trees	hiking	year-round	p213
Waimea Bay Beach Park	glorious beach with incredible winter surf	surfing, swimming, snorkeling	seasons vary	p201
Waimea Valley Audubon Center	preserve of native plants and archaeological sites	hiking; swimming in waterfall pool	year-round	p202

The US Fish & Wildlife Service website (www .fws.gov/pacificislands /wesa/endspindex.html) showcases the beauty of Hawaii's one-of-a-kind endangered birds and animals.

of all native forest birds. Today fully half of Hawaii's approximately 2400 native flora and fauna species are either threatened or endangered.

Vast tracts of native forest have long been cleared to give way to the monocrop cultures of sugarcane and pineapple. In the 1960s the advent of mass tourism posed new challenges to the environment, most notably in the rampant development of land-hungry golf courses. In recent decades the number of golf courses on O'ahu has jumped from just a handful to 37, and the total acreage given over to these golf courses now rivals that used for agriculture.

In terms of air quality, O'ahu has no polluting heavy industry. However, Honolulu, being on the dry and less windy leeward side of the island, occasionally has moderate levels of vehicle-related pollution. As for general aesthetics, roadside billboards are not allowed and overall the level of environmental awareness is more advanced here than on much of the US mainland.

On a grassroots level, a wide coalition of scientists, activists and residents has made island conservation efforts a slow, but steady success. There are more than 150 environmental groups in Hawaii, running the gamut from chapters of international organizations fighting to save the rain forests to neighborhood groups working to protect local beaches from impending development.

One of the most broad-based environmental groups is the Hawaii chapter of the **Sierra Club** (☎ 538-6616; www.hi.sierraclub.org). Its activities range from political activism on local environmental issues to weekend outings for eradicating invasive plants from the island's native forests. Its current Blue Water Campaign is working to protect Hawaii ocean waters from agricultural and golf course runoff and other types of land-based pollution. It is also fighting to control urban sprawl, using legal challenges to block developers from turning hundreds of acres of agricultural land in Central O'ahu into housing lots.

Also in the forefront is the **Earthjustice Legal Defense Fund** (☎ 599-2436; www .earthjustice.org), which plays a leading role in protecting Hawaii's fragile environment through court action. Over the years the group's Honolulu office has successfully sued to prohibit jet skis in waters used by humpback whales, and to stop the killing of sea turtles by the longline fishing

---

TREAD LIGHTLY

Hawaii's natural ecosystem has been ravaged by non-native plants and animals ever since the first contact with foreign ships. Seeds caught in the soles of your shoes or bugs left hiding out in the bottom of your backpack can potentially be a threat – so make sure your gear is clean before tramping into the woods.

You'll see countless 'No Trespassing – Kapu' signs around the island. Although you may be tempted to push on through that closed gate just to see what's beyond it, don't – unless of course a trustworthy local says it's actually OK. Respect the privacy of residents, whose quality of life is continually being encroached upon by tourist development. Practice respect for the 'aina (land). Leave nothing but footprints when walking in the forest or along beaches (snorkelers and divers shouldn't leave so much as a single toe print on fragile coral). Take out all your garbage.

Do not approach or otherwise disturb any endangered creatures, especially marine species, such as whales, dolphins, seals and sea turtles; doing so is not only illegal, but subjects trespassers to a hefty fine.

For volunteer opportunities – everything from public-awareness campaigns to counting migrating whales – contact **Malama Hawaii** (www.malamahawaii.org), a partnership network of environmental groups and other community organizations.

industry. Currently it's suing to prevent the introduction of a cobalt-60 nuclear irradiator at Honolulu International Airport proposed to treat produce for fruit flies.

A different approach is taken by the **Nature Conservancy of Hawaii** (☎ 537-4508; www.tnc.org), which protects Hawaii's rarest ecosystems by buying up tracts of land and working out long-term stewardships with prominent landholders. On O'ahu, the Nature Conservancy manages 'Ihi'ihilauakea Preserve, a 30-acre site containing a crater with a unique vernal pool above Hanauma Bay, and the Honouliuli Preserve, a 3692-acre tract on the southeastern slope of the Wai'anae Range, which is home to dozens of rare plant and animal species.

For a good source of the latest environmental issues facing the island, check the investigative journal *Environment Hawaii* at www.environment-hawaii.org.

O'ahu Outdoors

Now that you've made it to O'ahu, the real action begins. Sure, it might be fun to whittle away a day on the beach, but there's no need to stop there – an oceanful of adventures is just a Frisbee-toss away.

O'ahu is a great place for most anything that has to do with the water, including swimming, snorkeling, diving, surfing, windsurfing and kayaking. One great thing about the island is that every one of these activities has options suitable for all levels of experience, from someone who's trying the sport for the first time to a pro looking for top-notch conditions.

Take surfing (p54), for example, a sport where O'ahu reigns supreme. Some of the world's top action occurs on the North Shore – and with names like Banzai Pipeline, Avalanche and Himalayas, you can tell these towering surf breaks are not for neophytes. But that's only one side of the island's surf scene – in Waikiki, gentle waves and patient instructors can show a first-time surfer how to ride a wave in just an hour.

As a general rule, these activities require no advance planning before landing on the island – most of the time you can just show up, look around and decide.

O'ahu has a plethora of alluring land-based activities as well. You can take a horseback ride on the beach, hike into a remote rain forest or drive a golf ball in a spectacular mountain setting. Or if you prefer to take to the sky, you could jump at the chance to skydive (p208).

HERE'S TO EDDIE

'Eddie Would Go,' say the bumper stickers on half the cars in O'ahu that sport surfboards on top. Eddie who? Go where?

Eddie Aikau was a full-blooded native Hawaiian who got turned on to surfing as a teenager, learning the ropes as he moved up from Waikiki's tame surf to the monster waves of the North Shore. He so loved surfing that in 1968 he took a job as a lifeguard working at the North Shore beaches from Waimea Bay to Sunset Beach. Even though the North Shore has the most dangerous waves on O'ahu, no one was ever lost when Eddie was on duty. It's estimated he saved hundreds of lives during his decade-long career. Not only was he undaunted by 30ft waves, but he was also a master at maintaining the peace between local surfers and upstart off-islanders competing for the best breaks.

In an effort to get more in tune with his Hawaiian heritage, in 1978 Eddie joined a rediscovery trip aboard the *Hokule'a*, the double-hulled canoe that replicated the boats the first Polynesians used to reach Hawaii. It was to be the second journey for the *Hokule'a*, which in 1976 had followed the ancient migrations from O'ahu 2400 miles to Tahiti and back again.

For this second journey, more than 10,000 people gathered at the tip of Magic Island to see them off. On the way out the boat had to go through the Moloka'i Channel, the roughest waterway in the Hawaiian Islands, and the *Hokule'a* capsized. Unable to right it, Eddie jumped on his surfboard and set out to paddle 12 miles across the treacherous channel to the island of Lana'i to get help. In the meantime a Hawaiian Air pilot spotted the capsized boat and rescuers were sent to pick up the crew. Eddie, however, was never seen again.

His brave life and tragic death became the stuff of legends. The excellent biography *Eddie Would Go* by Stuart Holmes Coleman details not only Eddie's life, but also the Hawaiian renaissance of the 1960s and '70s. Today the Quiksilver Big Wave Invitational in Memory of Eddie Aikau surf competition is held at Waimea Bay in winter – but only when waves reach monstrous heights.

WATER ACTIVITIES

You didn't forget your swimsuit now, did you? O'ahu sits smack in the middle of the vast Pacific Ocean, so it makes sense that playing in, on and under the water would be central to any island holiday.

WAVE RIDING
Surfing
O'ahu's surfing is in a class by itself. The island lies in the path of all the major swells that race unimpeded across the Pacific, which gives rise to awesome surfing conditions. See the boxed text on p54 for more information on this popular sport.

Bodysurfing & Boogie Boarding
Bodysurfers who really know their stuff and want to try the island's top shorebreaks should head for Sandy Beach Park (p168) and Makapu'u Beach Park (p169) in southeast O'ahu, and Makaha Beach Park (p223) in Leeward O'ahu. Other top shorebreaks are at Waimea Bay Beach Park (p201) on the North Shore; Kalama Beach (p179) in Kailua; and Malaekahana State Recreation Area (p192) and Pounders (p191) in La'ie.

O'ahu boasts some 594 defined surfing sites, nearly twice as many as any of the other Hawaiian Islands.

Waimanalo Beach Park (p170) and nearby Bellows Field Beach Park (p170) in Waimanalo, in Windward O'ahu, have gentle shorebreaks good for beginner bodysurfers.

The island's most popular boogie boarding venue is Kapahulu Groin (p119) in Waikiki.

Kiteboarding
A little like skateboarding or snowboarding on water, kiteboarding is actually a kind of surfing. If you can wakeboard or windsurf, that'll help. So will lots of muscles and stamina. While it may be impressive to watch, it's bloody hard to master. First you learn how to fly the kite, then you practice bodydragging (letting the kite pull you across the water) and finally you step on board. On O'ahu, the place to try your hand is Kailua (p178). The cost for a package of lessons that should get you on your way is $450.

Windsurfing
O'ahu has primo conditions for windsurfing. With a little instruction and practice, you can just step on a board and let the wind take you away.

The windsurfing action centers on Kailua (p178), where you'll find persistent year-round trade winds and some top-notch shops renting gear and offering instruction. Kailua Bay has superb conditions for all levels from beginner to pro, with flat-water and wave conditions in different sections of the bay. It's never a slacker but the very best winds typically occur in summer, when east-to-northeast trades run at 8 to 15 knots. And when high-pressure systems come in, they can easily double that – which makes for awesome speed.

Surf News Network (www.surfnewsnetwork .com) has everything from current surf conditions, swell forecasts and upcoming competitions to very cool webcams of O'ahu's best surf breaks.

Other good windsurfing spots include Diamond Head (p164), for speed and jumps; Malaekahana State Recreation Area (p192), for open-water cruising; Mokule'ia Beach Park (p208), for consistent North Shore winds; and Backyards (p198), off Sunset Beach, with the island's highest sailable waves. In Waikiki, Fort DeRussy Beach (p123) is the main windsurfing spot. Windsurfing gear rents for around $35 to $50 a day. A three-hour introductory lesson that ends up with sailing costs around $50.

O'AHU ACTIVITIES

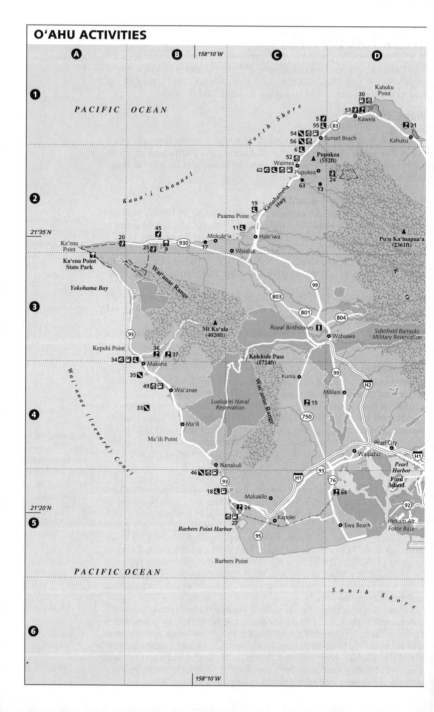

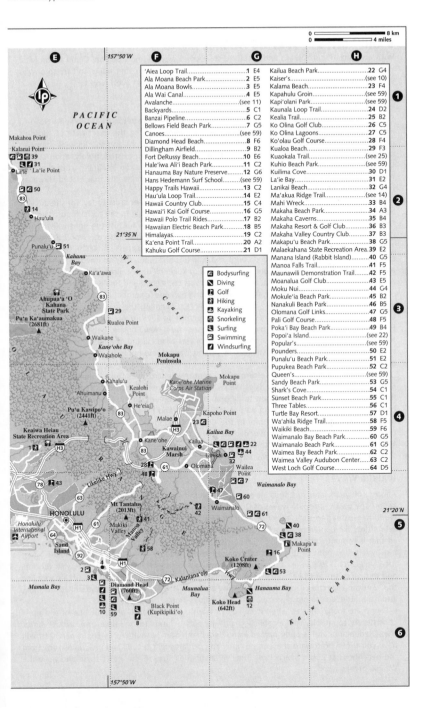

Legend

- 🅖 Bodysurfing
- 🄓 Diving
- 🄖 Golf
- 🄗 Hiking
- 🄚 Kayaking
- 🄢 Snorkeling
- 🄢 Surfing
- 🄢 Swimming
- 🄦 Windsurfing

O'AHU'S RITES OF SURFING PASSAGE *Jake Howard*

With a wealth of surf breaks and a culture steeped in wave-riding tradition, O'ahu is the ideal place to either be a surfer or learn to surf. As long as you know your limits and try to always surf with a smile, your next *surfari* to O'ahu will be one you won't soon forget.

EARLY RIDERS

Surfing in Hawaii goes back almost as far as the rainbows that stretch from Diamond Head to Ala Moana. Ancient Hawaiians lacked a written language, making the exact date of surfing's inception forever unknown, but researchers have traced petroglyphs and specific oral chants to approximately AD 1500, which leads them to believe that surfing existed in Polynesian culture long before that. One thing they do know is that wave riding was an integral part of the *kapu* (taboo) system of governing, which was more or less a feudal monarchy that placed Hawaiian royalty above the peasantry.

Just as driving through Beverly Hills in a Bentley screams upper crust today, for the ancient Hawaiians, the board you rode spoke volumes about where you sat in the social food chain. For the *ali'i* (ruling class), special craftsmen would search the jungles for just the right wiliwili tree, go through an intricate prayer ritual before felling the tree, then whittle the wood down to a 14ft to 16ft *olo* (a primitive long-board that usually weighed in excess of 100lb). Once ground smooth by *pohaku puna* (granulated coral) and *oahi* (rough stone), they adorned the board with a dark stain derived from ti root and polished it with kukui oil until a glossy finish was achieved. Another ceremony was then held, and the board was christened and finally ridden.

Minus the odd inter-island war, this all went along just fine for probably a couple of thousand years. Then Captain James Cook showed up in 1778, becoming the first Westerner to behold the sport of surfing. Despite Cook's unfortunate demise in 1779 (p24), word of the paradise in Hawaii was quick to get out, and by 1820 missionaries from New England began arriving. Just as they did on the mainland with all other aspects of Hawaiian culture, the missionaries promptly began to stamp out the 'hedonistic' act of surfing. Save a few holdouts, by 1890 surfing was all but extinct.

The most notable among those turn-of-the-century diehards was Duke Kahanamoku (p195). Kahanamoku grew up on the sands of Waikiki where, along with a handful of others, he swam, fished, dove and rode the reefs on traditional *olo*-style boards. In 1911 Duke and the Waikiki beachboys caught the attention of author Jack London, and being the prominent writer of the day that he was, London's accounts in the *Cruise of the Snark* almost immediately captured the imagination of the Western world. And there, practically surfing off the page, was Duke. Throughout the course of the 20th century Kahanamoku spread the gospel of surfing, traveling the world demonstrating the Hawaiian 'Sport of Kings.'

WAIKIKI WAVES

Almost 100 years later surfing is alive and well on the south shore of O'ahu. In Waikiki, the epicenter, the passive, sloping waves of Queen's, under the shadow of Diamond Head, is where the world has learned to surf. From Hawaiian kings and queens to throngs of Japanese tourists and celebrities, like Cameron Diaz and Kenny G, the slow, rolling waves of Queen's have embodied all that is romantic about Waikiki. Canoes is another hot spot when it comes to learning; this mushy left- and right-hander practically breaks in the shadow of the Duke Kahanamoku statue. After you catch a few waves, offer thanks by buying a fresh lei from one of the sidewalk vendors and throwing it over Duke's outstretched bronze arms. There's also Popular's. With a name like that you can expect a crowd, but it's a happy crowd. The waves are gentle, the smiles are wide, and from little kids to old diehards, everyone enjoys 'Pop's.'

There are many choices when it comes to learning to surf on O'ahu, but one of the most consistently reputable, well-established surf schools belongs to one-time professional surfer Hans Hedemann, and is aptly named Hans Hedemann Surf School (p123). The expert staff will have you trimming toward shore in no time. You can also rent boards and pick up lessons from the beachboys at Kuhio Beach Park. They've spent their lives in the water there and have the Waikiki breaks wired.

If you already have your feet under you and want to step it up, Ala Moana Bowls is where the local boys surf. If you're hankering to learn, be advised: this is *not* your spot. On a good south swell, the lefthander that breaks into the Ala Moana Harbor has a great tube section and can get heavy. Experience and local knowledge are musts here. Also, the parking lot's notorious for car break-ins, so either keep your valuables on you or leave them at the hotel.

Kaiser's is a hollow right reef that can hold sizable south swells. Like Ala Moana, it's popular with the locals, which makes it relatively unpopular with tourists from Wisconsin, but if you're respectful and wait your turn, it's a great place to catch summertime tubes. Then there is Diamond Head, a wide array of reef systems with all kinds of fun waves that break year-round. Because of the coastline's open-ocean exposure, Diamond Head picks up both long-period ground and choppier trade wind–generated swell. It does get windy out here, making windsurfing and kitesurfing equally popular pastimes.

ISLANDWIDE SURF SPOTS

When it comes to wave action, there's much more to O'ahu than just Waikiki. In fact, Waikiki is really at its peak only during the summer months, when low-pressure storms deep in the South Pacific send south swells its way.

East of Honolulu

To escape the over-crowded reefs of the south shore, or 'Town,' as it's been dubbed by island residents, head east on H1, out of Honolulu, past the snorkeling extravaganza that is Hanauma Bay Nature Preserve, and you'll arrive at the world-famous bodysurfing spot known as Sandy Beach (p168). The allure is the consistent, gin-clear tubes that break very close to shore on almost any swell. The danger is a bad bounce off the sand-covered bottom and a possible broken neck.

If you're not keen on this much of a spine-tingling adventure, just up the road is Makapu'u (p169), with its iconic lighthouse standing as a sentinel on the cliff above. The waves don't break as close to shore or as powerfully, and there's not nearly as much of a local vibe here (like Ala Moana, the parking lot at Sandy's is a reputed haven for break-in artists). Also, a hike out to the lighthouse (it takes about 20 minutes) offers a top-notch vista of the Pacific, with Maui off in the distance.

Legendary North Shore

When it comes to surf, nowhere on the planet gets as much attention as O'ahu's North Shore. Starting at the small hamlet of Hale'iwa and running approximately seven miles east on the Kamehameha Highway to Sunset Beach (p198), this stretch of coastline has been dubbed surfing's mecca.

While the south shore of O'ahu goes into hibernation during winter, the North Shore roars to life. During this time of year, powerful storms in the Gulf of Alaska send intense northwest swells in the general direction of 'the seven-mile miracle,' where occasionally the surf can top 30ft on the outer reefs. For three months pro surfers from all over the world arrive, hoping to catch a piece of the action. (If you're just starting off on a board, this certainly isn't the time or place to learn.)

On November 7, 1957, after years and years of spectating, a group of California surfers paddled out at Waimea Bay and ushered in the era of big-wave riding. Large waves had been surfed for a few years by this time, most visibly on the west side of O'ahu at Makaha, but Waimea was in a different league. The bravado and ability of Greg Noll, Pat Curren, James Jones, Eddie and Clyde Aikau, and a host of others would become the stuff of legends.

Several miles up the road and fewer than 10 years later, San Diego–born Butch Van Arsdalen rode the Banzai Pipeline for the first time, and with it another new gladiator pit was born. By the late 1960s and early '70s Gerry Lopez and Rory Russell emerged as the ultimate Pipeline stylists, defining the term 'getting tubed.'

Today there's no better place to watch all the action go down than at the Banzai Pipeline (p199). Breaking less than 100yd from shore, the cavernous tubes that detonate over a coral shelf in less than 3ft of water tempt surfers' fates every year, sometimes with lethal consequences. In

2005, 25-year-old Tahitian surfer Malik Joyeaux was killed after sustaining a particularly heavy wipeout.

The giant waves of Waimea Bay (p201) are always a crowd-pleaser, and the lifeguards there are a particularly good source of information, as well as being some of the toughest around. If you get bored on the sand, the Waimea Valley Audubon Center offers a pleasant walk, complete with beautiful rain forest and waterfall.

Every year surfers amass on the North Shore for a shot at winning the **Vans Triple Crown of Surfing** (www.triplecrownofsurfing.com). The three-contest series, held annually in November and December, begins with the OP Pro at Hale'iwa, then features the O'Neill World Cup at Sunset Beach and culminates with the Rip Curl Pipeline Masters. Kaua'i-born Andy Irons, three-time world champion, has displayed utter domination of the event for the past several years, putting an exclamation point on his statement in 2005 with a convincing victory at the Pipeline Masters.

GIRLS IN CURLS

Beyond big waves, a realm generally dominated by men, O'ahu has a tradition of exceptional girls in the curl. In the 1890s, as the flicker of surfing's light was just about to be extinguished, Princess Ka'iulani (who would later come to be celebrated in a Robert Louis Stevenson poem), riding her *olo*, almost single-handedly saved the sport. She would serve as an extremely influential figure for Duke and his contemporaries.

Later in the 20th century another woman would play a pivotal role in the lineup: Makaha's Rell Sunn, or 'Auntie Rell,' as she was known by so many. Before succumbing to cancer in 1998, Sunn made it a point to give the gift of surfing to as many underprivileged island children as she could, most notably through her annual *menehune* (the little people who built many of Hawaii's fishponds, heiau and other stonework, according to legend) contest, which she started in 1976 and ran up until her death. Even today Sunn embodies the true aloha spirit.

Following in Sunn's footsteps, China Uemura's Wahine Classic runs in Waikiki every year and continues to foster youth and women's surfing. The torch is also being passed to Honolulu's Carissa Moore. Only 13 years old, she's already being touted not only as a future world champion, but also as the girl who's going to redefine professional women's surfing.

KNOWING THE RULES: THE WAVES AND THE LOCALS

When it comes to dealing with the resident surfing populace, remember one simple word: respect. The rules of surfing etiquette are important and not very complicated; the gist is don't be a wave hog, and don't get in the way of other people while they're riding. If you're taking lessons, ask your instructor to explain the etiquette to you. Or if you're fending for yourself, don't be afraid to ask somebody in the water – they'll probably be happy to help and could end up giving you some local insight. Basically, be humble, be kind, share and always surf with a smile (even if you're on the verge of drowning).

For you island-bound surfers hungry to test your mettle in the Pacific power, knowing when and how big the next swell is can mean the difference between riding the wave of your life and picking your teeth out of the reef. This is where streaming webcams, surf reports and forecasts, like those found on **Wavewatch** (www.wavewatch.com) and **Surfline** (www.surfline.com), come in. Also, if you're just learning to surf, before you go jump in the hurricane surf of the century, take a look at the conditions so you don't get in over your head. Surfboard rentals are readily available near the beaches in Waikiki, Hale'iwa, Waimea, Kailua, La'ie and Makaha.

DIVING & SNORKELING

It's time to take the plunge! The waters around O'ahu offer spectacular scenery year-round, with excellent visibility and water temperatures ranging from 72°F to 80°F.

Of the 700 fish species that live in Hawaiian waters, nearly one-third of those are found nowhere else in the world. In addition to all those tropical fish, divers can often see spinner dolphins, green sea turtles and manta rays. The waters hold all sorts of hard and soft corals, waving anemones, unusual sponges and a variety of shellfish. Because of its volcanic origins, O'ahu also has some cool underwater caves and caverns.

Snorkeling

All you have to do to turn the beach into an underwater aquarium is don a mask and snorkel. It's easy, you don't need any experience, and snorkel gear can be rented near the main snorkeling venues for around $10 a day.

O'ahu's nearshore waters teem with colorful fish. Snorkelers can expect to see large rainbow-colored parrotfish munching coral on the sea floor, schools of silver needlefish glimmering near the surface, brilliant yellow tangs, odd-shaped filefish and ballooning puffer fish.

The island's year-round snorkeling mecca is at scenic Hanauma Bay Nature Preserve (p166), which has a deeply protected bay and is easily accessible from Waikiki. When waters are calm on the North Shore, Waimea Bay (p201) and Pupukea Beach Park (p201) provide excellent snorkeling in pristine conditions with far less activity than there is at Hanauma. The catch is that these North Shore sites can only be snorkeled when the waters are tranquil, which is roughly from May to October; the rest of the year the waters can be outright treacherous.

Scuba Diving

Whatever you're looking for, and whether you're an old pro or just a beginner, O'ahu has plenty to offer: boat dives, shore dives, night dives, reef dives, cave dives and wreck dives.

Experienced divers needn't bring anything other than a swimsuit and their certification card. Two-tank boat dives average $100 and include all gear.

If you want to experience diving for the first time, several dive operators offer a short beginner's 'try scuba' course for nondivers, which includes a brief instruction, followed by a shallow beach or boat dive. The cost is generally around $100, depending upon the operation and whether a boat is used.

A number of shops offer full open-water certification courses, which can sometimes be completed in as little as three days and cost around $400. The **Professional Association of Diving Instructors** (PADI; ☎ 800-729-7234; www .padi.com) certifies scuba divers.

O'ahu's top summer dive spots include the caves and ledges at Three Tables (p201) and Shark's Cove (p201) on the North Shore, and the Makaha Caverns off Makaha Beach (p223). For wreck diving, the sunken 165ft ship

For more information on dive spots, pick up Lonely Planet's *Diving & Snorkeling Hawaii*, which includes color photos of sites and fish.

Divers Alert Network (www.diversalertnetwork .org) gives advice on diving emergencies, insurance, decompression services, illness and injury.

OCEAN SAFETY

Drowning is the leading cause of accidental death for visitors. If you're not familiar with water conditions, please ask around. It's best not to swim alone in unfamiliar places.

Rip Currents Rips, or rip currents, are fast-flowing ocean currents that can drag swimmers out into deeper water. Anyone caught in one should either go with the flow until it loses power or swim parallel to shore to slip out of it.

Rogue Waves Never turn your back on the ocean. Waves don't all come in with equal height or strength, and sometimes a wave can sweep over a shoreline ledge and drag sunbathers from the beach into the ocean.

Shorebreaks If waves that are breaking close to the shore are only a couple of feet high, they're generally fine for novice bodysurfers. Large shorebreaks, though, can hit hard with a slamming downward force.

Undertows Common along steeply sloped beaches, undertows occur where large waves wash back directly into incoming surf. Swimmers caught up in one can be pulled underwater. Don't panic; go with the current until you get beyond the wave.

RESPONSIBLE DIVING

The popularity of diving is placing immense pressure on many sites. Please consider the following tips when diving to help preserve the ecology and beauty of reefs.

- Do not use reef anchors and take care not to ground boats on coral. Encourage dive operators to establish permanent moorings at popular sites.

- Avoid touching living marine organisms with your body or dragging equipment across the reef. Polyps can be damaged by even the gentlest contact. Never stand on coral. If you must hold on to the reef, only touch exposed rock or dead coral.

- Be conscious of your fins. Even without contact, the surge from heavy fin strokes near the reef can damage delicate organisms. When treading water in shallow reef areas, take care not to kick up clouds of sand. Settling sand can easily smother the delicate organisms of the reef.

- Practice and maintain proper buoyancy control. Major damage can be done by divers descending too fast and colliding with the reef. Make sure you are correctly weighted and that your weight belt is positioned so that you stay horizontal. Be aware that buoyancy can change over the period of an extended trip: initially you may breathe harder and need more weight; a few days later you may breathe more easily and need less weight.

- Take care in underwater caves. Spend as little time within them as possible, as your air bubbles may be caught within the roof and thereby leave previously submerged organisms high and dry.

- Resist the temptation to collect or buy coral or shells. Aside from the ecological damage, taking home marine souvenirs depletes the beauty of a site and spoils the enjoyment for others.

- Ensure that you take home all your rubbish and any other litter you may find. Plastics in particular are a serious threat to marine life. Turtles can mistake plastic for jellyfish and eat it.

- Do not feed fish. You may disturb their normal eating habits, encourage aggressive behavior or feed them food that is detrimental to their health.

- Minimize your disturbance of marine animals. It is illegal to approach endangered marine species too closely; these include whales, dolphins, sea turtles and the Hawaiian monk seal. In particular, do not ride on the backs of turtles, as this causes them great anxiety.

Mahi off Makaha Beach is a prize. Numerous spots between Honolulu and Hanauma Bay provide good winter diving.

There are dive shops all around O'ahu. If you're staying in Waikiki, some shops will provide transportation from your hotel.

KAYAKING

Get your paddle out. On O'ahu, the favorite kayaking spot is Kailua Beach, which has three uninhabited nearshore islands within the reef that you can paddle to. Landings are allowed on two of the islands: Moku Nui, which has a beautiful beach good for sunbathing and snorkeling, and Popoi'a Island (Flat Island), where there are some inviting footpaths. And it's all so easy – with advance reservations, you can rent a kayak right at Kailua Beach Park (p177). And although Waikiki doesn't have the same *Robinson Crusoe* element, kayak rentals are also readily available at Fort DeRussy Beach (p123). Kayaks are available in both single and tandem and cost around $50 a day.

SWIMMING

O'ahu is ringed with beautiful white-sand beaches, ranging from crowded resort strands to quiet hidden coves. The island has more than 50 beach parks, most with rest rooms and showers; about half are patrolled by lifeguards.

O'ahu has four distinct coastal areas, each with its own peculiar seasonal water conditions. When it's rough on one side, it's generally calm on another, which means you can find places to swim year-round. As a general rule, the best places to swim in winter are along the south shore, and in summer, the North Shore.

The south shore, which extends from Barbers Point to Makapu'u Point, encompasses some of the most popular beaches on the island, including legendary Waikiki Beach. The North Shore has spectacular waves in winter but can be as calm as a lake during the summer. The leeward Wai'anae Coast typically has conditions similar to those of the North Shore, with big surf in winter and suitable swimming conditions in summer, but you'll find protected year-round swimming at Poka'i Bay Beach Park in Wai'anae. Or go south to the calm waters of Ko Olina Lagoons (p218).

If you're a distance swimmer, the best place in Honolulu to swim laps is at Ala Moana Beach Park (p82).

> Ten days after the full moon, jellyfish swim into the shallow waters of leeward beaches, including Waikiki – usually for a one-day stay.

LAND ACTIVITIES

Landlubbers will find lots of fun things to do in O'ahu, whether you enjoy taking to the woods, manicured golf greens or the back of a horse.

HIKING

O'ahu offers an amazing variety of hiking trails, from short nature strolls on the edge of the city to walks through tropical jungles where you're unlikely to see another soul.

> Lonely Planet's *Hiking in Hawaii* is a comprehensive, independent hiking guide with good maps and clear directions. What else would you expect?

Trails

The most popular hike on O'ahu is the short but steep trail to the summit of Diamond Head Crater (p163), which is easy to reach from Waikiki and ends with a panoramic city view.

TIME TO REJUVENATE

Spa tourism is hot – hot as in *'ili'ili* therapy (with hot lava stones), that is. Modern Hawaiian spa treatments often sound a bit whimsical, but are loosely based on herbal traditions. Popular body wraps use wild ginger to remedy colds or jet lag and seaweed to detoxify. Body scrubs make use of coffee or sea salts to exfoliate and ti leaf or aloe to heal sunburns.

Other tropical treatments sound good enough to eat: *lomilomi* (which comes from the word *lomi*, to rub) is a traditional Hawaiian massage. Then there are coconut-milk baths, Kona-coffee scrubs, *kukui*-nut reflexology, and *'awapuhi* (wild ginger) or *limu* (seaweed) body wraps. Or maybe you're ready for a delicious chocolate macadamia nut scrub. And if you want to bring your honey, there are also couples' massages.

If you don't have the necessary $100 or so to spend on these delights, pick up a bottle of coconut oil to try at home. Otherwise, head to these top picks:

- Ihilani Spa – JW Marriott Ihilani Resort & Spa (p220)
- Abhasa Spa – Royal Hawaiian Hotel (p131)
- Mandara Spa – Hilton Hawaiian Village (p132)
- SpaHalekulani – Halekulani Hotel (p131)
- SpaSuites – Kahala Mandarin Oriental Hawaii (p164)
- Na Hoola Spa – Hyatt Regency Waikiki Resort (p132)
- Spa Luana – Turtle Bay Resort (p198)

The less-trodden Manoa Falls Trail (p91) offers a peaceful walk through an abandoned arboretum of lofty trees, ending at a waterfall – for the effort, there's no finer trail on the island.

The Tantalus and Makiki Valley area (p88) has the most extensive trail network, with fine views of Honolulu and surrounding valleys. Amazingly, though it's just 2 miles above the city hustle and bustle, this lush forest reserve is unspoiled and offers quiet solitude. The lesser-known Wa'ahila Ridge Trail (p90), on the east side of Manoa Valley, offers a different perspective on the area and good birding possibilities.

A real prize for nature lovers is the Ka'ena Point Trail (p227), a coastal hike through a windswept natural reserve on the uninhabited northwestern tip of O'ahu.

On O'ahu's windward side, a pleasant hour-long hike to Makapu'u lighthouse (see p169) often rewards hikers with a view of frolicking whales in winter. For a hardier walk on the windward coast, the 2.5-mile Hau'ula Loop Trail (p190) takes you deep into the forest.

Guided Hikes

By joining one of these outings, you get to meet and hike with ecologically minded islanders and it can also be a good way to get to the backwoods if you don't have a car. Wear sturdy shoes and, for the longer hikes, bring lunch and water.

Na Ala Hele (www.hawaiitrails.org) maintains public trails throughout O'ahu and marks trailheads with their distinctive signpost using a Hawaiian petroglyph logo.

Sierra Club (☎ 538-6616; www.hi.sierraclub.org; per person $5) Leads hikes and other outings on weekends.

Hawaii Audubon Society (☎ 528-1432; www.hawaiiaudubon.com; suggested donation $2) Leads bird-watching hikes once a month, usually on a weekend, meeting at a trailhead.

Hawaiian Trail & Mountain Club (http://htmclub.org/index.html; donation $2) Leads informal hikes every weekend.

Mauka Makai Excursions (☎ 255-2206; www.hawaiianecotours.net; hiking tours $43-75) A Hawaiian-owned cultural ecotour company offering full- and half-day field trips to cultural and archaeological sites around O'ahu.

O'ahu Nature Tours (☎ 924-2473; www.oahunaturetours.com; tours $20-52) Offers small half-day tours to hidden rain forest waterfalls, gardens and coastal seabird sanctuaries.

Safety

O'ahu has no snakes, no poison ivy, no poison oak and few wild animals that will fuss with hikers. There's a slim possibility of meeting up with a large boar in the backwoods, but they're unlikely to be a problem unless cornered.

Flash floods can be a real danger in many of the steep, narrow valleys that require stream crossings. Warning signs include a distant rumbling, the smell of fresh earth and a sudden increase in the river's current. If the water begins to rise, get to higher ground immediately. A walking stick is good for bracing yourself on slippery approaches, gaining leverage and testing the depth of streams.

Be alert to the possibility of landslides, falling rocks and exposed tree roots that are easy to trip over. Be wary of swimming under waterfalls, as rocks can dislodge from the top, and be careful on the edge of steep cliffs, since cliffside rock in Hawaii tends to be crumbly.

Darkness falls fast in Hawaii once the sun sets and ridge-top trails are no place to be caught unprepared in the dark. Always carry a flashlight just in case. Long pants offer protection from overgrown parts of the trail, and sturdy footwear with good traction is a must. Pack 2L of water per person for a day hike, carry a whistle to alert rescue workers should the need arise, wear sunscreen and, above all, start out early.

MOUNTAIN BIKING & CYCLING

Cycling has gained in popularity in O'ahu. The county publishes a nifty free *Bike O'ahu* map that shows which roads are suitable for novices and which are for experienced cyclists. All public buses have bike racks, making it easy to head out one way by bike and return by bus.

Although cycling along roads isn't a problem – other than traffic and the shortage of bike lanes – getting off the beaten path is a bit more complicated, since access to public forests and trails is limited. One excellent forest trail open to mountain bikers is the Maunawili Demonstration Trail (p175), a scenic 10-mile trek that connects the mountain crest at the Nu'uanu Pali Lookout with Waimanalo in windward O'ahu. Another popular mountain-bike trail is the 'Aiea Loop Trail (p159) in Keaiwa Heiau State Recreation Area above Pearl Harbor.

The **Hawaii Bicycling League** (☎ 735-5756; www.hbl.org) holds bike rides around O'ahu nearly every weekend, ranging from 10-mile jaunts to 60-mile treks. Some outings are geared strictly to road travel and others include off-road sites. Rides are free and open to the public.

For information on getting around O'ahu by bike, including bicycle rentals, see p247.

Mountain Biking the Hawaiian Islands by O'ahu resident John Alford is the bible for mountain bikers, covering public trails open to bikers, with maps and descriptions.

GOLF & TENNIS

If you feel like teeing off in paradise, O'ahu has nearly 40 golf courses to choose from, ranging from unpretentious municipal courses with affordable fees and relaxed settings to members-only private country clubs with resident pros and ultramanicured surroundings. High-rated standouts with greens open to the public include the Ko'olau Golf Course (p184) in Kane'ohe; Ko Olina Golf Club (p219) in Kapolei; and Turtle Bay Golf at Turtle Bay Golf Resort (p197) at the island's northern tip. The usual green fees at these courses cost about $135 to $165 for 18 holes, but if you don't mind teeing off in the afternoon ask about 'twilight discounts' that can lower the fees to less than $100.

O'ahu has 181 public tennis courts at county parks throughout the island. If you're staying in Waikiki, the most convenient locations are the courts at Ala Moana Beach Park (p82); at the Diamond Head Tennis Center (p122), at the Diamond Head end of Kapi'olani Park; and at the Kapi'olani Park (p122) courts, opposite the Waikiki Aquarium. Court time at these county facilities is free and on a first-come, first-served basis.

MOVE OVER, TIGER

No woman has ever rocked the golf world like teenage phenom Michelle Wie.

Born in Honolulu in 1989, she began playing golf at the age of four. At 10 she became the youngest player to ever qualify for a USGA amateur championship event, and from there went on to win most of the junior events she entered. At 12 she became the youngest female ever to qualify for an LPGA tournament. By the ripe old age of 13 she was one of the longest hitters on the LPGA tour, typically driving the ball a good 20yd past everybody else.

In 2004 she played in her first PGA event, the Sony Open, missing the cut by just one stroke – she was the youngest person, and just the fourth female ever, to play with the pro men in any PGA tournament.

In October 2005 Michelle Wie turned pro, a week before her 16th birthday. She now has endorsements from Nike and Sony, estimated at about $10 million a year, making her the highest-paid female golfer in the world. Her news conference to announce she was turning pro was held at 8am, so she'd still have to time to get to her first class at Punahou High School in Honolulu.

HORSEBACK RIDING

Got a hankering to saddle up? O'ahu has some recommendable stables along the North Shore. If you want to ride along the beach with the wind blowing in your hair, head up to Hawaii Polo Trail Rides (p209) in Mokule'ia or the Turtle Bay Resort (p197) in the north. If you want to ride in the mountains, Happy Trails Hawaii (p203) above Waimea is the place; it's also very kid-friendly. Trail rides typically cost $50 to $75.

JOGGING

Islanders are big on jogging, and the cool early morning hours are particularly well suited for running. Kapi'olani Park (p121), Ala Moana Beach Park (p82) and the Ala Wai Canal are favorite jogging spots in the Waikiki area. There's also a 4.8-mile run around Diamond Head crater that's a well-beaten track.

It's estimated that Honolulu has more joggers per capita than any other city in the world.

O'ahu has about 75 road races each year, from 1-mile fun runs and 5-mile jogs to competitive marathons, biathlons and triathlons. For an annual schedule of running events with times, dates and contact addresses, check out the **Running Room** (www.runningroomhawaii.com) and click 'Oahu Races.'

O'ahu's best-known race is the Honolulu Marathon, which in recent years has mushroomed into the third-largest marathon in the USA. Held in mid-December, it's an open-entry event, with an estimated half of the 25,000 entrants being first-time marathon runners. For information, contact **Honolulu Marathon Association** (www.honolulumarathon.org) to download an entry form from its website.

Food & Drink

Your tastebuds are in for a treat. The island's ethnic diversity gives rise to hundreds of different cuisines – every kind of Japanese food, an array of regional Chinese dishes, and native Hawaiian, Thai and Vietnamese food. Food is central to any gathering in Hawaii. Whether it's a day at the beach or a night on the town, a tasty spread is going to be part of the event. Foodies, you're in the right place. *Bon appétit!*

STAPLES & SPECIALTIES
Native Hawaiian
Kalua pig and poi are the 'meat and potatoes' – so to speak – of native Hawaiian food. Poi is served with everything Hawaiian. The purple paste is pounded from cooked taro roots, with water added to make it pudding-like. Its consistency is measured in one-, two- or three-finger poi – which indicates how many fingers are required to scoop it from bowl to mouth. Poi is nutritious and easily digestible, but for many nonlocals it's an acquired taste. *Kalua* pig is pig that is slow-cooked in an underground pit, using a traditional method of cooking.

Another common Hawaiian staple is *laulau,* a preparation of fish, pork and taro wrapped in a ti-leaf bundle and steamed until the leaf is soft. *Lomi* salmon is made by marinating minced raw salmon with diced tomatoes and green onions. Other Hawaiian foods include baked *'ulu* (breadfruit), *limu* (seaweed), *'opihi* (the tiny limpet shells that fishers pick off the reef at low tide) and *pipi kaula* (beef jerky). *Haupia,* the standard dessert for a Hawaiian meal, is a firm pudding made of coconut cream thickened with cornstarch or arrowroot.

Because it's harder to find than other ethnic cuisines, many visitors only taste traditional Hawaiian food at tourist luau or by sampling a dollop of poi at one of the hotel buffets. Still, O'ahu does have a few neighborhood restaurants that specialize in Hawaiian food, including Ono Hawaiian Food (p132) and Helena's Hawaiian Food (p104).

Local Food
The distinct style of food called 'local' usually refers to a fixed-plate lunch with 'two scoop rice,' a scoop of macaroni salad, and a serving of beef stew, mahimahi or teriyaki chicken, generally scoffed down with chopsticks. A breakfast plate might have Spam, eggs, kimchi (a vegetable pickle) and, always, two scoops of rice.

These plate meals are the standard fare in diners and lunch wagons. If it's full of starches, fats and gravies, you're probably eating local.

Pupu is the local term used for all kinds of munchies or hors d'oeuvres. Boiled peanuts, soy-flavored rice crackers called *kaki mochi* and sashimi are common *pupu.*

Hawaii's Best Local Desserts by Jean Watanabe Hee reveals dozens of recipes for gotta-be-homemade desserts, from *haupia* chocolate pie to macadamia nut angels.

TRAVEL YOUR TASTEBUDS

Forget candy bars. The most popular snack on O'ahu is crack seed, a Chinese food that can be sweet, sour, salty or some combination of the three. It's often made from dried fruits such as plums, apricots or pickled mangoes. The most popular – and most overwhelming to the uninitiated – is *li hing mui.* Sour enough to pucker the most stoic of faces, these days *li hing mui* is used to spice up everything from fresh apples to margaritas.

COMFORT FOOD IN A CAN

Hawaii is the Spam capital of the USA, and locals consume a whopping four million cans per year, or 10,958 cans per day (3½ times more than any other state consumes!). While US foodmaker Hormel's Spam, a pork-based luncheon meat, is the butt of jokes almost everywhere, there's little stigma in Hawaii. Rather, Spam is a comfort food – always eaten cooked, not straight from the can.

Why Spam? No one knows exactly. Some people say it simply goes well with rice, Hawaii's ubiquitous starch. Others claim it's a legacy of plantation cookery, when fresh meat was not always available. Even today, whenever the islands are threatened by a hurricane or dock-workers' strike, locals stock up on water, batteries, toilet paper, 20lb bags of rice and...Spam.

A local favorite is Spam *musubi*: a block of rice with a slice of fried Spam on top (or in the middle), wrapped with a strip of black sushi nori. Originated in the 1960s or '70s, it has become a classic, and thousands of *musubi* are sold daily at grocers, lunch counters and convenience stores. The Spam *musubi* phenomenon has even reached Hormel, which in 2004 released a collector's edition can called 'Hawaiian Spam' with a recipe for you-know-what on the back.

Another favorite is *poke* – raw fish marinated in soy sauce, oil, chili peppers, green onions and seaweed. It comes in many varieties – sesame *'ahi* (yellowfin tuna) is particularly delicious and goes well with beer.

> You can join the official Spam Club, read Spam trivia or find Spam recipes at www.spam.com.

Hawaii residents love their shave ice, a treat that's as common on the islands as ice cream is elsewhere. Shave ice is a snow cone taken to the next level. The ice is shaved as fine as powdery snow, packed into a paper cone and drenched with sweet, fruit-flavored syrups in eye-popping hues. Kids usually opt for the colorfully striped rainbow shave ice.

Hawaii Regional Cuisine

In recent years O'ahu has become a darling of gourmands and their magazines. It was from O'ahu that the movement dubbed 'Hawaii Regional Cuisine' took off and its pioneering chefs became celebrities. This type of cooking incorporates fresh island ingredients, borrows liberally from Hawaii's various ethnic groups and is marked by creative combinations such as Peking duck in ginger-*liliko'i* sauce. Roy Yamaguchi, the forerunner of the movement, opened his original Roy's restaurant (p166) in Hawai'i Kai in 1988. Alan Wong's namesake restaurant (p102), founded in 1995, is widely considered Hawaii's finest, and critics nationwide marvel at his imaginative signature starter – a shot glass filled with *'opihi* (limpet) in a light bath of tomato broth, fennel and basil.

> Hawaii Regional Cuisine master Roy Yamaguchi gives away his secret recipes in *Roy's Feasts from Hawaii*, with gorgeous photos of the dishes he prepares and the people who harvest O'ahu's abundant crops.

DRINKS
Alcoholic Drinks

Beer is the drink of choice in Hawaii, and the best beer produced on the islands is made by the Kona Brewing Company on the Big Island but readily available on O'ahu. Microbreweries are alive and well on O'ahu, the most popular being the waterfront Gordon Biersch (p105) at the Aloha Tower Marketplace in Honolulu, which brews good German-style lagers. Also worthy of a taste test are the Big Aloha Brewery at Sam Choy's (p104) and Brew Moon (p105).

All upscale restaurants have extensive wine lists of Californian and European vintages. Wine-tasting parties and clubs are not uncommon, wine sales have skyrocketed and wine bars, such as Formaggio (p105), have opened in Honolulu.

And, of course, at every beachside bar you can order one of those colorful tropical drinks topped with a fruit garnish. Three favorites are piña colada, made with rum, pineapple juice and cream of coconut; mai tai, a mix of rum, grenadine and lemon and pineapple juices; and blue Hawaii, a vodka drink colored with blue curaçao.

Nonalcoholic Drinks

Cans of Hawaiian-made fruit juices such as guava-orange or passion fruit can readily be found at most stores. If you're touring around, you might want to toss a couple of cans in your day pack.

Still, Hawaii's favorite homegrown drink is coffee. Although coffee is grown on several islands, including on the North Shore of O'ahu, the finest hands down is the Kona coffee grown on hillslopes on the Big Island. O'ahu coffee, known as Waialua coffee, has only been grown for about a decade; the first harvests were disappointing but the latest beans are worth a taste.

Hawaii is the only state in the USA where coffee is grown.

CELEBRATIONS

The traditional Hawaiian feast marking special events is the luau. Local luau are still commonplace in modern Hawaii for baby christenings and similar events. Typically big bashes that include extended family, co-workers and friends, in spirit these local luau are far more authentic than anything you'll see at a tourist luau, but the short-stay visitor would be lucky indeed to get an invitation to one.

The main dish at any luau is *kalua* pig, which is roasted in a pitlike earthen oven called an *imu*. The *imu* is readied for cooking by building a fire and heating rocks in the pit. When the rocks are glowing red, layers of moisture-laden banana trunks and green ti leaves are placed over the stones. A pig that has been slit open is filled with hot rocks and laid on top of the bed.

Homesick locals living on the mainland share their recipe collections on-line at www.alohaworld.com/ono.

Other foods wrapped in ti and banana leaves are placed around it. It's all covered with more ti leaves and a layer of coconut-frond mats and topped with dirt to seal in the heat, which then bakes and steams the food. The process takes about four to eight hours depending on the size of the pig and the amount of food added. Anything cooked in this style is called *kalua*.

Food plays center stage in many other Hawaiian celebrations and festivities. On Sundays the beach parks are packed full of large family gatherings, picnic tables stacked high with potluck-style plates. Even visitors can get in on the action, with Brunch on the Beach (p136), a food festival that turns Waikiki's beachfront drag into a huge outdoor café on the third Sunday of the month. If you're lucky enough to be in Honolulu on the last weekend of June, you can sample all sorts of local foods, from home cooking to gourmet, at the Taste of Honolulu (p96) festival.

O'AHU'S TOP FIVE

Ritzy Restaurants

- Alan Wong's (p102)
- L'Uraku (p102)
- Orchids (p136)
- Roy's (p166)
- Lucy's Grill & Bar (p181)

Plate Lunch Places

- Ono-Loa (p186)
- Kalapawai Market (p180)
- Kaka'ako Kitchen (p100)
- Romy's Kahuku Prawns (p193)
- Poke Stop (p220)

WHERE TO EAT & DRINK

The choices are endless. For local multiethnic food, Chinatown abounds with interesting Asian eateries. Want to hit the café scene? Head to the Kaimuki region of greater Honolulu. And if you're ready to fine dine at some of the best restaurants in the Pacific, you can start your explorations right in Waikiki. As for enjoying a drink on the waterfront, Waikiki is as good as it gets, adding sunset views and hula dancers to the scene.

VEGETARIANS & VEGANS

While most locals are omnivores, vegetarians and vegans can feast well on O'ahu, too. The Asian influence in local cuisine guarantees lots of vegetable and tofu options all around the island.

That said, vegetarians aren't the target market: a plate lunch without meat or fish is not quite a plate lunch, and top-end restaurants do tend to highlight seafood. But the trend toward meatless diets is growing slowly, mostly among mainland transplants, and many tourist-oriented restaurants now add a couple of vegetarian choices to their menu listings. Overall, locals have a 'live and let live' attitude and respect other people's eating habits and diets. When ordering at a restaurant, be sure to ask whether a dish is indeed meatless, as local cooks might inadvertently overlook those bacon bits on the spinach salad or that chicken broth in the risotto.

This book uses the **V** symbol in reviews for restaurants that are noteworthy for their vegetarian choices. Vegetarians shouldn't miss Legend Vegetarian Restaurant (p100) in Chinatown, which offers an amazing array of creative meatless Chinese dishes.

> Ti leaves to Hawaiian chefs are like a biodegradable combination of aluminum foil and paper plates: food is wrapped in it, cooked in it and served on it.

EATING WITH KIDS

Families will find plenty of dining options, from hamburger joints and pizza places to festive luau and pick-what-you-like buffets. This book uses the 👶 symbol to indicate restaurants that are particularly kid-friendly.

HABITS & CUSTOMS

Hawaii residents tend to eat at set hours – 6am, noon and 6pm – so that's when you can expect the most competition for a table in a restaurant. Locals tend to be big eaters; 'super size' was popular here long before it became a term on the mainland. Feel free to split a meal or take home leftovers.

> Never trust a skinny chef? That's the motto of celebrity chef Sam Choy, who shares a few favorite recipes at www.samchoy.com.

COOKING COURSES

Food critic and former celebrity chef Matthew Gray runs his own **Hawaii Food Tours** (☎ 926-3663, 800-715-2468; www.hawaiifoodtours.com) introducing visitors to the unique delights of island cuisine. His Hole in the Wall Tour ($59) visits mom-and-pop *bento* (Japanese-style box lunch) and plate lunch joints; the Hawaiian Feast in Paradise Tour ($99) concentrates on poi and other traditional Hawaiian food; and the Gourmet Triology Food

---

DOS & DON'TS

- A tip to your waitperson of 15% to 20% is expected whenever you have table service. Don't tip if you pick up your order at the counter.

- If you're invited to a Hawaiian home for a meal, always remove your shoes before entering.

- Don't even think of lighting up. Smoking is not allowed in O'ahu restaurants.

& Wine Lovers Tour ($149) is a dinner night out, visiting three top Honolulu restaurants.

If you don't know your mai tai from a blue Hawaii, maybe it's time to take a course from a pro. Top mixologist Dale DeGroff offers courses in preparing luscious tropical drinks at Lewers Lounge (p125), Waikiki's premier drinking spot.

EAT YOUR WORDS

If someone offers you a *broke da mout malasada* or *ono kine poke,* would you try it? Don't miss out because you're stumped by the lingo. Here's a list of common food terms; for pidgin and Hawaiian pronunciation tips, see p257.

Food Glossary

'a'ama	black crab
'ahi	yellowfin tuna
aku	skipjack tuna
a'u	swordfish, marlin
'awa	kava, a native plant used to make an intoxicating drink
bento	Japanese-style box lunch
broke da mout	delicious
crack seed	Chinese preserved fruit; a salty, sweet or sour snack
donburi	large bowl of rice and main dish
grind	to eat
grinds	food; *'ono kine grinds* is good food
guava	green-yellow fruit with moist pink flesh and lots of edible seeds
gyoza	grilled dumpling usually containing minced pork or shrimp
haupia	coconut pudding
he'e	octopus; also called *tako* in Japanese
imu	underground earthen oven used to cook *kalua* pig and other luau food
inamona	ground and roasted *kukui* (candlenut), used to flavor dishes such as *poke*
kaki mochi	shoyu-flavored rice crackers
kalo	taro
kalua	traditional method of cooking in an underground pit
kamaboko	a block of puréed, steamed fish
katsu	deep-fried fillets
kaukau	food
laulau	a bundle made of pork or chicken and salted butterfish, wrapped in taro and ti leaves and steamed
li hing mui	sour crack seed
liliko'i	passion fruit
loco moco	dish of rice, fried egg and hamburger patty topped with gravy or other condiments
lomi salmon	minced, salted salmon, diced tomato and green onion
luau	Hawaiian feast
mahimahi	white-fleshed fish also called 'dolphin' (not the mammal)
mai tai	alcoholic drink made from rum, grenadine, and lemon and pineapple juices
malasada	Portuguese fried dough, served warm and sugar-coated
manju	Japanese cake filled with sweet bean paste
mano	shark
mochi	Japanese sticky-rice cake
nishime	stew of root vegetables and seaweed
nori	Japanese seaweed, usually dried
ogo	seaweed

onaga	mild-tasting red snapper
ono	wahoo fish
'ono	delicious
'ono kine grinds	good food
opah	moonfish
'opakapaka	pink snapper
'opihi	edible limpet
pad thai	rice noodles stir-fried with tofu, vegetables, egg and peanuts
papio or ulua	jack fish
pipi kaula	Hawaiian beef jerky
poha	gooseberry
poi	staple Hawaiian starch made of steamed, mashed taro
poka	a fruit in the passion fruit family
poke	cubed raw fish mixed with shoyu, sesame oil, salt, chili pepper or other condiments
pupu	snack or appetizer; also a type of cowry shell
saimin	local-style noodle soup
shoyu	soy sauce
soba	buckwheat noodles
star fruit	translucent yellow-green fruit with five ribs like the points of a star and sweet, juicy pulp
taro	plant with edible corm used to make poi
teishoku	fixed, multicourse Japanese meal
teppanyaki	Japanese style of cooking with an iron grill
tonkatsu	breaded and fried pork cutlets, also prepared as chicken *katsu*
tsukemono	pickled vegetables
'uala	sweet potato
uhu	parrotfish
uku	gray snapper
'ulu	breadfruit, a starchy fruit prepared much like a potato
ume	Japanese pickled plum
unagi	eel
wana	sea urchin

Honolulu

The pulse of Hawaii beats from Honolulu. Whether you're talking politics, culture or business, this vibrant, cosmopolitan city is at the center of it all. In fact, one-third of all the people in the state make Honolulu their home.

At a crossroads between East and West, Honolulu lays claim to being *the* most culturally diverse city in the USA. The rich collage of backgrounds and ethnicities shines in its cuisine and festivals, its temples and museums. Visitors will find an amalgam of lively neighborhoods to explore, from the hip enclaves around the University of Hawai'i to colorful Chinatown, which so fully brims with the sights, sounds and flavors of Asia that you have to remind yourself you're not on some backstreet in Hong Kong.

The heart of the city, downtown Honolulu, offers a mixed plate of past and present – and an inimitable jumble of landmark sites. At its epicenter, within sight of one another, stands a stately 19th-century royal palace, a modernistic state capitol, a New England missionary church and a Spanish-style city hall. Toss in a busy commercial harbor, throw in some sandy beaches, back it up with green mountains itching to be trod, and you've got yourself a city to explore.

Did we mention the food? Lick your chops and dive in, munching your way through exquisite plate lunches, fresh-off-the-boat sushi, piquant Asian curries and artistic Pacific Rim delights from some of the most celebrated chefs on the planet. As for nightlife, many of Hawaii's hottest musicians rock the city after dark – so don't forget your dancing shoes!

HIGHLIGHTS

- Touring elegant **'Iolani Palace** (p74), home of Hawaii's last monarchs
- Hiking through a forest of lofty trees to awe-inspiring **Manoa Falls** (p91)
- Exploring the gallery scene and lively street markets in **Chinatown** (p80)
- Browsing the fascinating collections at the **Bishop Museum** (p88)
- Swimming and sunbathing away an afternoon at glorious **Ala Moana Beach Park** (p82)

★ Bishop Museum   Manoa Falls ★

★ Chinatown

★ 'Iolani Palace

★ Ala Moana Beach Park

■ POPULATION: 373,000   ■ AREA: 105 SQ KM

HISTORY

Honolulu, which means 'Sheltered Bay,' sprang to life with the arrival of foreign merchant ships in the 1790s. Vigorous trade soon developed, a harborside village sprouted up and the town quickly became Hawaii's center of commerce. Kamehameha I soon moved his royal court to Honolulu Harbor, setting up residence at what is today the southern end of Bethel St, where he could keep an eye on business and collect trade duties.

In the 1820s whaling ships arrived in force, and Honolulu's first bars and brothels opened almost overnight. Christian missionaries began coming ashore at the same time, albeit with different intents. Both groups left their mark. Hawaii's first missionary church is just a stone's throw from the royal palace. And downtown Honolulu still holds the headquarters of the corporations that controlled Hawaii's commerce by the end of the 19th century. It's no coincidence that their lists of corporate board members – Alexander, Baldwin, Cooke and Dole – read like rosters from the first mission ships.

The whalers left a different legacy. Hotel St, a line of bars and strip joints a few blocks from the harbor, remains the city's red-light district.

After Honolulu became the official capital in 1845, virtually everything of political significance in Hawaii took place in the heart of this city. Kings were coronated, queens were overthrown and coups were played out all within the confines of Honolulu's city center.

ORIENTATION

Unlike other large American cities, Honolulu doesn't have a separate municipal government – the entire island of O'ahu is governed as the City & County of Honolulu. Consequently, Honolulu's boundaries are not cut and dried. Still, the city proper is generally considered to extend west to the airport and east to Kaimuki, and that's the area covered in this chapter.

Downtown Honolulu contains all of O'ahu's state and federal government buildings, including the state capitol; it's also home to many of its most important historic sights. The landmark Aloha Tower and cruise-ship terminals are a few blocks west of the capitol.

Chinatown is immediately north of downtown Honolulu, roughly bounded by Honolulu Harbor, Bethel St, Vineyard Blvd and River St.

Waikiki, the tourist epicenter, is southeast of downtown Honolulu (see p111). Ala Moana Blvd (Hwy 92) connects Chinatown and the Ala Moana Center with Waikiki.

King St (a one-way street heading southeast) and Beretania St (one way heading northwest) connect downtown Honolulu with the university area.

H1, the main south shore freeway, passes east–west through Honolulu, linking the city to the airport and all other freeways on the island.

See p109 for more on getting to or from the city.

INFORMATION

Bookstores

Bestsellers (Map pp76-7; ☎ 528-2378; 1001 Bishop St; ☼ 7:30am-5:30pm Mon-Fri, 9am-3pm Sat) This downtown bookstore has a good selection of travel guides, novels and maps.

Book Shelf (Map p86; ☎ 944-2665; 2600 S King St; ☼ 9am-11pm Mon-Thu, to midnight Fri & Sat) A great source for used titles, including hard-to-find Hawaiiana and comics.

Borders Books & Music (Map pp84-5; ☎ 591-8995; Ward Centre, 1200 Ala Moana Blvd; ☼ 9am-10pm) Extensive news and travel sections.

Native Books Na Mea Hawaii (Map pp84-5; ☎ 596-8885; 1st fl, Ward Warehouse, 1050 Ala Moana Blvd; ☼ 10am-9pm Mon-Sat, to 5pm Sun) Specializes in Hawaiiana titles.

Rainbow Books & Records (Map p86; ☎ 955-7994; 1010 University Ave; ☼ 10am-10pm Sun-Thu, to 11pm Fri & Sat) Carries both new and used books, including an excellent Hawaiian section.

UH Manoa Campus Bookstore (Map p86; ☎ 956-8022; 2465 Campus Rd; ☼ 8:15am-4:45pm Mon-Fri, to 11:45am Sat) In the university's Campus Center.

Emergency

Police (☎ 529-3111) For non-emergencies.

Police, Fire & Ambulance (☎ 911) For all emergencies.

Suicide & Crisis Line (☎ 832-3100) Operates 24 hours.

Internet Access

Café 2600 (Map p86; ☎ 955-2683; 2600 S King St; per min 9¢; ☼ 7am-midnight Mon-Thu, to 10pm Fri & Sat) A casual cybercafé near the University of Hawai'i. Free wi-fi, sandwiches and coffee to choose from.

HONOLULU IN TWO DAYS

You can get a good taste of what Honolulu has to offer in a couple of days.

Start your first day exploring the market scene in **Chinatown** (p80); join the locals over noodles at lunch and then stroll through **Foster Botanical Garden** (p82), Hawaii's finest collection of towering trees and flowering plants. Make your way to the downtown area, taking time to tour the **Hawai'i State Art Museum** (p75) and **'Iolani Palace** (p74). When the dinner bell rings, head to the Aloha Tower Marketplace, catch the grand view from the **Aloha Tower** (p79) and enjoy a thoroughly Hawaiian dinner show at **Chai's Island Bistro** (p106).

On day two spend the morning at the **Bishop Museum** (p88) and at lunchtime see what homemade Hawaiian cooking is all about at **Helena's Hawaiian Food** (p104). In the afternoon explore the **Hawai'i Maritime Center** (p80) and then head to **Ala Moana Beach Park** (p82) for a swim and a sunset walk around **Magic Island** (p82). End the day by treating yourself to the delights of Pacific Rim cuisine at Honolulu's finest restaurant, **Alan Wong's** (p102).

Coffee Talk (Map pp72-3; ☎ 737-7444; 3601 Wai'alae Ave; per min 15¢; ⏲ 5am-11pm Sun-Thu, to midnight Fri & Sat) This trendy Kaimuki café has fast terminals for Web mail, plus a free-use wi-fi setup. If nothing else, you can get wired on the coffee drinks, all of which are double shots.

Honolulu Coffee Company (Map pp76-7; ☎ 521-4400; 1001 Bishop St; ⏲ 6am-5:30pm Mon-Fri, 7am-noon Sat) Tucked away in a leafy courtyard setting at Tamarind Sq, on the corner of S King St, this is one of the more pleasant wi-fi places in downtown Honolulu. Wi-fi is free with any purchase, and the pastries and heady coffee are hard to resist.

Net Stop Coffee (Map p86; ☎ 955-1020; 2615 S King St; per min 9¢; ⏲ 8:30am-midnight Mon-Fri, 9:30am-midnight Sat & Sun) This state-of-the-art cybercafé near the University of Hawai'i has ultrafast T1 connections and a full array of services.

Libraries

Hawaii State Library (Map pp76-7; ☎ 586-3500; 478 S King St; ⏲ 9am-5pm Tue, Fri & Sat, 10am-5pm Wed, 9am-8pm Thu) O'ahu's main library, adjacent to 'Iolani Palace, with a sunny central courtyard ideal for leafing through a good book. Its collection of over half a million titles is the state's best, with comprehensive Hawaii sections.

Media

NEWSPAPERS & MAGAZINES

Honolulu Advertiser (www.honoluluadvertiser.com) Honolulu's largest and most substantial daily newspaper; it comes out in the morning.

Honolulu Star-Bulletin (www.starbulletin.com) Honolulu's other daily newspaper comes out in the afternoon.

Honolulu Weekly (www.honoluluweekly.com) The more useful weekly paper; it's progressive, has an extensive entertainment section and is available free around the island.

Spotlight's O'ahu Gold Free weekly tourist magazine that has some interesting feature stories, and is chock-full of discount coupons for everything from hamburgers to sunset cruises.

RADIO & TV

KHPR (88.1 FM) Hawaii Public Radio.

KINE (105.1 FM) Tune here for the best in classic and contemporary Hawaiian music.

KIPO (89.3 FM) Hawaii Public Radio.

KKUA (90.7 FM) Hawaii Public Radio.

KTUH (90.3 FM) Broadcasting from the University of Hawai'i.

Channel 2 For some local flavor, watch Honolulu's favorite evening news broadcast, which ends with some fine slack-key guitar music by Keola and Kapono Beamer, and clips of people waving the *shaka* (Hawaiian hand greeting) sign.

Channels 10 & 11 Both TV channels feature 24-hour visitor information and ads geared to tourists.

Medical Services

Queen's Medical Center (Map pp76-7; ☎ 538-9011; 1301 Punchbowl St) One of O'ahu's several hospitals with 24-hour emergency services.

Straub Clinic & Hospital (Map pp84-5; ☎ 522-4000; 888 S King St) Offers 24-hour emergency services; on the corner of Ward Ave.

Money

Bank of Hawaii Ala Moana (Map pp84-5; ☎ 942-6111; Ala Moana Center, 1450 Ala Moana Blvd); Chinatown (Map pp76-7; ☎ 532-2480; 101 N King St); Downtown (Map pp76-7; ☎ 538-4171; 111 S King St); University of Hawai'i area (Map p86; ☎ 973-4460; 1010 University Ave)

First Hawaiian Bank Chinatown (Map pp76-7; ☎ 525-6888; 2 N King St); Downtown (Map pp76-7; ☎ 844-4444; First Hawaiian Center, 999 Bishop St)

HONOLULU

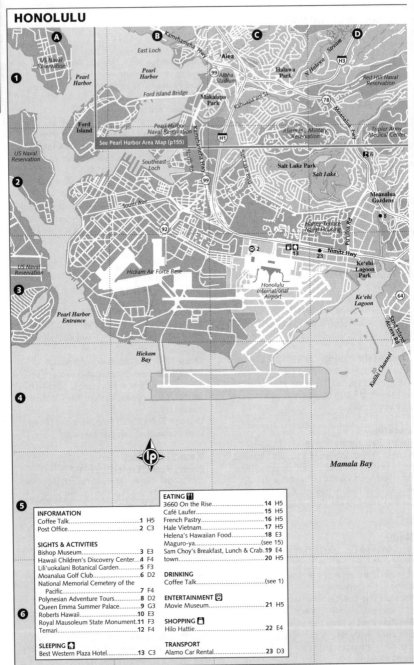

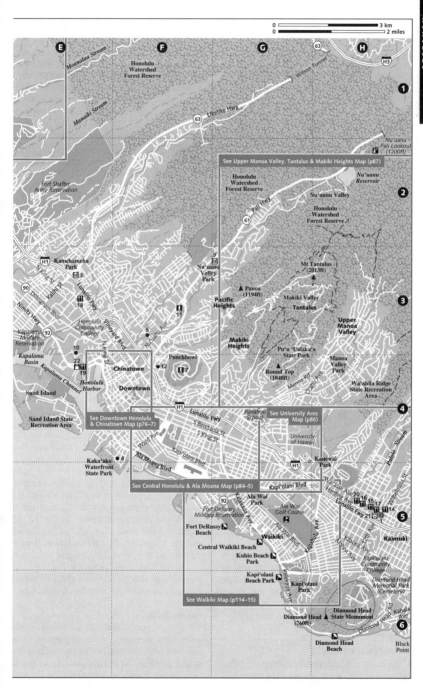

0 — 3 km
0 — 2 miles

Moanalua Stream

Honolulu
Watershed
Forest Reserve

Manaiki Stream

Wilson Tunnel

Likelike Hwy

H3

Nu'uanu
Pali Lookout
(1200ft)

See Upper Manoa Valley, Tantalus & Makiki Heights Map (p87)

Fort Shafter
Army Reservation

Honolulu
Watershed
Forest Reserve

Nu'uanu
Reservoir

Nu'uanu Valley

Pali Hwy

Honolulu
Watershed
Forest Reserve

Kamehameha
Park

N King St
Kalihi St
Lunalilo Fwy
Dillingham Blvd
Nimitz Hwy
Kapalama
Military
Reservation

Nu'uanu
Valley
Park

Pauoa
(1194ft)

Mt Tantalus
(2013ft)

Pacific
Heights

Makiki Valley

Tantalus

Upper
Manoa
Valley

Honolulu
Community
College
Vineyard Blvd

Nu'uanu Ave

Makiki
Heights

Pu'u 'Ualaka'a
State Park

Manoa Valley Rd

Manoa
Valley
Park

Kapalama
Basin

Kapalama Channel

N King St

Chinatown

Downtown

Punchbowl

Round Top
(1048ft)

Manoa Rd

O'ahu Ave

Wa'ahila Ridge
State Recreation
Area

Sand Island

Honolulu
Harbor

Sand Island State
Recreation Area

See Downtown Honolulu
& Chinatown Map (p76–7)

Lunalilo Pwy

Ward Ave

S Beretania St
S King St

Punahou
School

See University Area
Map (p86)

University
of Hawaii

Palolo Stream

Kaka'ako
Waterfront
State Park

Ala Moana Blvd

Kapi'olani Blvd

Kanewai
Park

Kapi'olani Blvd

See Central Honolulu & Ala Moana Map (p84–5)

Ala Wai
Park

Ala Wai
Golf Course

Wai'alae Ave
Harding Ave
Lunalilo Fwy

Kaimuki

Fort DeRussy
Military
Reservation

Kalakaua Ave

Ala Wai Blvd

Kapahulu Ave

Kilauea Ave

Kapi'olani
Community
College

Fort DeRussy
Beach

Waikiki

Central Waikiki Beach

Kuhio Beach
Park

Kapi'olani
Beach Park

Kapi'olani
Park

Kalakaua Ave

Diamond Head
Memorial Park
(Cemetery)

See Waikiki Map (p114–15)

Diamond Head ▲ State Monument
(760ft)

Diamond Head
Beach

Diamond Head Rd

Kahala Ave

Black
Point

Post

Ala Moana Post Office (Map pp84-5; ☎ 800-275-8777; Ala Moana Center, 1450 Ala Moana Blvd; ☻ 8:30am-5pm Mon-Fri, to 4:15pm Sat) On the ground floor on the inland side of the shopping center, this post office has longer hours than most.

Chinatown Post Office (Map pp76-7; ☎ 800-275-8777; Chinatown Cultural Plaza, River St)

Downtown Post Office (Map pp76-7; ☎ 800-275-8777; 335 Merchant St) In the Old Federal Building, on the corner of Richards St.

Main Post Office (Map pp72-3; ☎ 800-275-8777; Honolulu International Airport, 3600 Aolele St, Honolulu, HI 96820; ☻ 7:30am-8pm Mon-Fri, 8am-4pm Sat) If you're expecting to receive mail by general delivery (poste restante), it is accepted only at this post office, adjacent to the airport, and it's held no more than 30 days.

University of Hawai'i Post Office (Map p86; ☎ 800-275-8777; Administrative Services Bldg) At the west side of the Campus Center building.

Toilets

There are public toilets at shopping centers, museums and Ala Moana Beach Park and, for patrons, at restaurants and bars.

Tourist Information

You can pick up all sorts of tourist brochures at the visitor booths at Honolulu International Airport.

The **O'ahu Visitors Bureau** (☎ 523-8802, 877-525-6248; www.visit-oahu.com) has an excellent website, and staff can answer questions over the phone.

Travel Agencies

The following reputable travel agencies specialize in discount air tickets:

King's Travel (Map pp84-5; ☎ 593-4481; www.kings travel.com; 725 Kapi'olani Blvd)

Non-Stop Travel (Map pp84-5; ☎ 593-0700, 800-551-1226; www.nonstophawaii.com; 1350 S King St)

DANGERS & ANNOYANCES

Drug dealing and nighttime youth gang activity are prevalent at the north side of Chinatown along the Nu'uanu Stream, so that neighborhood, including the River Street pedestrian mall, should be avoided after dark.

SIGHTS

Downtown Honolulu

If the historic buildings of downtown Honolulu could talk, what a story they could tell!

This compact area was center stage for the political intrigue and social upheavals that changed the fabric of Hawaii in the 19th and 20th centuries. The main players ruled here, revolted here, worshipped here and still rest, however restlessly, in the graveyards here.

But not everything enshrines history. Indeed, one of the delights of downtown is the juxtaposition of past and present, with stately Victorian-era buildings mirrored in the black glass of sleek high-rises. So whether you're in the mood to catch a concert by the Royal Hawaiian Band on the palace lawn or up for browsing at the state's finest contemporary art museum, you'll find plenty to vie for your interest in the heart of Honolulu.

'IOLANI PALACE

There's simply no other place that evokes a more poignant sense of Hawaii's history than 'Iolani Palace (Map pp76–7), a place where royalty feasted, the haole (Caucasian) business community steamed, and plots and counterplots simmered. So much happened within the walls of the palace, involving monarchs and those who overthrew them, that you can almost sense the spirits of those who were once here.

The palace was the official residence of King Kalakaua and Queen Kapi'olani from 1882 to 1891, and of Queen Lili'uokalani for two years after that. Following the overthrow of the Hawaiian kingdom in 1893, the palace became the capitol – first for the republic, then for the territory and later for the state of Hawaii.

It wasn't until 1969 that Hawaii's state legislators moved out of their cramped palace quarters. Until that time the senate had been meeting in the dining room and the House of Representatives in the throne room. By the time they left 'Iolani Palace was in shambles, the grand koa staircase termite-ridden, and the Douglas fir floors pitted and gouged. After a decade-long renovation, the palace was restored to its former glory and reopened as a museum.

Palace Tour

You must join a **tour** (☎ 522-0832; adult/child 5-17yr $20/5, child under 5yr not admitted; ☻ 90min tours every half-hr 9am-2pm Tue-Sat) to see 'Iolani's grand interior. As the guides like to point out, 'Iolani Palace was modern for its day.

Every bedroom had its own bathroom with hot running water, and electric lights replaced the gas lamps a full four years before the White House in Washington installed electricity.

The red-and-gold throne room features the original thrones of the king and queen and a *kapu* (taboo) stick made of the spiraled ivory tusk of a narwhal. In addition to hosting celebrations full of pomp and pageantry, it was in the throne room that King Kalakaua danced his favorite Western dances – the waltz and the Virginia reel – into the wee hours of the morning.

Not all the events that took place here were joyous. Two years after she was dethroned, Queen Lili'uokalani was brought back to the throne room and tried for treason. In a move calculated to humiliate the Hawaiian people, she spent nine months as a prisoner in 'Iolani Palace, her former home.

Palace Grounds

The palace grounds, open during daylight hours and free of charge, are also history-laden and fun to explore. The former **barracks** of the Royal Household Guards, a building that looks oddly like the uppermost layer of a medieval fort that's been sliced off and plopped on the ground, now contains the palace ticket window.

A focal point on the grounds is the **domed pavilion**, originally built for the coronation of King Kalakaua in 1883 and still used for governor inaugurations. Swing by the pavilion at noon on Friday to hear the Royal Hawaiian Band (p106), which hails back to the days of Kalakaua, performing some of the king's favorite tunes.

The **grassy mound** that is surrounded by a wrought-iron fence contained the tombs of Kamehameha II and Queen Kamamalu (who both died in 1824) until they were moved to the Royal Mausoleum in Nu'uanu.

STATE CAPITOL

Built in the 1960s, Hawaii's **state capitol** (Map pp76-7; ☎ 587-0666; 415 S Beretania St; ☼ 8am-5pm Mon-Fri) is an acquired architectural taste for some, and certainly not your standard gold dome. A grandiose attempt at a theme design, its two central legislative chambers are cone-shaped to represent volcanoes; the supporting columns symbolize palm trees; the rotunda is open to let trade winds

---

FAVORITE BREAKFAST SPOTS

If you are heading into Honolulu early to do some downtown sightseeing, visit Great Harvest (p98), which bakes mouthwatering cinnamon rolls and pastries in the morning. Should you be near the shopping district, the open-air Pagoda Restaurant (p101) has the right wake-up-gently atmosphere, with its balmy breezes, encircling carp pond and thoroughly family-friendly atmosphere. If Chinatown is your destination, go local with luscious dim sum at Golden Palace Seafood Restaurant (p99).

---

blow through; and the whole structure is encircled by a pool representing the ocean surrounding Hawaii.

Visitors are free to walk through the rotunda and peer through viewing windows into the legislative chambers. Take the elevator to the top (5th) floor for a splendid view of downtown Honolulu.

In front of the capitol is a **statue of Father Damien**, the Belgian priest who worked among Hawaii's lepers in the late 19th century before dying of the disease himself. The stylized sculpture was created by Venezuelan artist Marisol Escubar.

QUEEN LILI'UOKALANI STATUE

A life-sized bronze statue of Hawaii's last queen (Map pp76–7), Queen Lili'uokalani, stands between 'Iolani Palace and the state capitol, and is facing Washington Place, Lili'uokalani's place of exile for more than 20 years. Lili'uokalani holds a copy of the Hawaiian constitution, which she wrote in 1893 in an attempt to strengthen Hawaiian rule (and which US businessmen used as an excuse to overthrow her); the *Aloha 'Oe*, a patriotic hymn she composed; and *Kumulipo*, the Hawaiian chant of creation. The statue is invariably draped with fresh hibiscus and maile lei, a sign of how revered the queen remains to Hawaiians.

HAWAI'I STATE ART MUSEUM

The superb state art **museum** (Map pp76-7; ☎ 586-0900; www.hawaii.gov/sfca; No 1 Capitol District Bldg, 250 S Hotel St; admission free; ☼ 10am-4pm Tue-Sat, 5-9pm first Friday of month) is a treasure waiting to be explored. For full details, see the boxed text Strokes of Brilliance (p78).

DOWNTOWN HONOLULU & CHINATOWN

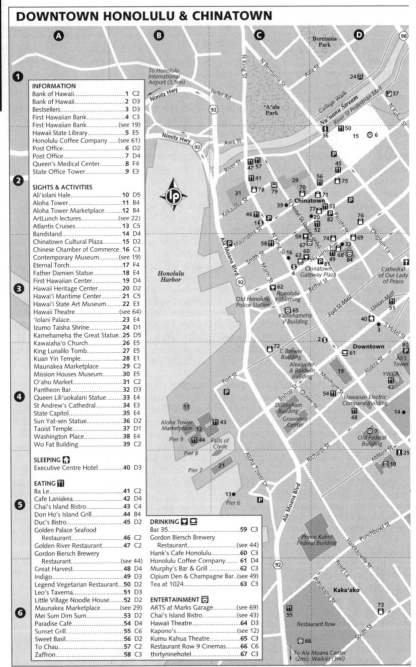

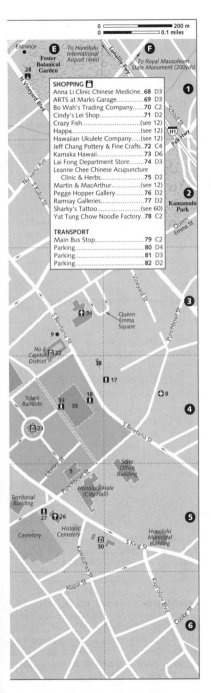

WASHINGTON PLACE

The governor's official residence (Map pp76–7) is a large colonial-style building surrounded by stately trees, built in 1846 by US sea captain John Dominis. The captain's son, also named John, became the governor of O'ahu and married the Hawaiian princess who later became Queen Lili'uokalani. After the queen was dethroned, she lived at Washington Place in exile until her death in 1917.

A plaque near the sidewalk on the left side of Washington Place is inscribed with the words to *Aloha Oe,* the anthem composed by Queen Lili'uokalani. The house can be viewed from the sidewalk, but is not open to the general public.

ST ANDREW'S CATHEDRAL

King Kamehameha IV, attracted by the royal trappings of the Church of England, decided to build his own cathedral in Hawaii. He and his consort, Queen Emma, founded the Anglican Church of Hawaii in 1858. The cathedral's cornerstone was finally laid in 1867 by King Kamehameha V, four years after the death of Kamehameha IV, who died on St Andrew's Day – hence the church's name.

The architecture of the **cathedral** (Map pp76-7; ☎ 524-2822; cnr Alakea & Beretania Sts; admission free; ☽ 9am-5pm) is French Gothic, using stone and glass shipped from England. Its most striking feature is the impressive window of handblown stained glass that forms the western facade and reaches from the floor to the eaves. In the right section of the glass you can see the Reverend Thomas Staley, the first bishop sent to Hawaii by Queen Victoria, alongside Kamehameha IV and Queen Emma.

ALI'IOLANI HALE

The first major government building constructed by the Hawaiian monarchy was **Ali'iolani Hale** (Map pp76-7; ☎ 539-4994; 417 S King St; admission free; ☽ 8am-4pm Mon-Fri), which in Hawaiian means House of Heavenly Kings. It was originally designed by Australian architect Thomas Rowe to be a royal palace, although it was never used as such. Instead, the building has housed the Hawaii Supreme Court since its construction in 1874 and was also once home to the state legislature.

HONOLULU

STROKES OF BRILLIANCE

A place that can really make you feel passionate about the arts, the Hawai'i State Art Museum should be high on your must-see list. Opened in 2002, the museum fulfills a 35-year effort by the State Foundation on Culture and the Arts to find a permanent home for its splendid collection of works by Hawaii artists. Some of the artists are island-born, while others arrived from far-flung places and fell in love with Hawaii's remarkable scenery and traditions.

The museum is superb not just for its fine collection, but also for its overall design. Works are displayed around themes that include island traditions, social issues, Hawaiian heritage, and the beauty of the land and sea. Hawaii's confluence of Asian, Pacific and American cultures is evident throughout, and the curators have done an excellent job of capturing the soul of the islands and the heart of the people.

The grand building itself is a work of art. Built directly across from 'Iolani Palace, it was designed in Spanish mission style by Emory, Webb and Rogers in 1928 and is now on the National Register of Historic Places.

Near the entrance, visitors see a model of the type of canoe that brought the first Polynesians to Hawaii, displayed with *The Discovery of Hawai'i*, a painting by Herb Kawainui Kane that shows the awed voyagers on that first canoe as they crest a wave and catch site of an erupting volcano. Among the highlights:

- A sculpture of shoes left on steps depicts *E Komo Mai*, the Hawaiian spirit of welcome, where anybody can remove their footwear and make themselves at home. The artist, George Kahumoku, is best known for his slack-key guitar playing.

- *Ronin Samurai*, part of a 1982 series by Masami Teraoka, uses traditional Japanese *ukiyoe* techniques to take a wry look at tourism. In this work a samurai and a geisha are shown snorkeling in Hanauma Bay.

- *Two Sisters of Old Hawaii*, a work by Madge Tennent, known for her bold paintings of Hawaiians in the early 20th century, is set off by a giant koa frame carved as a maile lei, itself a work of art.

- *Hakioawa Dance/Kaho'olawe Room*, a jarring lithograph, is Anne Miura's depiction of what her house on Maui felt like every time a US Navy test bomb exploded on nearby Kaho'olawe.

- *In the Troubled Rainbow*, photographs by Mark Hamasaki, continues the theme of social commentary that doesn't always favor the government. Here the assault on the land that marked the controversial construction of O'ahu's H3 highway in the 1990s is presented in stark black and white.

- Jean Charlot's *Ko Ke Kumulipo (The Drummer)* is a masterpiece by the painter who spent many years in the islands before his death in 1979. It depicts a local drummer intent on his music in a way that will have you sure you can hear it.

- Kids of all ages will love Doug Young's sculpture of a human-size gecko sunbathing in a lounge chair, part of the *Geckos in Paradise* series.

A visit to the museum can easily occupy a few hours, but the sensible admissions policy (it's free!) means that you can pop in after visiting the palace, do a little browsing and come back again. Some of the galleries feature changing exhibits, so there are always a few fun surprises.

It was on the steps of Ali'iolani Hale, in January 1893, that Sanford Dole proclaimed the establishment of a provisional government and the overthrow of the Hawaiian monarchy. Step inside to find a display on Hawaii's judicial history dating back to the time of Kamehameha the Great.

KAMEHAMEHA THE GREAT STATUE

A bronze statue of Kamehameha the Great (Map pp76–7) stands in front of Ali'iolani Hale, facing Iolani Palace. On June 11, a state holiday honoring Kamehameha, the statue is ceremoniously draped with layer upon layer of 12ft lei.

The Kamehameha statue was cast in 1880 in Florence, Italy, by American sculptor Thomas Gould. The current statue is actually a recast, however, as the first statue was lost at sea near the Falkland Islands. The original statue, which was recovered from the ocean floor after the second version was dedicated here in 1883, now stands in Kohala on the Big Island, where Kamehameha was born.

KAWAIAHA'O CHURCH
O'ahu's oldest **church** (Map pp76-7; ☎ 522-1333; 957 Punchbowl St; admission free; ☺ 8am-4pm) was built on the site where the first missionaries constructed a grass thatch church after their arrival in 1820. The original structure used woven mats instead of pews and seated 300 people.

Still, thatch wasn't quite what the missionaries had in mind, so they designed this typical New England Congregational church with simple Gothic influences. Completed in 1842, the church is made of 14,000 coral slabs, each weighing about 1000lb, which Hawaiian divers chiseled out of Honolulu's underwater reef – a task that took four years.

The clock tower was donated by Kamehameha III, and the old clock, installed in 1850, still keeps accurate time. The rear seats of the church, marked by *kahili* (feather) staffs and velvet padding, were for royalty and are still reserved for descendants of royalty today. Visitors are welcome to join the congregation for the 9am Sunday services, which include hymns in Hawaiian.

King Lunalilo Tomb
The tomb of King Lunalilo, the successor to Kamehameha V, is on the grounds of Kawaiaha'o Church at the main entrance. Lunalilo ruled for only one year before his death in 1874 at the age of 39.

Church Cemetery
The cemetery at the rear of Kawaiaha'o Church is an interesting place to poke around, a bit like a who's who of colonial history. You'll find the gravestones of early missionaries buried alongside other important Westerners of the day, including the infamous Sanford Dole, who overthrew Queen Lili'uokalani and went on to become the first territorial governor of Hawaii.

MISSION HOUSES MUSEUM
The old headquarters of the Sandwich Islands Mission has now been set aside as a **museum** (Map pp76-7; ☎ 531-0481; 553 S King St; tours adult/child $10/6; ☺ tours 11am, 1pm & 2:45pm Tue-Sat).

The first missionaries packed more than their bags when they left Boston – they actually brought a prefabricated wooden house, called the **Frame House**, around the Horn with them! Designed to withstand frigid New England winter winds, the house's small windows instead block out Honolulu's cooling trade winds, keeping the interior hot and stuffy. Erected in 1821, it's the oldest wooden structure in Hawaii.

The coral-block **Chamberlain House** was the mission storeroom, a necessity as Honolulu had few shops in those days. It holds old storage crates and the desk and quill pen storekeeper Levi Chamberlain used to tally the supplies he doled out to missionary families.

FIRST HAWAIIAN CENTER
The headquarters of the First Hawaiian Bank houses the downtown gallery of the **Contemporary Museum** (Map pp76-7; ☎ 526-0232; 999 Bishop St; admission free; ☺ 8:30am-4pm Mon-Thu, to 6pm Fri), which features quality exhibits of modern Hawaiian art. Honolulu's tallest high-rise, the sleek building itself incorporates artwork, including a four story–high glass wall containing 185 prisms designed by famed New York glass artist Jamie Carpenter. Also take a look at *Enchanting Garden,* a flowing-water sculpture by Satoru Abe, at the King St entrance.

ALOHA TOWER
Built in 1926 at the edge of the downtown district, the 10-story Aloha Tower (Map pp76–7) is a Honolulu landmark that for years was the city's tallest building. In the days when all tourists arrived by ship, this icon of pre-war Hawaii – with its four-sided clock tower inscribed with 'Aloha' – greeted every visitor. These days cruise ships still disembark at the terminal beneath the tower.

Take a look at the interior of the cruise-ship terminal, which has wall-to-wall murals depicting early-20th-century Honolulu life. The scenes include hula dancers, Hawaiian kids diving off the pier and mainland passengers disembarking from one of the San Francisco–Honolulu ships that docked here during that era.

Be sure to take the elevator to the top of the Aloha Tower, where an **observation deck** (☎ 537-9260; Pier 9; admission free; ✆ 9am-5pm; 🚌 19 & 20) offers a sweeping 360-degree view of Honolulu and the waterfront. It's a great way to get a perspective on the entire city. Interpretive plaques point out the landmarks and provide some fun trivia.

In addition to the cruise-ship terminal and the tower itself, the complex holds the **Aloha Tower Marketplace** (p108), a shopping center with numerous stores and eateries. Fittingly, many of the shops specialize in Hawaiiana items, and most of the places to eat have harbor views.

HAWAI'I MARITIME CENTER
A great place to get a sense of Hawaii's history is the **Hawai'i Maritime Center** (Map pp76-7; ☎ 536-6373; Pier 7; adult/child 4-12yr $7.50/4.50; ✆ 8:30am-5pm; 🚌 19 & 20). Museum displays cover everything from the arrival of Captain Cook to modern-day windsurfing, with lots of tidbits that you won't find anywhere else. The whaling section masterfully conveys a sense of the era as it affected Hawaii.

Interesting displays on early tourism include a reproduction of a Matson liner stateroom and photos of Waikiki in the days when just the Royal Hawaiian and the Moana hotels shared the shore with Diamond Head. Matson built both hotels in the early 1900s

to accommodate the passengers they carried on their cruises. Ironically, Matson sold the hotels off to the Sheraton chain in 1959, just before the jet age launched sleepy tourism into a booming industry.

Museum visitors can also climb aboard the *Falls of Clyde*, the world's last four-masted, four-rigged ship. Built in 1878, the ship once carried sugar and passengers between Hilo and San Francisco, and is now a National Historic Landmark.

Chinatown
The buzz of street vendors, the scent of burning incense and the chatter of bargaining shoppers – Chinatown's streets burst with life like no place else on O'ahu. The sights and sounds of this colorful neighborhood richly reflect the Asian roots of its residents. Chinese characters mark prices in the market, fire-breathing dragons spiral up the columns of buildings and steaming dim sum awakens even the sleepiest of appetites. Take time to explore: wander through the markets, consult with a herbalist and rub shoulders with the locals over a bowl of noodles.

And if you're beginning to think Chinatown is all hustle and bustle, just mosey on over to Foster Botanical Garden – the city's finest – for a meditative stroll.

HAWAII THEATRE
This neoclassical **theatre** (Map pp76-7; ☎ 528-0506; 1130 Bethel St) first opened in 1922 with

---

RISING PHOENIX

Around 1860 Chinese immigrants who had worked off their sugarcane plantation contracts began settling in Chinatown and opening up small businesses. In December 1899 the bubonic plague broke out in Chinatown. The 7000 Chinese, Hawaiians and Japanese who made the crowded neighborhood their home were cordoned off and forbidden to leave. As more plague cases arose, the board of health decided to conduct controlled burns of infected homes.

On January 20, 1900, the fire brigade set fire to a building on the corner of Beretania St and Nu'uanu Ave. The wind suddenly picked up and the fire spread out of control, racing toward the waterfront. To make matters worse, police guards stationed inside the plague area attempted to stop quarantined residents from fleeing. Nearly 40 acres of Chinatown burned to the ground.

Not everyone thought the speard of the fire was accidental. Just the year before, Chinese immigration into Hawaii had been halted by the US annexation of the islands, and Chinatown itself was prime real estate on the edge of the burgeoning downtown district. Despite the adverse climate, the residents of Chinatown held their own and a new Chinatown arose from the ashes.

In the 1940s, thousands of American GIs walked the streets of Chinatown before being shipped off to Iwo Jima and Guadalcanal. Many spent their last days of freedom in Chinatown's 'body houses,' pool halls and tattoo parlors.

silent films playing to the tunes of a pipe organ. Dubbed the 'Pride of the Pacific,' it ran continuous shows during WWII, but the development of mall cinemas in the 1970s brought down the curtain.

After closing in 1984, the theater's future looked dim, even though it was on the National Register of Historic Places. Theater buffs came to the rescue, purchased the property and spearheaded an extensive multimillion-dollar restoration.

The 1400-seat theater has a lovely interior, with trompe-l'oeil mosaics and bas-relief scenes of Shakespearean plays. It reopened in 1996 for dance, drama and music performances, and is now one of the leading entertainment venues in Honolulu.

One-hour guided tours, with insights on the history and architecture of the place and a demonstration of the old organ, are offered at 11am every Tuesday ($5).

CHINATOWN MARKETS
Chinatown's focal point, **O'ahu Market** (Map pp76-7; cnr Kekaulike & N King Sts; 7am-5pm), has been a Honolulu institution since 1904. Some of the city's finest chefs start their day here wrangling over fish that's so fresh it's still wriggling. And just about anything else that hits a pot can be found here, from pig heads and fresh octopus to bok choy and green papayas. The market is unique in that it's owned by the vendors, who in 1984 pooled their money together and purchased the property to keep it from falling into the hands of developers.

Another fun place to test your bargaining skills is the **Maunakea Marketplace** (Map pp76-7; 1120 Maunakea St; 7am-5pm), a run of ramshackle stands and small shops surrounding an enclosed courtyard, with a popular food court full of little mom-and-pop stalls.

CHINATOWN CULTURAL PLAZA
This plaza (Map pp76-7), covering the better part of a block, is bordered by N Beretania St, Maunakea and River Sts. The modern complex doesn't have the character of Chinatown's older shops, but inside it's still quintessential Chinatown, with tailors, acupuncturists and calligraphers alongside travel agencies and restaurants. In the small courtyard, elderly Chinese come daily to light incense and leave mangoes at a statue of Kuan Yin.

TRADITIONAL FLOWER POWER

Chinatown herbalists are both physicians and pharmacists, with walls full of small wooden drawers each filled with a different herb. They'll size you up, feel your pulse and listen to you describe your ailments before deciding which drawers to open, mixing herbs and flowers and wrapping them for you to take home and boil together. The object is to balance yin and yang forces. You can find herbalists at the Chinatown Cultural Plaza and elsewhere around Chinatown, including **Leanne Chee Chinese Acupuncture Clinic & Herbs** (Map pp76-7; 533-2498; 1159 Maunakea St; 9am-4pm Mon-Sat) and **Anna Li Clinic Chinese Medicine** (Map pp76-7; 537-1133; 1121 Nu'uanu Ave; 9am-noon Mon-Sat & 2-5pm Mon-Fri).

TEMPLES & SHRINES
Kuan Yin Temple
Near the entrance of Foster Botanical Garden you'll find this brightly adorned Chinese **temple** (Map pp76-7; 533-6361; 170 N Vineyard Blvd; sunrise-sunset), the oldest in Honolulu. The richly carved interior overflows with the sweet, pervasive scent of burning incense.

The temple is dedicated to Kuan Yin Bodhisattva, goddess of mercy, whose statue is the largest in the prayer hall. Devotees burn paper 'money' for prosperity and good luck. Offerings of fresh flowers and fruit are placed at the altar. The large citrus fruit that is stacked pyramid-style is the pomelo, considered a symbol of fertility because of its many seeds.

Honolulu's Buddhist community worships at the temple, and respectful visitors are welcome.

Taoist Temple
Founded in 1889, the Lum Sai Ho Tong Society was one of more than 100 societies started by Chinese immigrants in Hawaii to help preserve their cultural identity. This one was for the Lum clan, which hails from an area west of the Yellow River. At one time the society had more than 4000 members, and even now there are nearly a thousand Lums in the Honolulu phone book.

The society's **Taoist temple** (Map pp76-7; cnr River & Kukui Sts) honors the goddess Tin Hau, a Lum child who rescued her father from drowning and was later deified. Many Chinese claim to see her apparition when they travel by boat. The temple is not usually open to the general public, but you can admire the building from the outside.

Izumo Taisha Shrine

Across the river from the Taoist temple is a wooden Shinto **shrine** (Map pp76-7; ☎ 538-7778; 215 N Kukui St; ☺ 9am-5pm) built by Japanese immigrants in 1923. It was confiscated during WWII by the city of Honolulu and wasn't returned to its congregation until 1962.

Incidentally, the 100lb sacks of rice that sit near the altar symbolize good health, and ringing the bell placed at the shrine entrance is considered an act of purification for those who come to pray.

FOSTER BOTANICAL GARDEN

If you need a reprieve from the city, this impressive 14-acre **botanical garden** (Map pp76-7; ☎ 522-7066; 180 N Vineyard Blvd; adult/child 6-12yr $5/1; ☺ 9am-4pm) offers shady strolls along scented paths.

The garden first took root in 1850. Among its rare specimens are the native Hawaiian loulu palm, taken from Oʻahu's Nuʻuanu Valley, and the evening-blooming East African *Gigasiphon macrosiphon.* Both are thought to be extinct in the wild.

Several of the garden's towering trees are the largest of their kind in the USA. Oddities include a double coconut palm capable of producing a 50lb nut – watch your head! Let your nose lead you through fragrant vanilla vines and cinnamon trees in the spice garden, and bring along a camera for some great close-up photo-ops in the orchid section.

You can pick up a self-guided tour booklet at the entrance or join an hour-long walking tour, included in the admission price, at 1pm Monday to Saturday.

Central Honolulu & Ala Moana

Ala Moana means 'Path to the Sea' and its namesake road, Ala Moana Blvd (Hwy 92), connects the coast between Waikiki and Honolulu, clear out to the airport. Although when most people think Ala Moana they think shopping, that's only one part of what you'll find here. Ala Moana Beach Park is a gem that has few rivals anywhere – in Hawaii or beyond. Two stellar museums, one for

keiki (children) and the other for art connoisseurs, ensure that even when the sun fails to shine, there are cheery places to go.

ALA MOANA CENTER

Hawaii's biggest shopping center, the **Ala Moana Center** (Map pp84-5; 1450 Ala Moana Blvd), boasts nearly 300 shops and eateries. When outer islanders fly to Honolulu to shop, they go to Ala Moana. It's also Honolulu's major bus transfer point and tens of thousands of passengers transit through daily, so even if you weren't planning to go to the center, you're likely to end up there anyway.

Ala Moana has typical mall anchor stores, such as Sears and Macy's, as well as lots of fun, local-spun specialty shops. A favorite for local color is the Crack Seed Center, where you can scoop from jars full of pickled mangoes, candied ginger and banzai mix. There are also airline offices, banks, a supermarket and a food court with scores of ethnic fast-food stalls.

ALA MOANA BEACH PARK

Opposite the Ala Moana Center, this fabulous city park (Map pp84–5) has much less hustle and bustle than Waikiki. The park is fronted by a broad, golden-sand beach, nearly a mile long, which is buffered from the traffic noise of Ala Moana Blvd by a spacious, grassy area with shade trees.

This is where Honolulu residents go to jog after work, play volleyball and enjoy weekend picnics. The park has full beach facilities, several softball fields, tennis courts and free parking. It's a very popular park, yet big enough that it never feels crowded.

Ala Moana is an ideal choice for distance swimmers. However, at low tide the deep channel that runs the length of the beach can be a hazard to poor swimmers who don't realize it's there. A former boat channel, it drops off suddenly to overhead depths. If you want to measure laps, it's 500m between the lifeguard tower at the Waikiki end and the white post in the water midway between the third and fourth lifeguard towers.

MAGIC ISLAND

The 43-acre peninsula jutting from the eastern side of the park is the ʻAina Moana State Recreation Area, more commonly known as Magic Island (Map pp84–5). During the school year you can often find high-school outrigger canoe teams practicing here in the late afternoon. There's a pleasant walk around the perimeter of Magic Island, and sunsets can be picture-perfect, with sailboats pulling in and out of the adjoining Ala Wai Yacht Harbor. This is also a hot summer surf spot.

HAWAII CHILDREN'S DISCOVERY CENTER
This extensive hands-on **museum** (Map pp72-3; ☎ 524-5437; www.discoverycenterhawaii.org; 111 'Ohe St; adult/child 2-17yr $8/6.75, child under 2yr free; ☼ 9am-1pm Tue-Fri, 10am-3pm Sat & Sun; ☒ 8 & 20) is a great place to take the kids on a rainy day.

It all starts at the entry, where the **Toy Box** introduces children to the center via a video puppet show. **Fantastic You** explores the human body, allowing kids to walk through a mock stomach. More traditional displays can be found in the **Your Town** section, where kids can drive an interactive fire engine or become a TV interviewer. The **Hawaiian Rainbows** and **Rainbow World** sections relate specifically to life in Hawaii, allowing children to navigate a ship and swim with dolphins. Older kids may find some of the displays interesting, but the museum is primarily geared to capture the interest of pre-teen children.

HONOLULU ACADEMY OF ARTS
This exceptional fine arts **museum** (Map pp84-5; ☎ 532-8700; www.honoluluacademy.org; 900 S Beretania St; adult/senior or student $7/4, child under 13yr free; ☼ 10am-

---

DETOUR: LILI'UOKALANI BOTANICAL GARDEN

A waterfall in the center of Honolulu? You bet, right in the heart of this city **park** (Map pp72-3; ☎ 522-7060; 123 N Kuakini St; admission free; ☼ 9am-5pm) that extends along eight flowing acres of Nu'uanu Stream. Named for Queen Lili'uokalani, who once tended the park as her own private garden, this makes a fun diversion if you're looking for a place in town to break out a picnic lunch. To get there from Chinatown, take Nu'uanu Ave north and after crossing over the H1, continue for 0.25 miles and then turn left onto Kuakini St. The garden entrance is on the left just 200yd up the street.

4:30pm Tue-Sat, 1-5pm Sun; ☒ 2), with solid Asian, European and Pacific collections, houses nearly 40,000 pieces of artwork.

The museum, dating to 1927, has a classical facade that's invitingly open and airy, with galleries branching off a series of garden courtyards. Exhibits, which reflect the various cultures that make up current-day Hawaii, include one of America's finest Asian art collections with everything from peaceful Buddhas to fierce samurai armor. A highlight is the striking contemporary wing with Hawaiian works on its upper level, and modern art by such luminaries as Henry Moore and Georgia O'Keeffe below.

This is a place to relax and move slowly. Consider pairing your browsing with lunch at the museum's courtyard café (p101).

KAKA'AKO WATERFRONT PARK
Near downtown Honolulu and just off Ala Moana Blvd at the end of Cooke St, little Kaka'ako Waterfront Park (Map pp72–3) feels like it's far from town; a small grassy rise protects it from much of the city noise. Rollerbladers cruise along the rock-fringed promenade, which offers clear views of Diamond Head and Honolulu Harbor. The 28-acre park attracts experienced surfers in the morning and picnickers in the afternoon. It's not a safe swimming beach, but the tricky surf break is near the shore, making Kaka'ako a great place to watch surfers up close.

University Area
A happening college scene and some interesting dining options are in store in this neighborhood in the foothills of Manoa Valley.

UNIVERSITY OF HAWAI'I
Just 2 miles north of Waikiki, the **University of Hawai'i** (UH; Map p86; ☎ 956-8111; cnr University Ave & Dole St; ☒ 4 & 6) at Manoa is the central campus of the statewide university system.

The university has strong programs in astronomy, geophysics, marine sciences, and Hawaiian and Pacific studies, and the campus attracts students from islands throughout the Pacific. It has approximately 19,000 students and offers degrees in 90 fields of study.

Staff at the **information center** (Map p86; ☎ 956-7235; Room 212; ☼ 8:30am-4:30pm Mon-Fri) in

CENTRAL HONOLULU & ALA MOANA

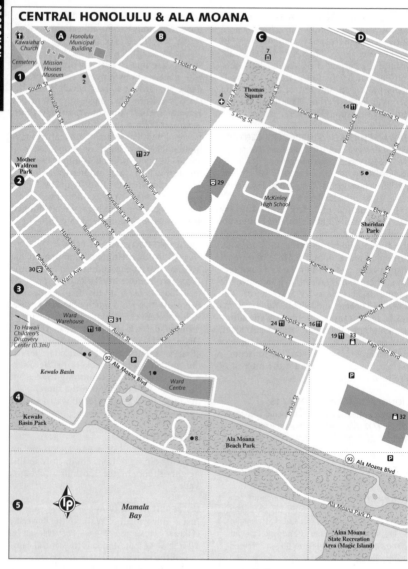

the Campus Center provide campus maps, give tours and can answer any questions you have about the university. Free one-hour **walking tours** of the campus, emphasizing history and architecture, leave from the Campus Center at 2pm Monday, Wednesday and Friday; to join, simply arrive 10 minutes before the tour begins.

EAST-WEST CENTER

At the eastern side of the University of Hawai'i campus is the **East-West Center** (Map p86; ☎ 944-7111; 1777 East-West Rd; ☐ 4, 6), an internationally recognized education and research organization established by the US Congress in 1960 to promote mutual understanding among the peoples of Asia, the

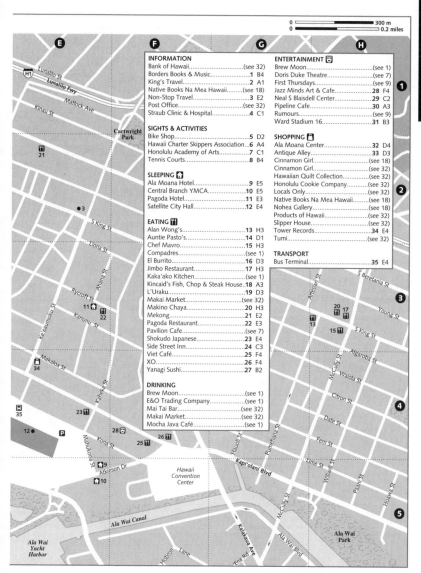

Pacific and the USA. Some 2000 researchers and graduate students work and study at the center, examining development policy, the environment and other Pacific issues.

Changing exhibits on Asian culture and art are displayed in the East-West Center's Gallery in **Burns Hall** (Map p86; ☎ 944-7111; cnr Dole St & East-West Rd; admission free; ☽ 8am-5pm Mon-Fri, noon-4pm Sun). The center occasionally has other multicultural programs open to the public, such as music concerts, dance performances and seminars.

JOHN YOUNG MUSEUM
The little campus **John Young Museum** (Map p86; ☎ 956-8866; Room 002, Krauss Hall; admission free;

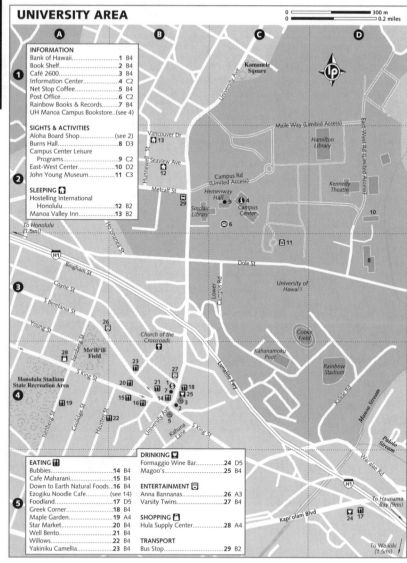

UNIVERSITY AREA

0 ——————— 300 m
0 ——————— 0.2 miles

INFORMATION
Bank of Hawaii.............................1 B4
Book Shelf....................................2 B4
Café 2600....................................3 B4
Information Center.......................4 C2
Net Stop Coffee...........................5 B4
Post Office...................................6 C2
Rainbow Books & Records..........7 B4
UH Manoa Campus Bookstore..(see 4)

SIGHTS & ACTIVITIES
Aloha Board Shop...................(see 2)
Burns Hall....................................8 D3
Campus Center Leisure
    Programs.................................9 C2
East-West Center.......................10 D2
John Young Museum..................11 C3

SLEEPING
Hostelling International
    Honolulu...............................12 B2
Manoa Valley Inn.....................13 B2

EATING
Bubbies.......................................14 B4
Cafe Maharani...........................15 B4
Down to Earth Natural Foods....16 B4
Ezogiku Noodle Cafe.............(see 14)
Foodland....................................17 D5
Greek Corner..............................18 B4
Maple Garden.............................19 A4
Star Market.................................20 B4
Well Bento..................................21 B4
Willows......................................22 B4
Yakiniku Camellia.......................23 B4

DRINKING
Formaggio Wine Bar...................24 D5
Magoo's......................................25 B4

ENTERTAINMENT
Anna Bannanas...........................26 A3
Varsity Twins..............................27 B4

SHOPPING
Hula Supply Center.....................28 A4

TRANSPORT
Bus Stop.....................................29 B2

11am-2pm Mon-Fri, 1-4pm Sun) is dedicated to Hawaii artist John Young, who died in 1998. The museum features Young's collection of artifacts from Pacific islands and Asia. While this is not one of Honolulu's more outstanding museums, it''s definitely worth a visit if you are already in the area.

Upper Manoa Valley

The Upper Manoa Valley climbs beyond the university into forest reserve land in the mountains above Honolulu. It's a perfect place to commune with nature. The road up the valley runs through a well-to-do residential neighborhood before reaching the trailhead to Manoa Falls and the Lyon

Arboretum. For the ideal combination, take the hike to Manoa Falls in the morning and then stop by the arboretum to identify trees you've seen along the trail.

If coming by bus, take the No 5 Manoa Valley to the end of the line, at the junction of Manoa Rd and Kumuone St. From there, it's a 10-minute walk (half a mile) to the end of Manoa Rd, where the Manoa Falls Trail begins. Lyon Arboretum is at the end of the short drive just to the left of the trailhead.

To reach this area by car, drive to the end of Manoa Rd. Lyon Arboretum has parking for its visitors. There's room to park at the trailhead, but broken windshield glass confirms that it's not a secure place. A better option is to park in the residential area shortly

before the end of Manoa Rd. Either way, don't leave anything valuable in the car.

MANOA FALLS

The prettiest waterfall in Honolulu is the 100ft cascade of Manoa Falls (Map p87), which spills out of the Waihi Stream in the Upper Manoa Valley. The only way to reach the waterfall is along a 0.75-mile trail (p91) through a lush rain forest of grand trees.

LYON ARBORETUM

This 193-acre **arboretum** (Map p87; ☎ 988-0456; 3860 Manoa Rd; admission by donation; ✆ 9am-4pm Mon-Fri; 🚌 5) is the handiwork of Dr Harold Lyon, who introduced 10,000 exotic trees and plants to Hawaii. Approximately half

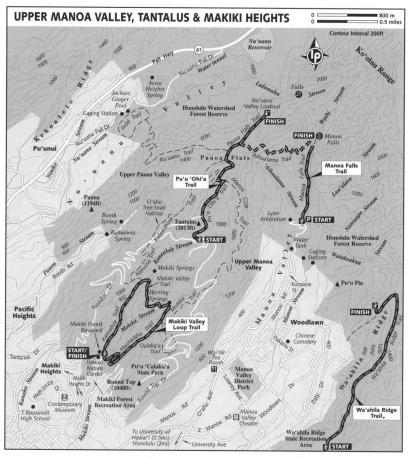

UPPER MANOA VALLEY, TANTALUS & MAKIKI HEIGHTS

are represented in this arboretum managed by the University of Hawai'i.

Related species are clustered in a semi-natural state. Key plants in the Hawaiian ethnobotanical garden include breadfruit and taro; *ko,* the sugarcane brought by early Polynesian settlers; *kukui,* which produced lantern oil; and ti, which was used for medicinal purposes during ancient times and for making moonshine after Westerners arrived.

For the best of the arboretum's short trails take the 20-minute walk up to **Inspiration Point**, which offers valley views, inviting stone benches and abundant birdsong. The path loops through fragrant magnolias and passes tall trees, including a bo tree thought to be a descendant of the tree Gautama Buddha sat under when he received enlightenment. How's that for inspiration!

Tantalus & Makiki Heights

Two miles from downtown Honolulu, a narrow switchback road cuts its way up the forest reserve land of Tantalus and the Makiki Valley. The road climbs almost to the top of 2013ft Mt Tantalus, with swank mountainside homes tucked in along the way.

Although the road is one continuous loop, the western side is called Tantalus Dr and the eastern side Round Top Dr. The 8.5-mile circuit is Honolulu's finest scenic drive; it offers splendid views of the city below.

The route is winding, narrow and steep, but it's a good paved road. Among the dense tropical growth, bamboo, ginger, elephant-ear taro and fragrant eucalyptus trees are easily identified. Jungle vines climb to the top of telephone poles and twist their way across the wires.

A network of hiking trails (p90) runs between Tantalus Dr and Round Top Dr and throughout the forest reserve. The Makiki Heights area below the forest reserve is one of the most exclusive residential areas in Honolulu. There's a bus service as far as Makiki Heights and the Contemporary Museum, but none around the Tantalus–Round Top loop road.

PU'U 'UALAKA'A STATE PARK

For an unparalleled panorama view of Honolulu, visit **Pu'u 'Ualaka'a State Park** (Map p87; ⊗ 7am-7:45pm Apr-Sep, to 6:45pm Oct-Mar), 2.5 miles up Round Top Dr from Makiki St.

The sweeping view extends from Kahala and Diamond Head on the far left, across Waikiki and downtown Honolulu, to the Wai'anae Range on the far right. To the southeast is the University of Hawai'i at Manoa, easily recognizable by its sports stadium; to the southwest you can see clearly into the green mound of Punchbowl Crater; the airport is visible on the edge of the coast and Pearl Harbor beyond that.

If you're taking photos, the best time is during the day. However, this is also a fine place to watch evening settle over the city; arrive at least 30 minutes prior to sunset to see the hills before they're in shadow.

CONTEMPORARY MUSEUM

This engaging modern-art **museum** (☎ 526-1322; www.tcmhi.org; 2411 Makiki Heights Dr; adult $5, child under 13yr free; ⊗ 10am-4pm Tue-Sat, noon-4pm Sun; ☐ 15) occupies an estate with 3.5 acres of sculpture-dotted gardens.

The estate house was constructed in 1925 for Anna Rice Cooke, whose other former home is the present site of the Honolulu Academy of Arts. An influential newspaper heiress, she played a founding role in both museums.

The main galleries feature changing exhibits of paintings, sculpture and other contemporary artwork by both national and international artists. A newer building on the lawn holds the museum's most prized piece, a vivid environmental installation by David Hockney based on his sets for *L'Enfant et les Sortilèges,* Ravel's 1925 opera.

Docent-led tours, at 1:30pm, are included in the price of admission. There's an excellent café (p104) serving lunch and drinks.

Elsewhere in Honolulu

BISHOP MUSEUM

Hands down the finest Polynesian anthropological museum in the world, the **Bishop Museum** (Map pp72-3; ☎ 847-3511; www.bishopmuseum.org; 1525 Bernice St; adult/child 4-12yr $14.95/11.95; ⊗ 9am-5pm; ☐ 2) showcases a remarkable array of cultural exhibits. And it's staying current, too, with a new and very cool $17 million center dedicated to Hawaii's awesome natural environment.

To get to the Bishop Museum by bus from Waikiki or downtown Honolulu, take the No 2 School St bus to Kapalama St, and turn right on Bernice St. By car, take exit

20B off H1, go inland on Houghtailing St and turn left on Bernice St.

Collections

The main gallery, the **Hawaiian Hall**, dedicates three floors to the cultural history of Hawaii. The 1st floor covers pre-Western Hawaii, displaying a full-sized *pili* grass–thatched house, carved temple images and shark-tooth war clubs. The foremost treasure is a feather cloak worn by Kamehameha the Great and created entirely of the yellow feathers of the now-extinct *mamo*, a predominately black bird with a yellow upper tail. Some 80,000 birds were caught and plucked to create this single cloak. To get a sense of just how few feathers each bird had, look at the nearby taxidermic *mamo* to the left of the Queen Lili'uokalani exhibit.

Missionary-inspired quilt work, whaling paraphernalia and other 19th-century influences are highlighted on the 2nd floor. The top floor spotlights the ethnic groups that comprise Hawaii today. Like Hawaii itself, it has a bit of everything, including samurai armor, Portuguese festival costumes and a Hawaiian ukulele made from coconut shells.

The **Kahili Room**, off the main hall, features portraits of Hawaiian royalty and a display of *kahili,* the feathered staffs used at coronations and royal funerals. Other exhibits cover the cultures of Polynesia, Micronesia and Melanesia.

Science Adventure Center

An eye-popping treat, this state-of-the-art center lets you walk through an erupting volcano, take a mini-submarine dive and play your hand at all sorts of interactive gadgets. While most of it is geared to entertain and enlighten folks of all ages, there are some fun things set aside just for kids, like the tree house and mock-insect costumes.

Planetarium

The museum is also home to O'ahu's only planetarium, which highlights traditional Polynesian methods of navigation, such as wave patterns and the position of the stars. Shows are held at noon, 12:45pm, 1:30pm and 3:30pm, and are included in the museum admission price. If you want to see what's unique in the night sky above Hawaii, catch the noon show.

PUNCHBOWL

The bowl-shaped remnant of a long-extinct volcanic crater, Punchbowl (Map pp72–3) sits a mile northeast of the downtown district, at an elevation of 500ft.

Early Hawaiians called the crater Puowaina, the 'hill of human sacrifices.' It's believed there was a heiau at the crater and that the slain bodies of *kapu* breakers were brought here to be cremated upon the altar. Today people come to Punchbowl to visit the war memorial and enjoy the panoramic views.

If you're driving to Punchbowl, take the H1 to the Pali Hwy. There's a marked exit as you start up the Pali Hwy; watch closely, because it comes up quickly! From there, drive slowly and follow the signs as you wind through narrow streets.

By bus, take the No 2 from Waikiki to downtown Honolulu and get off at Beretania and Alapa'i Sts, where you'll transfer to bus 15. Ask the driver where to get off. It's about a 15-minute walk to Punchbowl from the bus stop.

National Memorial Cemetery of the Pacific

The 115-acre **National Memorial Cemetery of the Pacific** (Map pp72-3; ☎ 532-3720; 2177 Puowaina Dr; admission free; ☉ 8am-5:30pm Oct-Feb, to 6:30pm Mar-Sep) is located at Punchbowl. The remains of Hawaiians sacrificed to appease

---

GRAVESPOTTING

The remains of Ernie Pyle, the famous war correspondent who covered both world wars and was hit by machine gunfire on Ie Shima during the final days of WWII, lie in section D, grave 109, at the National Memorial Cemetery of the Pacific. Five stones to the left, at grave D-1, is the marker for astronaut Ellison Onizuka, the Big Island native who perished in the 1986 *Challenger* space shuttle disaster. Henry Oliver Hansen, one of the Marines who raised the US flag on Iwo Jima at the end of WWII – a shot of which became one of the most recognized photographs of the war – is buried across the road in section O, grave 392. All of their resting places are marked with the same style of flat granite stone that marks each of the cemetery's graves.

the gods now share the crater floor with the bodies of over 33,000 soldiers, more than half of whom were killed in the Pacific during WWII.

A huge marble memorial at the rear of the cemetery has eight marble courts representing different Pacific regions. The memorial is inscribed with the names of the 26,289Americans missing in action from WWII and the Korean War. Two additional half courts contain the names of 2500 soldiers missing from the Vietnam War.

Lookout

Even without the war sights, Punchbowl would be worth the drive up for the view.

To get to the viewpoint, bear to the far left after entering the Punchbowl and go up to the top of the hill, where there's a lookout perched above the city, looking down on the state capitol and offering sweeping views clear out to Diamond Head and the Pacific beyond.

QUEEN EMMA SUMMER PALACE

In the heat of the summer, Queen Emma loved to slip away from her formal downtown home to this cooler hillside retreat. Her **summer palace** (Map pp72-3; ☎ 595-3167; www .daughtersofhawaii.org; 2913 Pali Hwy; adult/child under 18yr $6/1; ◷ 9am-4pm; 🚗 4) resembles an old plantation mansion, with a columned porch, high ceilings and louvered windows to catch the breeze. Inside is a repository of regal memorabilia and period furniture collected from five of Emma's homes.

There are lots of fun things to look at here, including a cathedral-shaped koa cabinet displaying a set of china from Queen Victoria; Emma's necklace of tiger claws, a gift from a maharaja of India; and feather cloaks and capes once worn by Hawaiian royalty. Queen Emma Summer Palace is on the Pali Hwy (Hwy 61) at the 2-mile marker.

MOANALUA GARDENS

This former vacation haunt for Hawaiian royalty makes a enjoyable diversion if you're in the area. The park (Map pp72–3), dotted with grand shade trees, has several hints of its regal past, including King Kamehameha V's gingerbread-trimmed summer cottage overlooking an ancient taro pond. Hawaiian culture takes center stage here each July when the park hosts the Prince Lot Hula

Festival (p96), one of the biggest festivals of its kind in Hawaii.

To get there, take the Pu'uloa Rd/Tripler Hospital exit off Hwy 78 and then make an immediate right turn into the gardens.

ACTIVITIES
Land Activities
HIKING

Everyone knows O'ahu abounds in ocean adventures, but most first-time visitors are surprised by the lightly trodden hiking trails that await in the lush green hillsides just above downtown Honolulu.

For information on guided hikes around the island, many of which depart from Honolulu, go to p59.

Wa'ahila Ridge Trail

Panoramic views of valleys, mountains and the city reward hikers who take this trail (Map p87), which ascends a ridge between Manoa and Palolo Valleys. The forest along the way is also a good place to spot two beautiful native birds, the 'apapane, a bright-red honeyeater with a black bill, and the yellow-green 'amakihi.

The 4.8-mile round-trip hike begins at the **Wa'ahila Ridge State Recreation Area** (☎ 587-0062; Ruth Pl; ◷ 7am-6:45pm; 🚗 14), where fine views of Manoa Valley start right at the parking lot. The trailhead, marked by a Na Ala Hele trail sign, starts in an ironwood forest just past the picnic tables. Bear left after the sign and you'll immediately start climbing the ridge and enjoying even broader views of the valley.

The trail continues uphill on a rutted dirt road past a water tank. Watch for a small arrow pointing to the left where the trail leaves the road and enters the forest reserve. Scattered with soft ironwood needles, the trail contours for a bit before sliding steeply downhill to a dry and rocky area.

Only partly shaded now, the trail labors up and down a series of small saddles and knobs, while granting views over the valley out to downtown Honolulu. At one point, the trail drops sharply over a series of boulders that require some minor scrambling, but then continues rhythmically on its roller-coaster pattern for another mile.

You'll see a big koa tree, its roots spreading across the trail, just before you make a more arduous, partly exposed climb to a

THE AUTHOR'S CHOICE

By far the most rewarding hour-long trek on O'ahu is the **Manoa Falls Trail** (Map p87; Upper Manoa Valley). If you're looking for something longer, you can turn it into a half-day hike by continuing on to Nu'uanu Valley Lookout, adding stellar views to your jungle jaunt.

Not only is the forested Manoa Falls Trail itself lovely, but it ends at a scenic waterfall and it's easily accessible from the city to boot. The trail runs for 0.75 miles above a rocky streambed before ending at the falls.

It's a relatively easy hike, with a 400ft gain in elevation. The trail is usually a bit muddy, but not too bad if it hasn't been raining recently. Be careful not to trip over exposed tree roots – they're potential ankle breakers, especially if you're moving at a quick pace. The packed clay can be slippery in some steep places, so take your time, pick up a walking stick and enjoy the trail.

Surrounded by lush vegetation and moss-covered stones, you get the feeling you are walking through a thick rain forest a long way from civilization. The sounds are purely natural: the chirping of birds and the rush of the stream and waterfall.

All sorts of trees line the path, including tall *Eucalyptus robusta,* with its soft, spongy, reddish bark; flowering orange African tulip trees; and other lofty varieties that creak like wooden doors in old houses. Many of them were planted by the nearby Lyon Arboretum, which at one time held a lease on the property.

Up ahead the vertical falls drop 100ft into a small pool. Wild purple orchids and red ginger grow nearby, adding a colorful element to the tranquil scene. The pool isn't deep enough for swimming, and falling rocks make it dangerous, so don't venture beyond the established viewing area.

About 50ft before Manoa Falls, the inconspicuous '**Aihualama Trail** starts to the west of a chain-link fence and scrambles over some boulders. After a couple of minutes the trail enters a tall bamboo forest with some massive old banyan trees and then contours around the ridge, offering broad views of Manoa Valley. Another mile of gradual switchbacks (ignore any shortcuts or misleading side trails) brings hikers to an intersection with the **Pauoa Flats Trail**, which ascends to the right for 0.5 miles over muddy tree roots to spectacular **Nu'uanu Valley Lookout**. Here atop the Ko'olau Range, where O'ahu's steep *pali* (cliffs) are visible all around, it's possible to peer through a gap out to windward O'ahu.

Round-trip distance is 1.5 miles if you do only the Manoa Falls Trail or 5.5 miles if you go all the way to the Nu'uanu Valley Lookout and back. For details on getting to the trailhead, see p86.

wide, grassy clearing with bird's-eye views of Manoa Valley and greater Honolulu. Beyond this clearing, the trail keeps going for only another five minutes, before it becomes muddy and overgrown and enters a restricted watershed area.

To get to the start of the trail, turn north off Wai'alae Ave onto St Louis Dr, turning right after 2.9 miles onto Peter St and then left after 0.5 miles onto Ruth Pl, which terminates at the park after 0.3 miles. If you come by bus, the nearest bus stop is at the intersection of Peter and Ruth Sts.

Makiki Valley Loop Trail

Three of the trails in the Tantalus area – Maunalaha Trail, Makiki Valley Trail and Kanealole Trail – can be combined to make the Makiki Valley Loop Trail (Map p87), a popular 2.5-mile hike.

The loop goes through a lush and varied tropical forest that begins and ends in Hawaii's first state nursery and arboretum. Here hundreds of thousands of trees were grown to replace the sandalwood forests that were leveled in Makiki Valley and elsewhere in Hawaii in the 19th century.

The **Maunalaha Trail** begins at the rest rooms below the parking lot of the Hawaii Nature Center. After crossing over a small stream and a few tame switchbacks, the trail makes a no-holds-barred ascent of the Makiki Valley's east ridge over a giant staircase of tree roots, passing Norfolk pines, banyans and taro patches along the way. Behind are views of Honolulu's skyscrapers and harbor.

After 0.75 miles, you'll come to a four-way junction. Follow the **Makiki Valley Trail** straight ahead and proceed uphill. The trail goes through small gulches and across gentle streams bordered with patches of ginger. Near the Moleka Stream crossing, there are mountain apple trees that flower in the spring and bear fruit in the summer. Edible yellow guava and strawberry guava also grow along the trail.

The **Kanealole Trail** begins as you cross Kanealole Stream and then follows the stream back to the baseyard, 0.75 miles away. The trail leads down through a field of Job's tears; the beadlike bracts of the female flowers of this tall grass are often used for lei. Kanealole Trail is usually muddy, so wear shoes with good traction and pick up a walking stick.

To reach the trailhead, turn left off Makiki St and go 0.5 miles up Makiki Heights Dr. Where the road makes a sharp bend, proceed straight ahead through a gate into the Makiki Forest Recreation Area and continue until you reach a gravel parking lot. You can also take the No 15 bus; get off near the intersection of Mott-Smith and Makiki Heights Drs and walk down Makiki Heights Dr. It's a mile-long walk between the bus stop and the trailhead.

Pu'u 'Ohi'a Trail

A network of interconnected trails crosses the Tantalus area, offering adventurous hiking with quiet forests and stunning views.

The **Pu'u 'Ohi'a Trail** (Map p87), in conjunction with the Pauoa Flats Trail, leads up to Nu'uanu Valley Lookout. It's nearly 2 miles one way and makes a hardy hike. The trailhead is at the very top of Tantalus Dr, 3.6 miles up from its intersection with Makiki Heights Dr. There's a large turnoff opposite the trailhead where you can park.

The Pu'u 'Ohi'a Trail begins with reinforced log steps and leads past fragrant ginger, groves of bamboo that rustle musically in the wind and lots of eucalyptus, a fast-growing tree that was planted to protect the watershed. About 0.5 miles up, the trail reaches the top of 2013ft Mt Tantalus, also known as Pu'u 'Ohi'a.

From Mt Tantalus, the trail leads to a service road. Continue on the road to its end, where there's a telephone company building. The trail picks up again behind the left side of the building.

Continue down the trail until it reaches the **Manoa Cliff Trail** and go left. Walk for a

short distance until you come to another intersection, where you'll turn right onto the **Pauoa Flats Trail**. This trail leads down into Pauoa Flats and on to the **Nu'uanu Valley Lookout**, with its sweeping view of windward O'ahu. The flats area can be muddy; be careful not to trip on exposed tree roots.

You'll pass two trailheads before reaching the lookout. The first is the **Nu'uanu Trail**, on the left, which runs 0.75 miles along the western side of Upper Pauoa Valley and offers broad views of Honolulu and the Wai'anae Range. The second is the **Aihualama Trail**, on the right, which leads to Manoa Falls.

CYCLING

The **Bike Shop** (Map pp84-5; ☎ 596-0588; 1149 S King St; per day $20-40; ☼ 9am-7pm Mon-Fri, to 5pm Sat, 10am-5pm Sun) rents a variety of quality bicycles and can give you a map showing suggested cycling routes to match your interest. Diehards often head up to Tantalus; expect a good workout, but the scenery is ample reward.

GOLF

Go swing a club at **Moanalua Golf Club** (Map pp72-3; ☎ 839-2411; 1250 Ala Aolani; per 18 holes $42; ☼ 5:30am-sunset), the oldest golf course in Hawaii and, for that matter, the oldest west of the Rockies. Built in 1898 by a missionary family, it's a relatively quick par 36 course, with an elevated green, straight fairway and nine holes that can be played twice around.

TENNIS

Ala Moana Beach Park (p82) has 10 tennis courts and it's an ideal place to play. If you hit the court during the day you can cool off with a dip in the ocean afterward; if you come at night, the courts are lit up. Court time at these public facilities is free and on a first-come, first-served basis.

ART LECTURES

At the Hawai'i State Art Museum (p75), **ArtLunch lectures** (☎ 586-0900; No 1 Capitol District Bldg, 250 S Hotel St; admission free; ☼ noon-1pm last Tue of month) offer visitors the chance to listen to and chat with artists who have their works on display at the museum. Feel free to bring your own packed lunch, as many of the downtown art patrons do.

Water Activities

SWIMMING
For Honolulu's best ocean swimming head to Ala Moana Beach Park (p82). Those who prefer a freshwater swim will generally need to look no further than their hotel lobby.

SURFING
There are surf breaks just off Ala Moana Beach Park (p82) suitable for intermediate surfers and off Kaka'ako Waterfront Park (p83) suitable for advanced surfers. Rent surfboards at **Aloha Board Shop** (Map p86; ☎ 955-6030; 2600 S King St; per day/week $25/100; 🕙 10am-7:30pm Mon-Sat, 11am-5pm Sun) in the university area.

CRUISES
Numerous sunset sails, dinner cruises and party boats leave daily from Kewalo Basin, just west of Ala Moana Beach Park. Many provide transport to and from Waikiki and advertise various specials; check the free tourist magazines for the latest offers.

Atlantis Cruises (Map pp76-7; ☎ 973-1311; Pier 6, Aloha Tower Dr) offers several cruise options aboard *Navatek I*, a sleek, high-tech catamaran designed to minimize rolling. Of most interest are the naturalist-led 2½-hour whale-watching cruises (adult/child aged two to 12 $52/26), which operate from late December to early April, leave at noon daily and include a buffet lunch.

DEEP-SEA FISHING
Hawaiian waters teem with sport fish, like Pacific blue marlin and yellowfin tuna, and if you want to try snagging one you can hop a fishing boat at Honolulu's Kewalo Basin. The cost is typically around $700 for a full-day charter that can accommodate up to six people, or $150 per person if you want to join a group. The price includes all gear, but not lunch or beverages. The **Hawaii Charter Skippers Association** (Map pp84-5; ☎ 591-9100; hcsa@msn.com; No 110, Kewalo Basin, 1085 Ala Moana Blvd) books outings on several boats; all are operated by coast guard–certified skippers.

WALKING TOURS
There's just no better way to explore the history-laden downtown district and vibrant Chinatown than by setting out on foot on the routes that follow.

Chinatown Walking Tour
Chinatown is one of the most intriguing quarters of the city to explore. This is best done in the daytime, not only because that's when the markets and shops are open, but also because the streets can get a little seedy after dark, particularly down by the river.

A good place to start your tour is **Chinatown Gateway Plaza (1)**, where stone lions, male and female, mark the official entrance to the plaza. Walk northeast along Bethel St to Pauahi St where you'll see the century-old **Hawaii Theatre** (**2**; p80), a restored neoclassical gem. Proceed up Pauahi St and make a left on Nu'uanu Ave, and you'll see the now-abandoned **Pantheon Bar (3)**, Honolulu's oldest watering hole and a favorite of sailors in days past. The granite-block sidewalks along Nu'uanu Ave are also a relic of an earlier day, built with the discarded ballasts of ships that brought tea from China in the 19th century.

Continue to the corner of N King St, and stroll into the lobby of the **First Hawaiian Bank (4)**, where the retro-architecture includes wooden teller cages with bars. So unique is the old lobby that it was used as the setting for filming Kate's bank robbery scene in TV's *Lost*.

> **WALK FACTS**
> **Distance** 1.5 miles
> **Duration** 2.5 hours

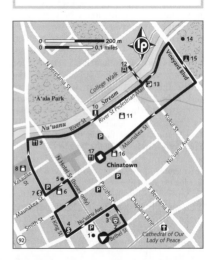

Go northwest on N King St, then after a block turn right on Smith St until you reach N Hotel St, where X-rated peep shows and strip bars recall Chinatown's seedier past, a sharp contrast to the creeping gentrification that marks the downtown edge of Chinatown.

Turn left on N Hotel St and go one block to Maunakea St, the heart of Chinatown, with its herbalists and noodle shops. Right on the corner is one of Chinatown's oldest structures, the century-old **Wo Fat Building (5)**, with its ornate facade resembling a Chinese temple. Continue down Maunakea St and stop at **Shung Chong Yuein (6)**, which specializes in delicious Chinese sweets, including candied ginger and lotus root and moon cakes that are out of this world.

At N King St turn right and walk past the **Bank of Hawaii (7)**, where fire-breathing dragons coil around the red pillars of its column facade, and after one block you'll reach the bustling **O'ahu Market (8**; p81), where boxes of iced fish and fresh produce await shoppers.

Continue to the intersection of N King and River Sts, where you'll find some wonderful neighborhood eateries. For authentic Vietnamese flavor, stop to slurp a bowl of soup at **To Chau (9**; p99), Chinatown's top *pho* restaurant. Continue walking northeast along River St, which soon turns into a pedestrian mall.

The **bronze statue (10)** of Chinese revolutionary leader Dr Sun Yat-sen stands watch near the start of the River St pedestrian mall and, just beyond, Chinatown seniors play checkers and mah-jongg on shaded benches along the Nu'uanu Stream. Duck into the **Chinatown Cultural Plaza (11**; p81) for a look at the bevy of shops and then take the bridge across the stream to the century-old **Izumo Taisha Shrine (12**; p82), which attracts school children from Japan who visit as a gesture of peace. Back on the mall, take a look at the facade of the Lum Sai Ho Tong Society's **Taoist temple (13**; p81), and continue to the end of River St, which terminates at the entrance to **Foster Botanical Garden (14**; p82).

After touring the gardens walk down Vineyard Blvd to **Kuan Yin Temple (15**; p81) and make an offering for good luck. Continue to Maunakea St and turn right. At the intersection of Maunakea and N Beretania Sts,

you'll find clusters of mom-and-pop **lei shops (16)**, where lei makers deftly string flowers and the heady fragrances of plumeria and jasmine fill the air. Go ahead, treat yourself – you won't find a fresher lei anywhere.

If hunger strikes, **Sweet Basil (17**; p100), Chinatown's hottest new restaurant, is a just a block away at Maunakea and Pauahi Sts.

Downtown Walking Tour

Forget the car. Downtown Honolulu makes ideal strolling, with its most handsome buildings within easy walking distance of each other. Although a quick tour could be made in a couple of hours, if you're up for more leisurely exploration, it's possible to spend the better part of a day poking around.

Start at **'Iolani Palace (1**; p74), the area's most pivotal spot, both historically and geographically. If time permits, join a guided palace tour for a glimpse into the royal past. In any case, be sure to stroll around the palace grounds. At the back side of the palace, en route to the **state capitol (2**; p75), you'll find the **statue of Queen Lili'uokalani (3**; p75). You can enter the capitol through the rear, and exit on the Beretania St side, opposite the **eternal torch (4)**, a memorial dedicated to soldiers who died in WWII.

WALK FACTS

Distance 1.5 miles
Duration 2–4 hours

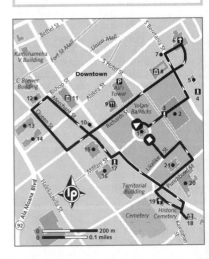

Turn left on Beretania St, stopping to take a look at **Washington Place** (**5**; p77) and **St Andrew's Cathedral** (**6**; p77). In the lobby of the **Leiopapa A Kamehameha Building (7)**, directly opposite the cathedral, you'll find a colorful tile mural depicting Hawaiian royalty. From there, walk down Richards St to **No 1 Capitol District (8)**, an elegant five-story period building that houses the Hawai'i State Art Museum (p75), one of Honolulu's premiere sights. Then continue along Richards St past the **YWCA (9)**, built in 1927 by Julia Morgan, the renowned architect who designed William Randolph Hearst's San Simeon estate in California. If it's lunchtime, treat yourself to a fine meal at Cafe Laniakea (p98), the Y's courtyard café.

Pass by the **Hawaiian Electric Company (10)**, a four-story administration building sporting Spanish colonial architecture, and turn right on Merchant St to see some of the historic buildings and modern skyscrapers that house Hawaii's largest corporations. Be sure to visit the art gallery in the **First Hawaiian Center** (**11**; p79), Honolulu's tallest high-rise.

Turn left on Bishop St and you'll pass the **Alexander & Baldwin Building** (**12**; c1929), which has a stone and tile facade incorporating tropical fruit, Hawaiian fish, and the Chinese characters for prosperity and longevity. The building is named after Samuel Alexander and Henry Baldwin, sons of missionaries who vaulted to prominence in the sugar industry and created one of Hawaii's biggest corporations.

Turn left on Queen St and you'll immediately see the four-story **Dillingham Building (13)**, built in 1929 in Italian Renaissance style, and now mirrored in the sleek reflective glass of the adjacent 30-story **Grosvenor Center (14)** – a true study in contrasts.

Make your way back to Merchant St and proceed south, where you'll find the Spanish colonial–style **Old Federal Building (15)**, **Ali'iolani Hale** (**16**; p77) and a **statue of Kamehameha the Great** (**17**; p78). Just beyond that is the **Mission Houses Museum** (**18**; p79) and the historic **Kawaiaha'o Church** (**19**; p79).

As you make your way back to 'Iolani Palace, take a look at two classic period buildings on Punchbowl St: **Honolulu Hale** (**20**; City Hall), which has a Spanish mission design and was built in 1927 by Hawaii's renowned architect CW Dickey, and the **Hawaii State Library** (**21**; p71), a beautiful early-20th-century building with a grand column facade.

COURSES

The University of Hawai'i's **Campus Center Leisure Programs** (Map p86; ☎ 956-6468; www.hawaii.edu/cclp/classes; Room 101, Hemenway Hall, University of Hawai'i, 2445 Campus Center Rd; courses $10-65) offers a variety of short-term courses open to the general public. It's a great way to meet students while learning a local skill. Some courses, like the bodyboarding class, are completed in a day, though most others, including hula, yoga and slack-key guitar classes, meet a couple of times a week during a month-long session.

Make your own colorful souvenir to take home at **Temari** (Map pp72-3; ☎ 536-4566; www.temaricenter.com; 1754 Lusitana St; courses $25-50), a nonprofit center that perpetuates traditional Asian-Pacific arts. The center offers one-day courses in such things as marbled paper-making, origami, lei making and esoteric art forms like *gyotaku*, which uses fish rubbings to create an image.

HONOLULU FOR CHILDREN

Up for a picnic on the beach? Take the kids to Honolulu's finest combination of grassy lawns, endless sand and calm waters at **Ala Moana Beach Park** (p82); it's convenient to Waikiki, and there are lifeguards and outdoor showers to wash the sand off little feet.

Young kids will find a treasure chest of amusing things to toy with at the **Hawaii Children's Discovery Center** (p83), a space designed specifically for knee-high visitors. Older kids will dig the **Hawai'i Maritime Center** (p80), where they can climb down into the hull of the *Falls of Clyde*. The **Bishop Museum** (p88) has plenty of entertainment – and a dash of enlightenment – for kids of all ages; shark-toothed war clubs await inspection, a planetarium chronicles star-guided navigational systems that guided Polynesians to Hawaii, and a stellar new science center lets visitors walk right through an erupting volcano.

TOURS

Although Chinatown is a fun place to poke around on your own, two organizations provide walking tours of the neighborhood that are peppered with historical insights and often take you into a few places that you'd be unable to visit by yourself. The wise old granddaddy of the tours is the one led by the **Chinese Chamber of Commerce** (Map pp76-7; ☎ 533-3181; 42 N King St; tours $10; ☺ 9:30am-noon Tue); just meet at the chamber office on the 2nd floor a few minutes before tour time. The **Hawaii Heritage Center** (Map pp76-7; ☎ 521-2749; 1040 Smith St; tours $10; ☺ 9:30-11:30am Tue & Fri) also does a good job, beginning its walking tours from its Chinatown office. No reservations are necessary for either tour.

Roberts Hawaii (☎ 539-9400, 800-831-5541; www .robertshawaii.com; 680 Iwilei Rd; 4hr tour $65) offers 'Discover Historic Honolulu' narrated walking tours that concentrate on downtown sites and include a tour of the 'Iolani Palace interior.

Polynesian Adventure Tours (☎ 833-3000; www .polyad.com; 1049 Kikowaena Pl; half-day tour $24) offers a more conventional bus tour that includes the main downtown Honolulu sights, Punchbowl Crater, the USS *Arizona* Memorial and Pearl Harbor.

For details of self-guided walking tours of Honolulu and Chinatown, see p93.

FESTIVALS & EVENTS

January

Chinese New Year On the second new moon after the Winter Solstice (mid-January to mid-February), Chinese New Year is celebrated with a parade from 'Iolani Palace to River St, complete with lion dances and crackling strings of firecrackers.

Hula Bowl The best of the best college all-star players meet for this nationally televised football game held at Aloha Stadium on the third Saturday in January.

February

NFL Pro Bowl The annual all-star game of the National Football League takes place at Aloha Stadium in early February.

Great Aloha Run (www.greatalaharun.com) A popular 8.2-mile fun run from Aloha Tower to Aloha Stadium held on Presidents Day.

May

50th State Fair Featuring games, rides and exhibits, this event runs for four weekends from late May into June at Aloha Stadium.

June

Pan-Pacific Festival (☎ 926-8177) Japanese-Americans celebrate their cross-cultural heritage on

---

ARTY WALK

If you're in town on the first Friday of the month, join the art aficionados making the rounds at the city's Gallery Walk, a self-guided stroll through the happening downtown Honolulu and Chinatown art scene, complete with free *pupu* (snacks), refreshments and entertainment. It all happens between 5pm and 9pm. Walking maps can be picked up at any of the two-dozen art galleries, the majority of which are clustered in a two-block area radiating out from the landmark Hawaii Theatre (Map pp76–7).

---

a weekend in early June, with everything from mochi-pounding (pounding sticky rice) and traditional Japanese dance to hula and ukulele performances at venues around Honolulu, including the Ala Moana Center's Centerstage.

King Kamehameha Day (☎ 586-0333) On the Friday preceding this public holiday in early June, the statue of Kamehameha opposite 'Iolani Palace is ceremoniously draped with lei as the Royal Hawaiian Band performs.

King Kamehameha Hula Competition One of Hawaii's biggest hula contests, with some 500 dancers competing, takes place at the Neal S Blaisdell Center in Honolulu in late June.

Taste of Honolulu (www.taste808.com) Sample the city's best cooking at this three-day food festival held on the last weekend in June at the Honolulu Civic Center. There's a bit of everything, from top-of-the-food-chain to humble mom-and-pop eateries. Live music keeps the place jumping, but island *grinds* (food) are what bring thousands of locals to this one-of-a-kind event.

July

Independence Day America's festive birthday party, on July 4, is celebrated with extravagant fireworks at Ala Moana Beach Park.

Prince Lot Hula Festival (www.mgf-hawaii.com) Held at Moanalua Gardens on the third Saturday of the month, this major hula event features competitions among Hawaii's leading hula schools.

Transpacific Yacht Race On the July 4 weekend of odd-numbered years, sailboats leave southern California and arrive in Honolulu 10 to 14 days later. The 'Transpac,' which has been held for nearly a century, is the country's oldest long-distance sailboat race.

Queen Lili'uokalani Keiki Hula Competition *Keiki* (children) hula troupes from throughout Hawaii come to Honolulu to compete in this annual hula competition Thursday through Saturday in the third week in July.

September

Aloha Festivals Downtown Mele Downtown Hawaii blocks off Bishop and Merchant Sts for a night of street music and dancing in honor of King David Kalakaua, the Merrie Monarch, on the third Friday in September.

October

Talk Story Festival (www.co.honolulu.hi.us/parks /programs) Storytellers gather at Ala Moana Park on a weekend in mid-October to spin their yarns to all who lend an ear. Generally Friday is spooky stories, Saturday is kid-kind stories and Sunday is for stories with a message.

December

Honolulu Marathon (www.honolulumarathon.org) Bring your running shoes and join the pack at the third-largest marathon in the USA. It's run on the second Sunday of the month along a 26-mile course from the Aloha Tower in Honolulu to Kapi'olani Park in Waikiki.

Christmas Early in the month a Christmas tree is festively lit at city hall and craft fairs are held throughout the month all around Honolulu.

Aloha Bowl This big collegiate football game is held at Aloha Stadium on Christmas Day and televised nationally.

New Year's Eve Aloha Tower Marketplace takes center stage with free entertainment throughout the evening and a straight-on view of the explosive midnight fireworks display over Honolulu Harbor.

SLEEPING

Nearly everyone staying in the Honolulu area stays in Waikiki, which is where you'll find the finest and most varied sleep options (see p126). If you need to be near the airport, there are a couple of nondescript chain hotels nearby.

Budget

Central Branch YMCA (Map pp84-5; ☎ 941-3344; www .ymcahonolulu.org; 401 Atkinson Dr; s with shared bathroom $35, r with private bathroom $59; P ⊠ ⊠) Conveniently located just outside Waikiki and opposite Ala Moana Beach Park, the YMCA has 114 rooms. The rooms with shared bathroom, which are available to men only, are small and simple, resembling those in a student dorm. Rooms with bathrooms, which are a bit nicer, are open to both men and women. Guests receive YMCA privileges, including free use of the sauna, pool and gym. There's a laundry, TV lounge and snack bar.

Hostelling International Honolulu (Map p86; ☎ 946-0591; www.hostelsaloha.com; 2323a Seaview Ave; dm nonmembers/HI members $19/16, r $48/42; ⊙ office 8am-noon & 4pm-midnight; P) This small, well-run hostel, in a quiet residential neighborhood near the university, has seven dorm rooms with bunk beds that can accommodate 43 travelers, with men and women in separate dorms. There are also two rooms for couples. It's a great place to mingle with travelers and foreign students, who have a house on the same property. The hostel has a TV lounge, common-use kitchen, lockers and bulletin boards loaded with handy information.

Midrange

Manoa Valley Inn (Map p86; ☎ 947-6019; manoavalley inn.com; 2001 Vancouver Dr; r incl breakfast with shared bathroom $120, with private bathroom $140-170; P ⊠) B&B aficionados will love this university-area Victorian inn on the National Register of Historic Places. The inn's common areas and the eight guest rooms are furnished with antiques, and the whole place drips with colonial character. The inn is away from the beach and sightseeing attractions, so it's best suited for people who prefer to be outside the main tourist scene.

Pagoda Hotel (Map pp84-5; ☎ 941-6143, 800-367-2373; www.pagodahotel.com; 1525 Rycroft St; r $115, 1-bedroom units $130-190; P ⊠) North of the Ala Moana Center, the Pagoda attracts families from the other Hawaiian Islands who come on shopping sprees and want to avoid jumping into the bustling Waikiki scene. And kids love the carp pond encircling the hotel's restaurant. The rooms in the hotel itself, where you'll find the front desk and central lobby, are quiet and have the expected amenities, including a refrigerator. There are also units with kitchens in a nearby apartment complex, but they can feel a bit removed from the main hotel – especially if you're checking in at night.

Ala Moana Hotel (Map pp84-5; ☎ 955-4811, 800-367-6025; www.alamoanahotel.com; 410 Atkinson Dr; r $170-260; P ⊠) Looming above the Ala Moana Center and convenient to the Hawaii Convention Center, this 35-story hotel offers well-appointed, but fairly identical rooms. The higher rates are for higher floors with straight-on views of beautiful Ala Moana Beach Park. The hotel is popular with business travelers, including overnighting airline crews.

Best Western Plaza Hotel (Map pp72-3; ☎ 836-3636, 800-528-1234; plaza hotel@aloha.net; 3253 N

Nimitz Hwy; r $145; (P X R) The best of the airport-area hotels, rooms are comfortable and offer the usual amenities, including a lounge and restaurant. The only drawback is the noise from the heavy traffic on the highway fronting the hotel – ask for a room at the rear. Free 24-hour airport transfers.

Top End

Executive Centre Hotel (Map pp76-7; ☎ 539-3000, 877-997-6667; www.resortquesthawaii.com; 1088 Bishop St; r $220-295; (P X R) Honolulu's only downtown hotel is geared for business travelers and features 100 suites, each large and comfortable with three phones, voice mail and two TVs. Pricier units add kitchen facilities. As the hotel is on the upper floors of a modern high-rise, most of the rooms have fine views. A fitness center, heated lap pool and business center with secretarial services round out the amenities.

EATING

Honolulu has an incredible variety of restaurants that mirror the city's multiethnic composition. The key is to get out of the tourist areas and eat where the locals do.

Downtown Honolulu

Downtown Honolulu, once the domain of bland quick-lunch eateries, has in recent years blossomed into a dining destination in its own right. You'll find some appealing cafés in the city center, while the Aloha Tower Marketplace offers solid waterfront options.

BUDGET

Great Harvest (Map pp76-7; ☎ 587-0017; 233 Merchant St; sandwiches $2.50-8; ⊙ 6:30am-4:30pm Mon-Fri; X V) It's impossible to walk by this place in the morning when the scent of freshly baked bread wafts out the door. Get a loaf of the '3 Cheese' fresh out of the oven and you'll never settle for a simple grilled cheese sandwich again. Innovative sandwiches, like the Tuscan chicken with melted provolone on focaccia, are the specialty, but these folks aren't snobby – kids of any age can order an old-fashioned peanut butter and jelly. It's mostly brown-bag service, but there's a small counter with a half-dozen stools.

Paradise Café (Map pp76-7; ☎ 599-8448; cnr Alakea & Merchant Sts; dishes $4-9; ⊙ 6:30am-4:30pm; X V) Whether you're looking for potent java to start the day or a healthy Mandarin chicken salad to keep it on course, this popular café makes the perfect stop. The menu covers a broad gamut, from mouthwatering rotisserie chicken to sandwiches and deli fare.

Leo's Taverna (Map pp76-7; ☎ 550-8443; 1116 Bishop St; dishes $5-9; ⊙ 8am-6pm Mon-Fri, 10am-3pm Sat; V) This popular Greek restaurant offers an extensive menu. Vegetarians can choose from falafel, Greek salad, stuffed grape leaves and the like. For meat eaters, there are tasty gyros of marinated beef and lamb.

Midrange

Cafe Laniakea (Map pp76-7; ☎ 524-8789; 1040 Richards St; dishes $8-13; ⊙ 11am-2pm Mon-Fri; V) Menu highlights at the classy courtyard café in the Julia Morgan–designed YWCA range from organic nalo salads and seared 'ahi sandwiches to chocolate cream puffs and passion fruit iced tea. While you're nibbling at your meal take a closer look at the pillared motif at the north side of the courtyard where the resemblance to Hearst Castle, Morgan's most famous work, is readily apparent.

Don Ho's Island Grill (Map pp76-7; ☎ 528-0807; Pier 9, Aloha Tower Marketplace; mains $10-24; ⊙ 11am-10pm) Campy island flavor at its best. Sit at a thatch-covered table and enjoy surfboard pizzas and local grinds, like Don Ho's Hawaiian-style plate complete with kalua pork and poi. Don Ho memorabilia adorns the walls and Hawaii's best-known musician occasionally appears in the flesh as well. If that's not enough to pique your interest, there's also an ocean view, $2 happy-hour (3pm to 6pm) beers and live Hawaiian music nightly.

Sunset Grill (Map pp76-7; ☎ 521-4409; Restaurant Row, 500 Ala Moana Blvd; lunch $10-15, dinner $16-37; ⊙ 11am-10pm Mon-Fri, 5-11pm Sat & Sun; X) Yes, it has blackened 'ahi and other grilled delights, but islanders flock here for the rack of rib dinner ($17), the biggest and best in Honolulu. The restaurant boasts an extensive wine list, including numerous selections by the glass. And if you're up for dinner and a movie, the Restaurant Row complex has Hawaii's second-biggest cineplex.

Gordon Biersch Brewery Restaurant (Map pp76-7; ☎ 599-4877; Pier 9, Aloha Tower Marketplace; light eats $5-12, mains $10-24; ⊙ 10am-11pm Sun-Thu, to midnight Fri & Sat; X) This waterfront microbrewery restaurant attracts a crowd by matching reliably good brews with innovative Hawaiian *pupu*. The crab cakes and 'ahi poke (cubed raw fish mixed with soy sauce, sesame oil and chili pepper) are favorites among the snacks, but if you're hungry don't stop there – the steaks weigh in at nearly a pound and the grilled seafood is also a winner. There's live music on weekends.

TOP END

Chai's Island Bistro (Map pp76-7; ☎ 585-0011; Pier 9, Aloha Tower Marketplace; lunch mains $12-25, dinner mains $26-43; ☒ 11am-4pm Tue-Fri, 4-10pm daily) This chef-driven restaurant draws accolades for both its food and presentation, but what really makes it a one-of-a-kind experience is the music that accompanies dinner. Come on a night when the Brothers Cazimero or Jerry Santos are playing – two of the top acts in Hawaii – and you're in for a real treat. The upmarket Pacific Rim cuisine, with such specialties as wok-seared lobster and brandy-glazed Mongolian lamb, is no slacker either.

Chinatown

With its lively markets overflowing with fresh produce, meats and fish, it's no surprise that Chinatown is a great place to head when you're hungry. Of course, there are plenty of Chinese restaurants, but it doesn't stop there – you'll find a wide variety of Vietnamese, Thai and other Asian fare as well.

BUDGET

Golden Palace Seafood Restaurant (Map pp76-7; ☎ 521-8268; 111 N King St; dim sum $1.50, other dishes $6-10; ☒ 7am-10pm; ☒) It says seafood on the sign outside, but the dim sum is what brings Chinatown's regulars here. Have a seat and wait for the carts filled with bamboo steamer boxes to roll by. You have to choose quickly, but keep an eye out for the steamed pork with bean curd and deep-fried shrimp-and-seaweed roll.

To Chau (Map76-7; ☎ 533-4549; 1007 River St; dishes $4-6; ☒ 8:30am-2:30pm) This Vietnamese restaurant serves fantastic *pho*, a delicious soup of beef broth, rice noodles and thin slices of beef. It comes with a second plate of fresh basil, mung bean sprouts and hot chili peppers that you add to your liking. A bowl of soup is a meal in itself, and the shrimp rolls are also excellent. It's so popular that even at 10am you may have to line up outside the door for one of the 16 tables. It's well worth the wait.

Golden River Restaurant (Map pp76-7; ☎ 531-1185; 198 N King St; dishes $4-8; ☒ 8am-4pm; ☒) Next door to To Chau, this tidy family-run restaurant also does a superb job with *pho*, and if someone in your party prefers full-plate meat and rice dishes instead of soup, it's served here, too.

Ba Le (Map pp76-7; ☎ 521-3973; 150 N King St; snacks $1-6; ☒ 6am-5pm Mon-Sat, to 3pm Sun; ☒ ☒) A good place for a quick, inexpensive bite. Vegetarian sandwiches – a tangy combo of crunchy carrots, daikon and cilantro – cost just $3.25, while meat selections, such as a lemongrass chicken sandwich, are $4. For a caffeine jolt, order the sweet, strong French coffee, either hot or cold.

Maunakea Marketplace (Map pp76-7; N Hotel St; meals $5; ☒ 7am-3:30pm) For a quintessentially local dining option, head to the food court in this marketplace, where you'll find about 20 stalls with vendors dishing out home-style Chinese, Filipino, Thai, Vietnamese, Korean and Japanese food. You can

---

THE AUTHOR'S CHOICE

Makino Chaya (Map pp84-5; ☎ 955-5966; 1936 S King St; lunch/dinner Mon-Thu $13/25, Fri-Sun $14/26; ☒ 11:30am-2pm Mon-Sun & 5:30-10pm Mon-Fri, 4:45-10pm Sat & Sun; ☒) Smart Japanese decor and paper umbrellas hanging from the ceiling set the tone at this cheery newcomer to the Honolulu dining scene. This place has it all – a fresh buffet spread of sushi, briny seafood delights and salads are just for starters. The waiter hands you a full menu and you can order to your heart's delight, with dozens of mains like grilled butterfish, shrimp tempura and chicken yakitori. And at dinner it even adds lobster – yep, you heard right, lobster. The only rule is that you order no more than three dishes to start with and you finish them before reordering – otherwise it's as much as you can eat and everything is made to order. Oh, and save room for the chocolate fountain. Makino Chaya is off the beaten path – as a matter of fact, unless locals are taking a visiting relative out for dinner, you may well be the only tourist in the place. But this is one secret that's too good to keep!

chow down at tiny wooden tables that are crowded into the central walkway.

MIDRANGE

Little Village Noodle House (Map pp76-7; ☎ 545-3008; 1113 Smith St; dishes $6-13; ☯ 10:30am-10:30pm Sun-Thu, to midnight Fri & Sat; ✖) An engaging atmosphere sets the tone at this award-winning pan-Chinese restaurant. Highlights on the eclectic menu include spicy shrimp, plump Shanghai noodles and sizzling butter-fish. For an interesting cross-cultural combo, try the roasted pork with taro. If you enjoy anything in black bean sauce, this is the gold standard for Honolulu. For sweets the crepe with red-bean paste is as good as it gets.

Sweet Basil (Map pp76-7; ☎ 545-5800; 1152 Mau-nakea St; mains $8-12; ☯ 10:30am-2pm; ✖ Ⓥ) This place has so much class it draws the business lunch crowd away from downtown Hono-lulu. And it is undoubtedly worth going out of your way for. Such delicacies as soft-shell crabs in Panang sauce spice up a menu that includes everything from spring rolls and satay to vegetarian curries. Save room for the signature coconut custard dessert.

Legend Vegetarian Restaurant (Map pp76-7; ☎ 532-8218; Chinatown Cultural Plaza; dishes $7-12; ☯ 10:30am-2pm Thu-Tue; ✖ Ⓥ) This 100% vege-tarian Chinese dining spot offers incongru-ously named dishes (vegetarian butterfish! sweet-and-sour vegetarian pork!) that cre-atively use tofu and wheat gluten to dupli-cate the flavors of meat and seafood. The menu is not only imaginative but extensive as well, and the restaurant consistently packs in a crowd.

Zaffron (Map pp76-7; ☎ 533-6635; 69 N King St; lunch/dinner $10/19; ☯ 11am-2pm Mon-Sat, 5-9pm Wed-Sat; ✖ Ⓥ) This tidy home-style Indian eatery on the southwest side of Chinatown offers tempting buffets that include such aromatic dishes as spicy curries, chicken and fish tikkas, saffron rice and naan.

Mei Sum Dim Sum (Map pp76-7; ☎ 531-3268; 65 N Pauahi St; dim sum $2-3.15, mains $6-12; ☯ 7am-9pm; ✖ Ⓥ) This cheery little place has a full menu of Chinese dishes, but the real treasure is the multitude of small plates that make for a memorable dim sum meal.

TOP END

Indigo (Map pp76-7; ☎ 521-2900; 1121 Nu'uanu Ave; mains $16-30; ☯ 11:30am-2pm Tue-Fri, 6-9:30pm Tue-Sat, bar menu to midnight Tue-Sat; ✖) Hobnob with the theater crowd at this smart place serv-ing contemporary Eurasian cuisine. The cre-ative dim sum appetizers, such as tempura 'ahi rolls and goat cheese wontons, are a special treat. Dinner features such dishes as tangerine-glazed ribs, ginger-miso salmon and mahogany duck. An award-winning wine list matches the inspired menu. Lunch buffet with dim sum costs $16.

Duc's Bistro (Map pp76-7; ☎ 531-6325; 1188 Mau-nakea St; lunch $10-17, dinner $14-30; ☯ 11:30am-1:30pm Mon-Fri, 5:30-10pm daily; ✖) This swank China-town bistro is mostly Paris, part Saigon, with a tiny Manhattan-like bar. French-Vietnamese fusion highlights include avocado and green papaya salad, noodles in lime sauce and seafood paella. A small jazz combo performs on most evenings.

Central Honolulu & Ala Moana

This area has an excellent selection of offer-ings in all price ranges, including Honolulu's best fine-dining restaurants.

BUDGET

Kaka'ako Kitchen (Map pp84-5; ☎ 596-7488; Ward Centre, 1200 Ala Moana Blvd; meals $6-12; ☯ 7am-9pm Mon-Thu, to 10pm Fri & Sat, to 5pm Sun; Ⓥ) A spin-off of the upscale restaurant 3660 On the Rise, Kaka'ako uses the same fresh ingre-dients and creative flair as its pricier par-ent operation. Here, however, the food is served plate-lunch style on styrofoam with brown rice and an organic salad. For the real gastronomic edge skip the local plates and order a gourmet plate, such as the mouthwatering seared 'ahi and shitake salad or the sautéed wild salmon stuffed with crabmeat.

Mai Tai Bar (Map pp84-5; ☎ 947-2900; Ala Moana Center, 1450 Ala Moana Blvd; light eats $6-10; ☯ 11am-1am) Head to this open-air bar on the top floor of the Ala Moana Center for Hono-lulu's best burger, made with beef from Hawaii-raised cattle. Wash it down with a bottle of Kona brew, listen to Hawaiian-style musicians (after 4pm) and enjoy the breeze that wafts through.

Makai Market (Map pp84-5; Ala Moana Center, 1450 Ala Moana Blvd; ☯ 8am-9pm Mon-Sat, 9am-6pm Sun; ✖ ♿ Ⓥ) The Ala Moana Center's food court, on the ocean side of the Ala Moana Center's ground floor, is a circus with neon signs, hundreds of tiny tables crowded to-gether and some 50 fast-food stalls. There's something for everyone, from salads to ice cream and warm cookies, and Chinese, Japanese, Hawaiian, Thai and Mexican food.

MIDRANGE

Shokudo Japanese (Map pp84-5; ☎ 941-3701; 1585 Kapi'olani Blvd; dishes $5-21; ☽ 5pm-2am; ☒) Don't be fooled by the sleek interior and rave reviews – this contemporary Japanese restaurant serves up its fine cuisine at reasonable prices. The menu focuses on small plates, allowing you to try unusual tastes, such as mochi cheese gratin, as well as more traditional noodle and sushi options. Not to be missed here is *ishiyaki*, a hot-stone cooking style that's served on a sizzling plate – the *unagi* (eel) rice is a winner.

Pavilion Cafe (Map pp84-5; ☎ 532-8734; Honolulu Academy of Arts, 900 S Beretania St; dishes $8-13; ☽ 11:30am-1:30pm Tue-Sat; ☒ Ⓥ) The setting doesn't get more artsy then at this courtyard café overlooking the museum's water fountains. Gourmet salads and sandwiches, a good wine selection and tempting desserts all combine to make this a wonderfully indulgent way to support the arts. Reservations are suggested, particularly if a special exhibit is taking place at the museum.

Side Street Inn (Map pp84-5; ☎ 591-0253; 1225 Hopaka St; dishes $6-18; ☽ 10am-1:30pm Mon-Fri, 4pm-1am daily; ☒) The outside looks like hell, but this late-night mecca near Ala Moana Center attracts Honolulu's best chefs, along with a faithful following who come for the hearty portions of island standards, like kalbi ribs and pan-fried pork chops. If you come for lunch, join the line of construction workers ordering plate lunches ($6 to $7) at the counter.

El Burrito (Map pp84-5; ☎ 596-8225; 550 Pi'ikoi St; combination plates $9-13; ☽ 11am-8pm Mon-Thu, to 9pm Fri & Sat; ☒) Near the Ala Moana Center, this hole-in-the-wall could be a neighborhood restaurant on a back street in Mexico City. It squeezes in about a dozen tables and serves authentic Mexican fare, with fellow diners as likely to be chatting in Spanish as English. The food is good, the crowd loyal and the dinner queues long – best you come at lunch.

Pagoda Restaurant (Map pp84-5; ☎ 941-6611; 1525 Rycroft St; breakfast dishes $5-9, lunch buffet $14-16, dinner buffet $24-26; ☽ 6:30-10:30am & 11am-2pm Mon-Sat, 4:30-9:30pm daily; ☖) The restaurant at the Pagoda Hotel offers a pleasant gardenlike

setting bordering a carp pond. Not surprisingly it's the island-inspired atmosphere that draws the crowd. The breakfast menu includes local favorites, like sweet-bread French toast. Lunch is a buffet of Japanese and American dishes, while dinner is a fancier buffet spread that includes prime rib, crab legs and sashimi.

Auntie Pasto's (Map pp84-5; ☎ 523-8855; 1099 S Beretania St; mains $8-20; ☽ 11am-10:30pm Mon-Fri, 4-11pm Sat & Sun; ☒ Ⓥ) It may be well off the tourist track, but this Italian eatery attracts a crowd with reliably good food at honest prices. Pasta is the specialty, with a number of vegetarian varieties, such as eggplant parmesan, as well as a full range of seafood and meat options. The only drawback is that you may have to wait for a table – particularly on the weekend.

Yanagi Sushi (Map pp84-5; ☎ 597-1525; 762 Kapi'olani Blvd; á la carte sushi $3-5, meals $16-24; ☽ 11am-2pm daily, 5:30pm-2am Mon-Sat, 5:30-10pm Sun; ☒) Popular with the after-hours club crowd, the food at Yanagi doesn't slack off as the night goes on. Not only is the sushi top-rate, but other Japanese dishes are also prepared to perfection. Ask about the 'late bird' dinner specials available after 10:30pm.

XO (Map pp84-5; ☎ 942-2020; 1718 Kapi'olani Blvd; mains $12-28; ☽ 11am-1am; ☒) Within easy walking distance of Waikiki, this smart, chef-driven Chinese restaurant specializes in delicious seafood dishes, like black-bean lobster. What's XO? A 'secret sauce' made in part with dried shrimp, garlic, chili, scallops and ham that's used to spice up everything from the rib-eye steak to the daily fish specials. Bet you haven't tried *that* before.

Compadres (Map pp84-5; ☎ 591-8307; Ward Centre, 1200 Ala Moana Blvd; mains $12-27; ☽ 11am-11pm Mon-Thu, 11am-midnight Fri & Sat, 11am-10pm Sun; ☒) On the Ward Centre's upper level, this bustling Mexican restaurant draws a crowd. It offers the expected chicken enchilada and steak fajita, and adds local seafood to the mix with fresh fish tacos, char-grilled to perfection and topped with spicy avocado.

Jimbo Restaurant (Map pp84-5; ☎ 947-2211; 1936 S King St; meals $9-14; ☽ 11am-3pm & 5-10pm; ☒) This local favorite has real home-style Japanese food and atmosphere. It makes its own udon noodles fresh daily and attracts one of the most loyal followings in

Honolulu. For the ultimate in comfort food, order the *oyako donburi* (chicken and egg on rice). No credit cards.

Mekong (Map pp84-5; ☎ 591-8841; 1295 S Beretania St; mains $8-12; ♥ 11am-2pm Mon-Fri, 5-9:30pm daily; ☒ **V**) One of the oldest Thai restaurants in Honolulu, this unpretentious place enjoys a solid reputation for good food at fair prices. The menu includes excellent spring rolls, tasty noodle dishes, and a variety of vegetarian and meat curries.

Viet Café (Map pp84-5; ☎ 949-8268; 1960 Kapi'olani Blvd; dishes $8-12; ♥ 10am-midnight; ☒ **V**) Within walking distance of the Ala Moana end of Waikiki via the McCully Bridge, this busy Vietnamese eatery is a favorite among Honolulu's Vietnamese community for its traditional sour soups, barbequed pork chops and late hours.

TOP END

Alan Wong's (Map pp84-5; ☎ 949-2526; 1857 S King St; www.alanwongs.com; mains $26-38, 5-course tasting menu $65; ♥ 5-10pm; ☒) The perennial winner of Hawaii's esteemed Hale 'Aina award, chef Alan Wong is the darling among Hawaii's elite chefs. This high-energy place specializes in upscale Hawaii Regional Cuisine with an emphasis on fresh local ingredients. For a sure winner, order ginger-crusted *onaga* (red snapper), Wong's time-honored signature dish, though you're unlikely to go wrong with anything on the menu. Reservations are essential and typically need to be made at least a few days in advance, but you can do it all on-line.

L'Uraku (Map pp84-5; ☎ 955-0552; 1341 Kapi'olani Blvd; mains $15-35; ♥ 11am-2pm & 5:30-10pm; ☒) This sparkling Japanese-European fusion eatery masterfully blends East and West flavors with local ingredients in such dishes as the miso-braised shortribs and the seared scallops with bacon-cabbage ragout and eel-stock sauce. For unbeatable value, try the three-course 'weekender' lunch ($17) or the 'dinner tasting' for a generous sampling of the best in the house ($39, with wine pairings $53).

Chef Mavro (Map pp84-5; ☎ 944-4714; 1969 S King St; 4-course dinner with/without wines $111/71; ♥ 6:30-9:30pm Tue-Sun; ☒) When you're ready to mix green tea–dusted zucchini blossom tempura with a glass of German mosel wine, you're ready for one of Honolulu's most elegant restaurants, known in particular for

its food and wine pairings. Meals change with the season, but include the likes of coriander-crusted strip loin and fresh catch with garlic-saffron sauce.

Kincaid's Fish, Chop & Steak House (☎ 591-2005; Ward Warehouse, cnr Ala Moana Blvd & Ward Ave; lunch $10-18, dinner mains $20-38; ♥ 11am-10pm, ☒) With creative seafood and steaks, a fine harbor view and reliable martinis, it's no surprise that this upscale restaurant is a favorite among the downtown business crowd. The dungeness crab cakes served with a sweet and sour Thai sauce is a savory house special.

University Area

Not surprisingly, the area around the University of Hawai'i at Manoa supports reasonably priced ethnic restaurants, coffee shops and health-food stores. The following places are within walking distance of the three-way intersection of King St, Beretania St and University Ave.

BUDGET

Well Bento (Map p86; ☎ 941-5261; 2nd fl, 2570 S Beretania St; dishes $7-10; ♥ 10:30am-9pm; **V**) This inconspicuous little take-out kitchen specializes in Zen macrobiotic meals free of refined sugar and dairy products. Tahini sauce and brown rice accompany anything from sliced tempeh and grilled tofu to Cajun chicken.

Ezogiku Noodle Cafe (Map p86; ☎ 942-3608; 1010 University Ave; dishes $6-8; ♥ 11am-11pm) Steaming bowls of Japanese ramen, curries and fried rice are the mainstay. It's cheap, fast and the closest you'll get to a subway noodle shop this side of Tokyo.

Bubbies (Map p86; ☎ 949-8984; 1010 University Ave; ice cream $3-5; ♥ noon-midnight Mon-Thu, noon-1am Fri & Sat, noon-11:30pm Sun) This ice-cream shop is a great place to go for homemade ice cream in luscious tropical flavors, such as papaya-ginger. Just as many people come to Bubbies for its chocolate mochi-with-espresso ice cream.

Down to Earth Natural Foods (Map p86; ☎ 947-7678; 2525 S King St; salad bar per lb $7; ♥ 7:30am-10pm, **V**) Honolulu's largest natural foods supermarket makes the ideal place to shop for everything from Indian chapatis to local organic produce. It also has a vegetarian deli with a salad bar and hot dishes, such as vegetable curry. There's a conventional

24-hour grocery store, Star Market, across the street.

MIDRANGE

Greek Corner (Map p86; ☎ 942-5503; 1025 University Ave; mains $10-14; ☺ 11am-3pm & 5-10pm Mon-Sat, 5-9pm Sun; ✿ Ⓥ) This inviting eatery has good Greek food and, being near the university, prices are cheaper than they'd be in trendier parts of town. Main dishes, which come with Greek salad, rice and pita bread, include popular standards like lamb kebab, moussaka and stuffed grape leaves, as well as plenty of other choices for vegetarians and meat-eaters alike.

Yakiniku Camellia (Map p86; ☎ 944-0449; 2494 S Beretania St; lunch/dinner buffet $12/16.75; ☺ 11am-2:30pm & 3-10pm; ✿) Forget those simple all-you-can-eat buffets; here the feature is an all-you-can-cook feast of authentic Korean food. The mainstay is pieces of chicken, pork and beef that you grill at your table. Accompanying this are salads, soups and scores of spicy marinated side dishes called kimchi – fire-eaters should note that the redder they are, the hotter they are.

Cafe Maharani (Map p86; ☎ 951-7447; 2509 S King St; dishes $9-12; ☺ 5-10pm; ✿ Ⓥ) Along with standard northern Indian dishes like tandoori chicken and lamb curry, this little family-run restaurant also serves excellent vegetarian dishes, such as eggplant tikka masala. When it comes to spiciness, dishes can be ordered any way you want, from mild to tongue-searing hot.

Maple Garden (Map p86; ☎ 941-6641; 909 Isenberg St; mains $8-12; ☺ 11am-2pm & 5:30-10pm; ✿ Ⓥ) Around the corner from S King St, this popular local Szechuan restaurant serves up generous potions of delicious food. There are scores of options, whether you prefer vegetarian, meat or seafood. If you like it hot, the eggplant in garlic sauce is a house specialty that will light up your tastebuds.

TOP END

Willows (Map p86; ☎ 952-9200; 901 Hausten St; lunch buffet Mon-Fri $17, Sat $20, Sun brunch $28, dinner buffet $28; ☺ 11am-2pm Mon-Fri, 10am-2pm Sat & Sun, 5:30-9pm daily) A favorite among Honolulu residents for its island atmosphere and all-you-can-eat Hawaiian buffet. A chef carves prime rib and suckling pig to accompany 'ahi poke, salads, crab legs, desserts and more. The open garden setting, complete with lily ponds, is family friendly throughout.

Kaimuki & Wai'alae Ave

It maybe off the beaten path but Kaimuki, at the eastern side of the city, is making its mark on the dining scene with an ever-increasing number of trendy urban restaurants attracting diners from all around Honolulu.

BUDGET & MIDRANGE

town (Map pp72-3; ☎ 735-5900; 3435 Wai'alae Ave; sandwiches $7-10; mains $15-22; ☺ 6:30am-9:30pm Mon-Sat) Sit at the outdoor tables at this hip bistro and watch the Kaimuki action buzz by. Its motto 'local first, organic whenever possible, with aloha always' characterizes the approach that won town instant recognition as one of Honolulu's best new restaurants. And when we're talking local, we're not just talking vegies and seafood – even the burgers and steaks are from O'ahu cattle, raised hormone-free on the North Shore.

Hale Vietnam (Map pp72-3; ☎ 735-7581; 1140 12th Ave; mains $7-22; ☺ 10am-10pm; ✿ Ⓥ) Grab a seat at this top-notch local favorite and enjoy home-style Vietnamese food at its finest. A delightful starter is the temple rolls, a combination of fresh basil, mint, tofu and yam rolled in rice paper. The yellow curries are also excellent and come in vegetarian, beef and chicken variations.

Maguro-ya (Map pp72-3; ☎ 732-3775; 3565 Wai'alae Ave; meals $12-32; ☺ 11am-1:45pm Tue-Sat, 5-9:30pm Tue-Sun; ✿) This handsome Japanese eatery is among Honolulu's best for sushi and traditional *teishoku* (combination) meals that include tempura, sashimi and sushi along with rice, salad and pickled vegetables.

Café Laufer (Map pp72-3; ☎ 735-7717; 3565 Wai'alae Ave; light eats $5-10; ☺ 10am-9pm, to 10pm Fri & Sat, closed Tue; ✿) Locals flock to this neighborhood café at lunchtime to order the Chinese chicken salad and top it off with lovely homemade desserts. If you're in the mood for sandwiches, you can order those, too.

French Pastry (Map pp72-3; ☎ 739-0993; 3447 Wai'alae Ave; snacks $1-7; ☺ 9am-7pm Mon-Thu, to 9pm Fri & Sat) In search of the perfect croissant? Look no further than this sweet bakery-café. Absolutely exquisite cakes and tarts are also served, along with good sandwiches and lattes.

HONOLULU

TOP END

3660 On the Rise (Map pp72-3; ☎ 737-1177; 3660 Wai'alae Ave; mains $20-28; 🕑 5:30-9pm Tue-Sun; ✖) Succulent grilled seafood and steaks are served alongside fresh local veggies at Kaimuki's top dinner restaurant. The cuisine, sometimes dubbed Euro-Island, flawlessly blends continental and Hawaiian flavors, running the gamut from snapper steamed in ti leaf to Black Angus garlic steak. Reservations are recommended.

Elsewhere in Honolulu

Helena's Hawaiian Food (Map pp72-3; ☎ 845-8044; 1240 N School St; meals $5-9; 🕑 10:30am-7:30pm Tue-Fri) Located out by the Bishop Museum, this Honolulu institution can claim its own history, dating back to 1946. Walking through the door is like stepping into another era. Octogenarian owner Helena Chock still handles the cash register and chats with customers, while her grandson commands the kitchen. Most people order á la carte. Start with poi and rice, add a couple of small plates of *lomi* salmon, smoky spareribs or *kalua* pig, and you've got a mini-luau for under $10.

Sam Choy's Breakfast, Lunch & Crab (Map pp72-3; ☎ 545-7979; 580 N Nimitz Hwy; breakfast & lunch $8-16, dinner $18-40, Sun brunch buffet $17; 🕑 6:30am-10pm; ✖) Sam offers huge portions of local specialties, such as fried noodles or *loco moco* (three hamburger patties and more, buried in gravy) for breakfast, and fresh crab, crab cakes or other sandwiches for lunch, and more crab for dinner. There's also a steak-and-lobster combo. The food is great, though Choy's rising stardom is reflected in his prices. The on-site Big Aloha Brewery pours some of the best microbrews in town.

Contemporary Museum (Map p87; ☎ 523-3362, 2411 Makiki Heights Dr; lunch mains $8-10; 🕑 11:30am-2:30pm Tue-Sat, noon-2:30pm Sun; Ⓥ) For a genteel treat, head up to the Makiki Valley and enjoy lunch at the enticing Contemporary Café, which spills onto the museum lawn. Chef-owner Noreen Lam prepares healthy salads and creative sandwiches, including grilled eggplant with feta, on European-style breads. It's not necessary to pay museum admission if you're just here for lunch – simply let the staff at the door know that you're visiting the café.

DRINKING
Cafés

Mocha Java Café (Map pp84-5; ☎ 591-9023; Ward Centre, 1200 Ala Moana Blvd; 🕑 7am-9pm Mon-Sat, 8am-6pm Sun) On the ground level of the Ward Centre, this hip café makes jolting macchiatos, foamy lattes and healthy fresh-fruit smoothies. Homemade crepes, café fare and free wi-fi go along with the drinks.

Tea at 1024 (Map pp76-7; ☎ 521-9596; 1024 Nu'uanu Ave; high tea $15; 🕑 11am-2pm Tue-Fri, to 3pm Sat) Sit in high-back rattan chairs sipping fragrant teas at this pastry chef–run tea salon located on the edge of Chinatown. For the best in local flavor, order the house-blend tea with lychee and chrysanthemum. High tea comes with sandwiches (the curried chicken is excellent), scones and jam. All in all it's a fun place with a touch of class.

Honolulu Coffee Company (Map pp76-7; ☎ 521-4400; 1001 Bishop St; 🕑 6am-5:30pm Mon-Fri, 7am-noon Sat) Overlooking Tamarind Sq, with its stellar view of the city skyline; take a break here from your downtown touring to enjoy sinfully delicious cakes, luscious fruit tart and a java jolt.

THE AUTHOR'S CHOICE

Wai'oli Tea Room (Map p87; ☎ 988-5800; 2950 Manoa Rd; high tea $18.75; 🕑 10:30am-3:30pm Mon-Fri, 8am-3:30pm Sat & Sun) If author Robert Louis Stevenson were still hanging around Honolulu today, this is where you'd find him. The grass shack in which he lived in the late 19th century stood in the garden here until just a few years ago, when it finally collapsed. Not surprisingly, this historic restaurant set in verdant Manoa Valley exudes period charm. The open-air dining room looks out onto gardens of red ginger and birds-of-paradise. Light eats are available at lunchtime, but the real event here is the afternoon high tea, which is served on the veranda from 10:30am to 3:30pm daily. It's an elegant affair offering exotic teas, finger sandwiches and homemade scones served on fine china. Reservations are required for high tea and need to be made a day in advance.

Coffee Talk (Map pp72-3; ☎ 737-7444; 3601 Wai'alae Ave; ⏱ 5am-11pm Sun-Thu, 5am-midnight Fri & Sat) A quintessential college hangout, this Kaimuki café is a great place to unwind over a chai latte and a blueberry scone, or wind back up with a double espresso. You can check your email while you're at it.

Bars

Formaggio Wine Bar (Map p86; ☎ 739-7719; 2919 Kapi'olani Blvd) It's hard to find, tucked back in the Market City Shopping Center, but worth the search. Set up to resemble a European wine cellar, this friendly spot attracts a mix of college students and young professionals, and serves everything from California Pinot Noir to French champagne by the glass. An excellent selection of world cheeses, panini sandwiches and Italian desserts make for a one-stop evening out.

Opium Den & Champagne Bar (Map pp76-7; ☎ 521-2900; 1121 Nu'uanu Ave) This bar at the Indigo restaurant is best known for its small army of martinis. Try the amazing lemon-drop martini if you dare. Being on the edge of Chinatown and near the Hawaii Theatre, it attracts both theatergoers and a downtown after-work crowd with drink specials ($2.75 martini madness from 4pm to 7pm Tuesday to Friday) and music Tuesday through Saturday, everything from tribal rhythmic jazz to funky techno.

Brew Moon (Map pp84-5; ☎ 593-0088; Ward Centre, 1200 Ala Moana Blvd) Ales brewed on-site range from a low-calorie 'moonlight' froth to a dark, full-bodied 'Black Hole' malt that packs a punch. To tantalize the tastebuds order the 24oz sampler ($6.50) of six different ales. This stylish, high-energy place also serves a solid bistro menu. Swing by between 3pm and 6pm for happy-hour discounts on drinks and food.

Murphy's Bar & Grill (Map pp76-7; ☎ 531-0422; 2 Merchant St) Honolulu's version of a *Cheers* bar, this friendly downtown pub pours both Irish stouts and Hawaii-brewed beers. Just a block from the waterfront, it hails back to days of the whalers and lays claim to being the oldest saloon in Honolulu.

Mai Tai Bar (Map pp84-5; ☎ 947-2900; Ala Moana Centre, 1450 Ala Moana Blvd) Oceanside on the top floor of the Ala Moana Center, this boisterous open-air bar packs a young singles crowd, particularly on weekends. Good drinks, and not just mai tais, though the

frozen mai tai is a knockout! Island-style music nightly.

E&O Trading Company (Map pp84-5; ☎ 591-9555; Ward Centre, 1200 Ala Moana Blvd; ⏱ 11:30am-10:30pm Sun-Thu, 11:30am-11:30pm Fri & Sat) Bamboo birdcages, silk pillows and a bar resembling an Asian teahouse make this a fun diversion for an exotic tea, fresh juice or alcoholic drink. Good satay and small-plate menu as well, and R&B music on Friday nights.

Gordon Biersch Brewery Restaurant (Map pp76-7; ☎ 599-4877; 1st fl, Aloha Tower Marketplace; ⏱ 10am-11pm Sun-Thu, 10am-midnight Fri & Sat) Hawaii's first and most successful microbrewery features fresh lagers made according to Germany's centuries-old purity laws. A fine ocean view, good food, and live rhythm and blues from 9pm on Friday and Saturday nights.

Magoo's (Map p86; ☎ 946-8830; 1015 University Ave) University students hang at this open-air sidewalk bar to watch the action passing by. The beer's cheap, the conversation's loose, and the pizza and snack menus match. A real buzz of activity on Friday evenings.

Hank's Cafe Honolulu (Map pp76-7; ☎ 526-1410; 1038 Nu'uanu Ave) You can't get more low-key than at this friendly neighborhood bar on the edge of Chinatown. There's a piano bar or other live music nightly, and the dim walls are brightened with the paintings of owner Hank Taufaasau.

Bar 35 (Map pp76-7; ☎ 537-3535; 35 S Hotel St) This New York–style bar and lounge, next to Chinatown's thirtyninehotel, is a good place to go if you can't make up your mind. There's more than 100 bottled beers to choose from and good pizza to go along with the brew.

ENTERTAINMENT

No matter what your interest, you'll find a plethora of tantalizing nightlife options in this lively city. Updated weekly entertainment listings can be found in the free *Honolulu Weekly*, which is easily picked up throughout the city, and the TGIF insert in the Friday edition of the *Honolulu Advertiser*.

Live Music

Pipeline Cafe (Map pp84-5; ☎ 589-1999; www.pipelinecafe.net; 805 Pohukaina St; admission up to $25) The edgiest place in town has a punk rock heart but also showcases hip-hop and heavy metal bands. You don't need multiple face

THE AUTHOR'S CHOICE

Kapono's (Map pp76-7; ☎ 536-2161; Aloha Tower Marketplace; ☼ 11am-2am Tue-Sat) The club's namesake, Henry Kapono, the most popular musician on O'ahu, rocks on the stage here most Wednesday and Friday nights. The rest of the week he hands the scene over to other bands, but whoever's playing, there's always a crowd at this cool oceanfront amphitheater. Happy 'hour' is a daylong event, running from 11am to 8pm and featuring $2 draft beers.

piercings to blend in, but it doesn't hurt. There's often an admission charge, but it depends on the band.

Jazz Minds Art & Cafe (Map pp84-5; ☎ 945-0800; 1661 Kapi'olani Blvd) Every big city needs a venue dedicated solely to jazz, and this is Honolulu's. The music covers everything from big band and bebop to fiery salsa and cutting-edge minimalist. It's cozy with almost a speakeasy ambiance that just invites good jazz.

Brew Moon (Map pp84-5; ☎ 593-0088; Ward Centre, 1200 Ala Moana Blvd) This brew pub with a cool ocean view has live music Thursday to Sunday nights; typically jazz with a little Hawaiian slipped in from time to time. On Wednesday local comedian Andy Bumatai offers side-splitting takes on all things Hawaii.

Anna Bannanas (Map p86; ☎ 946-5190; 2440 S Beretania St; ☼ 9pm-2am Thu-Sat) A hot dance place not far from the university, featuring blues, ska and reggae bands.

Rumours (Map pp84-5; ☎ 955-4811; Ala Moana Hotel, 410 Atkinson Dr; ☼ 9pm-4am Fri & Sat) Dancing to DJ music, focusing on Top 40, '70s and '80s music.

Chai's Island Bistro (Map pp76-7; ☎ 585-0011; Aloha Tower Marketplace) Chai's not only features some of Hawaii's finest musicians for its diners, but it also lets loose on Saturday nights, transforming itself into the NJOY dance party with DJs at 10pm.

Theater & Concerts

Honolulu boasts a symphony, ballet troupes, chamber orchestras, and over a dozen community theater groups performing everything from Broadway musicals to David Mamet satires and pidgin fairy tales.

Hawaii Theatre (Map pp76-7; ☎ 528-0506; www.hawaiitheatre.com; 1130 Bethel St) Beautifully restored, this grand dame of O'ahu's theater scene is a major venue for dance, music and theater. Performances include top Hawaiian musicians like the Makaha Sons, modern dance, contemporary plays and international acts, like the Shanghai circus.

Neal S Blaisdell Center (Map pp84-5; ☎ 591-2211; www.blaisdellcenter.com; 777 Ward Ave) This modern complex hosts concerts ranging from island artists, like the Brothers Cazimero, to visiting rock stars, such as the Eagles and Tower of Power. It's also the venue for Broadway shows, the Ice Capades and other family events.

Kumu Kahua Theatre (Map pp76-7; ☎ 536-4441; www.kumukahua.org; 46 Merchant St) It holds just 100 seats but this little treasure in the restored Kamehameha V Post Office building packs a solid Hawaiian punch. Dedicated to works by Hawaiian playwrights, it focuses on cultural themes, such as 'David Carradine Not Chinese,' and fun musicals richly peppered with Hawaiian pidgin.

Manoa Valley Theatre (Map p87; ☎ 988-6131; 2833 E Manoa Rd) An intimate venue, this 150-seat theater near the University of Hawai'i is a wonderful place to see top-quality performances that cater to a college audience.

Doris Duke Theatre (Map pp84-5; ☎ 532-8768; www.honoluluacademy.org; 900 S Beretania St) At the Honolulu Academy of Arts, this theater presents multicultural performing arts and concerts along the lines of Chinese opera and Japanese *koto* music, and art house films.

East-West Center (Map p86; ☎ 944-7111; www.eastwestcenter.org; 1601 East-West Rd) Adjacent to the University of Hawai'i, this educational center hosts multicultural theater and concerts.

Aloha Stadium (Map p155; ☎ 486-9300) On the western outskirts of Honolulu, Aloha Stadium has the island's largest audience capacity and is the site for some of the biggest big-name concerts. The Rolling Stones in Hawaii? Yep, this is where they'd show up.

Free Entertainment

'Iolani Palace (Map pp76-7; ☎ 922-5331; admission free; ☼ noon-1pm Fri Sep-Jul) The Royal Hawaiian Band, which dates back to the days of the Hawaiian monarchy, still performs as it did a century ago in the bandstand on the palace lawn. Not surprisingly, watching the band here is a bit like reliving history. Some of the music the band performs was written by Queen Lili'uokalani, Hawaii's last queen, who both ruled from the palace and later was a prisoner there.

Ala Moana Center (Map pp84-5; ☎ 955-9517; 1450 Ala Moana Blvd) The shopping center's courtyard area called Centerstage is the venue for all sorts of local entertainment, including free performances by hula dancers, gospel groups, ballet troupes, local bands and the like. There's something happening almost daily – look for the schedule in the Ala Moana Center's free shopping magazine.

Mayor's Office of Culture & Arts (☎ 527-5666; www.honolulu.gov/moca) The city sponsors numerous free performances, art exhibits and musical events, from street musicians in city parks to seasonal band concerts in various locales around Honolulu. Call for a recorded list of upcoming events.

Poetry & Performance Art

ARTS at Marks Garage (Map pp76-7; ☎ 521-2903; www.artsatmarks.com; 1159 Nu'uanu Ave; ☒ 11am-6pm Tue-Sat) This art gallery and performance venue draws people to Chinatown with a wide range of special performances that can include art, dance, poetry and jazz. A fun event if you happen to be on the island on the last Tuesday of the month is reVERSES, a night of poetry featuring readings by well-known island poets and an open mike for beginners.

thirtyninehotel (Map pp76-7; ☎ 599-2552; 39 N Hotel St; ☒ hr vary) At this cool multimedia gallery in Chinatown, artist Gelareh Khoie does everything from exhibiting art and hosting theater performances to spinning discs for dance parties. Call to see what's happening – there's always something going on.

First Thursdays (Map pp84-5; ☎ 387-9664; Hawaiian Hut, Ala Moana Hotel, 410 Atkinson Dr; admission $3-5; ☒ 8:30pm first Thu of month) Monthly poetry slam features local poets and a few visiting nationally known ones as well. It's one of the biggest slams in the country, typically with hundreds of people in attendance, and it's a fun bash that mixes in other entertainment, with live painters, musicians and DJs sharing the stage.

Cinemas

Honolulu has several large multiplexes showing first-run feature films and a couple of atmospheric art house cinemas.

Restaurant Row 9 Cinemas (Map pp76-7; ☎ 526-4171; 500 Ala Moana Blvd) For dinner and a movie, this nine-screen multiplex at Restaurant Row makes a good choice.

Ward Stadium 16 (Map pp84-5; ☎ 593-3000; Auahi & Kamakee Sts) You'll find lots to choose from at this cinema with 16 screens.

Movie Museum (Map pp72-3; ☎ 735-8771; 3566 Harding Ave) For a cozier scene, the Movie Museum is a fun place to watch classic oldies, such as *Citizen Kane* and *Casablanca*, in a cinema with just 20 comfy chairs. Reservations are recommended.

Varsity Twins (Map p86; ☎ 593-3000; 1006 University Ave) Near the University of Hawai'i, this classic two-screen cinema designed by the famed architect CW Dickey shows foreign, art house and other alternative films.

SHOPPING
Ala Moana Center

Hawaii's biggest shopping center, the **Ala Moana Center** (Map pp84-5; ☎ 955-9517; 1450 Ala Moana Blvd; ☒ 9:30am-9pm Mon-Sat, 10am-7pm Sun) has 200 stores, from chain department stores to fashionable boutiques and specialty shops.

LOCAL GIRL MAKES GOOD

A home-grown success story, Cinnamon Girl women's wear is one sweet operation. The fragrance of cinnamon wafts through the air as you walk through the door, and the atmosphere from the natural wood floors to the cheery staff is as engaging as it gets. It's all the handiwork of O'ahu resident Jonelle Fujita, who in the past decade has gone from selling her handmade dresses at craft fairs to running a multimillion-dollar business with more than 100 employees. Her shops sell necklaces, sandals and other accessories, but the signature product is women's rayon dresses in feminine styles that resemble a fusion of Laura Ashley and sexy sundress. All of the dresses are designed by Fujita, who now has three shops on O'ahu and has opened up branches on the other Hawaiian islands. Her O'ahu shops are at the Ala Moana Center (p108), Ward Warehouse (Map pp84–5) and Pearlridge Shopping Center.

Some of the most interesting shops in the center include the following:

Slipper House (☎ 949-0155) Since 1952 the Slipper House has been the sole (!) of Hawaii, selling everything from rubber reef walkers to slippers with rhinestones and heels.

Honolulu Cookie Company (☎ 845-1778) For a one-of-a-kind taste of Hawaiian flavor you've got to try the pineapple-shaped cookies blended with macadamia nuts, mango and Kona coffee and dipped in chocolate. The cookie kiosk is at the edge of the Makai Market food court.

Hawaiian Quilt Collection (☎ 946-2233) If you want to pick up a Hawaiian quilt, or just see what's unique about them, this is the place. Not just quilts, but quilted pillows and wall hangings, and kits to make your own.

Products of Hawaii (☎ 949-6866) Take home some island-style treats from this souvenir shop that sells everything from Hawaii-made chocolates to T-shirts and coffee mugs with aloha designs.

Cinnamon Girl (☎ 947-4332) Stylish dresses that are cool, contemporary and island-made are featured at this homegrown shop. For more details, see the boxed text Local Girl Makes Good (p107).

Locals Only (☎ 942-1555) A good place to pick up swimwear, vintage aloha shirts and sportswear that reflects Hawaii's lifestyle.

Tumi (☎ 949-7089) This innovative travel-gear company has lots of cool luggage, handbags and business cases to choose from.

Chinatown

Chinatown's a fun place to do some offbeat shopping, and a good area to browse for art and antiques.

Bo Wah's Trading Company (Map pp76-7; ☎ 537-2017; 1037 Maunakea St) Here you can find all things Chinese, from rice bowls to jasmine soap and Oriental cookie molds. Other nearby shops in the neighborhood sell snuff bottles, cloisonné jewelry and freshwater rice pearls.

Pegge Hopper Gallery (Map pp76-7; ☎ 524-1160; 1164 Nu'uanu Ave; ☷ 11am-4pm Tue-Fri, to 3pm Sat) Perhaps no artist is more widely recognized on the islands than Pegge Hopper, whose prints of voluptuous Hawaiian women adorn many a wall.

Ramsay Galleries (Map pp76-7; ☎ 537-2787; 1128 Smith St; ☷ 10am-5pm Mon-Fri, to 4pm Sat) Stop here

to peruse the finely detailed pen-and-ink drawings of Honolulu by internationally known artist Ramsay, as well as changing collections of works by other local artists.

Lai Fong Department Store (Map pp76-7; ☎ 781-8140; 1118 Nu'uanu Ave) This landmark shop sells a curious variety of antiques and knick-knacks, including Chinese silk clothing, Oriental porcelain and vintage postcards of Hawaii dating back to the first half of the 20th century.

Sharky's Tattoo (Map pp76-7; ☎ 585-0076; 1038 Nu'uanu Ave; ☷ noon-10pm Mon-Sat, to 6pm Sun) More than just a tattoo parlor, Sharky's also displays and sells tattoo-related art in acrylic, watercolor and pencil. You'll find it upstairs from Hank's Cafe Honolulu (p105), which also sells artwork.

ARTS at Marks Garage (Map pp76-7; ☎ 521-2903; 1159 Nu'uanu Ave; ☷ 11am-6pm Tue-Sat) This eclectic community exhibit and performance center sells the works of up-and-coming island artists in a wide variety of mediums.

Cindy's Lei Shop (Map pp76-7; ☎ 536-6538; 1034 Maunakea St; ☷ 6am-8pm Mon-Sat, to 6pm Sun) An inviting little place with lei made of maile (a native twining plant), lantern 'ilima (a native flower) and ginger, in addition to more common orchids and plumeria. Scores of other lei shops can be found near the intersection of Maunakea and N Beretania Sts. Pick one up for as little as $3. The shops will pack them, too, for you to carry home on the plane.

Aloha Tower Marketplace

Overlooking Honolulu Harbor, the **Aloha Tower Marketplace** (Map pp76-7; ☎ 528-5700; Pier 9; ☷ 9am-9pm Mon-Sat, to 6pm Sun) has some 50 shops, with barely an off-island chain among

---

OODLES OF NOODLES

If you look inside one of the half-dozen noodle factories in Chinatown, you'll see clouds of white flour hanging in the air and thin sheets of dough running around rollers and coming out as noodles. One easy-to-find but very small shop, **Yat Tung Chow Noodle Factory** (Map pp76-7; ☎ 531-7982; 150 N King St; ☷ 6am-3pm Mon-Sat, to 1pm Sun), makes nine sizes of noodles, from skinny golden thread to fat udon. If you want to try the real deal, pick up a pound (80¢ to $1.60).

them, as well as kiosks selling Hawaiian-made foods, jewelry and knickknacks.

Martin & MacArthur (☎ 524-6066) You'll find a standout selection of upmarket Hawaiiana products here, including koa boxes and bowls, Hawaiian quilts, etched glass and handmade dolls. Many of the items are museum quality and it's a great place to browse, even if you're not up for shopping.

Happa (☎ 528-0395) Check out the cool, classic nostalgia posters of early Hawaii tourist scenes, complete with clipper planes, steamships and grass-skirted hula dancers waiting for passengers to embark. You'll also find Hawaii-made sandals and purses.

Hawaiian Ukulele Company (☎ 536-3228) A good place to find the full range of ukulele options, from inexpensive Chinese imports to handcrafted Hawaii-made ukuleles.

Crazy Fish (☎ 524-3119) Women's and girls' clothing in bright, cheerful prints and florals, many handpainted, all made in Hawaii, all lovely.

Elsewhere Around Honolulu

Native Books Na Mea Hawaii (Map pp84-5; ☎ 596-8885; 1st fl, Ward Warehouse, 1050 Ala Moana Blvd; 10am-9pm Mon-Sat, to 5pm Sun) If you're looking for beautiful Hawaiian crafts and souvenirs to bring home, start here. The variety and quality are top-notch. You'll find silk-screened fabrics, bamboo flutes, Hawaiian quilts and much more.

Antique Alley (Map pp84-5; ☎ 941-8551; 1347 Kapi'olani Blvd; 11am-5pm Mon-Sat) Its motto, 'variety is the spice of life,' gives a hint at the plethora of collectibles you'll find at this place inland of the Ala Moana Center. Eight vendors work under the same roof, selling everything from poi pounders and vintage hula dolls to ceramics and estate jewelry. Lots of fun, this place.

Nohea Gallery (Map pp84-5; ☎ 596-0074; 1st fl, Ward Warehouse, 1050 Ala Moana Blvd) This high-end gallery sells gorgeous handcrafted jewelry, glassware, pottery and woodwork, the vast majority of it made in Hawaii.

Hula Supply Center (Map p86; 941-5379; 2346 S King St) Hawaiian musicians and dancers come here to get their feather lei, calabash drum gourds, hula skirts, nose flutes and the like. Any one of these items would make an interesting souvenir to take home.

Kamaka Hawaii (Map pp76-7; ☎ 531-3165; 550 South St) If you've been hankering to make your own music, this shop specializes in handcrafted ukuleles made on O'ahu, with prices starting at around $500.

Jeff Chang Pottery & Fine Crafts (Map pp76-7; ☎ 599-2502; 808 Fort St Mall; 9am-6pm Mon-Fri, to 3pm Sat) Everything here is island-made. The striking raku pottery is made by Chang himself, and you'll also find exquisite hand-turned bowls of Hawaiian woods, art jewelry and blown glass by some of Hawaii's finest artisans.

Hilo Hattie (Map pp72-3; ☎ 535-6500; 700 Nimitz Hwy; 8am-6pm) Everyone's heard of Hilo Hattie, the warehouse-style shop selling Hawaiian gifts of all types: aloha shirts, matching muumuu, macadamia nuts, puka shell necklaces and on and on. Very touristy, more than a little kitschy, but the shop has good deals. There's also a branch at the Ala Moana Center.

Tower Records (Map pp84-5; ☎ 941-7774; 611 Ke'eaumoku St) You'll find a good collection of classic and contemporary Hawaiian CDs at this shop just north of the Ala Moana Center. Handy headphone setups allow you to listen to song cuts before you buy.

Queen Emma Summer Palace (Map pp72-3; ☎ 595-3167; 2913 Pali Hwy; 9am-4pm) The gift shop in the back of this museum specializes in Hawaii-made books and crafts, such as koa bracelets, jewelry boxes made from native woods and watercolor paintings of island scenes.

GETTING THERE & AWAY

For information on flights to/from Honolulu, see p244. Honolulu International Airport is a 9-mile, 25-minute drive northwest of downtown via Ala Moana Blvd/Nimitz Hwy (92) or the H1.

GETTING AROUND

If visiting downtown Honolulu or Chinatown on a weekday, consider taking the bus even if you have a car. It's more convenient. Not only will you spare yourself heavy traffic and challenging parking, but you can also start your touring in one area and hop on a bus home from another without having to circle back to where you've parked.

Bus

The Ala Moana Center on Ala Moana Blvd is the central bus terminal for TheBus (p248), the island's public bus network.

From Ala Moana you can connect with a broad network of buses to points around the island.

Most people heading into Honolulu will be coming from Waikiki and there are several direct bus routes that don't require transferring at Ala Moana. If you're heading to the 'Iolani Palace area from Waikiki, the most frequent and convenient bus is No 2. To go directly to waterfront locales, such as the Aloha Tower Marketplace from Waikiki, take bus 19 or 20. To get to the center of Chinatown from Waikiki, take bus 2 to N Hotel St. Private trolley buses (p152) also connect Honolulu with Waikiki.

Car & Motorcycle

Parking is available at several municipal lots in the downtown Honolulu area.

Chinatown is full of one-way streets, traffic is thick and parking can be tight, so consider taking the bus even if you have a car. However, there are public parking garages, including at the Chinatown Gateway Plaza on Bethel St and the Ali'i Tower on Alakea St. Note that N Hotel St is open to bus traffic only.

Downtown Honolulu and Chinatown also have street-side metered parking; it's reasonably easy to find an empty street-side space on weekends but nearly impossible on a weekday.

All of the major shopping centers, such as the Ala Moana Center and the Ward Warehouse, have free parking for their customers.

Traffic in Honolulu can jam up during rush hour, from 7am to 9am and 3pm to 6pm Monday to Friday. You can also expect heavy traffic when heading toward Honolulu in the morning and away in the late afternoon on the Pali and Likelike Hwys.

Taxi

Taxis are readily available at the airport, but are otherwise generally hard to find and you may have to call. To book a taxi, phone **TheCab** (☎ 422-2222), **Charley's** (☎ 955-2211) or **City Taxi** (☎ 524-2121).

Waikiki

Fringed by white sands and basking in year-round sunshine, Waikiki lures visitors from far and wide. Once the domain of Hawaiian royalty, today it swarms with lively masses of humanity. Surfers and sun worshippers share the beach; music and laughter waft from seaside bars; and vacationers take turns snapping Kodak moments.

True, high-rise hotels are lined up cheek to jowl along the center of the beach, but there are plenty of quieter niches as well. It may come as a surprise, but nearly half of Waikiki's beaches are backed by green parks. And the whole place has had a major face-lift, with handsome results. A mile of the beachfront has been expanded, adding pocket parks, water fountains and bronze statues.

The changes are so dramatic that if you've haven't been to Waikiki lately you simply haven't been to Waikiki. And those who have never been are in for a treat. Package tourism is still here (where else would it go? Some 95% of the island's hotels are in Waikiki), but much of the ersatz that once dominated has been replaced with the real deal. Islanders who previously avoided Waikiki now join vacationers to watch O'ahu's top hula troupes perform nightly on the beach and listen to some of Hawaii's best musicians work their magic on steel guitars and ukuleles.

Waikiki is all about fun. Take a surfing lesson from a bronzed beachboy, sip a fruity mai tai as the sun drops into the sea, indulge in some of the best people-watching on the planet. It's for good reason everyone's here.

WAIKIKI

HIGHLIGHTS

- Digging your toes into the sand at **Queen's Surf Beach** (p119) as the sunset unfolds

- Feasting on a luscious Sunday brunch at **Orchids** (p136)

- Basking in aloha at the nightly hula show at **Kuhio Beach Torch Lighting & Hula Show** (p148)

- Taking a surfing lesson from one of Waikiki's beachboys at **Central Waikiki Beach** (p123)

- Joining the party scene at **Duke's Canoe Club** (p146)

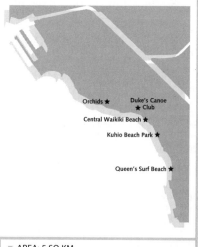

Orchids ★

Duke's Canoe ★ Club

Central Waikiki Beach ★

Kuhio Beach Park ★

Queen's Surf Beach ★

| ▪ POPULATION: 26,000 | ▪ AREA: 5 SQ KM |

WAIKIKI

WAIKIKI IN TWO DAYS

Waikiki is all about the beach. Here's a suggested plan if you have just a couple of days.

Start your first day with breakfast on the beach at the **Hau Tree Lanai** (p133). From there it's just steps to the calm waters of **Sans Souci Beach** (p119) and Waikiki's best snorkeling. In the afternoon take a **surfing lesson** (p123) from one of the beachboys at Kuhio Beach Park. Cap off the day with a sunset dinner at **Shore Bird Beach Broiler** (p133).

On day two catch a **catamaran sail** (p123), then take a **walking tour** (p124) and do a little **shopping** (p149) along the way. In the late afternoon find your way to Kuhio Beach Park hula mound and enjoy an authentic **hula show** (p148) to the backdrop of a sunset. Later mosey on over to the **Beach Bar at Banyan Court** (p145), order a tall tropical drink and enjoy the live Hawaiian music. When you're ready to eat, head down the beach to **Duke's Canoe Club** (p133).

HISTORY

When you look at Waikiki today, it's hard to imagine that just 125 years ago this tourist mecca was almost entirely wetlands, filled with fishponds, taro patches and rice paddies. Fed by mountain streams from Manoa Valley, Waikiki, which in Hawaiian means 'spouting water,' was one of the most fertile areas on O'ahu.

By the late 19th century Waikiki began attracting Honolulu's more well-to-do citizens, who built gingerbread-trimmed cottages along the narrow beachfront.

Tourism took root in 1901, when the Moana opened its doors as Waikiki's first hotel. A tram line was built to connect Waikiki to downtown Honolulu, and city folk crowded aboard for weekend beach outings. Tiring quickly of the pesky mosquitoes that thrived in the wetlands, these early beachgoers petitioned to have Waikiki's 'swamps' brought under control.

In 1922 the Ala Wai Canal was dug to divert the streams that flowed into Waikiki and to dry out the wetlands. Water buffaloes were replaced by tourists, and within a couple of years Waikiki's second hotel, the Royal Hawaiian, opened to serve passengers arriving on luxury ocean liners from San Francisco. Dubbed the Pink Palace, the hotel's guest list read like a who's who on the celebrity scene – royalty and Rockefellers wined and dined along with the likes of Charlie Chaplin and Babe Ruth.

The Depression and WWII put a damper on tourism, and as late as 1950 Waikiki had only 1400 hotel rooms. Surfers could drive their cars right up to the beach and park on the sand. In the 1960s, however, tourism took over in earnest. By 1968 Waikiki had some 13,000 hotel rooms, and in the following two decades that number more than doubled. The lack of available land finally halted the boom, but not before Waikiki's real estate prices vaulted to a level second only to those in central Tokyo.

ORIENTATION

Waikiki is bounded on two sides by the Ala Wai Canal, on another by the ocean and on the fourth by Kapi'olani Park. Three parallel roads cross Waikiki: Kalakaua Ave, the beach road named after King David Kalakaua; Kuhio Ave, the main drag for Waikiki's buses, which is named after Prince Jonah Kuhio Kalaniana'ole; and Ala Wai Blvd, which borders the Ala Wai Canal.

Commercial vehicles have restricted access on Kalakaua Ave, and the traffic on this multilane road is one way, so it's relatively smooth for driving. However, pedestrians need to be cautious, as cars tend to zoom by at a fairly fast clip.

Walking along the beach is an alternative to using the crowded sidewalks. It's possible to walk the full length of Waikiki along the sand and seaside footpaths. The beach is particularly romantic to stroll along at night, enhanced by both the city skyline and the surf lapping at the shore.

See p152 for more on getting around Waikiki.

INFORMATION
Bookstores

Bestsellers (☎ 953-2378; Hilton Hawaiian Village, 2005 Kalia Rd; ☷ 8am-10pm) Hawaiian books, travel guides and paperback fiction.

Borders Express (☎ 922-4154; Waikiki Shopping Plaza, 2270 Kalakaua Ave; ☷ 9:30am-9:30pm) A smaller but well-stocked version of the larger Borders stores.

Emergency

Police, Fire & Ambulance (☎ 911) For all emergencies.
Police Substation (☎ 529-3801; 2405 Kalakaua Ave;
⌣ 24hr) If you need help, or just friendly directions,
there's a small police station in front of Kuhio Beach Park.

Internet Access

Caffe G (☎ 979-2299; 1888 Kalakaua Ave; per 10min
$1; ⌣ 8am-11pm Mon-Fri, to 10pm Sat & Sun) This is the
place to go if you're staying at the western end of Waikiki.
Daily Buzz Internet Cafe (☎ 924-2223; 150 Ka'iulani
Ave; first 10min $3, per 1min thereafter 15¢; ⌣ 6am-
2pm) Just off the lobby of the Ohana East hotel, this is a
good place to check your email over a light breakfast.
Fishbowl Internet Cafe (☎ 922-7565; 2463 Kuhio
Ave; per 10min $1; ⌣ 8am-midnight) Bustling little place
in the Aqua Resort hotel.
Paradise Computers (☎ 923-8800; 420 Nahua St; per
20min $2; ⌣ 8am-11pm) Super-fast computers and more
privacy than most places.
Waikiki Beachside Hostel (☎ 923-9566; 2556 Lemon
Rd; per 10min $1; ⌣ 24hr) The Internet computer room is
accessible to both guests and nonguests and available 24/7.
Waikiki Net Surf (☎ 922-0000; Waikiki Shore, 2161
Kalia Rd; first 10min $2, per 10min thereafter $1;
⌣ 8am-8pm Mon-Sat, to 5pm Sun) Handy if you're
at Fort DeRussy Beach.
WikiWiki CyberCafe (☎ 923-9797; Waikiki Town
Center, 2301 Kuhio Ave; per 1min 10¢, minimum $1;
⌣ 8am-10pm Mon & Thu-Sat, 10am-10pm Tue-Wed,
noon-10pm Sun) Friendly little place that's perfect for
a quick email check.

Laundry

The great majority of Waikiki hotels and
hostels offer coin-operated laundry facilities
for their guests. A few hotels have larger
coin-operated laundry facilities that are also
open to nonguests, including the **Ohana East**
(☎ 922-5353; 150 Kai'ulani Ave; ⌣ 7am-10pm) and
the **Ohana Maile Sky Court** (☎ 947-2828; 2058 Kukio
Ave; ⌣ 7am-10pm). If you don't feel like waiting around to do your own laundry, you
can drop it off at **Campbell Highlander Laundry**
(☎ 732-5630; 3340b Campbell Ave; per lb 90¢; ⌣ 6:30am-
9pm) in the morning and pick it up later the
same day. If you do your laundry yourself,
expect to pay about $5 per load to wash and
dry. If you drop it off at Campbell, expect to
pay about double that.

Libraries

Waikiki-Kapahulu Public Library (☎ 733-8488;
400 Kapahulu Ave; ⌣ 10am-5pm Tue, Wed, Fri & Sat,
noon-7pm Thu) The Waikiki-Kapahulu Public Library is

a relatively small library, but it does carry mainland and
Honolulu newspapers.

Media

101 Things to Do Found at the free tourist brochure
racks around Waikiki, this magazine has lots of interesting
suggestions and descriptions of things to see and do.
This Week O'ahu This ubiquitous free tourist magazine,
which can be found on every other street corner in Waikiki,
can be a good source of visitor information and has scores
of discount coupons.

Medical Services

Longs Drugs (☎ 947-2651; 2220 S King St; ⌣ 24hr)
The nearest 24-hour pharmacy to Waikiki, between
McCully St and University Ave.
Straub Doctors on Call (☎ 971-6000; 120 Ka'iulani
Ave) A 24-hour clinic with X-ray and lab facilities in the
Sheraton Princess Kaiulani hotel. The charge for an office
visit is a minimum $125 if you don't have health insurance.

Money

There are ATMs all over Waikiki, including
at these full-service banks.
Bank of Hawaii (☎ 543-6900; 2220 Kalakaua Ave)
First Hawaiian Bank (☎ 943-4670; 2181 Kalakaua Ave)

THE CRANES HAVE RETURNED

The old joke goes like this: What's the state
bird of Hawaii? The answer: The construction
crane. Well now, after a long hibernation,
the flock has returned to Waikiki.

Waikiki Beach Walk, the largest development project to be undertaken in Waikiki
in 30 years, is demolishing an aging 8-acre
span along Lewers St between Kalakaua
Ave and Kalia Rd, and turning it into a
sparkling new center. Two former budget
hotels, which had a total of 900 rooms, are
being redeveloped into a 420-room condo-
style Embassy Suites hotel, and another tired
480-room hotel is being transformed into a
195-condo time-share development to be
operated by upscale Fairfield Resorts. The
focal point of this $460-million development
is an entertainment center that incorporates
a Hawaiian design theme with an outdoor
plaza. A highlight among the 40 new shops
and eateries moving in is a new restaurant
by Roy Yamaguchi, the O'ahu chef who put
Hawaii Regional Cuisine on the map. It should
be well worth a visit.

WAIKIKI

WAIKIKI

A Ala Moana Beach Park
To Downtown **B** Honolulu (2mi); Kapolei (23mi)
Ala Wai Canal
C
To Longs **D** Drugs (0.8mi)
Ala Wai Park

Ala Moana Park Dr

92

128

43

Ala Wai Yacht Harbor

Hobron Lane
Hobron Lane
Etna Rd
Kalakaua Ave
Ala Wai Blvd
McCully St
Hoana St
Lime St
Kenheki St

2

Paul St

86

108 140
104
39

117

141

16

Rainbow Dr
Kalia Rd

Hilton Lagoon

45
82

Pier

Kahanamoku Beach

41

14

Maluhia Rd

Kalia Rd

91
55
67
Nimahana St
Olohana St

59
92
Kalakaua Ave

Kuamoo St
Reonana St

Kalaimoku St

Kuhio Ave
Launiu St
Kaiolu St

38

135

Fort DeRussy Military Reservation

10

44
131
113
76
58
Lewers St

Saratoga Rd
Beach Walk

35
126
115
105
81
106

122
133

110
144

139

118
116

27

Fort DeRussy Beach

56
57

51

29

62 60
77

42

123
69
61

119

Gray's Beach

Pier

Mamala Bay

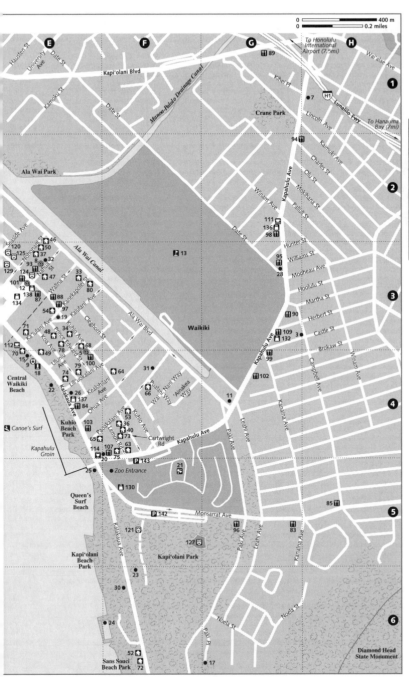

WAIKIKI

Post
Waikiki Post Office (☎ 973-7515; 330 Saratoga Rd;
⏱ 8am-4:30pm Mon-Fri, 9am-1pm Sat) The Waikiki
Post Office is located in the center of Waikiki. The post
office gets pretty busy, but there iss free parking available.
There's no general delivery service here; any mail
addressed as such will be sent to the main post office (p74)
near the airport.

Tourist Information
Hawaii Visitors & Convention Bureau (☎ 923-
1811; www.gohawaii.com; 8th fl, Waikiki Business Plaza,
2270 Kalakaua Ave; ⏱ 8am-4:30pm Mon-Fri) The
administrative office of the Hawaii Visitors & Convention
Bureau has some handouts and can answer questions, but
truth be told, you'll find a newer and a more extensive
selection of tourist brochures at the airport, so stock up
there before heading off.

Travel Agencies
Panda Travel (☎ 734-1961, 888-726-3288; www
.pandaonline.com; 1017 Kapahulu Ave; ⏱ 8am-5:30pm
Mon-Fri, 9am-1pm Sat) This travel agency is a reliable
full-service place that sells discounted air tickets, and
handles everything from cruises to currency exchange and
travel insurance.

DANGERS & ANNOYANCES
Be careful with your belongings; don't leave
valuables unattended on the beach or they
may grow a quick pair of legs and run off
without you.

There's been a clampdown on the hus-
tlers who once pushed time-shares and con
deals on Waikiki street corners. They're not
totally gone – there are just far fewer of
them, and some have metamorphized into
'activity centers.' If you see a sign touting
car rentals for $5 a day, you've probably
found one. Time-share salespeople will
offer you all sorts of deals, from a free luau
to sunset cruises, if you'll just come to hear
their 'no obligation' pitch. Caveat emptor.

At night you can expect to see a few pro-
vocatively dressed prostitutes cruising for
well-dressed Japanese businessmen. Still,
when all is said and done, Waikiki is fairly
tame, and the average visitor is unlikely to
encounter any problems.

SIGHTS
Beaches
Ahhh, beaches, the very essence of Waikiki.
Forget ancient temples and great museums
(they can be found elsewhere on the island);
this tourist mecca is all about the beach.
The glorious 2-mile stretch of white sand
that runs from the Hilton Hawaiian Village
to Kapi'olani Park is commonly referred
to as Waikiki Beach, but different sections
along the way have their own names and
characteristics.

In the early morning the beach belongs
to walkers and joggers, and it's surprisingly
quiet. Strolling down the beach toward Diamond Head at sunrise can actually be a
meditative experience.

By midmorning it looks like a normal
resort beach, with water-sports conces-
sionaires setting up shop and catamarans
pulling up on the beach offering $25 sails.
By noon it's packed with sun worshippers,
and the challenge is to walk along the beach
without stepping on anyone.

Waikiki Beach is good for swimming,
boogie boarding, surfing, sailing and other
beach activities most of the year. Between
May and September, summer swells can
make the water a little rough for swimming, but they also make it the best season for surfing. For windsurfing go to Fort
DeRussy Beach, and for snorkeling head
to the less-crowded Queen's Surf and Sans
Souci Beaches. There are lifeguards and
showers at many places along the entire
Waikiki beachfront.

KAHANAMOKU BEACH
Fronting the Hilton Hawaiian Village, Kahanamoku Beach is the westernmost beach
in Waikiki. It takes its name from Duke
Kahanamoku (1890–1968), whose family owned the land where the Hilton now
stands. Hawaii's legendary surfer and Olympic gold-medal winner learned to swim
right here, and this beach is still a great
place for kids to take the plunge. Protected
by a breakwater and a coral reef, the beach
offers calm swimming conditions and a
sandy bottom that slopes gradually.

FORT DERUSSY BEACH
This one is an overlooked beauty. Seldom
crowded, Fort DeRussy Beach extends some
1800ft along the shore of the Fort DeRussy
Military Reservation. Like all beaches in Hawaii, it's public; the federal government provides lifeguards, showers and a slew of other
facilities. Arbor-covered picnic tables and a
grassy lawn with shade trees offer inviting

WAIKIKI

WAIKIKI

alternatives to frying in the sand. The only area off-limits to civvies is Hale Koa, a military hotel backing onto the beach, though if you get the munchies, the hotel's poolside snack bar has good burgers and sells to all beachgoers – no military ID necessary, just a swimsuit.

The water is typically calm and good for swimming, though at low tide it can be a bit shallow. When conditions are right, this is a good place for windsurfing, boogie boarding and board surfing.

GRAY'S BEACH

The beach near the Halekulani Hotel, Gray's Beach was named after a boarding house called Gray's-by-the-Sea that stood on the site in the 1920s. In the 1930s it was home to the original Halekulani, a lovely mansion that was the predecessor of today's swank high-rise hotel.

Because the seawall in front of the Halekulani Hotel is so close to the waterline, the beach sand fronting the hotel is often totally submerged by the surf, but the waters off the beach are shallow and calm, offering good conditions for swimming.

CENTRAL WAIKIKI BEACH

The generous stretch of beach between the Royal Hawaiian Hotel and Kuhio Beach Park is Waikiki's busiest section of sand and surf, great for sunbathing, swimming and people-watching. Most of the beach has a shallow bottom with a gradual slope. The only drawback for swimmers is the beach's popularity with other swimmers, beginning surfers and the occasional catamaran, so keep your eyes open when you're in the water.

Queen's Surf and Canoe's Surf, Waikiki's best-known surf breaks, are just offshore and on a good day there can be hundreds of surfers lined up on the horizon waiting to catch a wave.

Waikiki Beach Center

Opposite the Hyatt Regency Waikiki, the Waikiki Beach Center offers a plethora of facilities, including rest rooms, showers, a snack bar, a police station, surfboard lockers and rental concession stands.

Wizard Stones of Kapaemahu

On the Diamond Head side of the police station you'll see four boulders known as the Wizard Stones of Kapaemahu, which are said to contain the secrets and healing powers of four Tahitian sorcerers named Kapaemahu, Kinohi, Kapuni and Kahaloa, who visited from Tahiti in ancient times. Before returning to their homeland, the sorcerers transferred their powers to these stones.

Duke Kahanamoku Statue

Just east of the Wizard Stones is a bronze statue of Duke Kahanamoku (1890–1968), Hawaii's most decorated athlete, standing with one of his long boards. Considered the 'father of modern surfing,' Duke, who made his home in Waikiki, gave surfing demonstrations on beaches around the world from Sydney, Australia, to Rockaway Beach, New York. Many local surfers took issue with the placement of the statue, which has Duke standing with his back to the sea – a position they say he never would have taken in real life. In response, the city moved the statue as close to the sidewalk as possible, thus moving it further from the water.

KUHIO BEACH PARK

This delightful beach park offers everything from protected swimming to outrigger canoe rides and hula shows.

The beach park is marked on its eastern end by Kapahulu Groin, a walled storm drain with a walkway on top that juts out into the ocean. A low stone breakwater, called the Wall, runs about 1300ft out from Kapahulu Groin, parallel to the beach. This breakwater was built to control sand erosion and, in the process, two nearly enclosed swimming pools were formed. Local kids

---

CATCH A WAVE WITH THE DUKE

OK, so why *are* all those people standing in front of the Duke Kahanamoku statue and waving wildly up at the sky? Could it be they're hip to the location of Waikiki's most popular webcam?

If you too want to prove to your mates that you've made it to America's most celebrated beach resort, have them log onto the Duke's live streaming video webcam at www.honolulu.gov/cameras/waikiki_beach/waikiki.htm. Prearrange a time when they can be on-line and you can be at the Duke's statue – then smile at the folks back home.

PEOPLE'S PARK

Kuhio Beach Park has always been a special place for islanders. The distinguished Hawaiian statesman Prince Jonah Kuhio Kalaniana'ole, who fought his entire life for Hawaiian rights, maintained his residence on this beach. He bequeathed his property to the public. His house, named Pualeilani (Flower from the Wreath of Heaven), was torn down in 1936, 14 years after his death, in order to expand the beach.

In the 1990s the city spent millions of dollars removing one lane of Kalakaua Ave fronting Kuhio Beach Park, and in its place extended the beach and added water fountains, statues, gardens and a hula mound. Between the old-timers who gather each afternoon to play chess and cribbage at Kuhio's sidewalk pavilions and the kids who race down here after school each day to boogie board off the Kapahulu Groin, this section of the beach has as much local color as tourist influence. It's a true people's park, something that undoubtedly would have made Prince Kuhio proud.

---

walk out on the Wall, but it can be dangerous to the uninitiated due to a slippery surface and breaking surf.

The pool closest to Kapahulu Groin is best for swimming, with the water near the breakwater reaching overhead depths. However, because circulation is limited, the water gets murky with a noticeable film of suntan oil. The 'Watch Out Deep Holes' sign refers to holes in the pool's sandy bottom created by swirling currents, so waders should be cautious in the deeper part of the pool.

Kapahulu Groin

Kapahulu Groin is one of Waikiki's hottest boogie boarding spots. If the surf's right, you can find a few dozen boogie boarders, mostly teenagers, riding the waves. The kids ride straight for the groin's cement wall and then veer away at the last moment, drawing 'oohs' and 'ahs' from the tourists who gather to watch them. Kapahulu Groin is also a great place to catch one of Waikiki's spectacular sunsets.

KAPI'OLANI BEACH PARK

Inviting Kapi'olani Beach Park extends from the Kapahulu Groin to the Natatorium. This stretch of beach, backed by a green space of banyan trees and grassy lawns, offers a relaxing niche with none of the frenzied activity found on the beaches fronting the Waikiki hotel strip. It's a popular weekend picnicking spot for local families, who unload the kids to splash in the water as they line up the barbecue grills. A footpath runs along the entire beach, attracting walkers, joggers and mothers with

baby carriages. Facilities include a snack bar, rest rooms and showers.

Queen's Surf Beach

Queen's Surf Beach is the name given to the northern end of Kapi'olani Beach. It is the most popular beach on O'ahu with the gay community and has good swimming. Snorkeling is good here, too – just swim out in the direction of the last buoy on the left and you'll find large unicorn tangs, butterfly fish and moray eels sticking their heads out of rock crevices.

Natatorium

At the Diamond Head end of Kapi'olani Beach Park, this 100m-long saltwater swimming pool was constructed in the 1920s as a memorial for soldiers who died in WWI. There were once hopes of hosting an Olympics on O'ahu, with this pool as the focal point. Although the Olympic competitions were never held here, two Olympic gold medalists – Johnny Weissmuller and Duke Kahanamoku – both trained in this tide-fed pool.

The Natatorium is on the National Register of Historic Places. In the late 1990s the city spent a hefty $11 million for restoration work that spiffed up the Natatorium's exterior, but the money dried up before the pool itself could be restored.

SANS SOUCI BEACH PARK

Bordered by the New Otani Kaimana Beach Hotel, Sans Souci is a prime sandy beach away from the main tourist scene. A shallow reef close to shore makes for calm, protected waters and provides good snorkeling.

For the best action, snorkel in the direction of the Natatorium and you'll find large parrotfish and other colorful tropicals.

Local residents come to Sans Souci Beach Park for their daily swims. Strong swimmers can follow the Kapua Channel that cuts through the reef; be aware that currents can pick up in the channel. Check conditions with the lifeguard before heading out.

Historic Hotels

Waikiki's two historic hotels, the Royal Hawaiian and the Moana (now the Sheraton Moana Surfrider), retain their original period character and are well worth a visit. Both are on the National Register of Historic Places and are a short walk from each other on Kalakaua Ave.

ROYAL HAWAIIAN HOTEL

With pink turrets and Moorish architecture, the Royal Hawaiin Hotel (p131) is a throwback to the era when Rudolph Valentino was *the* romantic idol and travel to Hawaii was by luxury liner. Inside, the hotel is lovely and airy, with high ceilings and chandeliers and everything in rose colors befitting the hotel's nickname, the Pink Palace.

The hotel site was once a royal coconut grove with some 10,000 trees and the very spot where Kamehameha the Great camped before beginning his battle to conquer O'ahu in 1795. A few of the coconut trees can still be found in the small garden at the rear of the hotel along with lots of flowering plants. Ask the concierge for the **self-guided garden walking tour** brochure, which identifies what you'll see there, and go take a stroll.

To learn more about the hotel's fascinating past, join one of the free **historical tours** that start at 2pm on Monday, Wednesday and Friday in the lobby, across from the front desk. No reservations are necessary; just show up.

SHERATON MOANA SURFRIDER

The elder statesman of the Waikiki scene, the Moana (p129) dates back to 1901. The Victorian-style hotel, which underwent an amazing $50-million restoration a few years back, retains the aura of an old plantation inn. Just walking into the lobby is like stepping back in time. On the 2nd floor, just up the stairs from the lobby, there's an interesting **display of memorabilia** from the early

hotel days. Here you'll find everything from scripts from the 'Hawaii Calls' radio show and woolen bathing suits, to period photographs and a short video of Waikiki back in the days when this was the only hotel on the horizon.

At 11am and 5pm on Monday, Wednesday and Friday, visitors can join a free hourlong **historical tour** of the hotel; just show up in the lobby – reservations aren't necessary.

Fort DeRussy

Although Fort DeRussy Military Reservation is a recreation center for the US armed forces, this gorgeous stretch of military turf is not reserved solely for soldiers. The hotel on the property is open only to military personnel, but there's public access to the rest of the property, including Fort DeRussy Beach and the US Army Museum of Hawaii. The section of Fort DeRussy between Kalia Rd and Kalakaua Ave has public footpaths that provide a shortcut between the two roads.

US ARMY MUSEUM OF HAWAII

This **museum** (☎ 955-9552; Fort DeRussy; admission free; ☼ 10am-4:15pm Tue-Sun) showcases a surprisingly interesting array of military paraphernalia as it relates to Hawaii's history, starting with shark-tooth clubs that Kamehameha the Great used to win control of the island chain two centuries ago. Most other exhibits concentrate on the US military presence in Hawaii, beginning in 1898 with the Philippines-bound army troops that used O'ahu as a waystation.

The extensive WWII exhibits include displays you might not expect in a military museum, such as coverage of the discriminatory treatment that Japanese-Americans were subjected to during this period. Also worth a look are the displays on the 442nd, the Japanese-American regiment that became the most decorated regiment in WWII, and the display on Hawaii native son General Eric K Shinseki, the Army chief of staff who withstood political pressure and spoke up against the White House's plan to invade Iraq in 2003.

Bishop Museum at Kalia

This **museum** (☎ 947-2458; Hilton Hawaiian Village, 2005 Kalia Rd; adult/child under 12yr $7/free; ☼ 10am-5pm), in the hotel's Kalia Tower, is intended for people who can't make it over to the

A MONUMENT TO ITSELF

In 1911, to provide protection for Honolulu Harbor, the US Army Corps of Engineers snatched up a prime chunk of Waikiki beachfront and erected Battery Randolph at what is now known as Fort DeRussy Beach. To make the fortress impenetrable from would-be attackers, reinforced concrete was used throughout. The ceilings, a hefty 12ft thick, were outfitted with two 14in diameter disappearing guns that had an 11-mile range and were designed to recoil down into the concrete walls for reloading after each firing. A 55-ton lead counterweight would then return the carriage to position. When these powerful guns were fired, the entire neighborhood shook.

After WWII the obsolete battery no longer served any function, and in 1969 the military tried to demolish it. Those hefty walls proved too formidable for the wrecking ball, however, and the use of dynamite was ruled out by the objections of anxious neighbors. It was obvious this fortress wasn't coming down, so the military put the best face on things and on December 7, 1976, the 35th anniversary of the bombing of Pearl Harbor, reopened it as the US Army Museum of Hawaii.

main Bishop Museum on the western side of Honolulu.

Although this Waikiki collection is significantly smaller, it is nonetheless of high quality, including Hawaiian artefacts such as stone adzes, feather capes, a replica *pili* grass hut, one of Duke Kahanamoku's 10ft wooden surfboards, and some insightful displays on the Hawaiian monarchy, Polynesian migration and the early days of Waikiki tourism.

You can get a good introduction to Hawaii's cultural heritage here, but if you have time to get outside Waikiki and really want to dip deep, the Bishop Museum (p88) and the Hawai'i Maritime Center (p80) are better options.

Kapi'olani Park

The only US park to be dedicated by a king, Kapi'olani Park has an enviable location in the shadow of Diamond Head and along the shores of Waikiki. The nearly 200-acre park was a gift from King Kalakaua to the people of O'ahu in 1877. Hawaii's first public park, it was named in honor of Kalakaua's wife, Queen Kapi'olani.

In its early days horse racing and band concerts were the park's biggest attractions. Although the racetrack is long gone, the concerts continue, and Kapi'olani Park is still the venue for a wide range of community activities.

The park contains the Waikiki Aquarium (right), the Honolulu Zoo, Kapi'olani Beach Park (p119), the Kapi'olani Bandstand (p147) and the Waikiki Shell (p149), an outdoor amphitheater that serves as a

venue for symphony, jazz and rock concerts. The Royal Hawaiian Band presents free afternoon concerts every Sunday at the bandstand, and other activities also take place there throughout the year.

An octagonal memorial near the zoo's entrance contains the skeletal remains of some 200 native Hawaiians unearthed over the years by construction projects in Waikiki. Kapi'olani Park also has sports fields, tennis courts, tall banyan trees and expansive lawns ideal for just lazing about.

WAIKIKI AQUARIUM

On the Waikiki shoreline, this modern **aquarium** (☎ 923-9741; www.waquarium.org; 2777 Kalakaua Ave; adult/child 5-12yr/child 13-17yr $9/2/4; 9am-5pm) features an impressive shark gallery, where visitors can watch circling reef and zebra sharks through a 14ft window.

This is an ideal place to identify colorful coral and fish you've seen while snorkeling or diving. Tanks recreate various Hawaiian reef habitats, including those of a sheltered reef, a deep reef and an ancient reef. You'll see rare Hawaiian fish with names such as the bearded armorhead and the slingjawed wrasse, along with moray eels, giant groupers and flash-back cuttlefish wavering with pulses of light.

The aquarium was the first to breed the Palauan chambered nautilus in captivity, and you can see these creatures, with their unique spiral chambered shells, in the South Pacific section. Also look for the giant Palauan clams that were raised from dime-sized hatchlings in 1982 and now measure over 2ft, the largest in the USA.

WAIKIKI

The aquarium's outdoor tank is home to a pair of rare Hawaiian monk seals.

HONOLULU ZOO

The respectable **Honolulu Zoo** (☎ 971-7171; adult/child 6-12yr $6/1; ☻ 9am-4:30pm), at the northern end of Kapi'olani Park, features some 300 species spread across 42 acres of tropical greenery. A highlight is the naturalized African Savanna section, which has lions, cheetahs, white rhinos, giraffes, zebras, hippos and monkeys. There's also an interesting reptile section and a small petting zoo just for the little ones.

Hawaii has no indigenous land mammals, but if you head over to the aviary you can see some of its native birds, including the ae'o (Hawaiian stilt), the nene (Hawaiian goose) and the 'apapane, a bright-red forest bird. The entire zoo is accessible to baby strollers and wheelchairs.

Oceanarium

The **Pacific Beach Hotel** (☎ 922-1233; 2490 Kalakaua Ave; ☻ 24hr) houses an impressive three-story 280,000-gallon aquarium that forms the backdrop for two of the hotel restaurants. Even if you're not dining here, you can view the aquarium from the hotel lobby. Divers enter the oceanarium to feed the tropical fish daily at noon, 1pm, 6:30pm and 8pm. Bon appétit!

Ala Wai Canal

Built in the 1920s to collect rainwater away from Waikiki, diverting it out to sea via the Kapahulu Groin on one end and the Ala Wai Yacht Harbor at the other, the Ala Wai Canal resembles a giant moat. Its original intention was merely to turn Waikiki from a wetland swamp to a recreation area, but the canal itself has become a recreation area in its own right.

Every day at dawn people jog and power walk along the Ala Wai Canal, which forms the northern boundary of Waikiki. Late in the afternoon outrigger canoe teams paddle along the canal and out to the Ala Wai Yacht Harbor, offering photo opportunities for passersby. The palm tree–lined canal is bordered by a footpath that goes all the way from Kapahulu Ave at one end of Waikiki to the yacht harbor at the other end, with drinking fountains and benches along the way. Incidentally, those black fish

that school in the canal and blow kisses at the surface are tilapia, a fish that thrives in brackish waters around Hawaii.

ACTIVITIES

You never have to look far for something to do in Waikiki. Although its ocean activities are legendary, landlubbers will find plenty of fun in the sun, too.

Land Activities

GOLF

The **Ala Wai Golf Course** (☎ 733-7387; 404 Kapahulu Ave; per 18 holes $42; ☻ 6am-6pm) scores a Guinness World Record for being the busiest golf course in the world. If that weren't challenging enough, local golfers are allowed to book earlier in the week and grab all the starting times, leaving none for visitors. But there is a way to get onto this green haven. Just get there early in the day and put yourself on the waiting list; as long as your entire golfing party waits at the course, you'll get playing time. Clubs can be rented for $25. Golf carts cost $16.

TENNIS

If you're traveling with a racquet, head over to the Diamond Head Tennis Center, at the Diamond Head end of Kapi'olani Park, where you'll find 10 courts. Or, for night play, go to the Kapi'olani Park courts, opposite the Waikiki Aquarium, where all four courts have lights. Court time at these county facilities is free and on a first-come, first-served basis.

JOGGING

If you're into jogging, you're in good company. It's estimated that Honolulu has more joggers per capita than any other city on the planet. Two of the best places to break out your running shoes are at Kapi'olani Park and the Ala Wai Canal.

A Honolulu Marathon Clinic is held by the **Department of Parks & Recreation** (☎ 973-7250) year-round at 7am on Sunday at the Kapi'olani Park Bandstand. It's free and open to everyone from beginners to seasoned marathon runners, with participants joining groups of their own speed.

CYCLING

You can rent bicycles from several places in Waikiki. **Go Nuts Hawaii** (☎ 926-3367; 159 Ka'iulani

Ave; 8am-11pm) rents bicycles for $15/60 per day/week. **Coconut Cruisers** (924-1644; 2301 Kalakaua Ave), at the Diamond Head side of the Royal Hawaiian Shopping Center, rents bicycles for $20 a day. **Blue Sky Rentals** (947-0101; 1920 Ala Moana Blvd) rents bicycles for $15/20 per half/full day.

Water Activities

SURFING & OUTRIGGER CANOE RIDES

Waikiki has year-round surfing, with the largest waves coming in during summer. During winter the breaks are gentle and well suited for beginners.

Surfing lessons can be arranged from the beach concession stands at Kuhio Beach Park. The going rate for a 1¼-hour lesson is $35. The concession stands also rent surfboards for $10/25 per hour/half day. The stands also offer $15 outrigger canoe rides that take off from the beach and ride the tossin' waves home – kids love 'em.

Also highly recommended is **Hans Hedemann Surf** (924-7778; www.hhsurf.com; Kapahulu Ave; 2hr group/private lesson $75/150; 9am-5pm), just 100yd up the street from Kapahulu Groin. Those who already have the technique down can rent surfboards from Hedemann for $10/25 per hour/half day.

If you want to rent for a longer period, check out **Go Nuts Hawaii** (926-3367; 159 Ka'iulani Ave; 8am-11pm), which rents surfboards for $75 to $99 per week.

BOOGIE BOARDING

The top boogie boarding venue in Waikiki is at the Kapahulu Groin. The most convenient rental choice is Ohana Rentals, a little stand at the Diamond Head side of at Kapahulu Groin, which rents boogie boards with fins for $7/20 per hour/day.

Aqua Zone (923-3483; Outrigger Waikiki hotel, 2335 Kalakaua Ave) rents boogie boards with fins for $18 a day. If you don't mind walking a couple of blocks inland, you can get a better deal at **Go Nuts Hawaii** (926-3367; 159 Ka'iulani Ave; 8am-11pm), which rents boogie boards for $12/50 per day/week.

SNORKELING

Because of all the action in the water, much of Waikiki Beach is not particularly good for snorkeling, so you'll need to pick your spot carefully. The best two choices are Sans Souci and Queen's Surf Beaches, both at Waikiki's southeastern side, where you'll find some live coral and a good variety of colorful fish.

Aqua Zone (923-3483; Outrigger Waikiki hotel, 2335 Kalakaua Ave) rents snorkel sets for $10 to $18 a day.

Snorkel Bob's (735-7944; 702 Kapahulu Ave; 8am-5pm), about a mile inland, rents snorkel sets from $4 to $8 a day or $10 to $32 a week, depending on the quality.

Go Nuts Hawaii (926-3367; 159 Ka'iulani Ave; 8am-11pm) rents snorkel gear for $5/20 per day/week.

DIVING

To really see the gorgeous stuff – the coral gardens, manta rays and large tropical fish – forget the shore dives and go out on a boat dive.

Waikiki Diving Center (922-2121; www.waikiki diving.com; 424 Nahua St; 2-tank dives $99, wreck dives $115; 9am-5pm), a reliable, full-service operation, offers boat dives suited for every ability and keeps it at a personal level, taking a maximum of 10 divers out at any time. It also offers free pickup from Waikiki hotels.

WINDSURFING

Fort DeRussy Beach is the main windsurfing spot in Waikiki. **Waikiki Pacific Windsurfing** (949-8952; 1hr group/private lesson $40/60; 9am-5pm), which operates out of the Prime Time Sports concession stand at Fort DeRussy Beach, rents windsurfing equipment for $25 an hour or $50 for five hours, and also gives lessons.

KAYAKING

Busy Waikiki is not the most ideal place for kayaking, but there are kayak rentals available right on the beach. Fort DeRussy Beach has fewer swimmers and catamarans to share the water with, which makes it a better bet for kayaking than the central Waikiki Beach strip. The best place to rent kayaks is from the **Prime Time Sports** (949-8952; 1-/2-person kayaks per hr $10/20; 9am-5pm) concession stand on Fort DeRussy Beach.

CRUISES

Forget the tour bus scene – get a glimpse of paradise from a dolphin's angle. Several catamaran sails leave from Waikiki Beach. Just walk down to the beach, step into the surf and hop on board.

WAIKIKI

WAIKIKI

Maita'i Catamaran (☎ 922-5665; www.leahi.com), which pulls up on the beach at the southeast side of the Halekulani Hotel (p131), offers the widest variety of sails, from 90-minute cruises off Waikiki at 11am, 1pm and 3pm for $23/12 per adult/child to a sunset mai-tai sail at 5pm for $34/17. If the kids are looking for something different to do, try the underwater adventure sail at 10:30am on Monday, Wednesday and Friday (adult/child $45/27), which includes snorkeling above a reef and an onboard picnic.

Na Hoku II (www.nahokuii.com), distinctive with its Hawaiian yellow-and-red striped sails, departs five times a day between 9:30am and 5:30pm, shoving off from the beach in front of Duke's Canoe Club (p133). The 90-minute cruise costs $25, including free mai tais and beer. Just go down to the beach and get on.

See the world from a porthole aboard **Atlantis Submarines** (☎ 973-9811; www.atlantisadventures.com; Kahanamoku Beach; adult/child $79/42). The sub dives to a depth of 120ft near a reef off Waikiki, offering views of exotic sea creatures that are otherwise reserved for divers

only. Tour times vary with demand but there are several sailings daily.

WALKING TOUR

Compact Waikiki is best explored on foot. Not surprisingly, its leading sights are on or near the shore; an enjoyable walking tour combines a stroll on the beach with a walk along Kalakaua Ave. You can walk the full length of Waikiki right along the sand. Although the beach gets crowded at noon, at other times it's usually less packed than the sidewalks along Kalakaua Ave.

A good place to begin the walk is the **Kapahulu Groin** (**1**; p119), where Waikiki's top boogie boarders thrill onlookers. Walk north up the beach, through **Kuhio Beach Park** (**2**; p118), with its fountains and hula mound. You'll soon see people lining up to take photos in front of the **Duke Kahanamoku**

WALK FACTS

Distance 2 miles
Duration 3 hours

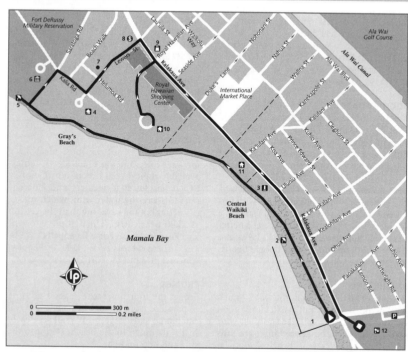

statue (**3**; p118), as well as endless racks of surfboards belonging to Waikiki's current-day surf riders. Continue along the beach until you reach the genteel **Halekulani Hotel** (**4**; p131) and its alfresco beachfront bar known as House Without a Key – Charlie Chan fans will want to stop for a frosty drink.

Back along the waterfront, it's just a few minutes to **Fort DeRussy Beach** (**5**; p117), with all sorts of water activities, and the adjacent **US Army Museum of Hawaii** (**6**; p120). Now it's time to head inland, taking Kalia Ave over to Lewers St, where you'll find the hotels and shops comprising the **Waikiki Beach Walk** (**7**; p113), the newest addition to the Waikiki skyline. On the corner of Lewers St and Kalakaua Ave stop at the **First Hawaiian Bank (8)**, whose lobby is richly decorated with Hawaiiana murals by the renowned fresco artist Jean Charlot; get a free brochure describing the artwork at the bank's information desk.

A walk-through plexiglass aquarium with frolicking sharks and rays is the bait that hooks passersby at the nearby duty-free **DFS Galleria (9)** shopping center – it's a fun diversion and the shopping is optional! Continue southeast ('go Diamond Head' as they say here) down Kalakaua Ave, stopping to discover why the historic **Royal Hawaiian Hotel** (**10**; p120) is called the Pink Lady. Then take a stroll through the airy lobby of **Sheraton Moana Surfrider** (**11**; p120), pausing to enjoy the music in its time-honored banyan courtyard. Upon returning to your starting point at Kapahulu Groin, you might want to visit the **Honolulu Zoo** (**12**; p122) across the street.

COURSES

Royal Hawaiian Shopping Center (☎ 922-2299; Kalakaua Ave) offers a bevy of classes in Hawaiian arts and crafts. All are free, though supplies must be purchased for the quilting class. The Hawaiian quilting lessons are from 9:30am to 11:30am on Tuesday and Thursday. Hula dance lessons are from 10am to 11am on Monday and Friday. Ukulele lessons are from 10am to 11am on Tuesday and Thursday, and from 11:30am to 12:30pm on Monday, Wednesday and Friday. Lei-making lessons are from 1pm to 2pm on Wednesday.

Waikiki Community Center (☎ 923-1802; www .waikikicommunitycenter.org; 310 Paoakalani Ave) lets you try your hand at mah-jongg, the ukulele, hula, tai chi, and a variety of arts and crafts. The instructors at this homespun community center are brimming with aloha and although most of the students are islanders, visitors are welcome to join in on a per-lesson basis. Fees range from $2 to $7, depending on the course. The frequency varies, but most classes are offered several days a week. Call or go on-line for the schedule.

Lewers Lounge (☎ 931-5040; Halekulani Hotel; 2199 Kalia Rd; seminar $50; ☺ Tue & Wed) focuses on libations (see p145). Here you can get your pointers from a true pro. 'King of Cocktails' Dale DeGroff made a reputation for himself as head bartender at New York's famed Rainbow Room before moving to paradise. Now the Halekulani's resident mixologist, he shares his secrets in cocktail-making seminars a couple of times a week.

WAIKIKI FOR CHILDREN

Kids, you're in for a treat, and it all starts at the beach. In just an hour you can learn how to stand up on a board and **surf** (p123) a wave. Or rent a **boogie board** (p123) and ride on your belly. Another fun way to ride the waves is to take an **outrigger canoe ride** (p118) and paddle into shore.

Want to see the world from beneath the waves? Don a snorkel and take a look at the colorful fish at **Queen's Surf Beach** (p119) or take a ride on the **Atlantis submarine** (opposite) and see it all through a peephole.

The **Waikiki Aquarium** (p121), with its colorful array of tropical fish and reef sharks, is fascinating for kids of all ages, but there are lots of fun things just for *keiki* (children) as well. Inquire about the current schedule for kids' programs with names like 'Home of the Hermit Crab' and 'Fish School.'

The **Honolulu Zoo** (p122) offers several activities just for kids, including a petting zoo where children can get eye-to-eye with tamer creatures and special 'twilight tours' that are geared for children aged five and older and take place from 5:30pm to 7:30pm on Saturday.

And then there are the numerous hula shows with a lively drum beat and cool dancing, including the nightly show at **Kuhio Beach Park** (p148) and a show at the **Waikiki Town Center** (2301 Kuhio Ave; admission free; ☺ 7pm Mon, Wed, Fri & Sat).

WAIKIKI

DETOUR: FIREWORKS ON THE BEACH

Want a front-row seat to Waikiki's spectacular pyrotechnics? Then pull into the Ala Wai Yacht Harbor on Friday evenings and get ready to enjoy the show. To get there, turn *makai* (oceanward) on Hobron Lane and then bear left around the yacht harbor until you reach the rear parking lot at the road's end. Parking is free. From the lot, walk 300yd east to the beach fronting the Hilton Hawaiian Village. Spread out a towel, lay back and watch the grand fireworks display that shoots off every Friday at 7pm.

And what kid can resist fireworks? Head to the Hilton Hawaiian Village on Friday at 6:30pm and you can watch a Polynesian song and dance show, complete with Samoan fire dancing, that tops off with a grand **fireworks display** (above) on the beach.

FESTIVALS & EVENTS

Waikiki loves a party, and the following celebrations are Waikiki's biggies:

January
New Year's Eve An extravagant fireworks display is shot off above Waikiki, lighting up the sky at the stroke of midnight.
Ala Wai Challenge Held the last Sunday in January, this Hawaiian cultural festival includes outrigger canoe races on the Ala Wai Canal and festivities at Ala Wai Park.

March
Honolulu Festival (www.honolulufestival.com) Held during the second weekend in March, festivities include plays, street performances, kite making, Japanese *bon odori* (dances) and a parade through Waikiki.
St Patrick's Day March 17 is celebrated with a parade of bagpipers and marching bands from Fort DeRussy, down Kalakaua Ave to Kapi'olani Park.

April
Hawaii Invitational International Music Festival High-school and college bands from far and wide compete in mid-April at the Kapi'olani Bandstand and Waikiki Shell in Kapi'olani Park.
Waikiki Spam Jam (www.spamjamhawaii.com) Join thousands of Spam aficionados celebrating O'ahu's quintessential people's food at this festive event held on a Saturday in late April.

May
May Day Known as Lei Day in Hawaii, on the first day of May you'll find lei-making competitions and the crowning of a queen at Kapi'olani Park.

June
Pan-Pacific Festival Held over a weekend in early June, this Japanese-American festival is celebrated throughout Waikiki with street performances, *taiko* drumming and other cultural festivities.

August
Obon The culminating event of this weeks-long Japanese summer festival is a floating lantern ceremony at the Ala Wai Canal on the evening of August 15.

September
Aloha Festivals Waikiki Waikiki celebrates Hawaiian culture in a huge evening block party along the beach on the second Friday in September with food, entertainment, live music and dancing on the beach.
Na Wahine o Ke Kai (www.holoholo.org/wahine) Hawaii's major annual women's outrigger canoe race, held near the end of September, starts at sunrise on the island of Moloka'i and ends 40 miles later at Waikiki's Fort DeRussy Beach.

October
Princess Kaiulani Commemoration Week Held throughout the third week in October, this event honors Hawaii's last princess with festivities, hula shows and other activities in Waikiki.
Na Moloka'i Hoe (www.holoholo.org) Hawaii's major men's outrigger canoe race, held midmonth, starts after sunrise on Moloka'i and finishes at Waikiki's Fort DeRussy Beach about five hours later. Six-person outrigger teams from as far away as Australia join Hawaiian teams in this annual competition.

SLEEPING

Waikiki's main beachfront strip, Kalakaua Ave, is lined with hotels with $300-plus rooms. Some of them are beauties with quiet gardens and seaside courtyards and others are high-rise megahotels catering to the package-tour crowd.

If stepping out of your room and digging your toes in the sand isn't a must, there are some inviting small hotels on the backstreets, where prices drop proportionally as you get further away from the beach. Some hotels in the Kuhio Ave area and up near the Ala Wai Canal have rooms as nice as many of the beachfront hotels at half the price – if you don't mind walking 10 minutes to the beach, you can really save a bundle.

In many hotels, the rooms and amenities are the same, with only the views varying. Generally, the higher the floor, the higher the price, and an ocean view will commonly bump up the bill by 50%. If you're paying extra for a view, you might want to ask to see the room first, since Waikiki certainly doesn't have any truth-in-labeling laws governing when a hotel can call a room 'ocean view.' Although many 'ocean views' are the real thing, others are mere glimpses of the water as seen through a series of high-rise buildings.

Waikiki has far more hotel rooms than condos, though a trend of hotel-to-condo conversions promises to add more condos to the scene. Outside of the condos listed in the following section, the best way to find a condo in Waikiki is to contact one of the vacation rental agencies that handle bookings for individual condo owners; their offers ebb and flow depending on supply and demand. A good place to start is **Aloha Waikiki Vacation Condos** (☎ 923-4402, 800-655-6055; www.waikiki-condos.com). Other agencies include **Pacific Islands Reservations** (☎ 808-262-8133; www.waikiki-condo-rentals.com) and **Super Waikiki Suites** (☎ 922-3311, 800-615-7050; www.waikiki-rentals.com). Another source of condo information is the 'Vacation Rentals' section of the two daily newspapers (p71), though it's typically slim pickings.

Budget
HOSTELS
Hostelling International Waikiki (☎ 926-8313; www.hostelsaloha.com; 2417 Prince Edward St; dm/d $20/48; ☺ reception 7am-3am; P 🖳) This friendly little hostel occupies a converted apartment complex just a few short blocks from Waikiki Beach. If you prefer your own private space to a dorm, you can find that here, too – request one of the five double rooms. The maximum stay is seven nights and there's a $3 surcharge if you're not an HI member. Unlike most other HI hostels, there's no dorm lockout or curfew. As there are only 60 beds, advance reservations are usually essential.

Waikiki Beachside Hostel (☎ 923-9566, 866-478-3888; www.waikikibeachsidehostel.com; 2556 Lemon Rd; dm $25-35, r $75; P 🖳) Waikiki's best private hostel attracts an international crowd

and offers plenty of perks, from a 24-hour Internet room to cheap island tours where you can meet like-minded travelers. The hostel occupies an older apartment complex, so each unit has a kitchen, bathroom, semi-private room and a few dorm beds.

HOTELS
Waikiki Prince Hotel (☎ 922-1544; www.waikikiprince.com; 2431 Prince Edward St; r $55-60, with kitchenette $80-90; P 🞬) Friendly managers with an eye on comfort have turned the 24 units in this six-story building into Waikiki's best-value budget hotel. The rooms are compact but cheery, and they are equipped with TV, micro-refrigerators and coffeemakers; for $20 extra you can opt for one with cooking facilities and a bit more space. Ask about weekly discounts. It's just a couple of minutes' walk to the beach.

Royal Grove Hotel (☎ 923-7691; www.royalgrovehotel.com; 151 Uluniu Ave; r $45-75; P 🞬 🖳) No frills but plenty of heart characterize this 85-room hotel that attracts so many returning snowbirds it's nearly impossible to get a room in winter without advance reservations. Rooms in the main wing are simple but perfectly adequate and even have lanai. Avoid rooms in the old Mauka Wing, which are small, noisy and without air-con. All rooms have kitchenettes; ask about discounts for longer stays.

Coconut Plaza Hotel (☎ 923-8828, 800-922-7866; www.resortquesthawaii.com; 450 Lewers St; r from $90; P 🞬 🖳) OK, it's just about as far from the beach as you can get in Waikiki, but there are some fine views of the Ala Wai Canal and the low price more than makes up for the 15-minute walk to the surf. Romantic types may enjoy the wall of mirrors and a sunset drink on their private lanai. You can also do some minor food prep here, as each room has a microwave and mini-refrigerator.

Breakers (☎ 923-3181, 800-426-0494; www.breakers-hawaii.com; 250 Beach Walk; studios $99-105; P 🞬 🖳) In a neighborhood dominated by high-rise hotels, this Polynesian-style place is a delightful throwback to earlier times. Staff are friendly; rooms are unassuming but fully adequate and each has a kitchenette. Request one of the 2nd-floor units, which adds a lanai for only $6 more.

Honolulu Prince (☎ 922-1616, 800-922-7866; www.honoluluprince.com; 317 Nahua St; r from $80; P 🞬) Clean, simple rooms at an affordable price is the mantra at this value-minded hotel. Just around the corner from Kuhio St, the location is convenient to restaurants and entertainment, and about a 10-minute walk from the beach. Standard rooms are adequate, but for $18 more you can upgrade to a commodious 'superior' room, which has two double beds, a sofa bed and a lanai.

Holiday Surf (☎ 923-8488; www.holidaysurfhotel .com; 2303 Ala Wai Blvd; studios per week $525-850; ✇) If you're looking for a deal on a weekly stay, this family-run place near the Ala Wai Canal has 30 units with kitchens. The cheapest rooms have thrift store–quality furnishings, while the pricier ones have upgraded decor and little extras like DVDs and VCRs.

Midrange
NEAR THE BEACH

Waikiki Parc Hotel (☎ 921-7272, 800-422-0450; www .waikikiparc.com; 2233 Helumoa Rd; r $196, with ocean view $219; P ✇ 🖥 ✇) Affordable elegance is in store here at the Halekulani's sister operation. The staff are pampering, the rooms bright and cool. The main thing you give up over the Halekulani (p131) is the beachfront locale – if you stay at the Parc you'll have to walk across the street to dig your feet into the sand. Request the 'Parc Sunrise' deal, which includes breakfast at no additional charge.

ResortQuest Waikiki Beach Hotel (☎ 922-2511, 800-922-7866; www.resortquesthawaii.com; 2570 Kalakaua Ave; r from $150; P ✇ ✇) From the surf-and-hula decor to the tiki torch–lit rooftop bar, this hotel is hip and fun. And it doesn't hurt to be opposite Kuhio Beach Park and surrounded by lots of nightlife and shopping options, either. In the morning the hotel hands out cool-pack bags that you can fill with complimentary breakfast goodies and take to the beach.

New Otani Kaimana Beach Hotel (☎ 923-1555, 800-356-8264; www.kaimana.com; 2863 Kalakaua Ave; r/ studios from $150/175; P ✇ 🖥) It's all about location, location, location. The staff are friendly and the rooms won't leave you wanting, but it's the quiet setting right on sweet Sans Souci Beach that makes this a stellar choice. Book early, because this low-key hotel is very popular with return visitors who know they've got a 'find.' No pool, but at this price and with this beach, who needs one?

Outrigger Waikiki Shore (☎ 923-3111, 800-688-7444; www.outrigger.com; 2161 Kalia Rd; studios from $230; P ✇ ✇) Watch glorious sunsets from your lanai at Waikiki's only beachfront condominium. Ask for one of the units facing Fort DeRussy Beach and the unobstructed view will be awash with palm trees and glistening sand. These spiffy units have cooking facilities and everything else you'll need, right down to a washer-dryer.

Queen Kapiolani Hotel (☎ 922-1941, 800-367-2317; www.queenkapiolani.com; 150 Kapahulu Ave; r $140-220; P ✇ ✇) A regal theme prevails at this older hotel located at the quieter eastern end of Waikiki. Chandeliers, high ceilings and paintings of Hawaiian royalty adorn the halls, and Kapi'olani Park and Queen's Surf Beach are a mere stone's throw away. Treat yourself to an ocean-view room for splendid unobstructed views of Diamond Head and the surf action from your lanai.

Imperial of Waikiki (☎ 923-1827, 800-347-2582; www.imperialofwaikiki.com; 205 Lewers St; studios $185, 1-bedroom units from $220; P ✇ ✇) Just a stone's throw from the beach (well, if you have a strong arm), this all-suites place offers comfy digs in a trendy neighborhood. A low-profile, little-known option, the Imperial is a time-share operation that rents out unfilled rooms on a space-available basis. The studios have limited cooking facilities, while the roomier one-bedroom suites have a full kitchen and enough space to sleep four people. Great stargazing from the rooftop hot tub!

Waikiki Resort Hotel (☎ 922-4911, 800-367-5116; www.waikikiresort.com; 2460 Koa Ave; r $139-179; P ✇ ✇) Just one short block from the water, this smaller hotel is much cozier than the nearby mega-resorts dominating the beachfront road. And although rooms won't provide great ocean views, they do offer all the other expected amenities, including mini-refrigerators, room safes and lanai. It's also set back a bit from the road, so traffic noise is minimal. All in all, fine value.

Ohana Royal Islander (☎ 922-1961, 800-462-6262; 2164 Kalia Rd; r from $159; P ✇) Friendly staff and a convenient location near Fort DeRussy Beach make this cozy hotel – the smallest in the Ohana group – a winner. The rooms are on the small side, but are pleasant and have all the expected amenities. The best rooms for ocean views are the

WAIKIKI

THE AUTHOR'S CHOICE

Sheraton Moana Surfrider (☎ 922-3111, 800-325-3535; www.moana-surfrider.com; 2365 Kalakaua Ave; r from $310, with ocean view $485; P ⊗ ☐ ⊠) If you love colonial-style hotels, you're in for a treat. Hawaii's first beachfront hotel, built in 1901, this grand establishment has been painstakingly restored right down to the elegantly carved columns of the porte-cochere. As in the old days, each floor has furnishings made from a different wood – koa on the 5th and cherry on the 6th, for example – and the graceful guest rooms retain their period look, with modern conveniences such as TVs and refrigerators discreetly concealed behind armoire doors. Hawaiian quilts adorn the airy lobby and a line of rocking chairs invite lazing on the front porch. The hotel embraces a seaside courtyard with a big banyan tree and a wraparound veranda, where island musicians sing hula songs each evening, just like in the 1920s when the 'Hawaii Calls' radio show was broadcast from here. Be sure to request the historic Banyan Wing, not the modern side wings, when you reserve. On-line discounts can sometimes lower the rates by about a third.

---

upper-floor corner ones, all of which end in the numbers 01.

Waikiki Circle Hotel (☎ 923-1571, 800-922-7866; www.astonhotels.com; 2464 Kalakaua Ave; r $170-200; P ⊗) Tired of all those square boxes? This sweet little circular building spirals up 13 floors with just a handful of rooms on each level. Go for one of the ocean-view rooms and you'll be able to watch the nightly hula show on Kuhio Beach while enjoying a drink on your lanai.

Outrigger Reef (☎ 923-3111, 800-688-7444; 2169 Kalia Rd; r from $230; P ⊗ ⊠) The well-appointed Outrigger Reef sports a great location right on the beach, near the expansive sands of Fort DeRussy and convenient to windsurfing and kayaking. The emphasis is on Hawaiiana, with a handcrafted outrigger canoe gracing the lobby and free lei-making and hula lessons available to guests.

Ewa Hotel Waikiki (☎ 922-1677, 800-359-8639; www.ewahotel.com; 2555 Cartwright Rd; r $95-105, with kitchenette $120-140, 2-bedroom units $270; P ⊗) Stylish pastel and rattan decor sets the tone at this backstreet boutique hotel on the eastern end of Waikiki. It's mostly a younger Japanese crowd, but the place also attracts a fair number of European travelers. Restaurants, the beach and bus stops are within easy walking distance. Generously discounted weekly rates are available.

Hawaiiana Hotel (☎ 923-3811, 800-367-5122; www.hawaiianahotelatwaikiki.com; 260 Beach Walk; r $105-215; P ⊗ ⊠) Walk through the gate and it's like stepping back 50 years. Yes, the furnishings may be a bit faded but the friendly Hawaiian staff at this low-key hotel shine. And just like in days past, none of the buildings on these grounds

rise higher than a coconut tree! If you're sensitive to traffic noise, avoid the rooms closest to busy Saratoga Rd.

Sheraton Princess Kaiulani (☎ 922-5811, 800-325-3535; www.sheraton-hawaii.com; 120 Ka'iulani Ave; r from $175; P ⊗ ⊠) One of Waikiki's earliest hotels, the Princess Kaiulani was built in the 1950s by the steamship company Matson Navigation in an effort to turn Waikiki into a major tourist destination. Needless to say, it worked – and half a century later vacationers are still lounging around the pool. The rooms are renovated and inviting. The location, opposite the beach in the busy heart of Waikiki, puts you in the midst of the action.

Ohana Reef Lanai (☎ 923-3881, 800-462-6262; www.ohanahotels.com; 225 Saratoga Rd; r from $219; P ⊗) One hundred percent smoke-free – and we're not just talking rooms. Even the bar at this hotel is nicotine-free. There's no pool, but beautiful Fort DeRussy Beach is just a short stroll away. For just $10 more, you can get a room with a kitchenette.

Waikiki Grand Hotel (☎ 923-1814, 888-336-4368; www.queenssurf.com; 134 Kapahulu Ave; r $159-189; ⊗ ⊠) Renovations have spiffed up this small hotel, which is best known as the home of Hula's, Waikiki's hottest gay spot. Rooms are compact, but have all the usual amenities and limited cooking facilities as well. It's just a minute's walk to the beach.

Hale Koa Hotel (☎ 955-0555, 800-367-6027; www.halekoa.com; 2055 Kalia Rd; r from $70; P ⊗ ⊠) Set on beautiful Fort DeRussy Beach, this modern, 1st-class hotel is reserved for US military personnel (both active and retired) and their families. Rates vary by the floor and by the guest's rank. There's a fitness center, three swimming pools and an array of activities for guests, making it an excellent value for those who qualify.

INLAND
B&BS
Diamond Head B&B (☎ 923-3360; www.diamondhead bnb.com; 3240 Noela St; r $130-145; P) Sleep like royalty in a jumbo-size koa bed that once belonged to Princess Ruth. And that's just one of the many perks of staying at this friendly B&B in an exclusive neighborhood above Kapi'olani Park. Beautiful views, a lovely garden and a hearty breakfast are also in store. The proprietor often joins guests over coffee and can give you the insider's scoop on the art scene. One of the three rooms is disability accessible. Call ahead for reservations.

Hotels
Ilima Hotel (☎ 923-1877, 800-801-9366; www.ilima .com; 445 Nohonani St; studios $157-179, 2-bedroom units $300-325; P ⚄ 🖳 🕮) Fusion at its finest, this all-suite hotel pairs the conveniences of a condo with the amenities of a hotel. Set in a less-hurried section of Waikiki, it's a serene niche yet a mere 10-minute walk to the beach. Opt for one of the higher floors for a fine view of the mountains and nearby Ala Wai Canal, as well as free high-speed Internet connections. One caveat: book early – there are only 99 rooms and they often fill with business travelers and other return visitors.

Waikiki Sand Villa Hotel (☎ 922-4744, 800-247-1903; www.waikikisandvillahotel.com; 2375 Ala Wai Blvd; r from $130; P ⚄ 🖳 🕮) Overlooking the Ala Wai Canal, this laid-back place, popular with young Japanese tourists, offers comfortable rooms and decent amenities. An on-site dive operation and a lobby-side Internet café are just a few of the perks. Request one of the corner rooms (those ending in 01 and 02) for the best views. If you stay by the week, you'll find enticing discounts.

Bamboo (☎ 922-7777, 866-406-2782; www.aqua bamboo.com; 2425 Kuhio Ave; r $155, 1-bedroom units $215-275; P ⚄ 🕮) A tranquil bamboo motif and amiable staff have transformed this former Waikiki hostel into an intimate Asian-style boutique hotel. There are a few hints of its less glorious past, but if you're looking for a meditative space in the midst of the

urban jungle it shouldn't disappoint. Need to unwind even more? Ask about the shiatsu massage offered at the poolside spa.

Royal Garden at Waikiki (☎ 943-0202, 800-367-5666; www.royalgardens.com; 440 Olohana St; r $150-275; P ⚄ 🕮) The marble lobby of this hotel is so classy it was used as the set in TV's *Lost* to portray the exclusive Seoul hotel where Jin had his doorman job. With just 200 rooms, this independent-run hotel is small enough to be personable. The lowest rate is for rooms on the lower floors; as the elevator climbs, so do the prices.

Aloha Surf Hotel (☎ 923-0222; www.aquaresorts .com; 444 Kanekapolei St; r from $120; P 🖳 🕮) A lively surf theme prevails at this 200-room hotel about a 10-minute walk from the beach. The lobby is fun, with surf videos and hanging surfboards. Although the rooms are on the small side, they have kitchenettes and free breakfast fare is provided. Be sure to ask for a renovated room, as a couple of floors are overdue for renovation.

Waikiki Joy Hotel (☎ 923-2300, 800-922-7866; www.waikikijoyhotel.com; 320 Lewers St; r $165-205, 1-bedroom units $295; P ⚄ 🕮) A lobby-side koi pond sets the tone at this soothing boutique hotel. Each of the rooms has its own JVC sound system and a bubbly Jacuzzi where you can soak those tired muscles after a hard day in the surf. Other amenities at this little oasis, just steps from bustling Kuhio St, include a fitness club, sauna and complimentary morning pastries.

Ohana Waikiki Malia (☎ 923-7621, 800-462-6262; www.ohanahotels.com; 2211 Kuhio Ave; r $179, 1-bedroom ste $229; P ⚄ ♿) Tennis with a view? A rooftop court is just one of the perks at this family-friendly place. The one-bedroom suites have room for a couple of kids; if you need more space, many of the rooms have connecting doors. When booking, look for simple saver rates, which drop room prices to as low as $89.

Outrigger Luana Waikiki (☎ 955-6000, 800-688-7444; www.outrigger.com; 2045 Kalakaua Ave; studios from $210; P ⚄ 🕮) Beautifully furnished studios are in store at this condominium-hotel, which has been totally refurbished to the tune of $11 million. It makes a good choice if you want to do your own cooking and don't need to be close to the beach.

Ohana East (☎ 922-5353, 800-462-6262; www.oh anahotels.com; 150 Ka'iulani Ave; r from $219, with kitchenette from $229; P ⚄ 🖳 🕮 ♿) Come here if you want a central location and a full array of amenities, including a fitness center, high-speed Internet access and a 24-hour business center. Fourteen floors of this hotel are entirely nonsmoking, and the place attracts as many families as business travelers. Ask about the half-price simple saver rate.

Celebrity Resorts Waikiki (☎ 923-7336, 800-588-2651; www.celebrityresorts.com; 431 Nohonani St; studios $199, 1-bedroom units $255; P 🏊) Impromptu pizza nights and sing-alongs by the pool – guests at this old-fashioned place act just like neighbors who've known each other for years. Set in a quieter low-rise section of Waikiki, the hotel offers unusual amenities like weekly hula lessons, coconut painting and a barbecue with live Hawaiian music. Rooms are basic, however, which makes it pricy unless you find a good on-line deal.

Radisson Prince Kuhio (☎ 922-0811, 800-333-3333; www.radisson.com/waikikihi; 2500 Kuhio Ave; r from $179; P 🏊 🖥 🍽) This smart-looking hotel with large, well-appointed rooms is good value for this price range. There's wi-fi throughout the hotel, a business center and fitness facilities.

Ohana Maile Sky Court (☎ 947-2828, 800-462-6262; 2058 Kuhio Ave; r from $159; P 🏊 🍽) This hotel features an inviting lobby and a central location convenient to restaurants and shops. Some of the rooms are so small that once you open your suitcase, you may have to dance sideward a bit to get around the beds, but they're otherwise pleasant. And for just $10 more you can get one with a well-equipped kitchenette.

Doubletree Alana Hotel Waikiki (☎ 941-7275, 800-222-8733; www.alana-doubletree.com; 1956 Ala Moana Blvd; r/ste from $159/219; P 🏊 🍽) Hawaiian artwork adorns the lobby of this stylish but affordable hotel on the western side of Waikiki. The rooms have all the expected amenities, including minibars and lanai, and if jet lag has you on your own schedule you can hit the treadmill in the hotel's 24-hour fitness center.

Ocean Resort Hotel Waikiki (☎ 922-3861, 800-367-2317; www.oceanresort.com; 175 Paoakalani Ave; r $147-173, studios $193-230; P 🏊 🍽) Just a short walk from the beach, this midsize hotel offers good amenities at a fair price. Non-smoking rooms are available on request. Opt for a higher floor for the largest and quietest rooms. When things are slow, it

offers walk-in rates as low as $80 – a real deal for this standard of hotel.

ResortQuest Waikiki Sunset (☎ 931-1400, 800-922-7866; www.resortquesthawaii.com; 229 Paoakalani Ave; 1-bedroom units $240-285; P 🏊 🖥 🍽) Many of the rooms in this condo hotel feature huge floor-to-ceiling windows offering some of the widest sunset views imaginable. Then there are the little extras, like a sauna and free tennis. Ask about promotions that offer handsome discounts off the standard rates.

Top End

Halekulani Hotel (☎ 923-2311, 800-367-2343; www.halekulani.com; 2199 Kalia Rd; r from $360; P 🏊 🖥 🍽) Elegant rooms and acres of gleaming marble are the fashion at Waikiki's premier oceanfront hotel. Guest rooms have deep soaking tubs and lovely touches, such as terry bathrobes and fresh flowers, but the pampering doesn't stop there. The service throughout this hotel, and at its exquisite restaurants, is so highly regarded it's been awarded top recognition by travel icons like *Travel & Leisure* magazine. And if by chance your budget knows no bounds, book yourself into the new luxury suite created by renowned designer Vera Wang.

W Honolulu Diamond Head (☎ 922-1700; www.whotels.com; 2885 Kalakaua Ave; r $430-530; P 🏊 🖥) The W, as everyone calls this polished gem, exudes sophistication like no other place in Waikiki. High-end amenities include down-feather bedding, 27in TVs, high-speed Internet access and a coddling 'whatever/whenever' service motto. It's also home to one of Waikiki's hottest restaurants and its most fashionable lounge. Of course, it's right on the beach, too

Royal Hawaiian Hotel (☎ 923-7311, 800-325-3535; www.royal-hawaiian.com; 2259 Kalakaua Ave; r in historic wing/tower from $395/650; P 🏊 🖥 🍽) Waikiki's first luxury hotel, this pink Moorish-style landmark at the end of Royal Hawaiian Ave is a beauty – cool and airy and loaded with charm. The historic section maintains a classic appeal, with some of the rooms having quiet garden views. This section is easier to book, too, as most guests prefer the modern high-rise wing with its ocean views.

Outrigger Waikiki (☎ 923-0711, 800-688-7444; www.outrigger.com; 2335 Kalakaua Ave; r from $300; P 🏊 🖥 🍽) You couldn't be more in the thick of things than at this seaside babe, the Outrigger's flagship hotel. Set on a prime stretch of sand, you can hit the surf in the morning, join the party crowd at Duke's Canoe Club in the afternoon and unwind over dinner as you watch the sun set. For the best views and quietest digs, request a room on an upper floor.

Hyatt Regency Waikiki (☎ 921-6026, 800-233-1234; www.hyattwaikiki.com; 2424 Kalakaua Ave; r from $265; P ⊠ ⌨ ⌸) Unlike many of its neighbors, this central hotel incorporates a generous dose of open space into its layout with an atrium of resplendent gardens separating two towers. Each tower has a max of 18 rooms per floor, making it feel quieter and more exclusive than other hotels its size. Agreeable tropical room decor and good amenities round out the package.

Hawaii Prince Hotel (☎ 944-4411, 800-321-6248; www.princeresortshawaii.com; 100 Holomoana St; r from $250; P ⊠ ⌨ ⌸) If sleek is what you seek, this ultramodern hotel overlooking the yacht harbor fits the bill. Each of the rooms boasts a fine ocean view, the service is superb and the on-site restaurants are notable. And for those mixing a little work with play, there's a business center complete with secretarial services.

Hilton Hawaiian Village (☎ 949-4321, 800-445-8667; www.hiltonhawaiianvillage.com; 2005 Kalia Rd; r $249-500; P ⊠ ⌨ ⌸ 👶) Yep, this one really is a mega-resort, Hawaii's largest hotel with more than 3000 rooms. Yet somehow, between the swan ponds, penguin pools and other eye candy spread around the grounds, it just doesn't seem that massive. And the numerous amenities, including some excellent restaurants and a thunderous Friday-night fireworks display, offer guests endless options. There's a full array of activities geared just for kids, too.

EATING

Waikiki is chock-full of places to eat, ranging from unpretentious local eateries to some of Hawaii's most acclaimed restaurants. Many of the better restaurants are right on the beach, offering splendid ocean views and unforgettable sunset dining.

Budget

Ono Hawaiian Food (☎ 737-2275; 726 Kapahulu Ave; meals $8-10; ⏰ 11am-7:45pm Mon-Sat) This is the real deal, traditional Hawaiian food served

Hawaiian-style. It's a simple little diner, crowded with aging tables and decorated with sports paraphernalia, but at dinnertime people line up on the sidewalk waiting to get in. A favorite is the *kalua* pig plate, which comes with *lomi* salmon, *pipi kaula* beef jerky, *haupia* (coconut pudding) and either rice or poi. Ono makes an unbeatable place to enjoy a truly local meal. The best way to avoid the crowd is to arrive before 5:30pm.

Diamond Head Market & Grill (☎ 732-0077; 3158 Monsarrat Ave; take-out dishes $7-9; ⏰ grill 10:30am-9pm, deli 7:30am-9pm) If you're up for a picnic in the park, head first to this neighborhood gem. At the deli side, you can order creative salads like fennel-citrus by the pound. At the adjacent grill, a take-out window dishes out gourmet-quality plate lunches – don't miss the grilled *'ahi* (yellowfin tuna) salad.

Leonard's (☎ 737-5591; 933 Kapahulu Ave; pastries 70¢-$1; ⏰ 6am-9pm) It's just plain hard to go by Leonard's without stopping. This Portuguese bakery is famous throughout O'ahu for its *malasadas*, a sweet fried dough rolled in sugar and served warm – like a doughnut without the hole. Order the *haupia malasada*, filled with an addictive coconut cream, and you'll be hooked.

Teddy's Bigger Burgers (☎ 926-3444; 134 Kapahulu Ave; burgers $4-8.50; ⏰ 10:30am-9pm) Cool retro black-and-white checkered decor and good hand-formed burgers. Diehards should order the monster double-patty burger – weighing in at over 1lb, it provides unequivocal testimony that Teddy indeed has *the* bigger burger! Wash it down with an old-fashioned root beer float – but skip the greasy fries.

Fatty's Chinese Kitchen (☎ 922-9600; 2345 Kuhio Ave; meals $4-6; ⏰ 10:30am-10:30pm) Who says Waikiki has to be expensive? This hole-in-the-wall eatery serves good Chinese fare at bargain prices. Island favorites like shoyu chicken and pineapple shrimp come with rice or chow mein. The atmosphere is purely local, with a dozen stools lining a long bar and the cook on the other side chopping away.

Rainbow Drive-In (☎ 737-0177; cnr Kapahulu & Kanaina Aves; snacks $2-6; ⏰ 7:30am-9pm) A throwback to an earlier era, this drive-in eatery is where surfers stop for a quick bite after a day on the waves. Burgers, plate lunches, malts and saimin shore up the menu.

THE AUTHOR'S CHOICE

Shore Bird Beach Broiler (☎ 922-2887; Outrigger Reef, 2169 Kalia Rd; breakfast $10, lunch $11, dinner $12-22; ⏰ 7am-1pm & 4:30-10pm) This place has it all – open air, right on the ocean, live Hawaiian dinner music and a one-of-a-kind setup that lets you be your own chef as you chat away with the neighbors. At one end of the dining room there's a big common grill where you barbecue your own order – fresh fish, juicy steaks or chicken. When you've cooked it to your liking take your plate to the generous buffet spread, which includes the usual barbecue sides like salad fixings, chili and rice, and then perks things up with Hawaiian favorites like poi, pickled octopus and *lomi* salmon. It's a busy place, so unless you get there early, expect to wait for a table. However, this is scarcely a hardship, as you can hang out on the beach until your name's called. Shore Bird has good breakfast and lunch buffets, too, but a sunset dinner at the barbie is unbeatable.

Waiola Bakery & Shave Ice (☎ 949-2269; 525 Kapahulu Ave; snacks $1.50-3; ⏰ noon-5:30pm Mon-Fri, 11am-6pm Sat & Sun) Up for a cool treat? This unassuming shop has been serving super-fine shave ice since 1940, so you'd better believe it's got it right. It's also the place to try another Hawaiian speciality, taro bread.

Eggs 'n' Things (☎ 949-0820; 1911 Kalakaua Ave; dishes $3-10; ⏰ 11pm-2pm) Never found empty, this bustling all-nighter specializes in reliable breakfast fare, from pancakes topped with tropical syrups to fluffy omelettes. The most popular deal is the 'early riser' special of three pancakes and two eggs, which is offered from 5am to 9am for just $3.75.

Saint Germain (☎ 924-4305; 2301 Kuhio Ave; snacks $2-6; ⏰ 6:30am-10pm) Vacationers longing for French-style pastries will find tempting croissants and cakes at this bakery. At the counter you can order vegetarian or meat sandwiches made to order with your choice of bread, including a crispy baguette.

Ruffage Natural Foods (☎ 922-2042; 2443 Kuhio Ave; snacks $5-6; ⏰ 9am-6pm Mon-Sat) For a quick, healthy snack, this pint-size health-food store has made-to-order sandwiches, burritos and smoothies.

Food Pantry (☎ 923-9831; 2370 Kuhio Ave; ⏰ 6am-1am) This is the best place to get groceries in Waikiki. Its prices are higher than those of the chain supermarkets, which are all outside Waikiki, but lower than those of Waikiki's numerous convenience stores. If you have a car, there's a 24-hour Foodland supermarket north of Waikiki, near the eastern intersection of King St and Kapi'olani Blvd. If you don't have a car, the most convenient full-service supermarkets are the ones in the Ala Moana Center.

Farmers Market (☎ 923-1802; Waikiki Community Center, 310 Paoakalani Ave; ⏰ 7am-1pm Tue & Fri) Get your island-fresh produce right in Waikiki at this little farmers market held at the community center twice a week.

Midrange
NEAR THE BEACH
Duke's Canoe Club (☎ 922-2268; Outrigger Waikiki, 2335 Kalakaua Ave; dinner mains $16-27; ⏰ 7am-10pm) Hands down Waikiki's most popular oceanfront restaurant and bar, this lively place takes its name from the late surfing icon Duke Kahanamoku. The surfing theme prevails in the decor of this casual open-air place and in the action on the beach it borders. A breakfast buffet ($13) offers fresh fruit and omelettes to order, while the buffet-style lunch ($12) centers around a salad bar and hot dishes like teriyaki chicken. Dinner focuses on fresh fish and steaks. There's live Hawaiian music nightly and on weekend afternoons.

Hau Tree Lanai (☎ 921-7066; New Otani Kaimana Beach Hotel, 2863 Kalakaua Ave; breakfast $9-15, lunch $12-20, dinner $28-36; ⏰ 7am-2pm & 5:30-9pm) A classic beachfront setting under an arbor of hau trees characterizes this delightful restaurant right on Sans Souci Beach. A favorite breakfast spot for islanders. The menu abounds in local flavor with everything from poi pancakes to seafood omelettes. At other meals the fresh-seared 'ahi is a treat not to be missed, and dinner, serenaded with the sound of the surf, is as romantic as it gets.

Sansei Seafood Restaurant & Sushi Bar (☎ 931-6286; 3rd fl, Waikiki Beach Marriott Resort, 2552 Kalakaua Ave; appetizers $4-15, mains $17-40; ⏰ 5:30-10pm; 🚼) The handiwork of one of Hawaii's hottest chefs, DK Kodama, Sansei features innovative Japanese-Hawaiian fare. The menu rolls out everything from traditional 'ahi sashimi to seared 'opakapaka (pink snapper) in a white truffle sauce. Not to be missed is the award-winning mango crab salad roll. Come for the early-bird special, between 5:30pm and 6pm Tuesday to Saturday, and you'll not only get 25% off all food, but you'll also nab a prime sunset view on the torch-lit veranda.

Beach Bar at Banyan Court (☎ 922-3111; Sheraton Moana Surfrider, 2365 Kalakaua Ave; meals $14-18; ☺ 10:30am-10pm) Here's why you want to be here: it's outdoors in the hotel's courtyard under the sprawling banyan tree, where you have a prime seat for watching hula dancers and Hawaiian musicians perform on the veranda. From 4pm the menu offers the likes of sugarcane shrimp brochettes and baby back ribs. Earlier in the day, it's sandwich fare minus the music.

Chuck's Steak House (☎ 923-1228; 2nd fl, Outrigger Waikiki, 2335 Kalakaua Ave; dinner $16-28; ☺ 4:45-10pm) Come early to score a table on the wrap-around lanai that hangs over Waikiki Beach and watch the sun set on all the playful seaside action. You'll also be rewarded with early-bird specials and cheap mai tais, but the real deal is the gorgeous view. What's for dinner? Well-prepared steak, chicken and seafood standards, with baked potato and a salad bar.

Sushikoh (☎ 923-5526; 255 Beachwalk; meals $7-20; ☺ 11:30am-2:30pm & 5-10pm) Step through the door and it's like walking into a neighborhood restaurant in Tokyo. The atmosphere, food and presentation are all first class in this friendly little chef-owned place. The traditional *teishoku*-style courses, served on lacquerware plates, make complete meals, or you can order sushi and sashimi à la carte.

Cheeseburger in Paradise (☎ 923-3731; 2500 Kalakaua Ave; mains $8-13; ☺ 7am-11pm Sun-Thu, to midnight Fri & Sat) If you enjoy tropical-themed kitsch, the grass-skirted waitresses and splashy 'old Hawaii' motif here will appeal. The house special is a Black Angus burger drowning in Jack and colby cheeses – get it topped in fresh guacamole and you won't be disappointed. Vegetarian gardenburgers and salads are available for less-carnivorous types.

Lulu's (☎ 926-5222; 2586 Kalakaua Ave; mains $8-22; ☺ 24hr; ⚐) Yep, that's right – Lulu's *never* closes. Surfboards on the wall set the mood at this hopping open-air restaurant and bar opposite Kuhio Beach Park. It can get a bit noisy but if you're in a high-energy mood it's pure fun. The extensive menu makes a broad sweep from fresh fish tacos to New York steaks. There's a kids menu, too.

Arancino (☎ 923-5557; 255 Beach Walk; mains $12-20; ☺ 11:30am-2:30pm & 5-10pm; ⚐) Italian food just the way mama would have made it. Whether you're sitting inside this cozy little restaurant or at one of the sidewalk tables, you'll be dining on delicious old-world fare. A good choice is the *spaghetti alla pescatore*, which abounds with shrimp, mussels and calamari in a hearty garlic sauce.

Oceanarium Restaurant (☎ 921-16111; Pacific Beach Hotel, 2490 Kalakaua Ave; breakfast buffet $13, lunch $8, dinner buffet $32; ☺ 6am-10pm; ⚐) This place is unforgettable not so much for its food but for its one-of-a-kind view. The dining room wraps around a stunning three-story aquarium brimming with colorful tropical fish, including some impressive sharks and rays. The buffets include everything but the aquarium fish!

INLAND

Keo's (☎ 922-9355; 2028 Kuhio Ave; mains $10-20; ☺ 5-10:30pm) *Bon Appétit* called it America's best Thai restaurant…need we say more? For nearly 30 years this place has been a magnet for Hollywood celebs, and even US presidents have surreptitiously stopped by to feast here. Chef Keo Sananikone starts with the basics, liberally spicing his dishes with herbs grown on his own farm. Expect lots of enticing seafood specials but don't overlook the local favorite: Evil Jungle Prince, a spicy coconut curry with fresh basil that can be ordered in vegetarian, meat or shrimp versions.

Irifune's (☎ 737-1141; 563 Kapahulu Ave; mains $10-15; ☺ 11:30am-1:30pm & 5:30-9:30pm Tue-Sat) Follow the locals to this bustling eatery, decorated with Japanese country kitsch and serving up creative island fare. A standout dinner choice is the *tataki 'ahi*, melt-in-your-mouth fresh tuna that's seared lightly on the outside and sashimi-like inside. Or opt for a combination dinner that pairs tempura with sashimi and other Japanese standards. Alcohol is not served, but you can bring your own beer.

Tanaka of Tokyo (☎ 922-4702; Waikiki Shopping Plaza, 2250 Kalakaua Ave; meals $18-38; ☺ 11:30am-2pm Mon-Fri, 5:30-10pm daily) This place is a blast, as much entertainment as it is a dining experience. Its U-shaped teppanyaki tables each have a central grill that's presided over by

PEOPLE'S OPEN MARKET

O'ahu's island-wide public market program, the People's Open Market, has been bringing fresh homegrown goodies to folks since the 1970s. Farmers truck their goods to various sites around the island and sell directly to customers. It's a great opportunity to support hard-working islanders while treating yourself to food that's both more fresh and cheaper than at grocery stores.

You'll find bargains on common fruits like papayas, oranges and avocados, as well as items such as passion fruit and exotic ethnic vegetables that simply aren't sold in supermarkets.

As for market etiquette, an air horn is sounded to start the market and the organizers prohibit any sales prior to that point. It's considered bad manners to ask a vendor to reserve anything for you before the market starts. Keep in mind that you're buying directly from the owner, so some of the testing that's commonplace in grocery stores – squeezing fruit, for instance – isn't going to make any friends here.

Try to arrive early. As a matter of fact, it's best to be there before the starting time, as once the horn blows, there's a big rush and people begin to scoop things up quickly. Everything typically wraps up within an hour.

There are 25 market sites in all around O'ahu, including at **Kapi'olani Park** (cnr Monsarrat & Paki Aves; ☉ 10-11am Wed). For information on locations elsewhere on the island call ☎ 522-7088 or check out www.co.honolulu.hi.us/parks/programs/pom.

a chef with 'flying knives,' who cooks and serves meals to the diners at his table. All meals include salad, an appetizer and dessert; prices depend upon the main dish you select, with options ranging from chicken to lobster tail.

Pyramids (☎ 737-2900; 758 Kapahulu Ave; lunch buffet $10, dinner mains $13-18; ☉ 11am-2pm & 5:30-10pm Mon-Sat, 5-9pm Sun) If you need a break from Pacific Rim cuisine, stop by here and enter another world. This atmospheric Egyptian restaurant offers a scrumptious lunch buffet of Mediterranean treats, including Greek salad, falafels and spicy meats cooked on a spit. Dinner is à la carte, with main dishes such as marinated lamb. You'll find vegetarian offerings on the menu, too, including a delicious eggplant moussaka. Belly dancers entertain nightly.

Singha Thai (☎ 941-2893; 1910 Ala Moana Blvd; mains $13-28; ☉ 5-11pm) Come here if you want to enjoy a dinner show along with award-winning Thai food. A troupe of graceful Thai dancers performs nightly from 7pm to 9pm. A sister operation of Honolulu's upscale Chai's Bistro, this place fuses Pacific Rim flavors and contemporary Thai cuisine, with luscious creations such as blacked 'ahi summer rolls or Hawaiian lobster tail in ginger-chili sauce. A solid choice for an exotic night out.

La Cucaracha (☎ 922-2288; 2310 Kuhio Ave; dishes $8-18, kids menu $4; ☉ noon-11pm; 🗷 🐧) Now, who would expect an authentic family-run

Mexican restaurant in the heart of Waikiki? Yet the food is excellent. All the dishes are lard-free and vegetarians will find several options designed just for them. Along with south-of-the-border standards, daily specials range from homemade tamales and chicken molé to fresh fish smothered in salsa verde. Wash it all down with a potent margarita, or Mexican beer on tap.

Todai (☎ 947-1000; 1910 Ala Moana Blvd; lunch/dinner buffet $15/27; ☉ 11:30am-2:30pm & 5:30-9:30pm) A seafood lover's dream, Todai lays out amazing buffet spreads with a near-endless variety of briny delights from the sea, from Alaskan crab legs to Hawaiian sashimi. Salads and mouthwatering desserts round it out. The place is always packed so it's wise to get there early, particularly at dinner.

Keoni's (☎ 922-9888; Ohana East, 2375 Kuhio Ave; breakfast & lunch $5-10, dinner $11-32; ☉ 7am-11pm; 🗷) Looking for the perfect place for families who can't agree on where to go? Keoni's, a sister operation of Keo's Thai restaurant, adds a fun twist to its menu, offering both Thai and American dishes. Whether you want a cheeseburger or Panang curry, you'll find it done right. And don't overlook breakfast, which is served until noon and features everything from macadamia nut pancakes to eggs Benedict.

Bogart's Cafe (☎ 739-0999; 3045 Monsarrat Ave; dishes $7-12; ☉ 6am-8pm Mon-Fri, to 6pm Sat & Sun) This bustling little eatery found just beyond Kapi'olani Park is a hot breakfast spot,

WAIKIKI

BRUNCH IN STYLE

Sunday is made for relaxing, right? So why not take a few hours to unwind over one of Waikiki's stellar Sunday brunch buffets, which are among the most indulgent imaginable.

In a class by itself is **Orchids** (☎ 923-2311; Halekulani Hotel, 2199 Kalia Rd; buffet $40; ☺ 9:30am-2:30pm), the most elegant Sunday brunch on O'ahu, if not in all of Hawaii. The grand spread includes sashimi, prime rib, smoked salmon, roast suckling pig, an array of salads and a thoroughly decadent dessert bar. In addition, there's a fine ocean view, orchid sprays on the tables and a soothing flute and harp duo to set the mood. It's best to make advance reservations, or you may encounter a long wait.

If you favor a historic colonial atmosphere over beachside dining, the Sunday brunch on the **Banyan Veranda** (☎ 922-8383; Sheraton Moana Surfrider, 2365 Kalakaua Ave; buffet $43; ☺ 9am-2pm) is the top choice. It features island favorites like *'ahi poke* (cubed raw yellowfin tuna mixed with shoyu, sesame oil, salt and chili pepper), Chinese dim sum, sashimi and *lomi* salmon, in addition to such brunch standards as prime rib, eggs Benedict, a waffle station and luscious desserts. The Banyan Veranda brunch is accompanied by live classical music.

For something less formal there's **Brunch on the Beach** (☎ 923-1094; ☺ 9am-1:30pm), a festive event that takes place on the third Sunday of the month and draws scores of locals and visitors alike. Oceanfront Kalakaua Ave, between Ka'iulani and Lili'uokalani Aves, is lined with umbrella-shaded tables and transformed into a huge outdoor café. Chefs from some of Waikiki's best restaurants set up food stands, and Hawaiian musicians perform along the beach. All you pay for is the cost of the food you choose. Sample whatever you like – grilled fish, spring rolls and dim sum are among the many selections – and most items cost just a couple of dollars, so you can easily eat your fill for less than $20.

---

with everything from thick Belgian waffles to crab and avocado omelettes. The lunch menu includes veggie wraps and innovative items like spinach and strawberry salad.

Moose McGillycuddy's (☎ 923-0751; 310 Lewers St; mains $6-13; ☺ 7:30am-10pm) Although best known as a nightspot, Moose also rakes in a breakfast crowd with huge omelettes. Try the Beach Boy: three eggs whipped up with ham, pineapple and cheese. Breakfast is available until 11am. At other times, the restaurant serves burgers, Mexican fare and steaks.

Perry's Smorgy (☎ 926-0184; 2380 Kuhio Ave; breakfast $7, lunch $9, dinner $11; ☺ 7-11am, 11:30am-2:30pm & 5-9pm) If you've worked up an appetite, Perry's offers affordable all-you-can-eat buffets in an agreeable gardenlike setting. The food isn't fancy but there's plenty to choose from, including ham, fresh tropical fruit and salad. Dinner adds a round of beef.

Top End

Reservations are always a good idea at any of Waikiki's top-end restaurants.

Golden Dragon (☎ 946-5336; Hilton Hawaiian Village, 2005 Kalia Rd; mains $17-35; ☺ 6-9:30pm Tue-Sat) Top fine-dining Chinese restaurant offering a full range of Cantonese and Szechuan dishes, including delicious stir-fried lobster tail with *haupia* and unbeatable crispy lemon chicken.

Order à la carte or select from generous three-course dinners ($34–50). Calorie-counters should check out the 'healthy menu' loaded with tempting low-fat treats.

Sam Choy's Diamond Head Restaurant (☎ 732-8645; 449 Kapahulu Ave; mains $21-34; ☺ 5:30-10pm Sun-Thu, 5-11pm Fri & Sat) If you've got a big appetite and want to indulge in flavorful Hawaii Regional Cuisine, this is the place. Unlike many other restaurateurs specializing in such fare, Choy serves huge portions and he loves to spice them up a notch as well. The menu covers the gamut from vegetarian to juicy steaks but the local favorite is the seafood *laulau*, a concoction of fresh fish, shrimp and scallops steamed to perfection in ti leaves. Skip the appetizers and save room for a slab of luscious pineapple cheesecake!

Bali By The Sea (☎ 941-2254; Hilton Hawaiian Village, 2005 Kalia Rd; mains $20-40; ☺ 6-9:30pm Mon-Sat) An award-winning food and wine list, chic decor and a splendid ocean view make Bali a sure bet. Tasty treats include the likes of Thai-spiced grilled tiger shrimp and the signature lime-sautéed *'opakapaka* with Moloka'i sweet potatoes. For your grand finale, don't miss the *liliko'i*-(passion fruit) topped chocolate custard cake.

(Continued on page 145)

The relatively easy Manoa Falls Trail (p91) rewards hikers with one of the island's most stunning waterfalls.

Though largely a bedroom community, the appeal of Kaneʻohe (p182) is in its magical Byodo-In temple and sailboat-friendly bay.

Hanauma Bay (p166) teems with countless varieties of fish and even some sea turtles, making for phenomenal snorkeling.

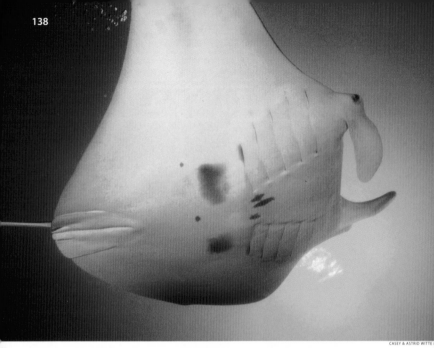

CASEY & ASTRID WITTE

O'ahu's waters harbor varied marine life (p43), including manta rays, green sea turtles, dolphins and humpback whales. Even endangered Hawaiian monk seals occasionally dock on the island's more remote northwest beaches. If you see them, keep your distance – at least 100ft, per federal and state laws that protect these once-thriving mammals.

JONATHAN BLAIR/CORBIS

KARL L

ANN CECIL

Pu'u 'Ualaka'a State Park (p88) offers sweeping views of Honolulu, Diamond Head, Pearl Harbor and beyond.

The ancient Polynesian sport of outrigger canoeing lives on in Hawaii, with clubs and races throughout the Islands. Not a paddler? Grab an outrigger canoe ride from Waikiki (p123).

CASEY & ASTRID WITTE MAHANEY

ANN CECIL

RICHARD

Waimea Bay Beach (p201), offers good snorkeling and swimming in summer.

O'ahu's premier bodysurfing and bodyboarding beach, Sandy Beach (p168) also sees more injuries and lifeguard rescues than any other on the island.

Opposite: Performers at the Polynesian Cultural Center (p191), Hawaii's top paid attraction, have entertained more than 30 million visitors since its founding in 1963.
JOHN BORTHWICK

Had enough of playing in the water? Get on it with a yacht or catamaran cruise out of Honolulu (p93) or Waikiki (p123).

LINE

ERIC L WH

Exploring Honolulu on foot (p93) reveals public-art gems like this wave mural, represented in the classic Japanese style.

Opposite: Iconic Diamond Head (p163) was named by British sailors who, upon first seeing the calcite crystals shimmering in the crater's lava rock, thought there were diamonds in the soil.

ANN CECIL

Most of O'ahu's cruise-ship passengers pass through Honolulu's Aloha Tower (p79).

In 1795 Kamehameha the Great (p26) united the individually ruled Hawaiian islands as a single kingdom.

ALISON WRIGHT

WOODS WHEA

142

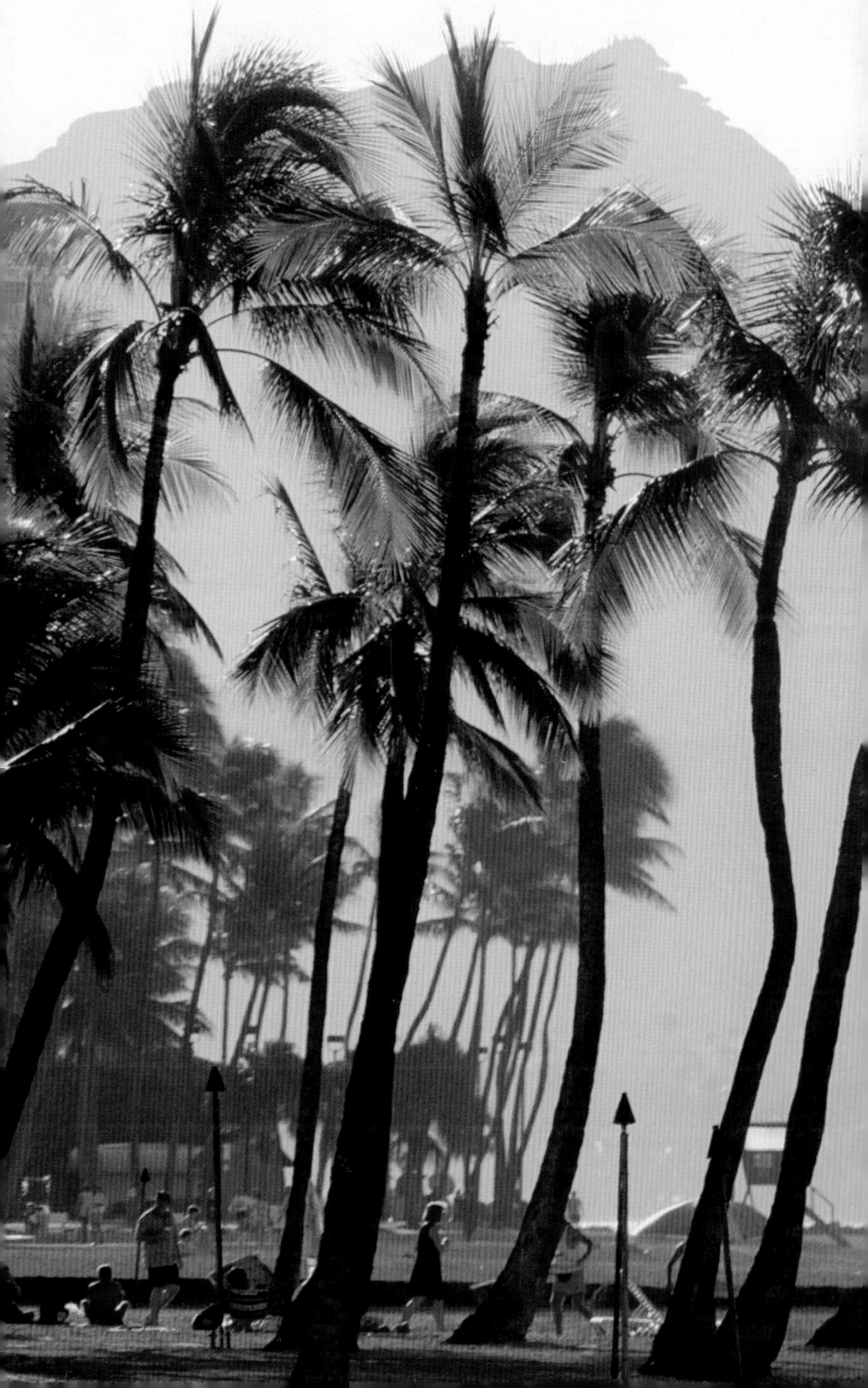

ALISON

Infamous Waikiki Beach (p117) stretches two glorious sandy miles. Each section is unique, so slather on the sunscreen and troll for a prime spot – of which there are countless.

If you're still up for a party, Waikiki Beach is a hotbed of beachfront bars (p145) and open-air entertainment (p146).

HOLGE

(Continued from page 136)

Banyan Veranda (☎ 921-4600; Sheraton Moana Surfrider, 2365 Kalakaua Ave; 4-course dinner $58; ⏰ 5:30-9pm) The setting on this hotel's historic courtyard veranda is a one-of-a-kind gem. The French- and Pacific Rim–influenced menu changes nightly but you can count on fresh Hawaiian seafood along with some traditional offerings like rack of lamb. Dinner is accompanied by Hawaiian music and hula dancing. All in all, the Banyan Veranda makes for a very romantic night out.

Prince Court (☎ 944-4494; 3rd fl, Hawaii Prince Hotel, 100 Holomoana St; lunch buffet $24, dinner buffet weekdays/weekend $40/42; ⏰ 11:30am-2pm Mon-Fri, 6-9:30pm Mon-Thu, 5:30-9:30pm Fri-Sun) A worthy treat. This sleek, contemporary restaurant offers a fine view of the yacht harbor and wonderful buffets of Asian and Western cuisine. All buffets have hot and cold mains, dim sum, fresh fish and tempting desserts; dinner adds lots of extras like crab legs and carved prime rib.

La Mer (☎ 923-2311; Halekulani Hotel, 2199 Kalia Rd; mains $35-48, 4-course dinner $85; ⏰ 6-10pm) The best of the best, La Mer is O'ahu's ultimate fine-dining restaurant, complete with a spectacular view of Diamond Head through swaying palms. A neoclassical French menu puts the emphasis on Provençal cuisine with the addition of fresh Hawaiian ingredients. The menu changes daily but typically features items such as 'ahi with caviar, bouillabaisse and filet mignon. Wines are perfectly matched. Formal is the byword and men must wear either a jacket or a long-sleeved shirt with a collar.

Kyo-ya (☎ 947-3911; 2057 Kalakaua Ave; lunch $15-20, dinner $20-55; ⏰ 11am-1:30pm Mon-Sat, 5:30-9:15pm daily) O'ahu's finest Japanese restaurant is the real deal, complete with kimono-clad waitresses and tables looking out onto a Zen rock garden. The food and presentation are as delightful as the setting. Meals are multicourse, with everything from salad to dessert included in the price. Expect to see more islanders here than tourists, as this is a favorite spot among locals for a special night out.

DRINKING
Cafés
Honolulu Coffee Company (☎ 533-1500; 2365 Kalakaua Ave; ⏰ 8am-10pm) Take a break from all the beach and shopping bustle to reju-

venate over a double espresso or an exotic tea. The gorgeous cakes and fruit tarts are so picture-perfect they could pose for the centerfold of a gourmet cookbook.

Marie's Organic Cafe (☎ 926-3900; 2155 Kalakaua Ave; ⏰ 10am-8pm Mon-Fri, 11am-8pm Sat) Hip meets healthy at this casual sidewalk café serving 100% organic Kona coffee and tasty fruit smoothies made from homegrown tropical fruit. And the tempting scones and chocolate pumpkin bread add some jazz to that organic label! You enter the cafe from Beach Walk.

Cydneybrooks Café & Bar (☎ 924-9100; 345 Royal Hawaiian Ave; ⏰ 8am-midnight Mon-Thu, 6pm-2am Fri & Sat) This stylish spot won an architectural award for its sleek design and wins kudos for its perfectly brewed coffee as well. It also serves lovely cool drinks like iced-honey café latte.

Hale Noa (☎ 735-4292; 766 Kapahulu Ave; ⏰ 8pm-midnight Mon-Sat) If you've never tried 'awa (kava) before, this is the place. A relaxing scene and a respect for the herb's roots in Hawaiian culture set the tone. This spicy elixir made from the *Piper methysticum* plant is mildly intoxicating, so it's suggested that you don't drink 'awa and drive.

Bars
Barefoot Bar (☎ 922-2268; Outrigger Waikiki, 2335 Kalakaua Ave) A spirited scene, this open-air bar at the side of Duke's Canoe Club is a hot spot for singles to meet. Even if you're not in the market, it's a good place to catch the nearby action on the beach and listen to live island music.

Beach Bar at Banyan Court (☎ 922-3111; Sheraton Moana Surfrider, 2365 Kalakaua Ave) Sit under the old banyan tree and sip a cool drink at this famous courtyard bar. For a fun alternative to the old mai tai, try the tropical itch, a flavorful concoction of Hawaiian passion fruit juice and rum. In the evening it's all accompanied by Hawaiian music and dance.

Lewers Lounge (☎ 923-2311; Halekulani Hotel; 2199 Kalia Rd; ⏰ 7:30pm-1am; 🎵) Dark woods, a jazz pianist and a thoroughly classy setting are in store at this venerable lounge. And this place takes its drinks seriously – there's not a canned mix in the house. Cocktails are made from scratch using fresh juices, including exotic tropical flavors like lychee and ginger. The martinis are second to none as well.

Lulu's (☎ 926-5222; 2586 Kalakaua Ave; ⏱ 24hr) An all-night party scene that gets more rambunctious as the night goes on. Spread across a big 2nd-floor veranda, Lulu's has a fine ocean view and a good *pupu* (snack) menu to go along with the drinks. The house special is the Big Lush, an oversized frozen mai tai, but this is also a good place to try Kona lager, Hawaii's finest homegrown beer.

Tiki's Grill & Bar (☎ 923-8454; ResortQuest Waikiki Beach Hotel, 2570 Kalakaua Ave) This hot, hip bar lit by tiki torches is a favorite place to enjoy a drink and *pupu*, and listen to live music as the sun sets over nearby Waikiki Beach.

Wonder Lounge (☎ 922-1700; W Honolulu Diamond Head, 2885 Kalakaua Ave) At Waikiki's swankiest lounge, well-dressed patrons sip drinks at an elegant bar featuring over 350 wines, munch great *pupu* and enjoy a stunning view of Diamond Head.

Coconut Willy's (☎ 923-9454; International Market Place, 2330 Kalakaua Ave; ⏱ 11am-1am) A great people-watching place and good party spot. There's plenty of action, with cover bands playing on and off from 3pm to midnight.

Hula Grill ☎ 923-4852; 2nd fl, Outrigger Waikiki, 2335 Kalakaua Ave) A good place for a quiet drink at sunset, the Hula Grill offers live Hawaiian music complete with hula dancers and a tiki torch–lit veranda overlooking the beach.

Top of Waikiki (☎ 923-3877; 21st fl, 2270 Kalakaua Ave; ⏱ 5-10:30pm) Your head will spin here even before you pick up a drink! This revolving bar atop the Waikiki Business Plaza offers a splendid 360° view of Waikiki, making a complete circle every 30 minutes.

Moana Terrace Bar (☎ 922-6611; Waikiki Beach Marriott Resort, 2552 Kalakaua Ave) A good choice if you're in a mellow mood, this poolside bar overlooking Kuhio Beach features sunset happy-hour drinks and live Hawaiian music from 6pm to 9pm nightly.

Ye Olde Fox & Hound (☎ 947-3776; Discovery Bay Center, 1178 Ala Moana Blvd) If you've a yearning for some Olde English flavor, head to this basement pub featuring English and Irish ales. Bangers and mash, shepherd's pie and other pub grub favorites go along with the brew.

ENTERTAINMENT

No surprise – Waikiki is entertainment central. Whether you just want to linger over one of those cool frosty drinks with the little umbrellas, yearn to hit the dance floor or are looking for a thoroughly island-style experience, you're in the right place.

In particular, there's a lot of stuff happening along the beachfront and it's there you'll find some of the best Hawaiian music to be heard anywhere. You can watch hula troupes sway at sunset at Kuhio Beach Park and listen to some of Hawaii's musical icons perform in the courtyard lounges of the oceanfront hotels.

A nice introduction on your first night out is to take a stroll along the central part of Waikiki Beach and sample the outdoor Hawaiian shows that take place overlooking the ocean. Take a leisurely wander past the musicians playing in the Sheraton Moana Surfrider's Banyan Veranda, watch beachside bands at Duke's Canoe Club, see the poolside performers at the Sheraton Waikiki Hotel's Sand Bar and so on down the line. Then go back and spend some time at whichever place catches your fancy.

For updated schedule information, check the free *Honolulu Weekly* newspaper, readily found around Waikiki, or the TGIF insert in the Friday edition of the *Honolulu Advertiser*.

Hawaiian Music

Hawaiian-style entertainment abounds in Waikiki, from rhythmic drums and hula dancers to mellow duos playing ukulele or slack-key guitar.

Duke's Canoe Club (☎ 922-2268; Outrigger Waikiki, 2335 Kalakaua Ave; ⏱ 4-6pm & 10pm-midnight) The seaside courtyard of this club is Waikiki's most popular venue for contemporary Hawaiian music, with the biggest names – including Henry Kapono – appearing on weekend afternoons. It's a great scene, especially on weekends when locals join the tourist crowd and the party spills over onto the beach.

Banyan Veranda (☎ 922-3111; Sheraton Moana Surfrider, 2365 Kalakaua Ave; ⏱ 5:30-10:30pm) Enjoy some of the finest in Hawaiian music and dance at this classic venue beneath the old banyan tree where *Hawaii Calls* has broadcasted its nationwide radio show for four decades, beginning in 1935. There's something happening every day. The performance schedule varies, but typically there's Hawaiian music and a hula dancer to 8:30pm, followed by a mix of Hawaiian and classical musicians later at night.

BEACH PARTY

How can you go wrong in a city where the mayor throws a beach party every weekend?

Every other weekend, on both Saturday and Sunday evenings, the Mayor's Office of Culture and the Arts for the City & County of Honolulu turns Queen's Surf Beach into a festive scene that attracts an equal measure of locals and visitors. Dubbed Sunset on the Beach, it's as much fun as a luau and everything is free – except for the food, and that's a bargain.

Hawaiian bands perform on a beachside stage from 4pm to sunset and then, when darkness falls, a huge screen is unscrolled above the stage and a feature movie is shown. Sometimes they opt for a movie with island connections, such as *Blue Hawaii* – the 1961 classic starring Elvis Presley – while on other nights it's a popular first-run Hollywood flick.

Tables and chairs are set up on the beach and out along the Kapahulu Groin. Waikiki restaurants operate food stalls along the beach, serving up everything from burgers and pizza to fancier treats like Panang chicken curry and savory seafood dishes. Nothing is over $6 and hey, kids, there's popcorn, too. It's all plenty of good fun and a great community experience.

House Without a Key (☎ 923-2311; Halekulani Hotel, 2199 Kalia Rd) No doubt that famous Charlie Chan novel set in Honolulu had some influence on the name, but truth be told, this delightful outdoor lounge simply has no doors to lock. It attracts a genteel crowd who gather daily for sunset cocktails, Hawaiian music and hula dancing by a former Miss Hawaii. Incidentally, the gracious woman doing the dancing doesn't work seven days a week – two former Miss Hawaii winners alternate nights.

Sand Bar (☎ 922-4422; Sheraton Waikiki, 2255 Kalakaua Ave) This circular cabana-like bar, overlooking the beach, has clear views of Diamond Head and live Hawaiian music nightly from 6pm to 8:30pm, including '*keiki* hula' every Sunday, when a children's hula group display their stuff.

Kapi'olani Bandstand (☎ 922-5331; Kapi'olani Park; ⏱ 2-3pm Sun Sep-Jul) An old-fashioned bandstand and rows of benches under sprawling shade trees provide the perfect venue for the time-honored Royal Hawaiian Band, which performs every Sunday afternoon except during August. Although not many visitors come this way, it's a great scene and a nice opportunity to rub shoulders with locals.

Paradise Lounge (☎ 949-4321; Hilton Hawaiian Village, 2005 Kalia Rd; ⏱ 5:30-10pm Sun-Thu, to midnight Fri & Sat) On Friday or Saturday night, head to the Hilton's Rainbow Tower to catch Jerry Santos and Olomana, one of the best Hawaiian groups performing on O'ahu today. If you go on Friday, you can also watch the Hilton's fireworks.

Mai Tai Bar (☎ 923-7311; 2259 Kalakaua Ave; ⏱ 10am-1am) At the Royal Hawaiian's low-key

bar you can catch great local groups, like Kelly Boy DeLima, from 4pm to 10pm nightly by the beach.

Royal Hawaiian Shopping Center (☎ 922-2299; Kalakaua Ave) Take a break from your shopping at this center, which sponsors free dance performances from 6:30pm to 9pm Monday and Tuesday by the local hula troupe Halau O Ka Hanu Lehua. The center is also the venue for mini-shows by performers from the Polynesian Cultural Center in La'ie; these take place from 6pm to 6:45pm Monday, Wednesday and Friday, and from 10am to 11:30am Tuesday, Thursday and Saturday.

LUAU

If your Hawaiian vacation just won't be complete without taking in a luau, you can choose from a cozy one right in Waikiki, or opt for a big party bash out of town but with free Waikiki hotel pickup. Either way, you'll be able to sample a wide array of Hawaiian foods, like *kalua* pig (pig cooked in an underground pit), *laulau* (a bundle of pork, chicken or fish wrapped in taro and ti leaves and steamed), *lomi* salmon (minced, salted salmon with diced tomato and green onion), poi (fermented taro) and that delicious pudding-like coconut dessert, *haupia*.

Royal Hawaiian Hotel (☎ 931-8383; 2259 Kalakaua Ave; show & buffet dinner adult/child 5-12yr $89/48; ⏱ 6-8:30pm Mon) This relatively small beachside luau, the only one in Waikiki, features a buffet-style dinner of Hawaiian food and a bar with mai tais and luau punch. A spirited Polynesian show with

WAIKIKI

contemporary Hawaiian hula and Samoan fire dancing accompanies it all. It's best to book in advance.

O'ahu's other two commercial luau, **Paradise Cove** (☎ 842-5911, 800-775-2683; www.paradisecove.com; 92-1089 Ali'inui Dr, Kapolei; adult/youth 13-18yr/child 3-12yr $73/63/53; ⏰ 5-9pm) and **Germaine's Luau** (☎ 949-6626, 800-367-5655; www.germainesluau.com; 440 Olai St, Kapolei; adult/youth 14-20yr/child 6-13yr $65/55/45; ⏰ 6-9pm), are both held nightly on the beach out in the Kapolei area. Guests are picked up at Waikiki hotels and taken by bus to the luau site (about one hour each way). Both shows are quite similar, with an *imu* ceremony (removal of the pig from the roasting pit), a buffet dinner of Hawaiian foods, and a Polynesian-style show complete with fire dances, hula and music. Paradise Cove adds some traditional arts and crafts and demonstrations of island games. Although they're both large operations, be aware that they often book up several days in advance, so early reservations are advised.

Dinner Shows
Don Ho Show (☎ 923-3981; Waikiki Beachcomber Hotel, 2300 Kalakaua Ave; show $32, show & dinner $52; ⏰ 7pm Sun-Thu) Want a jolt of 1960s nostalgia? If sing-alongs and getting invited on stage to be razzed with jokes sounds like fun, Don Ho is the way to go. This saucy Honolulu musician has been playing the Waikiki tourist scene since 1962. Sitting behind an organ, he bounces between witty banter, chatting with the audience and singing his classic pop hits, like *Tiny Bubbles* and *I'll Remember You*, offering a good dose of kitsch in the process.

Cirque Hawaii Theatre (☎ 922-0017; 325 Seaside Ave; show $57, show & dinner $99; ⏰ 6:30pm & 8:30pm) The latest addition to O'ahu's entertainment scene, Cirque Hawaii brings a flamboyant troupe of acrobats, contortionists and trapeze artists to Waikiki's former IMAX theater. And boy, does it beat watching big-screen nature flicks. The international cast, some 32 members in all, puts on a daredevil choreographed Las Vegas–style extravaganza that keeps the audience gaping.

Nightclubs
Wave Waikiki (☎ 941-0424; www.wavewaikiki.com; 1877 Kalakaua Ave; admission $5-8; ⏰ 9pm-4am) Waikiki's hottest nightclub has its edgiest scene, with the emphasis on hip-hop, funk and alternative music. There are two levels, two bars, and everything from hip DJs to live bands and launch parties. The minimum age is 18 on Monday and Wednesday, 21 on other nights.

Zanzabar Nightclub (☎ 924-3939; Waikiki Trade Center, 2255 Kuhio Ave; admission $10; ⏰ 9pm-4am) This fashion-conscious club has something happening nightly. There's always dancing but the scene varies with the day of the week. Some nights it's Latin with salsa and reggaeton, others it's hip-hop, house and trance. The minimum age is 18 on Thursday and Sunday, 21 on other nights.

Tsunami's (☎ 923-8848; 2260 Kuhio Ave; admission free; ⏰ 10pm-1am) With surfboard decor and a thatch-framed bar, Tsunami's is unpretentious fun with loud rock and a lively crowd. There are usually live bands on weekends, DJs on other nights. The minimum age is 21.

Scruples (☎ 923-9530; 2310 Kuhio Ave; admission 18-21yr $15, 21 & over $5; ☺ 8pm-4am) An old standby, this casual, disco-style, Top 40 dance club in the center of Waikiki attracts a singles crowd. The minimum age is 18.

Moose McGillycuddy's (☎ 923-0751; 310 Lewers St; admission free; ☺ 9pm-3am Mon-Sat) A restaurant by day, Moose turns into a raucous nightspot by night with live Top 40 bands and dancing, as well as the occasional bikini contest thrown in. You have to be 21 years of age to get in.

Concerts

The **Waikiki Shell** (Kapi'olani Park), a beautiful outdoor amphitheater, hosts both classical and contemporary twilight music concerts, with Diamond Head as a backdrop. The British reggae band UB40 and Hawaii's hottest ukulele star Jake Shimabukuro are among the folks who've recently taken the stage here. The shell's concerts are handled by the box office at the **Neal S Blaisdell Center** (Map pp84-5; ☎ 591-2211; www.blaisdellcenter.com; 777 Ward Ave, Honolulu), so contact them for the latest schedules.

Tea Ceremonies

Urasenke Foundation of Hawaii (☎ 923-3059; 245 Saratoga Rd; ☺ 10am Wed & Fri) Ensconced in a Japanese teahouse, this cultural organization presents a traditional tea ceremony two mornings a week, bringing a rare bit of serenity to busy Saratoga Rd. Students dressed in kimonos perform the ceremony on tatami mats in a formal tearoom; for visitors who are participating, it's a meditative experience. The ceremony lasts about 45 minutes, but the sense of harmony lingers throughout the day. For a donation of $3, guests are served green tea made from 400-year-old bushes. Although it's not always essential, reservations by phone are appreciated and allow the center to plan ahead. And visitors are asked to wear socks, because Japanese custom dictates you leave your shoes at the door.

SHOPPING

There are hundreds of shops in Waikiki vying for tourist dollars, including souvenir stalls, swimsuit shops and fancy boutiques. Numerous high-end shops located along Kalakaua Ave sell designer clothing and fashionable accessories. The simplest approach to shopping here is just to stroll along the street and see what catches your fancy, or peruse the lobby shops of the more expensive hotels.

You'll never be far from one of the ubiquitous ABC stores, which stand on nearly every other street corner. They're the handiest and cheapest place to pick up vacation necessities, such as beach mats, sunblock and sundry goods.

Clothing

Bailey's Antique Shop (☎ 734-7628; 517 Kapahulu Ave) There's simply no place else like Bailey's, which has without a doubt the finest aloha shirt collection on O'ahu. Rotating racks include hundreds – nay, thousands – of antique and used aloha shirts in all sorts of colors and styles, from paper-thin silk and 1930s classics to the orchid prints Tom Selleck wore in *Magnum PI*. There's something for everyone here, with prices varying from $5 to several thousand dollars. Bailey's Antique Shop is a great place to go and look around – very retro, very cool, almost like a museum.

Quiksilver Boardriders Club (☎ 922-5900; 2301 Kuhio Ave) Whether you're a surfer looking for a board or surf paraphernalia or just want to buy some new threads with hip surfing motifs, Quiksilver is always fun to browse. This is the place to get your 'Eddie Would Go' (see p50) T-shirt, too.

Newt at the Royal (☎ 922-0062; Royal Hawaiian Hotel, 2259 Kalakaua Ave) With stylish flair, Newt specializes in Montecristi Panama hats, classic fedoras, sportswear, and aloha shirts in '40s and '50s themes. Everything's tropical, neat as a pin and lavish in color.

Town & Country Surf Shop (☎ 971-5599; Pacific Beach Hotel, 2490 Kalakaua Ave) If it has to do with surfing, or just hanging on the beach and watching surfers, you'll find it here. Casual island-style beachwear, T-shirts and tops are sold alongside top-quality O'ahu-made surfboards.

Avanti Fashions (☎ 924-3232; 2164 Kalakaua Ave) Come here to find fabulous cotton and silk aloha shirts in classic patterns reminiscent of the days when travelers arrived by luxury liner. Vintage styles at their finest.

Crazy Fish (☎ 923-0288; Royal Hawaiian Shopping Center, Kalakaua Ave) Crazy Fish is a local shop that makes its own stylish clothing for women and girls, focusing on dresses with handpainted tropical motifs, but also handbags and sandals.

Gifts & Crafts

Na Lima Mili Hulu No'eau (☎ 732-0865; 762 Kapahulu Ave; ⊗ Mon-Sat) Specializing in handmade feather lei, this shop is unique not only to Waikiki but to Hawaii as a whole. Aunty Mary Louise Kaleonahenahe Kekuewa and her daughter Paulette keep alive the ancient craft of feather lei–making here. They also teach Hawaiian schoolchildren and have produced the book *Feather Lei as an Art* to encourage revival of this native craft. The shop's name translates as 'the skilled hands that touch the feathers,' and skilled indeed they are. It can take days to produce a single lei. Their work is truly amazing and the place is an authentic Hawaiian treasure.

Martin & MacArthur (☎ 923-5333; Hyatt Regency Waikiki, 2424 Kalakaua Ave) You may just want one of everything on display in this fantastic shop, which sells the works of some of Hawaii's top craftspeople. Specialties include top-quality island-made furniture, koa boxes and bowls, ceramics, etched glass and quilted items.

Hawaiian Quilt Collection (☎ 599-7766; Hyatt Regency Waikiki, 2424 Kalakaua Ave) Here's an entire shop dedicated to the craft of Hawaii quiltmaking. Unlike the usual patchwork styles found on the US mainland, traditional Hawaiian quilts feature stylized tropical flora on a white background. All of the high-quality quilts here are made in Hawaii, though there are imported lower-priced ones, so look at the labels carefully.

Natural Hawaiian (☎ 921-2129; 2490 Kalakaua Ave) Unlike most shops on the Waikiki Beach stretch, this place specializes in Hawaii-made products. You can buy local-label aloha shirts, island woodwork, fish wind chimes, photography and classic posters. The shop also has a convenient headphone setup that allows you to listen to Hawaii music CDs before buying.

Little Hawaiian Craft Shop (☎ 926-2662; Royal Hawaiian Shopping Center, Kalakaua Ave) Living up to its name, you'll find crafted items of all sorts here, many of them made by local artisans. Trinkets such as *kukui*-nut key chains share shelf space with Hawaiian quilt-pattern kits, shark-tooth club replicas, fine necklaces made of Ni'ihau shells and high-quality koa bowls.

Art Mart (Monsarrat Ave; ⊗ 9am-4pm Sat & Sun) Dozens of artists hang their works along the fence on the southern side of the Honolulu Zoo every weekend, weather permitting. It's mostly contemporary paintings and island photography, as often as not sold by the artists themselves. Many of Hawaii's better-known painters got their start at this informal market, so who knows, you might discover the next Paradise Picasso right here.

Bob's Ukulele (☎ 921-5365; Waikiki Beach Marriott Resort, 2552 Kalakaua Ave) This is the place in Waikiki to shop for that uniquely Hawaiian instrument, the ukulele. Skip the low-priced imports (you can get those anywhere) and take a look at the Hawaii-made ukes handcrafted from native woods.

Island Treasures Antiques (☎ 922-8223; 2145 Kuhio Ave; ☺ 4-10pm Tue-Fri, 2-6pm Sat & Sun) Eclectic antiques and collectibles. With some 3000 sq ft of displays there's everything from hip-shaking hula dolls, old Hawaii license plates and Hawaiiana kitsch, to jewelry, period glassware and Asian porcelain.

Shopping Centers

Waikiki has several shopping centers, though most are chock-full of the brand-label stores you'd find in any large city. You'll find a better dose of local flavor at the following two centers.

International Market Place (☎ 923-9871; Kalakaua Ave) For inexpensive souvenirs, visit this market set under a sprawling banyan tree in the center of Waikiki. Nearly a hundred stalls sell everything from seashell necklaces to T-shirts, sarongs and hibiscus-print handbags.

Royal Hawaiian Shopping Center (☎ 922-0588; Kalakaua Ave) This is Waikiki's biggest shopping center and the shopping center with the most Hawaiian flavor. It has over 100 stores selling jewelry, handicrafts, beachwear, casual clothing, and designer labels like Hermès and Chanel.

GETTING THERE & AWAY

All flights to O'ahu land at Honolulu International Airport. For information on flying to O'ahu, see p244.

To/From the Airport

From the airport you can get to Waikiki by local bus, by airport shuttle services, by taxi or by rental car. A taxi to Waikiki from the airport will cost approximately $25 to $30, depending on the hotel. The main car-rental

agencies have booths or courtesy phones in the airport baggage-claim area.

The easiest way to drive to Waikiki from the airport is to take Hwy 92, which starts out as Nimitz Hwy and turns into Ala Moana Blvd, leading directly into Waikiki. Just follow the 'To Waikiki' signs. Although this route joins more local traffic, it's hard to get lost on it.

If you're into life in the fast lane, connect instead with the H1 Fwy heading east.

On the return to the airport from Waikiki, beware of the poorly marked interchange where H1 and Hwy 78 split; if you're not in the right-hand lane at that point, you could easily end up on Hwy 78. It takes about 20 minutes to get from Waikiki to the airport via H1 if you don't catch heavy traffic, but give yourself twice as much time at rush hour.

PUBLIC BUS

Travel time between the airport and Waikiki on city bus 19 or 20 is about an hour. The fare is $2. The buses run about once every 20 minutes from 5am to 11:15pm Monday to Friday, and until 11:45pm Saturday and Sunday. The bus stops at the roadside median on the airport terminal's second level, in front of the airline counters. There are two stops but the bus sometimes fills up so it's best to catch it at the first one, which is in front of Lobby 4. The second stop is between Lobby 6 and 7. Luggage is limited to what you can hold on your lap or store under your seat, the latter comparable to the space under an airline seat. In Waikiki, the buses make stops every third block or so along Kalia Rd, Saratoga Rd and Kuhio Ave. For more information on public buses, see p248.

SHUTTLE BUS

A few private companies, including **Super Shuttle** (☎ 841-2928, 877-247-8737) and **Reliable Express** (☎ 924-9292), offer shuttle service between the airport and Waikiki hotels from 6am to 10pm. The ride averages 45 minutes, but can be longer or shorter depending on how many passengers are dropped off before reaching your hotel.

Board these buses at the roadside median on the ground level, in front of the baggage-claim areas. You don't need a reservation from the airport to Waikiki but you need to call at least a few hours in advance for the return van to the airport. If you buy a round-trip ticket when you board at the airport it costs $14, otherwise the cost is $8 one way.

GETTING AROUND
Bus

O'ahu's public bus system, **TheBus** (☎ 848-5555; www.thebus.org), runs frequent routes in Waikiki. The buses pick up at stops all along Kuhio Ave, the main bus route in Waikiki. Buses 8, 19, 20 and 58 run between Waikiki and the Ala Moana Center, Honolulu's central transfer point. It is hardly worth checking the bus timetables as these buses come by every few minutes throughout the day. If you're heading to the 'Iolani Palace area from Waikiki, the most frequent and convenient service is bus 2. To go directly to Aloha Tower Marketplace or the Hawai'i Maritime Center from Waikiki, take bus 19 or 20. To get to Chinatown by bus from Waikiki, you can take bus 2 or 13 to N Hotel St in the center of Chinatown, or bus 19 or 20 to River St on the northwestern edge of Chinatown. Bus 4 runs between Waikiki and the University of Hawai'i. The buses from Waikiki to downtown Honolulu, Chinatown and the university run about every 10 minutes. For more information about TheBus, see p248.

Car & Motorcycle

Major car-rental companies have branches in the larger hotels, but if you're renting a car you're better off picking up at the airport where the rates are invariably cheaper.

Another option is to tool around on a moped. **Go Nuts Hawaii** (☎ 926-3367; 159 Ka'iulani Ave; ⏰ 8am-11pm) rents mopeds for $35 a day, $99 for three days or $199 a week. **Blue Sky Rentals** (☎ 947-0101; 1920 Ala Moana Blvd) charges $40 to $50 a day.

Parking cheaply in Waikiki can be a challenge, but if you're willing to park on the outskirts of Waikiki, you can get by without having to even drop a dime. At the western end of Waikiki, there's a large public parking lot at Ala Wai Yacht Harbor that has free parking with a 24-hour limit. At the eastern end of Waikiki, there's a large parking lot along Monsarrat Ave at Kapi'olani Park that has free parking with no time limit. And the parking lot on Kapahulu Ave

adjacent to the Honolulu Zoo has Waikiki's lowest metered rates at just 25¢ an hour.

The parking garage at Waikiki Trade Center is central and inexpensive by Waikiki standards; enter from Seaside Ave. Parking costs $7 all day on Saturday and Sunday, and $7 for overnight parking on weekdays from 5pm to 6am. From 6am to 5pm on weekdays, however, it's $2 per half-hour. .

Taxi

Taxis are readily available at the larger hotels, though you can also call for one. The biggest company, **TheCab** (☎ 422-2222) has a 24-hour dispatch, as do several other companies, including **Charley's Taxi** (☎ 955-2211) and **City Taxi** (☎ 524-2121).

Trolley

The **Waikiki Trolley** (☎ 593-2822; www.waikikitrolley.com), an open-air trolley-style bus service, connects Waikiki with main tourist sights in Honolulu and southeast O'ahu. Services run along set routes, with pass-holders free to jump on and off the trolley as often as they like.

Its signature 'red line' follows a beaten path around Honolulu's main shopping and sightseeing attractions, including Ala Moana Center, Honolulu Academy of Arts, 'Iolani Palace, Bishop Museum, Chinatown and the Ward Centre. The 'blue line,' also dubbed the 'Ocean Coast Line,' goes east from Waikiki, stopping at the Honolulu Zoo, Waikiki Aquarium, Diamond Head Crater and Sea Life Park. The 'yellow line' focuses on shopping centers with stops at Ala Moana Center, Ward Centre and the Aloha Tower Marketplace, and the 'pink line' is a shuttle that simply runs between Waikiki and the Ala Moana Center.

The lines operate from around 9am to 6pm, though the exact start and stop times vary with the line. Frequency varies from every eight minutes on the pink line to once an hour for the blue line. The main ticket kiosk and departure point for the Waikiki Trolley is at the Royal Hawaiian Shopping Center in Waikiki. One-day passes cost $25/12 per adult/child and four-day passes cost $45/18 per adult/child; they are good for unlimited travel on all four lines.

Keep in mind that these are essentially daytime services, so if you're planning on doing a lot of traveling after sunset, the public bus – which also sells passes – may work out better for you and will certainly take you further afield.

The **Hilo Hattie Trolley** (☎ 537-2926) is a free shopping shuttle designed to get you from your Waikiki hotel to the retailer's superstore on Nimitz Hwy, with stops at Ala Moana Center and Aloha Tower Marketplace en route. It runs every 20 minutes between Waikiki hotels and the shopping centers, though you can end up waiting longer for one that's not full.

Pearl Harbor Area

Once a sleepy harbor best known for its lustrous pearl oysters, Pearl Harbor was thrust into the world history books on December 7, 1941, with the surprise attack that launched the US into WWII. Vestiges of that fateful day, which President Roosevelt declared would live on in infamy, serve as vivid reminders of the tragedy that occurred here and the Pacific War that followed in its wake. A visit to the USS *Arizona* Memorial, the sunken ship that still holds the remains of the sailors who died during the attack, can be an incredibly moving experience. The sense of history and of the people whose lives were sacrificed permeates the memorial with a poignancy that time has not erased. To this day, more visitors to Hawaii visit Pearl Harbor than any other sight in the entire state.

Two other nearby WWII sites are also worth a look – the USS *Bowfin* Submarine Museum and Park, which is adjacent to the USS *Arizona* Memorial, and the battleship USS *Missouri*, on whose deck General Douglas MacArthur accepted the Japanese surrender marking the end of WWII. Together the sites offer visitors a unique glimpse of the events that began and ended WWII for the US.

Those looking for a little peace and quiet can head into the hills above Pearl Harbor to Keaiwa Heiau State Recreation Area, which holds an ancient medicinal temple and scenic trails. Oh, and anyone who likes to bargain needs to head over to the Aloha Stadium Swap Meet, which is so extensive it runs the entire perimeter of this landmark football stadium.

HIGHLIGHTS

- Touring the **USS Arizona Memorial** (p156) for a poignant sense of the events that thrust the USA into WWII

- Walking the deck of the **USS Missouri** (p157), where the formal end of WWII took place

- Learning about traditional Hawaiian medicine at **Keaiwa Heiau** (p159), a healing temple

- Hiking or mountain biking the scenic **'Aiea Loop Trail** (p159)

- Bargaining for the best deals at the **Aloha Stadium Swap Meet** (p159)

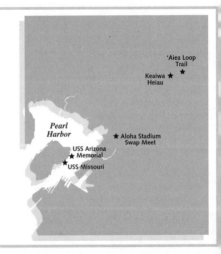

PEARL HARBOR AREA

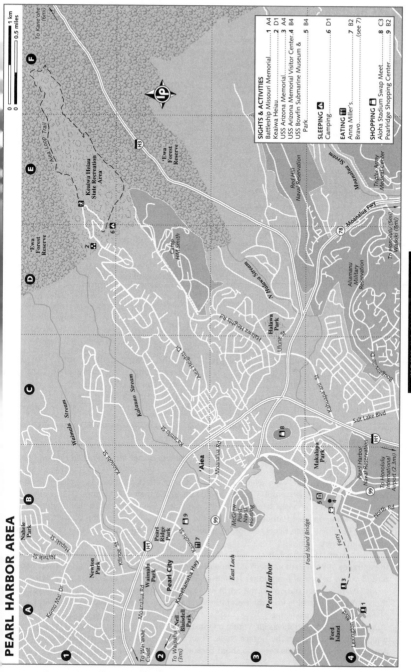

SIGHTS & ACTIVITIES
Battleship Missouri Memorial..........	1 A4
Keaiwa Heiau................................	2 D1
USS Arizona Memorial.....................	3 A4
USS Arizona Memorial Visitor Center.	4 B4
USS Bowfin Submarine Museum & Park.	5 B4

SLEEPING
Camping.......................................	6 D1

EATING
Anna Miller's.................................	7 B2
Bravo...	(see 7)

SHOPPING
Aloha Stadium Swap Meet..............	8 C3
Pearlridge Shopping Center............	9 B2

PEARL HARBOR

Of course, everyone affiliates the name Pearl Harbor with WWII, and indeed its trio of WWII memorials are the attraction here. But Pearl Harbor is a lot more than a tourist sight – it's the head of the US Pacific Naval Command, the largest naval operation in the world.

Sights & Activities

USS ARIZONA MEMORIAL

Over 1.5 million people 'remember Pearl Harbor' each year by visiting the USS *Arizona* Memorial, which is operated by the National Park Service.

The **visitor center** (☎ 422-2771, 24hr recorded information 422-0561; www.nps.gov/usar; admission free; ⏱ 7:30am-5pm daily except Thanksgiving, Christmas & New Year's Day) encompasses a museum and a theater, as well as the offshore memorial at the sunken USS *Arizona*. The 75-minute program includes a documentary film on the attack and a boat ride out to the memorial and back.

The 184ft memorial, built in 1962, sits directly over the *Arizona* but does not touch the sunken ship. The memorial contains the ship's bell and a wall inscribed with the names of the 1177 who perished onboard. The average age of the enlisted men on the Arizona was just 19.

From the memorial, the battleship is visible 8ft below the surface. The ship rests in about 40ft of water, and even now oozes a

gallon or two of oil each day. In the rush to recover from the attack and prepare for war, the navy exercised its option to leave the men in the sunken ship. They remain entombed in its hull, buried at sea.

Memorial Tour

Weather permitting, programs run every 15 minutes from 8am to 3pm (from 7:45am in summer) on a first-come, first-served basis. As soon as you arrive, pick up a ticket at the information booth (each person in the party must pick up their own ticket); the number printed on the ticket corresponds to the time the tour begins.

Generally, the shortest waits are in the morning, and if you arrive before the crowds, your wait may be less than half an hour; however, waits of a couple of hours are not uncommon. The summer months are the busiest, with an average of 4500 people taking the tour daily, and the day's allotment of tickets is often gone by noon.

Everything, including the boat ride, which is provided by the navy, is free. The memorial and all its facilities are accessible to the disabled.

Museum

Off the visitor center lobby, this little museum offers a glimpse of the era with photos from both Japanese and US military archives, showing Pearl Harbor before, during and after the attack. One photo is

---

SURPRISE ATTACK

On December 7, 1941, a wave of more than 350 Japanese planes attacked Pearl Harbor, home of the US Pacific Fleet.

Some 2335 US soldiers were killed during the two-hour attack. Of those, 1177 died in the battleship USS *Arizona* when it took a direct hit and sank in less than nine minutes. Twenty other US ships were sunk or seriously damaged and 347 airplanes were destroyed on that fateful day.

The attack upon Pearl Harbor, which jolted the USA into WWII, caught the US fleet totally by surprise. There had been two warnings, although the first occurred only 75 minutes before the attack. Both were dismissed.

At 6:40am on December 7, 1941, the USS *Ward* spotted a submarine conning tower approaching the entrance of Pearl Harbor. The *Ward* immediately attacked with depth charges and sank what turned out to be one of five midget Japanese submarines launched to penetrate the harbor.

At 7:02am a radar station on the north shore of O'ahu reported planes approaching. Even though they were coming from the west rather than the east, they were assumed to be American planes from the US mainland.

At 7:55am Pearl Harbor was hit. Within minutes the USS *Arizona* went down in a fiery inferno, trapping its crew beneath the surface. It wasn't until 15 minutes after the bombing started that American anti-aircraft guns began to shoot back at the Japanese warplanes.

CHECK YOUR BAGS AT THE TENT

Because of strictly enforced post-9/11 security measures, visitors to the USS *Arizona* Memorial and the USS *Missouri* Memorial face restrictions on what they can bring into these sites.

You are not allowed to bring into the USS *Arizona* Memorial visitor center, or onto either of the ship tours, *any* items that allow concealment, and this includes purses, camera bags, fanny packs, backpacks, diaper bags and the like. Also, cameras or video cameras larger than 12in are not allowed. It's not that these items are being searched and then allowed in; they simply can't be brought into the sites at all. Because of issues with theft from automobiles it is not advisable to lock any valuables in your car. Instead use the volunteer-run **storage facility** (6:30am-5:30pm) in the big tent at the Bowfin Park end of the parking lot, where they will store bags for $3 apiece.

---

of Harvard-educated Admiral Yamamoto, the brilliant military strategist who planned the attack on Pearl Harbor – even though he personally opposed going to war with the USA. Rather than relish the victory, Yamamoto stated after the attack that he feared Japan had 'awakened a sleeping giant and filled him with a terrible resolve.'

Pearl Harbor survivors, who act as volunteer historians, are sometimes available to talk with visitors about the day of the attack.

USS BOWFIN SUBMARINE MUSEUM & PARK

If you have to wait an hour or two for your USS *Arizona* Memorial tour to begin, take a stroll over to the adjacent **USS Bowfin Submarine Museum & Park** (423-1341; www.bowfin .org; admission to park free, admission to submarine & museum adult/child 4-12yr $10/3; 8am-5pm daily except Thanksgiving, Christmas & New Year's Day). The park contains the moored WWII submarine the USS *Bowfin*, as well as the Pacific Submarine Museum, which traces the development of submarines from their early origins to the nuclear age.

Commissioned in May 1943, the *Bowfin* sank 44 ships in the Pacific before the end of the war. Visitors can take a self-guided tour using a 30-minute recorded cassette. Children under four years of age are not allowed on the submarine for safety reasons.

You can stroll around the park for free, view the missiles and torpedoes displayed on the grounds, look through the periscopes and inspect a Japanese *kaiten*, a suicide torpedo. As the war was closing in on the Japanese homeland, the *kaiten* was developed in a last-ditch effort to ward off an invasion. It was the marine equivalent of the kamikaze pilot and his plane. A

volunteer was placed in the torpedo before it was fired, and he then piloted it to its target. The *kaiten* claimed at least one US ship, the USS *Mississinewa*, sunk off Ulithi Atoll in November 1944.

BATTLESHIP MISSOURI MEMORIAL

Walk the decks where General Douglas MacArthur accepted the Japanese surrender at the **Battleship Missouri Memorial** (973-2494; www.ussmissouri.org; Ford Island; self-guided tour adult/ child 4-12yr $16/8; 9am-5pm, ticket office 8am-4pm). You can poke about the USS *Missouri*'s officers' quarters, visit the wardroom that houses exhibits on the ship's history and examine the spot where a kamikaze pilot flew into the ship.

It's not possible to drive directly to Ford Island, because it's an active military facility. Instead, a trolleybus shuttles visitors to the *Missouri* from Bowfin Park, where the tickets are sold. If you're a history buff, the USS *Missouri* is a worthwhile sight, but if your time or money is more limited just visit the USS *Arizona* Memorial instead.

Festivals & Events

Memorial Day Held on the last Monday in May, this national public holiday honors soldiers killed in battle. The USS *Arizona* Memorial, which was dedicated on Memorial Day in 1962, has a special ceremony.

Pearl Harbor Day In commemoration of the 1941 Japanese attack on Pearl Harbor, special ceremonies are held at the USS *Arizona* Memorial on December 7, including a Hawaiian blessing, a wreath presentation and heartfelt accounts by survivors of the attack.

Getting There & Away

The USS *Arizona* Memorial visitor center and Bowfin Park are off Kamehameha Hwy (Hwy 99) on the Pearl Harbor Naval

---

MIGHTY MO

In 1998 the decommissioned USS *Missouri*, nicknamed 'Mighty Mo,' was brought to Ford Island by the nonprofit USS *Missouri* Memorial Association to add another element to Pearl Harbor's WWII sites.

The 887ft-long ship, one of four powerful Iowa-class battleships launched near the end of WWII, served as a flagship during the decisive battles of Iwo Jima and Okinawa. On September 2, 1945, the formal Japanese surrender that ended WWII took place on the battleship's deck. The USS *Missouri* is now docked just a few hundred yards from the sunken remains of the USS *Arizona;* together, the ships provide a unique set of historical bookends.

Launched in 1944, the *Missouri*, with its 13in-thick armor plating, enormous gun turrets and 65ft-long guns, was the last battleship ever built. In 1955, after service in the Korean War, it was placed in mothballs. Then, three decades later, it was awakened from rest during the heated Reagan-era military buildup, and after costly modernization, the *Missouri* was recommissioned in 1986. But the day of the battleship was gone, and this iconic battleship was finally and permanently decommissioned in 1992.

Several coastal cities clamored for the *Missouri*, but with the Pearl Harbor connection weighing heavily in its favor, Honolulu was chosen to become Mighty Mo's final home.

Reservation, southwest of the Aloha Stadium. If you're coming from Honolulu, take H1 west to exit 15A (*Arizona* Memorial/Stadium). Make sure to follow the highway signs for the USS *Arizona* Memorial, and not the signs for Pearl Harbor. There's plenty of free parking at the visitor center.

It's easy to get there by public bus. Bus 42 'Ewa Beach is the most direct bus from Waikiki, taking about an hour. Bus 20 covers the same route, but it makes a stop at the airport, adding about 15 minutes to the travel time.

The private **Hawaii Super Transit** (☎ 841-2989; one way/return $4/8) picks up people from hotels in Waikiki several times a day for a van ride to the visitor center. The ride takes about 40 minutes.

Avoid private boat cruises to Pearl Harbor that leave from Kewalo Basin, as they don't stop at the visitor center and their passengers are not allowed to board the USS *Arizona* Memorial.

PEARL CITY
pop 31,400
This urban enclave is home to lots of military personnel and civilians who work on the nearby military bases. Although it's usually written off by casual visitors, it does have a couple of good restaurants worth sniffing out and if you're up for a shopping spree, the Pearlridge Shopping Center is second only to Ala Moana Center in size.

If you're just passing through and not going to Pearl City itself, stay on H1 and avoid the parallel Kamehameha Hwy (Hwy 99), which is all stop-and-go traffic through blocks of fast-food restaurants and shopping malls.

Eating
Bravo (☎ 487-5544; 98-115 Kaonohi St; lunch specials $6-8, mains $8-18; ☺ 11am-10pm Sun-Thu, to 11pm Fri & Sat) This smart Italian-style eatery makes the perfect seafood fettuccine swimming with clams, shrimp and calamari, and also has some good-value lunch deals served until 2pm.

THE AUTHOR'S CHOICE

Anna Miller's (☎ 487-2421; Pearlridge Shopping Center, cnr Kaonohi St & Kamehameha Hwy; pie slice $3, mains $4-16; ☺ 24hr) This is *the* place to have breakfast, but you can pick your own hours as the bacon sizzles day and night. The huge omelettes and the delicious hot sandwiches are really just the side-show here. It's the luscious pies that pack the house. If you've been good today, reward yourself with a slice of the decadently delicious *haupia* chocolate pie, a cross-cultural delight that combines Hawaiian coconut pudding with Bavarian chocolate. Should the last piece be gone, fret not – the strawberry pie is no slacker either.

DETOUR: RIDE THE RAILS

A monorail in Hawaii? Yes it's true – though this baby runs barely a mile, connecting Uptown Pearlridge to Downtown Pearlridge, two wings of the Pearlridge Shopping Center. For just 50¢ you can hop aboard. Not only will you get a bird's-eye view of Pearl Harbor, but you'll also cross over the green oasis of O'ahu's largest watercress farm. To get to the Pearlridge Shopping Center from the west, take the Kamehameha Hwy and turn right on Kaonohi St.

Shopping

The **Pearlridge Shopping Center** (☎ 488-0981; 98-1005 Moanalua Rd), a massive shopping mall situated between the H1 and Kamehameha Hwy, has all of the usual mall stores, including a large Borders bookstore and some interesting local shops like Cinnamon Girl, which specializes in island-made women's wear (see the boxed text Local Girl Makes Good, p107).

KEAIWA HEIAU STATE RECREATION AREA

This 334-acre **state park** (☎ 483-2511; 'Aiea Heights Dr; admission free; ⏰ 7am-sunset) in 'Aiea, north of Pearl Harbor, contains an ancient medicinal temple, campgrounds, picnic facilities and a scenic trail.

From Honolulu, head west on Hwy 78 and then take the Stadium/Aiea turnoff onto Moanalua Rd. Turn right onto 'Aiea Heights Dr at the second traffic light. From here the road winds up 2.5 miles to the park.

Bus 11 (Honolulu–'Aiea Heights) serves this area; however, the bus stops 1.25 miles south of the park entrance, and it is another 600yd from the entrance to the campsites.

Sights & Activities
KEAIWA HEIAU

Marking the park entrance is Keaiwa Heiau, a 160ft-long stone temple built in the 1600s and used by *kahuna lapa'au* (herbalist healers). The kahuna used hundreds of medicinal plants and grew many on the grounds surrounding the heiau. Among those still found here are *noni*, whose pungent yellow fruits were used to treat heart disease; *kukui*, the nuts of which are an effective laxative; and ti leaves, which were wrapped around a sick person to break a fever. Not only did the herbs have medicinal value, but the heiau itself was also considered to possess life-giving energy, and the *kahuna lapa'au* was able to draw from the powers of both. Today people wishing to be healed still place offerings within the heiau. The offerings reflect the multiplicity of Hawaii's cultures: New Age crystals and sake cups sit beside flower lei and rocks wrapped in ti leaves.

'AIEA LOOP TRAIL

Popular with both hikers and mountain cyclists, the 'Aiea Loop Trail offers up

BARGAIN HUNTING

OK, so where's the best place to hunt for bamboo back scratchers, '50s kitsch ceramics and cheap aloha shirts? Hands-down the honors go to the **Aloha Stadium Swap Meet** (☎ 486-6704; 99-500 Salt Lake Blvd; admission 50¢; ⏰ 6am-3pm Wed, Sat & Sun; 🚍 20 & 42) at the Aloha Stadium in the Pearl Harbor area, a couple of blocks northwest of the USS *Arizona* Memorial.

The Aloha Stadium, best known as the host to nationally televised football games and top-name music concerts, transforms itself three days a week into Hawaii's biggest and best swap meet.

For local flavor, this flea market is hard to beat, with some 1500 vendors selling an amazing variety of items from macadamia nuts to collectibles, antiques and crafts. In keeping with the flea market's name, flowery aloha designs prevail on everything from daypacks and car-seat covers to bikinis, board shorts and beach towels. Oh, and then there are the endless racks of T-shirts – more than you might imagine one island could hold. It's also a fun place to mingle.

This is such a big event that there are private shuttle-bus services to the swap meet from Waikiki ($8 to $10 return) that operate every hour or so on meet days; for information call **Reliable Shuttle** (☎ 924-9292) or **Hawaii Super Transit** (☎ 841-2928).

By car, take the H1 west from Honolulu, get off at the Stadium/Halawa exit and follow signs for 'Stadium.'

sweeping vistas of Pearl Harbor, Diamond Head and the Ko'olau Range. The 4.5-mile 'Aiea Loop Trail begins at the top of the park's paved loop road, next to the rest rooms, and comes back out at the campground, about a third of a mile below the start of the trail. This easy hike takes 2½ to three hours.

The first part of the trail goes through a eucalyptus forest and runs along the ridge. Other trees on the way include ironwood, Norfolk Island pine, guava and native ohia lehua, which has fluffy, red flowers. About two-thirds of the way in, the wreckage of a C-47 cargo plane that crashed in 1943 can be spotted through the foliage on the eastern ridge.

Sleeping

Keaiwa Heiau State Recreation Area can accommodate 100 campers, most sites with their own picnic table and barbecue grill. Campsites are not crowded together, but because many are open, there's not a lot of privacy either. If you're camping in winter, make sure your gear is waterproof because it rains frequently at this 880ft elevation. The park has rest rooms, showers, a pay phone and drinking water. There's a resident caretaker by the front gate, and the gate is locked at night for security.

As with all O'ahu public campgrounds, camping is not permitted on Wednesday and Thursday, and permits must be obtained in advance. For details, see p230.

Southeast O'ahu

The scenery is so stunning along this crater-studded coast that virtually every TV show or movie that's ever filmed on O'ahu has levitated over to the island's southeast side to capture background footage. Bring a camera and see what they've come for. And bring a bathing suit, too, as the sights beneath the surface are equally awesome.

With mountains on one side and a sea full of bays and beaches on the other, the drive along the coast rates as the finest outing on the island. The highway rises and falls as it winds its way around the tip of the Ko'olau Range, looking down on boldly stratified rocks, lava sea cliffs and other fascinating geological formations. The hiking trail to the top of landmark Diamond Head crater, the snorkeling mecca at Hanauma Bay and the island's most famous bodysurfing beaches are all just a short ride from Waikiki.

There's no question that natural diversions and ooh-and-ah scenery take top honors, but southeast O'ahu offers other attractions. Kahala, the island's most exclusive haunt, houses O'ahu's premier getaway hotel for those with the means. Hawai'i Kai, a young community abounding in water views, is etching out a place for itself on the dining and nightlife scene. And then there's rural Waimanalo, an old-style Hawaiian community boasting gorgeous beaches and a breadbasket of small farms.

Explore the hidden treasures: a monument to a Hawaiian sumo champ, the mansion of an eccentric billionaire and a cactus garden in a forgotten crater. So go enjoy the views, but take your time – this ride is worthy of a whole day and then some.

HIGHLIGHTS

- Donning a snorkel and exploring the amazing sea life at **Hanauma Bay** (p166)
- Treating your tastebuds to Hawaii Regional Cuisine at **Roy's** (p166)
- Swimming to your heart's delight at beautiful **Waimanalo Bay** (p169)
- Climbing **Diamond Head Trail** (p163) for a top-notch view
- Tipping a mug of the finest Hawaiian suds at **Kona Brewing Company** (p165)

SOUTHEAST O'AHU

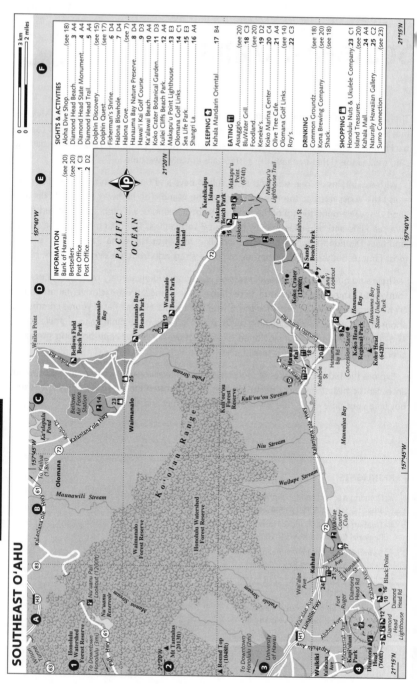

INFORMATION
Bank of Hawaii.....................(see 20)
Bestsellers........................(see 20)
Post Office...........................1 C3
Post Office...........................2 D2

SIGHTS & ACTIVITIES
Aloha Dive Shop....................(see 18)
Diamond Head Beach....................3 A4
Diamond Head State Monument....4 A4
Diamond Head Trail....................5 A4
Dolphin Discovery.................(see 15)
Dolphin Quest.....................(see 17)
Fisherman's Shrine....................6 D4
Halona Blowhole.......................7 D4
Halona Cove........................(see 7)
Hanauma Bay Nature Preserve......8 D4
Hawai'i Kai Golf Course...............9 D3
Ka'alawai Beach......................10 A4
Koko Crater Botanical Garden.......11 D3
Kuilei Cliffs Beach Park.............12 A4
Makapu'u Point Lighthouse.........13 E3
Olomana Golf Links...................14 C1
Sea Life Park........................15 E3
Shangri La...........................16 A4

SLEEPING
Kahala Mandarin Oriental.............17 B4

EATING
Assaggio...........................(see 20)
BluWater Grill.......................18 C3
Foodland...........................(see 20)
Keneke's.............................19 D2
Koko Marina Center...................20 C4
Olive Tree Cafe......................21 A4
Olomana Golf Links................(see 14)
Roy's................................22 C3

DRINKING
Common Groundz.....................(see 18)
Kona Brewing Company...............(see 20)
Shack..............................(see 18)

SHOPPING
Honolulu Nuts & Ukulele Company..23 C1
Island Treasures...................(see 20)
Kahala Mall..........................24 A4
Naturally Hawaiian Gallery...........25 C2
Sumo Connection....................(see 23)

DIAMOND HEAD

One of the best-known landmarks in the Pacific, Diamond Head is familiar to every visitor to O'ahu as the backdrop to Waikiki. The 760ft mountain is a tuff cone and crater formed by a violent steam explosion deep beneath the surface long after most of O'ahu's volcanic activity had stopped.

The Hawaiians called it Le'ahi and at its summit they built a *luakini* heiau, a type of temple used for human sacrifices. But ever since 1825, when British sailors found calcite crystals sparkling in the sun and mistakenly thought they'd struck it rich, it's been called Diamond Head.

In 1909 the US Army began building Fort Ruger at the edge of the crater. They constructed a network of tunnels and topped the rim with cannon emplacements, bunkers and observation posts. Reinforced during WWII, the fort is a silent sentinel whose guns have never been fired. Today there's a Hawaii National Guard base inside the crater.

More relevant to visitors, the crater is the site of **Diamond Head State Monument** (Diamond Head Rd; admission per person/vehicle $1/5; ☉ 6am-6pm; 🚌 22 & 58), a visitor facility with picnic tables and a hiking trail up to the crater summit. By car from Waikiki, take Monsarrat Ave to Diamond Head Rd and then take the right turn after Kapi'olani Community College into the crater.

Sights & Activities

DIAMOND HEAD TRAIL

The trail to Diamond Head summit was built in 1910 to service the military observation stations located along the crater rim. Today it's a popular hike.

Don't expect a walk in the park, as it's a fairly steep hike with a 560ft elevation gain. It is, however, only 0.75 miles to the top and plenty of people of all ages hike up. It takes about one hour return. The trail is open and hot, so wear sunscreen and pack water.

The crater is dry and scrubby with kiawe, native grasses and wildflowers. As you start

---

SHANGRI OOH LA LA

Tobacco heiress Doris Duke had a lifelong passion for Islamic art and architecture, inspired by a visit to the Taj Mahal on a voyage to India at the age of 23. Over the next half-century she traveled the globe from Indonesia to Istanbul, collecting some 3500 objects. In the 1930s she stopped on O'ahu on a worldwide cruise, fell in love with the island and decided to build **Shangri La** (☎ 866-385-3849; www.shangrilahawaii.org; tours $25; ☉ Wed-Sun Oct-Aug), her stunning home on Black Point, in the shadow of Diamond Head.

Duke's 15,000 sq ft home so uniquely incorporates Islamic design that it is like no other in Hawaii. Her bedroom, for example, adopts Mughal design from the Taj Mahal, including richly decorated marble entrances and intricately carved lattice window screens called *jalis*. Duke appreciated the finer points – the spirit more than the grand scale – of the wonders she had seen, and she made her Shangri La into a harmonious sanctuary rather than an ostentatious mansion. One of the true beauties of the place is the balance her home maintains with its environment. Duke's spirit of aloha expresses itself in the way the interiors open to embrace gardens and the ocean. One whole windowed wall of the living room looks out upon Diamond Head.

Duke's extensive collection of Islamic art includes vivid gemstone-studded enamels, glazed ceramic paintings and silk *suzanis*, intricate needlework tapestries that were part of young women's dowries. Throughout the estate, gardens and courtyards weave in and out of cool interiors and symmetrical fountains. Collections blend with the architecture to represent a theme or region as in the Damascus Room, the restored interior of a 19th-century Syrian house, and the Turkish Room, a sparkling array of mosaic floors and richly painted panels.

The house can be visited only by joining a tour. All tours leave from the Honolulu Academy of Arts (p83) and last 2½ hours, about 90 minutes of which is touring at Shangri La itself; the rest is spent watching a brief background video and traveling to and from Shangri La by van. Since the tours take a maximum of 12 people and are run only four to six times a day, reservations should be made well in advance. Shangri La is captivating not just for its collection but also for the unique glimpse it provides into the life of one of America's richest women, who, like her contemporary Howard Hughes, was eccentric, reclusive and absolutely fascinating.

up the trail, the summit is visible ahead, a bit to the left at roughly 11 o'clock. About 20 minutes up the trail, you enter a long, dark tunnel. Because the tunnel curves, you don't see light until you get close to the end. It's a little spooky, but there's a handrail and your eyes will adjust to make out shadows in the dark. Nevertheless, the park advises hikers to bring a flashlight.

When you step out into the light, you're immediately faced with a steep 99-step staircase, followed by a shorter tunnel, a narrow spiral staircase inside an unlit bunker and the last of the trail's 271 steps. Be careful when you reach the top – there are steep drops.

From the summit you're rewarded with a fantastic 360-degree view that takes in the southeastern coast to Koko Head and the leeward coast to Barbers Point, with Kapi'olani Park below. You can also see Diamond Head Lighthouse, coral reefs, sailboats and surfers waiting for waves on the coast below.

KUILEI CLIFFS BEACH PARK

In the shadow of Diamond Head, this **beach park** (Diamond Head Rd; 🚍 14) draws both surfers and windsurfers. Conditions are suitable for intermediate to advanced windsurfers, and when the swells are up it's a great place for wave riding. The beach has showers but no other facilities. You can access the beach from the parking lot just beyond the lighthouse. At the other end of the park, 0.5 miles further north, there's a little garden of flowering cacti and a good view across a turquoise sea all the way to Black Point and Kahala.

DIAMOND HEAD BEACH

This narrow sandy beach is popular with gay men, who pull off Diamond Head Rd onto the short, dead-end Beach Rd and then walk north along the shore about five minutes to find a little seclusion and sunbathe *au naturel* on the rocks.

KAHALA

The affluent seaside suburb of Kahala is home to many of Honolulu's wealthiest residents, the island's most exclusive resort hotel and the Waialae Country Club, a PGA tournament golf course.

The area's main drive, Kahala Ave, is lined with expensive waterfront homes,

though most are rather low-key. Don't expect to see much from the road, as hedges and estate fences keep the more exclusive properties out of sight, and the thick line of houses blocks out virtually any view of the sea. Between the homes, there are a half-dozen shoreline access points that provide a right-of-way to the beach, but the swimming conditions aren't notable – it's mostly shallow, with sparse pockets of sand.

Festivals & Events

The **Sony Open** in Hawaii, a PGA tour golf tournament, takes place in early January at the Waialae Country Club in Kahala, with a multimillion-dollar purse.

Sleeping

Kahala Mandarin Oriental (☎ 739-8888, 800-367-2525; www.mandarin-oriental.com; 5000 Kahala Ave; r from $345, with ocean view $735, presidential ste $4400; 🅿 🛇 🖳 🖳) Hang with the stars at O'ahu's top luxury hotel. On a private beach in swank Kahala, this is the favorite of celebs and other rich and famous, who love the paparazzi-free seclusion. The guest list is Hawaii's most regal and includes Britain's Prince Charles, Spain's King Juan Carlos and the last seven US presidents. Elegance and class reign supreme but this grand dame still maintains an appealing Hawaiian casualness. Staff who have been working here for decades and guests who return every year know each other by name, and it's that intimacy that really separates it from the Waikiki pack.

Eating

Olive Tree Cafe (☎ 737-0303; 4614 Kilauea Ave; mains $5-12; 🕑 5-10pm) The motto on the wall says it all at this busy eatery next to the Kahala Mall: 'Mostly Greek – not so fast food.' Highlights include fresh fish souvlaki and feta salads. Alcohol isn't served, but you can bring your own, and there's a Greek deli next door with a good selection of imported wines.

Shopping

Kahala Mall (☎ 732-7736; 4211 Wai'alae Ave; 🕑 10am-9pm Mon-Sat, to 5pm Sun) The area's largest mall has a bit of everything, from an eight-screen movie complex to nearly 100 shops, including a supermarket and a Barnes & Noble bookshop.

HAWAI'I KAI

Built around a marina and bordered by mountains, bays and parks, this suburban community designed by steel tycoon Henry J Kaiser (he's the Kai in Hawai'i Kai) may strike some to be a bit too meticulously planned, but for residents it certainly has it all: condos, houses, shopping centers, a golf course and an ever-increasing selection of good restaurants. As a central point for those traveling around southeast O'ahu it's an ideal place to stop and have a drink or a bite, and a couple of inviting B&Bs make it worth considering as a home base as well.

Information

Bank of Hawaii (☎ 397-4010; Koko Marina Center, 7192 Kalaniana'ole Hwy)

Bestsellers (☎ 394-2378; Koko Marina Center, 7192 Kalaniana'ole Hwy; ⏰ 9am-9pm)

Post Office (☎ 800-275-8777; 7040 Hawai'i Kai Dr)

Activities

Aloha Dive Shop (☎ 395-5922; www.alohadiveshop .com; Hawai'i Kai Shopping Center, 377 Keahole St; 2-tank dive $100; ⏰ 7am-5pm Mon-Sat) An established five-star PADI facility that offers boat dives for all levels around Maunalua Bay. If you've never dived before, staff will show you the ropes and take you to calm, relatively shallow waters. They'll also take snorkelers out on the boat for $40.

Hawai'i Kai Golf Course (☎ 395-2358; 8902 Kalaniana'ole Hwy; executive course green fees $38-43, championship course green fees $83-93; ⏰ 6:30am-6pm) Features two 18-hole courses: the par 72 championship course, which has the more challenging greens and best views, and the smaller par 54 executive course designed by Robert Trent Jones Sr. Ask about discounted twilight specials.

Sleeping

Aloha B&B (☎ 395-6694; http://home.hawaii.rr.com /alohaphyllis; 909 Kahauloa Pl; r with shared bathroom incl breakfast $60-75; P 🐕) See for yourself what life in Hawaii is really like at this contemporary home perched above Hawai'i Kai, just minutes from restaurants and the beach. The ocean view is fabulous, especially from the lanai, where a breakfast of homemade muffins and fruit is served each morning. Call in advance to make a reservation.

J&B's Haven (☎ 396-9462; http://home.hawaii.rr .com/jnbshaven; Kahena St; r incl breakfast $75-85;

DETOUR: KA'ALAWAI BEACH

Enjoy a taste of the good life at this quiet sandy beach sandwiched between Diamond Head and exclusive Black Point. To get there, take Diamond Head Rd northeast along the coast, past Kuilei Cliffs Beach Park, and at the point where it merges with Kahala Ave, turn right onto Kulamanu St. After 0.2 miles you'll reach Kulamanu Pl, the short road that leads to the beach. There's no parking on Kulamanu Pl but you can park on Kulamanu St and then walk down to the water.

P 🐕) Cozy accommodations, friendly hosts and terrific breakfasts are the hallmarks of this smoke-free B&B run by a mother and daughter team from England. Both guest rooms have floor-to-ceiling windows with mountain views; the pricier room also has air-con. Reservations must be made by calling in advance.

Eating

BluWater Grill (☎ 395-6224; Hawai'i Kai Shopping Center, 377 Keahole St; mains $14-20; ⏰ 11am-11pm Mon-Thu, to midnight Fri & Sat, 10am-11pm Sun) This breezy open-air restaurant overlooking the water serves superb kiawe-grilled fare with creative glazes and such delights as macadamia nut–crusted prawns with Thai chili. One of O'ahu's best new restaurants, it's a perfect place for a relaxing lunch or dinner.

Assaggio (☎ 396-0756; Koko Marina Center, 7192 Kalaniana'ole Hwy; mains $12-25; ⏰ 11:30am-2:30pm & 5-9:30pm Sun-Thu, to 10pm Fri & Sat) If you're in the mood for Italian, this waterfront restaurant boasts an extensive menu of reliable dishes from spicy clams casino to its signature chicken Assaggio spiked with garlic and wine. *Delizioso!*

Koko Marina Center (☎ 395-4737; 7192 Kalaniana'ole Hwy) For a quick eat on the run, stop here; you'll find a bevy of eateries selling ice cream, bagels and plate lunches. It also has a 24-hour Foodland supermarket.

Drinking & Entertainment

Kona Brewing Company (☎ 394-5662; Koko Marina Center, 7192 Kalaniana'ole Hwy; ⏰ 11am-11pm) Hang over the marina on the tiki torch–lit lanai and enjoy Hawaii's best brews, with names like Longboard Lager and Castaway IPA.

THE AUTHOR'S CHOICE

Roy's (☎ 396-7697; Hawai'i Kai Towne Plaza, 6700 Kalaniana'ole Hwy; pupu $7-12, mains $20-32; ⏱ 5:30-10pm Mon-Fri, 5-10pm Sat & Sun; 🗱) Foodies from far and wide flock to this high-energy place for a special night out or just to enjoy the delicious *pupu* (snacks) at the bar. Chef Roy Yamaguchi is a prominent force behind the popularity of Hawaii Regional Cuisine, which emphasizes using fresh local ingredients and blending the lighter aspects of European cooking with Polynesian and Asian influences. The restaurant centers around an exhibition kitchen where Roy orchestrates an impressive troupe of sous cooks and chefs. A melt-in-your-mouth treat that shouldn't be missed is the blackened *'ahi* (yellowfin tuna), seared outside, rare inside and served with a fiery wasabi sauce. If raw fish isn't your thing, the hibachi-grilled miso steak is a winner, too. For dessert, the hot chocolate soufflé is pure decadence – ask for two spoons and share it with a friend. Attentive service and perfectly matched wines by the glass add a cheery glow to the night. Ask about the nightly prix-fixe menu with a choice of appetizer, main and a dessert for just $33. Reservations are advised and can be made weeks in advance – request a table with a sunset view.

This is an unbeatable spot for a sunset drink. There's plenty to eat with your beer, too, from crab cakes to wood-fired pizza. There's live Hawaiian entertainment several nights a week.

Common Groundz (☎ 394-9777; Hawai'i Kai Shopping Center, 377 Keahole St; ⏱ 5:30am-9pm Mon-Fri, 6:30-9pm Sat & Sun) Organic free-trade coffee, homemade desserts and a cool view of the harbor set the tone at this progressive little coffee shop. A ukulele player performs some evenings.

Shack (☎ 396-1919; Hawai'i Kai Shopping Center, 377 Keahole St; ⏱ 11am-2am) This casual sports bar is the place to come if you want to watch the football game on a wall of TVs. Good fresh fish sandwiches and *pupu*, too.

Shopping

Island Treasures (☎ 396-8827; Koko Marina Center, 7192 Kalaniana'ole Hwy; ⏱ 10am-6pm Mon-Thu, to 8pm Fri & Sat, to 4pm Sun) You'll find a quality collection of koa woodwork, prints, etched glass and jewelry made by island artists at this little shop.

HANAUMA BAY NATURE PRESERVE

A wide, sheltered bay of sapphire and turquoise waters set in a rugged volcanic ring, Hanauma (Curved Bay) is a real gem. You come here for the scenery, you come here for the beach, but above all you come here to snorkel – and if you've never been snorkeling before, this is the perfect place to start.

Hanauma's biggest draw is the sheer number and variety of fish. From the overlook you can peer into crystal waters and view the entire coral reef that stretches across the width of the bay. You're bound to see schools of glittering silver fish, the bright blue flash of parrotfish and perhaps a sea turtle. To see an even more colorful scene, put on a mask, jump in and view it from beneath the surface.

Information

Hanauma is both a county beach park and a **state underwater park** (☎ 396-4229; admission $5, child under 13yr free; ⏱ 6am-6pm, to 7pm Apr-Oct, to 10pm Sat, closed Tue). It has a snack bar, lifeguards, showers, rest rooms and disabled access.

The beachside **concession stand** (☎ 394-6644; snorkel set per day $6; ⏱ 8am-5pm Nov-Mar, to 6pm Apr-Oct) rents snorkels, masks and fins. You'll need to hand over either $30, a credit card or your car-rental keys as a deposit. Dive-light rentals, for Saturday night snorkeling, cost $5.

Activities

There's a little center at the entrance to the nature preserve, where all guests are shown an eight-minute video illustrating the bay's ecology. Kids will also enjoy the center's hands-on interactive displays that highlight some of the more colorful creatures living in the bay.

SNORKELING

Snorkeling is good at Hanauma Bay year-round. Mornings are typically better than afternoons, as swimmers haven't yet stirred up the sand.

The large, sandy opening in the middle of the coral, known as the **Keyhole**, is the best place for novice snorkelers. The deepest water is 10ft, though it's very shallow over the coral – bring diving gloves if you have them. The Keyhole is well protected and usually swimming-pool calm.

For confident snorkelers, it's better on the outside of the reef, where there are larger coral heads, bigger fish and fewer people; to get there look for the channel at the southwestern end of the beach, or ask the lifeguard. Keep in mind that because of the channel current it's generally easier getting out than it is getting back in. Don't attempt to swim outside the reef when the water is rough or choppy. Not only will the channel current be strong, but the sand will be stirred up and visibility poor anyway.

DIVING
Divers have the whole bay to play in, with clear water, coral gardens, sea turtles and lots of fish. Beware of currents when the surf is up; surges near the Witches Brew, on the right-hand side; and the Moloka'i Express, a treacherous current that runs just outside the mouth of the bay.

TREAT IT WITH ALOHA

Once a favorite fishing spot, the fish population at Hanauma Bay had been nearly depleted by the time the bay was designated a marine-life conservation district in 1967. Once they were protected instead of hunted, the fish began to swarm back in by the thousands. The only problem was that the bay began to attract so many visitors that the ecological balance went topsy-turvy. Snorkelers feeding the fish peas and bread let to a burst in fish populations beyond naturally sustainable levels, and radically altered the variety of fish in the bay.

In the late 1990s the parks department instituted a second plan to save Hanauma Bay, this time from the people who were loving it to death. Among other things, it banned fish feeding by snorkelers, which has led to a more natural balance of fish species; it added entrance fees to help reduce the number of visitors (it had been in excess of two million a year – it's now half that); and it built an educational facility to teach snorkelers environmentally friendly ways of enjoying the bay's natural beauty. So tread lightly and have fun.

Getting There & Away
Hanauma Bay is about 10 miles from Waikiki via the Kalaniana'ole Hwy (Hwy 72). The parking lot ($1), which is at the east side of the driveway into the preserve, sometimes fills up before noon, so the earlier you get there the better.

Bus 22, called the Beachbus, runs between Waikiki and Hanauma Bay. Buses leave Waikiki from 8:15am to 4:25pm; the best place to pick one up is at the corner of Kuhio Ave and Namahana St, as that's the first stop and it often fills up shortly after. Buses leave from Hanauma Bay to return to Waikiki from 11am to 5:40pm. Buses in each direction run at least once an hour.

The Waikiki trolley (p152) also stops at Hanauma Bay.

KOKO HEAD REGIONAL PARK
The entire Koko Head area is a county regional park that includes Hanauma Bay, Koko Head, Halona Blowhole, Sandy Beach Park and Koko Crater. Note that public bus 22 stops at Hanauma Bay and Sandy Beach Park but makes no stops between the two.

Lana'i Lookout
About 0.75 miles past Hanauma, this roadside lookout rewards visitors with a view out to several Hawaiian islands: Lana'i to the right, Maui in the middle and Moloka'i to the left. It's also a good vantage point for getting a close-up look at the curious rock formations that form the sea cliffs along the coast here.

Fisherman's Shrine
Keep your eye peeled toward the ocean and on the highest point, on a sea cliff known locally as Bamboo Ridge, you'll spot a temple-like mound of rocks surrounding a statue of O-Jizosan, guardian of fishermen. This fishing shrine, decked in lei and surrounded by sake cups, was erected by Japanese fishermen to honor those lost while fishing off the point. There's a little roadside pull-off in front of the shrine.

Halona Cove
Take your lover down for a roll in the sand at this lovely pocket cove made famous in the 1953 movie *From Here to Eternity*. The steamy love scene that Burt Lancaster and Deborah Kerr enjoyed as the surf washed

over them on this beach is considered by many film critics as the finest ever captured on celluloid. You can gaze down onto the cove from the Halona Blowhole parking lot and if you look closely you'll be able to make out a faint path leading down to the beach. The path is steep but passable and begins just a few yards south of the Halona Blowhole parking lot.

Halona Blowhole

You can follow the tour buses to this one. At Halona Blowhole ocean waves surge through a submerged tunnel in the rock and spout up through a hole in the ledge. It's all preceded by a gushing sound, created by the air that's being forced out of the tunnel by rushing water. The action depends on water conditions – sometimes it's so barely discernible you'll wonder if it's even there, while at other times it's a real showstopper. Avoid the temptation to ignore the warning signs and walk down onto the ledge, as more than a few unsuspecting people have been tragically swept off the ledge by rogue waves.

Sandy Beach Park

Sandy Beach is the most dangerous beach on the island, when measured in terms of lifeguard rescues and broken necks. It has a punishing shorebreak, a powerful backwash and strong rip currents.

Needless to say, it's extremely popular with bodysurfers who know their stuff. It's equally popular with spectators, who gather to watch the bodysurfers being tossed around in the transparent waves.

WILD RIDE

Sandy Beach is the bodysurfer's ultimate challenge. When the tradewinds are strong here, a south swell pops up a riptide with a powerful backlash. Those riding it often get upended in the shorebreak, their bodies tossed inverted and head hanging upside down as the wave begins to crash back to the sand. Hundreds of people are injured at Sandy Beach each year, some with just broken arms and dislocated shoulders, but others with serious spinal injuries. The upside? Well, for experienced shorebreak riders, the action is a thrill that has no parallel anywhere else.

Sandy Beach is wide, very long and, yes, sandy. When the swells are big, board surfers hit the left side of the beach. Red flags flown on the beach indicate hazardous water conditions. Even if you don't notice the flags, always check with the lifeguards before entering the water.

Not all the action is in the water, however. The grassy strip on the inland side of the parking lot is used by people looking skyward for their thrills – it's both a hang glider landing site and a popular locale for kite flying.

Koko Crater

According to Hawaiian legend, Koko Crater is the imprint left by the magical flying vagina of Pele's sister Kapo, which was sent from the Big Island to lure the pig-god Kamapua'a away from Pele.

Today inside the crater you'll find the county-run **Koko Crater Botanical Garden** (admission free; ☉ 8am-sunset), with fragrant plumeria trees, oleander, cacti and other dryland plants. There are two connecting loop trails that lead through the garden. The first takes only about 10 minutes to walk and offers a close-up look at the garden specimens. Add on the second loop, which takes about an hour, for crater views.

To get there, take Kealahou St off the Kalaniana'ole Hwy, opposite the northern end of Sandy Beach. Just over half a mile in, turn left and continue a third of a mile to the garden.

MAKAPU'U POINT

The 647ft Makapu'u Point and its coastal **lighthouse** mark the easternmost point of O'ahu. At the north side of Makapu'u Point a **roadside lookout** affords a fine view down onto Makapu'u Beach Park, its aqua-blue waters outlined by white sand and black lava. It's an even more spectacular sight when hang gliders are taking off from the cliffs, O'ahu's top hang-gliding spot.

From the lookout you can see two offshore islands, the larger of which is **Manana Island**, also known as Rabbit Island. This aging volcanic crater is populated by feral rabbits and burrowing wedge-tailed shearwaters. The birds and rabbits coexist so closely that they sometimes even share the same burrows. Curiously, the island also looks vaguely like the head of a rabbit, and if you try hard you may see it, ears folded back. If that doesn't work, try to imagine it as a whale.

In front of it is the smaller **Kaohikaipu Island**, which won't tax the imagination – all it looks is flat. Divers sometimes explore the coral reef between the two islands, but to do so requires a boat.

Activities

The **Makapu'u Lighthouse Trail** follows a mile-long service road from the highway to the lighthouse. Although not difficult, it's an uphill walk and conditions can be hot and windy, but you'll be rewarded with fine coastal views along the way and at the lighthouse lookout. Furthermore, during winter whales are sometimes visible offshore. The trail to the lighthouse begins at a parking lot alongside the Kalaniana'ole Hwy just over a mile north of Sandy Beach.

MAKAPU'U BEACH PARK

Makapu'u Beach is one of the island's top winter bodysurfing spots, with waves reaching 12ft and higher. It also has the island's best shorebreak. As with Sandy Beach, Makapu'u is strictly the domain of experienced bodysurfers who can handle rough water conditions and dangerous currents. In summer, when the wave action disappears, the waters can be calm and good for swimming.

The beach, opposite Sea Life Park, is in a pretty setting, with cliffs in the background and a glimpse of the lighthouse. Two native Hawaiian plants – white-blossom *naupaka* by the beach and yellow-orange *'ilima*,

O'ahu's official flower – are plentiful by the parking lot.

SEA LIFE PARK

Hawaii's only **marine life park** (☎ 259-7933; 41-202 Kalaniana'ole Hwy; adult/child 4-12yr $25/13; ☻ 9:15am-5pm; ☐ 22, 57 & 58) offers a mixed bag of attractions. A former highlight, the 300,000-gallon aquarium containing fish, sea turtles and eagle rays is showing its age, and if you're interested in fishbowl gazing you're better off visiting the state-of-the-art Waikiki Aquarium.

There's the usual theme-park entertainment, with shows featuring imported Atlantic bottle-nosed dolphins giving choreographed performances, and a new pool where visitors can swim with dolphins (below). Other creature features include a pool of California sea lions and a penguin habitat.

Although the main attractions at Sea Life Park feature animals that aren't found in Hawaiian waters, the park also does some noteworthy rehabilitation work with injured and abandoned Hawaiian monk seal pups rescued from the wild; once they reach maturity, they're released back into their natural habitat.

WAIMANALO
pop 3675

The most Hawaiian town on the east side of the island, Waimanalo also enjoys one of the prettiest settings with the scalloped hills of the Ko'olau Range on one side and the crystal waters of Waimanalo Bay on the other. The bay has the longest continuous stretch of beach on O'ahu, with 5.5 miles

---

RUB NOSES WITH DOLPHINS

Who hasn't wanted to swim with dolphins? People who have experienced it often feel a close connection with the creatures – some even identify it as a mystical experience. Parents often feel it was *the* experience that gave their children a deep empathy for the animal world.

And then there's the other side of the issue – folks who argue that wild animals should be kept wild, and that the contact and captivity are harmful to the dolphins' well-being.

So weigh up the issues and decide for yourself.

If you decide to take the plunge, two reputable companies in southeast O'ahu offer programs that let visitors get up close, touch, feed and interact with Atlantic bottle-nosed dolphins, the type that are relatively gentle and easily trained for show in marine parks.

Dolphin Quest (☎ 739-8918; www.dolphinquest.org; 5000 Kahala Ave, Kahala) is at the Kahala Mandarin Oriental, and **Dolphin Discovery** (☎ 259-7933; www.dolphindiscovery.com; 41-202 Kalaniana'ole Hwy) takes place at Sea Life Park. Program fees cost $80 to $125, depending upon the time involved and the amount of interaction.

of white sand stretching from Makapu'u Point to Wailea Point. A long coral reef about a mile offshore breaks up the biggest waves, protecting much of the shore. Fans of the TV series *Magnum PI* may recognise the beach here, as it's where Magnum was often seen taking a swim after a hard day of sleuthing. Sometimes called Nalo by locals, Waimanalo has hillside farms that grow many of those wonderful fresh greens that are served in Honolulu's top restaurants.

Information

Post Office (☎ 800-275-8777; 41-859 Kalaniana'ole Hwy; ☺ 9am-4:30pm Mon-Fri, to 11am Sat)

Sights & Activities

WAIMANALO BEACH PARK

This park has an attractive beach of soft white sand, and the water is excellent for swimming. The park offers a slew of facilities, including a grassy picnic area, rest rooms, showers, baseball fields, basketball and volleyball courts, and a playground.

The park has ironwood trees, but overall it's more open than the other two Waimanalo parks to the north. Manana Island and Makapu'u Point are visible to the south. Bus 57, originating from the Ala Moana Shopping Center in Honolulu, stops at the park entrance.

WAIMANALO BAY BEACH PARK

This county park about a mile north of Waimanalo Beach Park has Waimanalo Bay's biggest waves, and is popular with board surfers and bodysurfers. Even if you're not planning to hit the water, stop by this beautiful broad sandy beach backed by ironwoods – not an iota of development in sight from the beach, just the ring of old Hawaii.

Note, though, that locals call the park 'Sherwood Forest' because thieves used to hang out here in days past – it hasn't totally shaken its reputation, so keep an eye on your belongings. There are barbecue grills, drinking water, showers, rest rooms and a lifeguard station.

Bus 57 stops on the main road in front of the park, and from there it's a third of a mile walk to the beach.

BELLOWS FIELD BEACH PARK

The beach fronting Bellows Air Force Station is open to civilian beachgoers and campers

on weekends only, from noon Friday until 8am Monday. This long beach has fine sand and a natural setting backed by ironwood trees. The small shore-break waves here are good for beginning bodysurfers and board surfers. There are showers, rest rooms, drinking water, a lifeguard, a caretaker and 50 campsites set among the trees.

The marked entrance to the park is 0.25 miles north of Waimanalo Bay Beach Park. Bus 57 stops in front of the entrance road and from there it's 1.5 miles to the beach.

GOLF

The **Olomana Golf Links** (☎ 259-7926; 41-1801 Kalaniana'ole Hwy; per 18 holes with electric cart $80; ☺ 7am-10pm, from 6am Mar-Oct) offers two challenging nine-hole courses that are played together as a regulation 18-hole course. Facilities include a driving range and a good restaurant.

Sleeping

Beach House Hawaii (☎ 259-7792, 866-625-6946; www.beachhousehawaii.com; house $85-600) Bask in Waimanalo aloha in one of the cottages and beach houses booked through this local agency.

The best place to camp in the area is Bellows Field Beach Park; for information on camping, see p230.

Eating

Olomano Golf Links (☎ 259-5163; 41-1801 Kalaniana'ole Hwy, Waimanalo; mains $8-14; ☺ 6am-6pm) This open-air clubhouse serves real – and real good – Hawaiian grinds, like *kalua*-style pork and teriyaki chicken with a dab of macaroni salad and pineapple slices.

Keneke's (☎ 259-5266; 41-857 Kalaniana'ole Hwy; plate lunches $5; ☺ 9am-5pm) The place to pick up quick plate-lunch meals to cart off to the beach.

There are food marts and fast-food eateries just south of Waimanalo Bay Beach Park and in a cluster of shops about a mile north of Bellows Field Beach Park.

Shopping

Sumo Connection (☎ 259-8646; Waimanalo Town Center, 41-1537 Kalaniana'ole Hwy; ☺ 9am-4pm Mon-Sat) This place is a monument to local-born Chad 'Akebono' Rowan, who made his fame as a *yokozuna* (grand champ) sumo wrestler in Japan in the 1990s. You simply can't miss this one – a lifesize bronze statue of Akebono greets you in the parking lot. Inside, Akebono's mom holds court with Japanese tourists who stop by to snap pictures with her. The shop sells Big Mama's Kona coffee, Sumo Connection T-shirts and other fun souvenirs.

Honolulu Nuts & Ukulele Company (☎ 259-7880; Waimanalo Town Center, 41-1537 Kalaniana'ole Hwy; ◷ 9am-6pm) Local flavor abounds at this shop selling everything from ukuleles and macadamia nuts to Hawaii-made shampoos and oils.

Naturally Hawaiian Galley (☎ 259-5354; 41-1025 Kalaniana'ole Hwy; ◷ 9am-6pm) Artist Patrick Ching, a former island park ranger and cowboy, sells his paintings, prints and illustrated books of Hawaii's natural wonders.

Windward O'ahu

Several of O'ahu's finest beaches, and a spicy mix of urban towns and rural villages, are just part of the allure of the island's eastern flank. The windsurfing mecca of Kailua offers one of the best alternative scenes to bustling Waikiki, with enticing restaurants and home-style accommodations. The charm of Kane'ohe may be less obvious, but it too harbors hidden gems as lovely as any on the island.

As you move north beyond Kane'ohe everything begins to slow down. Now you're in for a treat – a delicious slice of rural O'ahu, with its taro patches and quiet beaches. The Kamehameha Hwy – nothing more than a modest two-lane road – runs the length of the entire coast, doubling as Main St for each of the tiny towns along the way. You'll find loads of fruit stands, giving the drive a true feel of old Hawaii.

And, oh, the scenery. The beach-hugging road follows the dramatic Ko'olau Range along its entire length. In places these scalloped mountains loom a mile or two inland and in others they come so close to the shore that they nearly crowd the highway into the ocean. Whether you prefer the greens of a golf course or a trail through the woods, awesome sights await.

Not to forget this is windward O'ahu, where the trade winds propel anything with a sail. So if you've never tried windsurfing, or are aching to get back on a board, come here. Birders will find some great wing-watching sites – some require a kayak to reach, and with others you just need to know where to park.

HIGHLIGHTS

- Windsurfing and kayaking at sparkling **Kailua Beach Park** (p177)
- Getting blown away by the view at **Nu'uanu Pali Lookout** (p174)
- Munching on wiggle-fresh **shrimp** (p193) in Kahuku
- Beach-bumming an afternoon away at **Kualoa Regional Park** (p186)
- Enjoying tranquility and good fortune after ringing the bell at the **Byodo-In** (p182) temple in Kane'ohe

★ Kahuku

★ Kualoa Regional Park

Byodo-In ★

Kailua Beach Park ★

Nu'uanu Pali Lookout ★

WINDWARD O'AHU

Getting There & Away

Two highways cut through the Ko'olau Range from central Honolulu to windward O'ahu. The Pali Hwy (Hwy 61) goes straight into Kailua, while the Likelike Hwy (Hwy 63) runs directly into Kane'ohe. Although the Likelike (pronounced lee-kay-lee-kay) Hwy doesn't have the scenic stops the Pali

Hwy has, in some ways it is more dramatic. Driving away from Kane'ohe feels as if you're heading straight into towering fairy-tale mountains – then you suddenly shoot through a tunnel and emerge on the Honolulu side, the drama gone.

If you're driving both to and from windward O'ahu through the Ko'olau Range,

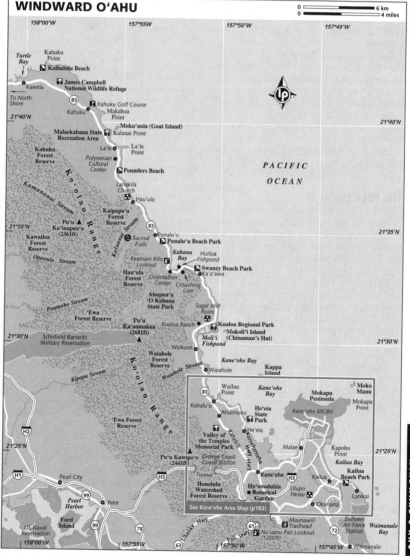

WINDWARD O'AHU

0 ___ 6 km
0 ___ 4 miles

PACIFIC OCEAN

Turtle Bay
Kahuku Point
Kaihalulu Beach
Kawela
James Campbell National Wildlife Refuge
To North Shore
Kahuku Golf Course
Kahuku
Makahoa Point
Moku'auia (Goat Island)
Malaekahana State Recreation Area
Kalanai Point
La'ie
La'ie Point
Kahuku Forest Reserve
Polynesian Cultural Center
Pounders Beach
Lanakila Church
Hau'ula
Kaipapa'u Forest Reserve
Pu'u Ka'inapua'a (2361ft)
Kawailoa Forest Reserve
Opaeula Stream
Sacred Falls
Punalu'u
Punalu'u Beach Park
Keaniani Kilo Lookout
Kahana Bay
Huilua Fishpond
Hau'ula Forest Reserve
Orientation Center
Swanzy Beach Park
Ka'a'awa
Crouching Lion
Ahupua'a 'O Kahana State Park
Poamoho Stream
'Ewa Forest Reserve
Pu'u Ka'aumakua (2681ft)
Sugar Mill Ruins
Kualoa Ranch
Kualoa Regional Park
Moli'i Fishpond
Mokoli'i Island (Chinaman's Hat)
Schofield Barracks Military Reservation
Waikane
Waiahole Forest Reserve
Kane'ohe Bay
Kappa Island
Kipapa Stream
Waiahole Stream
Waiahole
'Ewa Forest Reserve
Pu'u Kawipo'o (2441ft)
Omega Coast Guard Station
Tunnel
Honolulu Watershed Forest Reserve
Pearl City
Aiea
Pearl Harbor
Ford Island
US Naval Reservation

Ko'olau Range
Kamananui Stream
Kahana Stream

Wailau Point
Kahalu'u
Ahuimanu
He'eia State Park
He'eia
Valley of the Temples Memorial Park
Kane'ohe Bay
Mokapu Peninsula
Moko Manu
Mokapu Point
Kane'ohe MCBH
Malae
Kapoho Point
Kamehameha Hwy
Kane'ohe
Ho'omaluhia Botanical Garden
Ulupo Heiau
Olomana
Kailua Bay
Kailua
Kailua Beach Park
Lanikai

See Kane'ohe Area Map (p183)

Maunawili Trailhead
Nu'uanu Pali Lookout (1200ft)
Bellows Air Force Station
Waimanalo Bay
Waimanalo

158°00'W 157°55'W 157°50'W 157°45'W
21°40'N 21°35'N 21°30'N 21°25'N

H2 H1 99 78 63 61 72 83 H3

WINDWARD O'AHU

take the Pali Hwy up from Honolulu and the Likelike Hwy back to enjoy the best scenery of both.

Many Kailua residents commute to work over the Pali, so Honolulu-bound traffic can be heavy in the morning and outbound traffic heavy in the evening. It's less of a problem for visitors, however, as most day-trippers will be traveling against the traffic. Public buses travel the Pali Hwy between Honolulu and Kailua (see p181), but none stop at the Nu'uanu Pali Lookout.

Kane'ohe is the jumping-off point for travel north along the windward coast. Bus 55 services the Kamehameha Hwy from Kane'ohe to the Turtle Bay Resort at Kahuku Point. It runs approximately every 30 minutes from dawn to 6pm and then less frequently until 10:45pm. By bus from Kane'ohe, it takes about 30 minutes to reach Kualoa Regional Park, an hour to the Polynesian Cultural Center in La'ie and 1½ hours to the Turtle Bay Resort.

THE PALI HIGHWAY

The Pali Hwy (Hwy 61), which runs between Honolulu and Kailua, cuts through the spectacular Ko'olau Range. If it's been raining heavily, every fold and crevice in the mountains will have a lacy waterfall streaming down it.

Heading northeast up the Pali Hwy, just past the 4-mile marker, look up and to the right to see two notches cut about 15ft deep into the crest of the *pali* (cliff). These notches are thought to have been dug as cannon emplacements by Kamehameha the Great.

The original route between Honolulu and windward O'ahu was via an ancient footpath that wound its way perilously over these cliffs. In 1845 the path was widened into a horse trail and later into a cobblestone carriage road. In 1898 the Old Pali Hwy (as it's now called) was built in place of the carriage road. It was abandoned in the 1950s after tunnels were blasted through the Ko'olau Range and the present multilane Pali Hwy opened.

You can still drive a loop of the Old Pali Hwy (called Nu'uanu Pali Dr; right) and hike another mile of it from the Nu'uanu Pali Lookout. See opposite for information on hiking on the Old Pali Hwy trail.

FALLEN WARRIORS

In 1795 Kamehameha the Great routed O'ahu's warriors up the Nu'uanu Trail during his invasion of the island. On the steep cliffs, near the site of the Nu'uanu Pali Lookout, O'ahu's warriors made their last stand. Hundreds were thrown to their death over the *pali* (cliff) as they were overcome by Kamehameha's troops. A hundred years later, during the construction of the Old Pali Hwy, more than 500 skulls were found at the base of the cliffs.

Sights & Activities
NU'UANU PALI LOOKOUT

Whatever you do, don't miss the ridge-top Nu'uanu Pali Lookout with its sweeping vista of windward O'ahu from a height of 1200ft. From the lookout you can see Kane'ohe straight ahead, Kailua to the right, and Mokoli'i Island and the coastal fishpond at Kualoa Regional Park to the far left.

This is *windward* O'ahu – and the winds that funnel through the *pali* are so strong that you can sometimes lean against them. It gets cool enough to appreciate having a jacket.

When you return to the highway, it's easy to miss the sign leading you out of the parking lot, and instinct could send

---

DETOUR: NU'UANU PALI DRIVE

For a scenic side trip through a lush jungle scented with tropical flowers, turn off the Pali Hwy onto Nu'uanu Pali Dr, half a mile north of the 2-mile marker on the Pali Hwy.

The 2-mile Nu'uanu Pali Dr runs parallel to the Pali Hwy and then comes back out to the highway before the Nu'uanu Pali Lookout, so you don't miss out on any scenery by taking this side loop – in fact, quite the opposite.

Mature trees, all draped with hanging vines and wound with philodendrons, form a canopy overhead. All around are banyan trees with hanging aerial roots, tropical almond trees, bamboo groves, flowering impatiens, angel trumpets and golden cup – a climbing vine with large golden flowers.

WINDWARD O'AHU

you in the wrong direction. Go to the left if you're heading toward Kailua, to the right if heading toward Honolulu.

OLD PALI HWY TRAIL

The abandoned Old Pali Hwy winds down from the right side of the Nu'uanu Pali Lookout, ending at a barrier near the current highway about a mile away. Few people realize the road is here, let alone venture down it. It makes a nice walk, taking about 45 minutes return. There are good views looking back up at the jagged Ko'olau Range and out across the valley.

MAUNAWILI DEMONSTRATION TRAIL

The 10-mile Maunawili Demonstration Trail connects Nu'uanu Pali with Waimanalo on the coast. Popular with both hikers and mountain bikers, this scenic trail winds along the back side of Maunawili Valley, following the base of the lofty Ko'olau Range. Along the way, there are panoramic views of mountains and the windward coast.

This trail consists of many climbs up and down gulches, across streams and along ridges. Going in an easterly direction is the less strenuous way, as you will be following the trail from the mountain crest down to the coast. Even taking the trail for just a couple of miles will reward hikers with fine views of both the coast and Maunawili Valley's lush, forested interior.

Because the Maunawili Demonstration Trail is subject to erosion, mountain bikers are asked to stay off the trail when it's raining or if the trail is wet. If you come across muddy sections, dismount and walk your bike.

The trail can be accessed by driving about a mile north past the Nu'uanu Pali Lookout. Pull off to the right at the 'scenic point' turnout at the hairpin turn just before the 7-mile marker. There's trailhead parking here. Walk through the break in the guardrail where a footbridge takes you over a drainage ditch to begin the hike.

The trail can also be picked up from the Nu'uanu Pali Lookout by walking the mile-long stretch of the Old Pali Hwy Trail, which ends near the Maunawili Trailhead.

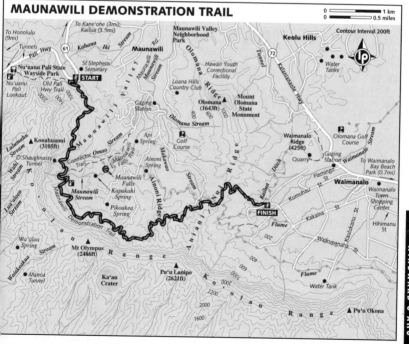

MAUNAWILI DEMONSTRATION TRAIL

KAILUA

pop 36,600

Windward O'ahu's largest town is lined with miles of lovely beaches that are ideal for a bevy of water activities. Kailua Beach has long been the hottest place on the island for windsurfers and kayakers. Now it's attracting ever increasing numbers of kiteboarding, a sport that was virtually created here by windsurfing legend Robbie Naish. Not surprisingly, the influx of visitors hot to hit the waves has given rise to surf shops, none more famous than the one run by Naish himself, and some solid low-profile accommodation options. There are no hotels, really no places with more than just a couple of rooms, and that's the beauty of it. Kailua doesn't draw package tourists – in this town everything is small and personable. With its agreeable mix of locals and visitors, Kailua makes a refreshing alternative to the resort scene.

History

In ancient times Kailua (meaning 'two seas') was a place of legends. It was home to a giant who turned into a mountain ridge, as well as the island's first *menehune* (the 'little people' who, according to legend, built many of Hawaii's fishponds and stonework) and numerous O'ahuan chiefs. Even Kamehameha the Great lived briefly in Kailua after his invasion of O'ahu. Rich in stream-fed agricultural land, fertile fishing grounds and protected canoe landings, Kailua once served as a political and economic center for the region. The area supported at least three *heiau* (ancient stone temple), one of which, Ulupo Heiau, you can still visit today.

Information

Bank of Hawaii (☎ 266-4600; 636 Kailua Rd) On the town's main road.

Bookends (☎ 261-1996; Kailua Shopping Center, 600 Kailua Rd; ☼ 9am-8pm Mon-Sat, to 5pm Sun) This independent bookstore has a good selection of new and used books, newspapers and maps.

Kailua Information Center & Chamber of Commerce (☎ 261-2727; www.kailuachamber.com; Kailua Shopping Center, 600 Kailua Rd; ☼ 10-4pm Mon-Fri, to 2pm Sat) Stop here to pick up free maps and information on Kailua accommodations and activities.

Kailua Laundromat (cnr Aulike & Uluniu Sts; ☼ 24hr)

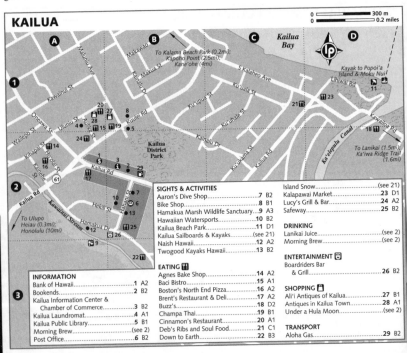

KAILUA

SIGHTS & ACTIVITIES	
Aaron's Dive Shop	7 B2
Bike Shop	8 B1
Hamakua Marsh Wildlife Sanctuary	9 A3
Hawaiian Watersports	10 B2
Kailua Beach Park	11 D1
Kailua Sailboards & Kayaks	(see 21)
Naish Hawaii	12 A2
Twogood Kayaks Hawaii	13 B2

EATING 🍴	
Agnes Bake Shop	14 A2
Baci Bistro	15 A1
Boston's North End Pizza	16 A2
Brent's Restaurant & Deli	17 A2
Buzz's	18 D2
Champa Thai	19 B1
Cinnamon's Restaurant	20 A1
Deb's Ribs and Soul Food	21 C1
Down to Earth	22 B3

Island Snow	(see 21)
Kalapawai Market	23 D1
Lucy's Grill & Bar	24 A2
Safeway	25 B2

DRINKING	
Lanikai Juice	(see 2)
Morning Brew	(see 2)

ENTERTAINMENT 🎭	
Boardriders Bar & Grill	26 B2

SHOPPING 🛍	
Ali'i Antiques of Kailua	27 B1
Antiques in Kailua Town	28 A1
Under a Hula Moon	(see 2)

TRANSPORT	
Aloha Gas	29 B2

INFORMATION	
Bank of Hawaii	1 A2
Bookends	2 B2
Kailua Information Center & Chamber of Commerce	3 B2
Kailua Laundromat	4 A1
Kailua Public Library	5 B1
Morning Brew	(see 2)
Post Office	6 B2

WINDWARD O'AHU

Kailua Post Office (☎ 266-3996; 335 Hahani St; ☺ 8am-6pm Mon-Fri, 9am-4pm Sat) Located in the town center.

Kailua Public Library (☎ 266-9911; 239 Kuulei Rd; ☺ 10am-5pm Mon, Wed, Fri & Sat, 1-8pm Tue & Thu) Has periodicals to browse.

Morning Brew (☎ 262-7770; Kailua Shopping Center, 600 Kailua Rd; per 30min $3; ☺ 6am-8pm) Offers Internet access and wi-fi connections for laptops.

Sights

KAILUA BEACH PARK

It's hard to imagine a more beautiful stretch of beach. Gracing the southeastern end of Kailua Bay, this glistening white-sand beach is long and broad with clear turquoise waters. It's perfect for leisurely walks, family outings and a full range of water activities, including windsurfing and kayaking.

Kailua Beach has a gently sloping sandy bottom with waters that are generally calm. Swimming conditions are good all year, but sunbathers beware – the breezes propel sand as well as windsurfers! The park has rest rooms, showers, lifeguards, a volleyball court and large grassy expanses shaded by ironwood trees.

Ka'elepulu Canal divides the park into two sections, although a sand bar usually prevents the canal waters from emptying into the bay. Windsurfing activities are centered to the west of the canal; there's a small boat ramp on the eastern side. The best time to come is on weekdays – mornings for swimmers, afternoons when breezes pick up for windsurfers. On sunny weekends it can be a challenge to find a parking space.

LANIKAI BEACH

If you follow the coastal road as it continues southeast from Kailua Beach Park, you'll shortly come to Lanikai, an exclusive residential neighborhood fronted by Lanikai Beach, a gorgeous stretch of powdery white sand overlooking two postcard-perfect islands. The sandy bottom slopes gently and the waters are calm, offering safe swimming conditions similar to those at Kailua. Unfortunately, the beach is shrinking, as nearly half of the sand has washed away in recent years as a result of retaining walls built to protect the multimillion-dollar homes constructed on the shore. Still, it's a beauty – see it while you can.

From Kailua Beach Park, the road turns into the one-way Aalapapa Dr, which comes back around as Mokulua Dr to make a 2.5-mile loop. There are 11 narrow beach access walkways off Mokulua Dr. For the best stretches of beach, try the walkway opposite Kualima Dr or any of the next three.

OFFSHORE ISLANDS

Three islands off Kailua and Lanikai are seabird sanctuaries and only accessible by kayak. Landings are allowed on **Popoi'a Island** (Flat Island), directly off the south end of Kailua Beach Park.

The twin **Mokulua Islands**, Moku Nui and Moku Iki, sit directly off Lanikai. It's possible to kayak from Kailua Beach Park to Moku Nui, but landings are prohibited on Moku Iki, the smaller of the two islands.

ULUPO HEIAU

The building of Ulupo Heiau, an imposing open-platform temple of stones piled 30ft high and 180ft long, is attributed to *menehune,* the little people who legends say created much of Hawaii's stonework, finishing each project in one night. Fittingly, Ulupo means 'night inspiration.' In front of the temple, thought to have been a *luakini* (type of heiau dedicated to the war god Ku and used for human sacrifices), is an artist's

---

LITTLE PEOPLE, BIG TASKS

Numerous Hawaiian legends tell of a tribe of happy, elflike people called *menehune* who came down out of the mountains to produce great engineering works in stone.

It seems likely that when the first wave of Tahitians arrived in Hawaii in around AD 1000, they conquered and subjugated Marquesan settlers who'd come to Hawaii centuries earlier, forcing them to build their temples, irrigation ditches and fishponds.

The Tahitian term for 'outcast' is *manahune,* and the diminutive social status the Marquesans had in the eyes of their conquerors may have given rise to tales of a dwarf-sized race.

The *menehune* may have created the temples, but the Tahitian settlers created the legends. While the stonework still remains, the true identity of Hawaii's 'little people' has slipped into obscurity.

rendition of the site as it appeared in the 18th century. From the path across the top of the heiau, there's a view of **Kawainui Marsh**, one of Hawaii's largest habitats for endangered waterbirds. Legend says the edible mud of the ancient fishpond was home to a *mo'o* (lizard spirit).

Ulupo Heiau is a mile south of Kailua center. Coming up the Pali Hwy (Hwy 61) from Honolulu, take Uluoa St, the first left after passing the Hwy 72 junction. Turn right on Manu Aloha St and right again onto Manuo'o St. The heiau is behind the YMCA.

HAMAKUA MARSH WILDLIFE SANCTUARY

Bird-watchers flock to this 22-acre sanctuary encompassing the marsh at the south side of the town center. Simply park behind the Down to Earth natural healthfood store on Hamakua Dr. The sanctuary begins at the back side of the parking lot, where you can readily spot rare Hawaiian birds in their natural habitat, including the *'alae 'ula* (Hawaii moorhen), *ae'o* (Hawaiian stilt) and *'alae ke'oke'o* (Hawaiian coot).

Activities

WINDSURFING

Thanks to strong onshore winds, windsurfers can sail at Kailua year-round. Different spots of the bay have different water conditions, some good for jumps and wave surfing, others for flatwater sails. Both companies listed here have shops in Kailua, but also give lessons and rent boards right at Kailua Beach Park on weekdays and Saturday mornings.

Naish Hawaii (☎ 262-6068, 800-767-6068; www .naish.com; 155 Hamakua Dr; ⏰ 9am-5:30pm) – as in windsurfing champion Robbie Naish – is the top dog in these parts. Rental rates vary with the board and rig: beginner equipment costs $35 per day, intermediate equipment $40 and advanced $55. Three-hour introductory lessons cost $50 if you take them with a small group, $75 for a private lesson; expect to spend half of the time learning the basics and half sailing.

The other major player is **Kailua Sailboards & Kayaks** (☎ 262-2555; www.kailuasailboards.com; Kailua Beach Center, 130 Kailua Rd; ⏰ 9am-5pm), which rents windsurfing equipment and gives lessons for prices comparable to Naish.

KITEBOARDING

Kind of like snowboarding, but on water and with a kite, kiteboarding (also called kitesurfing) is an exhilarating sport. It helps if you know how to wakeboard or windsurf, but all you really need to start is the ability to swim and wear a swimsuit that will stay on. It does take a lot of muscles and stamina. If you want to give it a shot, **Hawaiian Watersports** (☎ 262-5483; www.hawaiianwatersports .com; 354 Hahani St; 6hr lesson package $449; ⏰ 9am-6pm Mon-Sat, 9am-5pm Sun) gives lessons on Kailua Beach. It definitely doesn't come as easy as windsurfing – expect to take about six hours to learn enough to kiteboard on your own. About half of that will be lectures and learning techniques on land before you even hit the water.

KAYAKING

Kailua Beach, with its pretty little uninhabited nearshore islands within the reef, is the perfect place to wield a paddle. Landings are allowed on Moku Nui, which has a beautiful beach good for sunbathing and snorkeling, and on Popoi'a Island, which you can walk around.

Let the rental agent know your experience level and they can suggest you an itinerary to match your ability. If you feel more comfortable with a group, both companies listed here offer $89 guided kayak tours that last four hours, include a picnic lunch, and give you time for snorkeling and swimming. Both companies will deliver kayaks to the beach.

Kailua Sailboard & Kayaks (☎ 262-2555; www.kailua sailboards.com; Kailua Beach Center, 130 Kailua Rd; 1-/2-person kayak per day $49/59; ⏰ 9am-5pm)

Twogood Kayaks Hawaii (☎ 262-5656; 345 Hahani St; 1-/2-person kayak per half-day $39/49; ⏰ 9am-6pm Mon-Fri, 8am-6pm Sat & Sun)

HIKING

If you're up for a hike, the mile-long **Ka'iwa Ridge Trail** takes about one hour return, and offers exceptional ridge-top views of Kailua, Lanikai and the Ko'olau Range. It's best as a fair-weather trail as it's a bit steep and can get muddy after it rains. Good footwear is advised. To get there, turn right off Aalapapa Dr in Lanikai onto Ka'elepulu Dr and continue about 180yd until you reach the Mid-Pacific Country Club, then pull off and park just beyond it on the right side of the road. Walk up the side road across the street and opposite the yellow water hydrant you'll see the dirt trail, which starts between two chain-link fences.

SURFING
Kalama Beach Park, a small beach park north of Kailua Beach Park, has one of the largest shorebreaks in the bay. When the waves are up, both board surfers and bodysurfers can find decent conditions there. Board surfers also sometimes head to the northern end of Kailua Bay to Kapoho Point, which has a decent break during swells. Boards can be rented at **Kailua Sailboards & Kayaks** (☎ 262-2555; Kailua Beach Center, 130 Kailua Rd; surfboard rental per day $25; ⏱ 9am-5pm).

DIVING
Caves, lava tubes and coral gardens can all be explored by joining a boat dive with **Aaron's Dive Shop** (☎ 262-2333, 888-847-2822; www.hawaii-scuba.com; 307 Hahani St; 2-tank dive $114; ⏱ 6am-7pm Mon-Fri, 7am-6pm Sat, 7am-5pm Sun), a PADI five-star center.

Sleeping
Kailua has no hotels, but there's a good selection of beachfront houses, cottages and B&B-style rooms in private homes. Although the majority are handled by the vacation rental services listed on p229, the following places can be booked directly with the owners. Most don't allow smoking indoors.

Hawaii's Hidden Hideaway (☎ 262-6560, 877-443-3299; www.ahawaiibnb.com; 1369 Mokolea Dr; studio $110, ste $185) Bask in the good life at this upscale hideaway near Lanikai Beach. Each of the three units has a private entrance, lanai (porch) and kitchenette. The suite, which has a queen-sized canopy bed and a private Jacuzzi, would be a fun choice for honeymooners or those just looking for a romantic getaway. Special touches include a library of Hawaiiana books perfect for perusing in the evening, free use of beach gear, and a welcome basket of pastries, fruit and coffee. There's a three-day minimum stay.

Tee's at Kailua (☎ 261-0771; www.teesinn.com; 771 Wanaao Rd; d $145-195; ▣ ▣) This pampering getaway, just a five-minute walk from the beach, is a standout among Kailua's home-style B&Bs. There are two guest rooms, the larger with a king bed and a

Zen-like Asian decor, the other with a queen bed. Breakfast featuring organic goodies and the owner's own homegrown teas is served on the gardenside lanai.

Beachlane (☎ 262-8286; www.beachlane.com; 111 Hekili St; r $95, studio $125; ▣) Enjoy an ocean view from your bed at this sweet B&B just a minute's walk from the beach. The two guest rooms, both handsomely renovated in tropical style, share the upper floor of a contemporary home. Behind the main house are a pair of inviting studios with kitchenettes. All the units have queen beds, fans and cable TV. The owner speaks several languages, including Danish and German. Boogie boards and beach chairs await!

Manu Mele Bed & Breakfast (☎ 262-0016; www.pixi.com/~manumele; 153 Kailuana Place; r $70 & $90; ▣ ▣) Just steps from the beach, these attractive guest rooms in the contemporary home of English-born host Carol Isaacs have a lot of appeal. The largest sports a king bed, the smaller a queen bed. Each has a private entrance, refrigerator, microwave, coffeemaker, ceiling fan and cable TV. A basket of fruit and baked goods is provided on the first morning. The minimum stay is two days.

Sheffield House (☎ 262-0721; rachel@sheffieldhouse.com; 131 Kuulei Rd; r $85 & $105; ♿) A few minutes' walk from Kailua Beach, this kid-friendly place consists of two unassuming units in the home of the Sheffield family. There's a guest room with a wheelchair-accessible bathroom and a one-bedroom suite with a queen bed and a separate sitting area. Each unit has a private entrance, ceiling fans and kitchenette. Futons and a baby bed are available. There's a three-day minimum stay; a basket of pastries and coffee are provided on the first day.

Lanikai Plantations (☎ 561-1851; 1436 Aalapapa Dr; r $125, cottage $150) Just 500ft from the beach in Lanikai, this upscale plantation-style house has one private room with a queen bed and a cottage with a king bed. Guests have free use of a barbeque, double kayak and beach gear. Because of the prime location and the reasonable price, this place often books solid, so call well in advance.

Auntie Barbara's Vacation Rental (☎ 262-7420; http://hawaiiibjvacations.com; 516a North Kainalu Dr; studio $75, apt $105; ▣ ▣ ♿) Good value for a family, this apartment just a couple blocks from the beach sleeps up to five people and has all the comforts of home, including a full kitchen, a baby crib, and a washer and dryer. There's also a studio unit with a queen bed and kitchenette. Both units have private entrances and phones with free local calls.

Paradise Palms Bed & Breakfast (☎ 254-4234; www.paradisepalmshawaii.com; 804 Mokapu Rd; studios $85-95; ☒) On the northwestern end of Kailua, these cheery studios at the side of Marilyn and Jim Warman's home pack a lot of comfort for the money. The more expensive room has a king bed, the other a queen bed. Each has a private entrance, kitchenette and ceiling fans in addition to the air-con. Fruit, coffee and fresh-baked bread are provided upon arrival. The minimum stay is three days. There's a grocery store and several restaurants across the street.

Amanda's Vacation Rentals (☎ 262-8981; www .alternative-hawaii.com/amanda; 687 Paopua Loop; d $95-115, 3-5 people $135; ☒ ☐) A good choice if you need extra elbow room, these suites are huge and just a few minutes' walk from Kailua Beach. The two-bedroom unit offers 1000 sq ft of living space and sleeps five people comfortably. The one-bedroom suite has over 600 sq ft and can sleep four. Sea breezes and ceiling fans make the air-con optional, and there's an outdoor sitting area with a barbecue.

Papaya Paradise Bed & Breakfast (☎ 261-0316; www.kailuaoahuhawaii.com/papaya.htm; 395 Auwinala Rd; d $95, plus $15 each additional person; ☒ ☒) A 15-minute walk from Kailua Beach, this place consists of two rooms that are adjacent to the owner's home. Both units have two beds, a private entrance, ceiling fan and cable TV. Rates include light breakfast fare, and guests have access to a refrigerator and microwave. Boogie boards, coolers and beach chairs can be borrowed free. There's a three-day minimum stay.

Eating

NEAR THE BEACH

Kalapawai Market (☎ 262-4359; 305 S Kalaheo Ave; coffee $1, sandwiches $4-7; ☷ 6am-9pm) Everyone stops at this local landmark on the way to the beach to pick up their java fix and bagels. Not only are the coffees perfect, but so are the generous lunchtime sandwiches, made to order in every combo imaginable, from avocado vegetable to mile-high roast beef. Excellent wine selection as well.

Buzz's (☎ 261-4661; 413 Kawailoa Rd; lunch $8-12, dinner $15-32; ☷ 11am-3pm & 5-10pm) Opposite Kailua Beach Park, Buzz's serves up fresh fish sandwiches, burgers and salads at lunch. However, it is most popular as an evening steak house, with various cuts of steak grilled on kiawe charcoal shoring up the menu. Naturally there's also fresh fish, and meals include a salad bar. Credit cards are not accepted.

Deb's Ribs and Soul Food (☎ 262-3327; Kailua Beach Center, 130 Kailua Rd; mains $7-10; ☷ 11am-1:30pm Mon & Wed-Fri, 4:30-8:30pm Wed-Mon) Southern comfort food comes to Kailua at this home-style eatery serving catfish, collard greens and barbequed ribs. Makes for good picnic fare if you're on the way to the beach.

Island Snow (☎ 263-6339; Kailua Beach Center, 130 Kailua Rd; shave ice $2.50; ☷ 10am-6pm Mon-Fri, to 7pm Sat & Sun) If the heat's getting to you, cool off here with a Lanikai lime or a banzai banana shave ice.

TOWN CENTER

All of the following eateries are in Kailua's town center, within a mile of each other.

Baci Bistro (☎ 262-7555; 30 Aulike St; lunch specials $6-10, dinner mains $13-19; ☷ 11:30am-2pm Mon-Fri, 5:30-10pm daily) Old World atmosphere, traditional Italian fare and cheerful service add up to a perfect night out at this superb restaurant. The flavors are rich, from the nectar-like garlic soup to the *agnolotti d'aragosta*, a round pasta filled with ricotta, lobster and prosciutto and topped with cream sauce. Add a well-matched wine list and it's no wonder this place draws folks all the way from Honolulu.

Cinnamon's Restaurant (☎ 261-8724; 315 Uluniu St; mains $4-12; ☷ 7am-2pm daily, 5:30-8:30pm Thu-Sat; ☒) Locals in the know really pack this family-friendly place at breakfast to feast on standouts like eggs Benedict mahimahi (white fleshed fish) and frittatas with artichoke hearts. Save room for the homemade apple pie.

Boston's North End Pizza (☎ 263-7757; 29 Ho'olai St; pizza slices $4.25-6, pizza $17-24; ☷ 11am-8pm Mon-Fri, to 9pm Sat & Sun) Come here for windward O'ahu's best pizza. In addition to the enormous 19in pizza pies, this place sells slices that are each equal to a quarter of a pizza – big enough to make a meal in itself. The spinach and fresh garlic version is awesome.

Agnes Bake Shop (☎ 262-5367; 46 Ho'olai St; malasadas 60¢; ☷ 6am-6pm Tue-Sun) Taste the flavors of

---

THE AUTHOR'S CHOICE

Lucy's Grill & Bar (☎ 230-8188; 33 Aulike St; appetizers $7-13, dinner $16-28; ☽ 5-10pm) Decorated with blazing tiki torches, surfboards and saltwater fish tanks, this contemporary bistro encapsulates the laid-back Kailua beach vibe. The food celebrates Hawaii's multiethnic influences with an eclectic flair that knows few bounds. Europe meets Pacific Rim in such dishes as the macadamia nut-encrusted lamb shank and the spinach and caramelized onion pizza with *liliko'i* (passion fruit) puree. For a fiery treat, try the fish of the day in wasabi miso sauce. Come on Wednesday night when you can get a bottle of wine to accompany your meal at half the regular price.

If you're not up for a big meal, swing by anyway and sit at the bar, where you can munch on tasty appetizers and sip exotic drinks. The *'ahi* crab cakes and *kalua* pork tacos are nearly a meal in themselves. The bar drinks include some fun local concoctions, like the pineapple martini (with vodka-soaked fresh pineapple chunks) or *li hing mui* (named for a famous sweet and sour 'crack seed' snack) margarita. Still hungry? You won't be disappointed in the rich crème brûlée.

Portugal in this little bakery's sweet breads and pastries. Best of all are the *malasadas* (like a doughnut without a hole), which are made fresh, served hot and take about 10 minutes to fry up. The shop also sells hot drinks and Portuguese bean soup, and has half a dozen café tables where you can sit and eat.

Champa Thai (☎ 263-8281; 306 Kuulei Rd; dishes $7-10; ☽ 11am-2pm Mon-Fri & 5-9pm daily) This little family-run eatery cooks up Kailua's best Thai food. The signature Penang curry, with coconut milk and shrimp, is a spicy delight, and it also makes excellent pad Thai and summer rolls.

Brent's Restaurant & Deli (☎ 262-8588; 629a Kailua Rd; mains $5-11; ☽ 7am-2pm Mon-Fri, to 3pm Sat & Sun) From the smoked salmon and eggs, to the hefty corned-beef Reuben sandwiches, this New York–style deli is the closest you'll get to Manhattan, plus the weather's better.

Down To Earth (☎ 262-3838; 201 Hamakua Dr; ☽ 8am-9pm) Crunchy greens, all things organic and even a salad-and-hot-entrée bar (per pound $7) await at this large natural food store.

Safeway (☎ 266-5222; 200 Hamakua Dr; ☽ 24hr) A conventional supermarket, near Down to Earth.

Drinking

Lanikai Juice (☎ 262-2383; Kailua Shopping Center, 572 Kailua Rd; juice $3-5; ☽ 6am-8pm Mon-Fri, 8am-7pm Sat & Sun) A great place for a full range of fresh fruit smoothies with names like Da Kine, Mango Sunrise and Lanikai Splash. For a real lift, try the Pineapple Power, which spices freshly squeezed pineapple juice up with zinger herbs like ginseng.

Morning Brew (☎ 262-7770; 600 Kailua Rd; snacks $2-6; ☽ 6am-8pm) This bustling espresso bar serves everything from chai tea to 'Jump Start' double espressos. Good strawberry and whipped cream Belgian waffles, too.

Entertainment

Boardriders Bar & Grill (☎ 261-4600; 201 Hamakua Dr) This large bar and restaurant becomes a happening entertainment venue at night, when live bands take the stage and people take to the dance floor. Pool tables and dartboards, too. After 10pm you have to be 21 to get in.

Shopping

Ali'i Antiques of Kailua (☎ 261-1705; 21 Maluniu Ave; ☽ 10:30am-4:30pm Mon-Sat) An amazing mishmash of Victorian dolls, glassware, trinkets and all sorts of collectibles in wobbly stacks that tower above your head. Worth a look, but leave the kids outside.

Antiques in Kailua Town (☎ 263-1177; 315 Uluniu St; ☽ 9am-4pm Mon & Wed-Fri, to 2pm Tue, Sat & Sun) Across the parking lot from Ali'i Antiques, this spacious shop sells Asian and European antiques, including pottery, furniture and jewelry. It's a co-op, so you never know what you might find.

Under a Hula Moon (☎ 261-4252; Kailua Shopping Center, 600 Kailua Rd) Lots of quirky gift items with island themes, from shellacked blowfish to unusual paintings.

Getting There & Away

If traffic is light, by car it's a 20-minute drive along the Pali Hwy (Hwy 61) from Honolulu to Kailua. To get to Kailua Beach Park, simply stay on Kailua Rd, which begins at the

LET IT ROLL!

Test your knowledge of movies and TV shows filmed on O'ahu:

1. Where was the fictional home of Steve McGarrett's *Hawaii Five-O* crime-fighting unit?
2. Where was the Robins' Nest estate that served as *Magnum PI*'s home?
3. Name the three movies Elvis Presley made in Hawaii.
4. What hunk-and-babe lifeguard show filmed on the North Shore was the most widely broadcast TV show (150 countries) of its day?
5. What current blockbuster TV show about castaways is set on a North Shore beach?
6. What 1960s TV show about castaways used Coconut Island off Kane'ohe in its opening scene?
7. Why did Steven Spielberg move the setting of *Jurassic Park* from Kaua'i to windward O'ahu?
8. What 2005 film starring Drew Barrymore and Adam Sandler was filmed at Kualoa Ranch?
9. Who starred in the 2001 movie *Pearl Harbor*, one of Hollywood's biggest bombs?
10. Where did Kate Bosworth's character in *Blue Crush* (2002) work as a chambermaid?

See answers on p184.

end of the Pali Hwy and continues as the main road through town before reaching the coast.

Both buses 56 and 57 run between the Ala Moana Center in Honolulu and downtown Kailua roughly once every 15 minutes throughout the day; the trip takes about 40 minutes. To get to Kailua Beach Park or Lanikai, get off in downtown Kailua at the corner of Kailua Rd and Oneawa St and transfer to bus 70 Lanikai–Maunawili. However, check the schedule in advance, because bus 70 is not nearly as frequent.

KANE'OHE AREA

pop 35,000

Windward O'ahu's second largest town sits on scenic Kane'ohe Bay. The state's largest bay and reef-sheltered lagoon, Kane'ohe Bay stretches all the way from Mokapu Peninsula to Kualoa Point, 7 miles north of Kane'ohe. Although inshore it's largely silted and not good for swimming, the near-constant trade winds that sweep across the bay are ideal for sailing. Kane'ohe offers some worthwhile sights, but truth be told the town itself is largely a bedroom suburb that just doesn't pack the appeal of neighboring Kailua.

Orientation

Two highways run north–south through Kane'ohe. Kamehameha Hwy (Hwy 836) is both closer to the coast and more scenic and goes by He'eia State Park. The Kahekili Hwy (Hwy 83), which is further inland, intersects the Likelike Hwy (Hwy 63) and continues north past the Byodo-In temple. Kane'ohe Marine Corps Base Hawaii (MCBH) occupies the whole of Mokapu Peninsula; the H3 Fwy terminates at its gate.

Information

Borders Express (☎ 235-8044; Windward Mall, 46-056 Kamehameha Hwy) A good selection of Hawaii-related books, maps and novels, as well as some international newspapers.

First Hawaiian Bank (☎ 261-1898; Windward City Shopping Center, 45-480 Kane'ohe Bay Dr)

Kane'ohe Post Office (☎ 800-275-8777; 46-036 Kamehameha Hwy; ☒ 8am-6pm Mon-Fri, 9am-4pm Sat) Just southeast of the Windward Mall.

Sights

VALLEY OF THE TEMPLES & BYODO-IN

The Valley of the Temples, an interdenominational cemetery just off the Kahekili Hwy, is home to **Byodo-In** (☎ 239-8811; adult/child $2/1; ☒ 8am-5pm), a replica of a 900-year-old temple of the same name in Uji, Japan.

The temple's symmetry is a classic example of Japanese Heian architecture and garden design symbolizing the Pure Land of Mahayana Buddhism. The rich red of the temple against the verdant fluted cliffs of the Ko'olau Range is a watercolorist's dream, especially when mist settles in on the *pali*. In the main hall a 9ft-tall Buddha is positioned to catch the first rays of morning sunlight.

Wild peacocks roam the grounds and hang their tail feathers over the temple's upper railings. A carp pond with cruising bullfrogs fronts the temple, and the 3-ton brass bell beside it is said to bring tranquility and good fortune to those who ring it. It's all very Japanese, right down to the gift

WINDWARD O'AHU

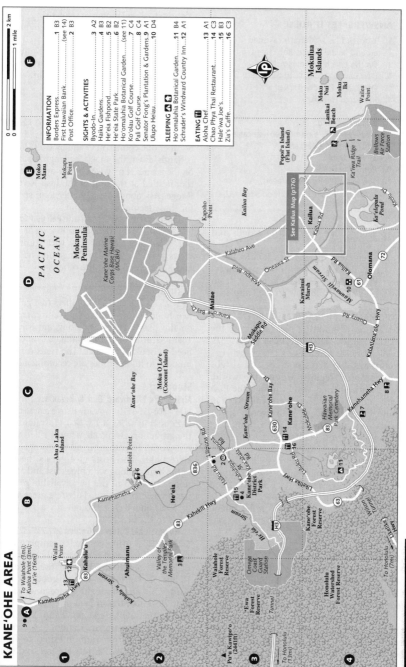

KANE'OHE AREA

INFORMATION	
Borders Express	1 B3
First Hawaiian Bank	(see 14)
Post Office	2 B3

SIGHTS & ACTIVITIES	
Byodo-In	3 A2
Haiku Gardens	4 B3
He'eia Fishpond	5 B2
He'eia State Park	6 B2
Ho'omaluhia Botanical Garden	(see 11)
Ko'olau Golf Course	7 C4
Pali Golf Course	8 C4
Senator Fong's Plantation & Gardens	9 A1
Ulupo Heiau	10 D4

SLEEPING	
Ho'omaluhia Botanical Garden	11 B4
Schrader's Windward Country Inn	12 A1

EATING	
Aloha Chef	13 A1
Chao Phya Thai Restaurant	14 C3
Hale'iwa Joe's	15 B3
Zia's Caffe	16 C3

WINDWARD O'AHU

shop selling sake cups, *daruma* dolls and happy Buddhas.

The cemetery entrance is 1.5 miles north of Haiku Rd. Bus 55 can drop passengers near the entrance on Kahekili Hwy, from where it's a 0.7-mile walk to the temple.

HO'OMALUHIA BOTANICAL GARDEN

Set against a stunning *pali* backdrop, the island's largest **botanical garden** (☎ 233-7323; 45-680 Luluku Rd; admission free; 9am-4pm) encompasses 400 acres of trees and shrubs from tropical regions around the world. A network of trails wind through the lush park and up to a 32-acre reservoir. Keep in mind the park's focus is on woody specimens – if you're looking for a romp past lots of flowering plants, head to Senator Fong's (opposite) instead.

A little visitor center has displays on Hawaiian ethnobotany and the history of the park, which was built to provide flood protection for the valley below. The park is at the end of Luluku Rd, 1.5 miles inland from Kamehameha Hwy. There's no bus service up to the park.

HAIKU GARDENS

A more meditative place is hard to imagine than **Haiku Gardens** (46-336 Haiku Rd; admission free; sunrise-sunset), a little valley containing a lily pond, an abundance of fragrant tropical flowers and lots of birdsong. The gardens, cradled by the Ko'olau Range, are picture perfect. The path starts at the side of Hale'iwa Joe's restaurant and takes only about 15 minutes down and back – though

it's apt to take longer if you bring your camera. To get there from Kamehameha Hwy, turn west on Haiku Rd just past the Windward Mall; after crossing Kahekili Hwy, continue on Haiku Rd a quarter of a mile. Haiku Gardens is on the right.

Activities
GOLF

Ko'olau Golf Course (☎ 236-4653; 45-550 Kionaole Rd; per 18 holes $135; 6am-5pm), named the number one course on O'ahu by *Golf Digest*, is hands-down the most challenging course on the island. It may well be the most scenic, too, nestled at the foot of the lush Ko'olau Range. Ask about the $79 afternoon special for those teeing off after 1pm.

The city-run par 72 hillside **Pali Golf Course** (☎ 266-7612; 45-050 Kamehameha Hwy; per 18 holes $42; 6am-6pm) also abounds with stunning views, with the Ko'olau Range on one side and Kane'ohe Bay on the other.

HIKING

Ho'omaluhia Botanical Garden offers free guided two-hour nature hikes, with commentary on the plants and trees along the way, at 10am Saturday and 1pm Sunday. You don't need to book in advance. The trails can get muddy, so hiking shoes are recommended.

Sleeping

Ali'i Bluffs Windward Bed & Breakfast (☎ 235-1124, 800-235-1151; www.hawaiiscene.com/aliibluffs; 46-251 Ikiiki St; tw $65, d $75;) Hospitality is the attraction at this cozy home filled with old-world furnishings, oil paintings and collectibles. The hosts give guests the run of the house, along with breakfast and afternoon tea. Each of the two available rooms has its own bathroom. There's a great view of Kane'ohe Bay, although it's a bit of a drive to the beach.

Ho'omaluhia Botanical Garden (☎ 233-7323; 45-680 Luluku Rd) A prime choice for campers who don't need to be on the beach, these grassy campsites set at the base of the Ko'olau Range offer great views and good hiking. And with an overnight guard and gates that close to noncampers after sunset, it's among the safest parks on O'ahu. You will need your own transportation, and camping is allowed from 9am on Friday to 4pm on Monday only. Permits are free and can be picked up right at the park.

Eating

Hale'iwa Joe's (☎ 247-6671; 46-336 Haiku Rd; mains $14-24; ⏰ 5:30-9:30pm Mon-Thu, to 10:30pm Fri & Sat) The Haiku Gardens location is half the attraction here – a romantic, open-air setting overlooking a lily pond tucked beneath the Ko'olau Range. The restaurant features excellent Pacific Rim fare, with the likes of coconut shrimp tempura and chicken satay, as well as juicy slabs of prime rib. The gardens are flood-lit at night.

Zia's Caffe (☎ 235-9427; 45-620 Kamehameha Hwy; main $8-20; ⏰ 11am-10pm Mon-Fri, 4-10pm Sat & Sun) Good Italian fare at honest prices draw lots of local families here. There's something for everyone, with a range of dishes that includes eggplant parmesan, shrimp scampi and an excellent chicken Caesar salad. A must for dessert is the white-chocolate tiramisu.

Chao Phya Thai Restaurant (☎ 235-3555; Windward Coast Shopping Center, 45-480 Kane'ohe Bay Dr; dishes $6-10; ⏰ 11am-2pm Mon-Sat, 5-9pm daily) This family-run eatery serves very decent northeastern Thai food, including green papaya salad and sticky rice, along with Thai standards like spring rolls and spicy curries. No liquor, but you can bring your own.

Getting There & Away

By car, the main route from Honolulu is the Likelike Hwy (Hwy 63), which leads into Kane'ohe's main commercial strip.

Kane'ohe is connected to Honolulu by buses 55 and 65, which leave from the Ala Moana Center a few times an hour and take about 35 minutes. Bus 56 connects Kailua with Kane'ohe about twice an hour and takes 20 minutes. You can also take bus 56 from the Ala Moana Center to Kane'ohe, but it takes much longer as it goes via Kailua.

KAHALU'U

This small enclave, at the north side of Kane'ohe, marks the start of the best bit of the windward coast drive.

Sights & Activities
HE'EIA STATE PARK
Stop at this little **state park** (⏰ sunrise-sunset) on Kealohi Point, just off the Kamehameha Hwy, to enjoy the good view of a fishpond and Coconut Island. **He'eia Fishpond**, an impressive survivor from the days when stone-walled ponds used for raising fish for royalty were common on Hawaiian shores,

remains largely intact despite the invasive mangrove that grows along its walls.

Coconut Island (Moku O Lo'e), just offshore to the southeast, was a royal playground, named for the coconut trees planted there by Princess Bernice Pauahi Bishop. In the 1930s it was the estate of Christian Holmes, heir to the Fleischmann Yeast fortune, who dredged it to double the island's size to 25 acres. Shots of Coconut Island appeared in opening scenes of the *Gilligan's Island* TV series. Today the University of Hawaii's marine biology department occupies much of the island.

SENATOR FONG'S PLANTATION & GARDENS
Names like the Eisenhower Plateau and Kennedy Valley are a hint of the background of these **gardens** (☎ 239-6775; 47-285 Pulama Rd; adult/child $14.50/9; ⏰ 10am-2pm), a labor of love of Hiram Fong, who served in the US Senate until 1977 and dedicated the rest of his life to preserving Hawaii's flora for future generations. Since Fong's death in 2004 at age 97, his family has taken over the 725-acre grounds and offers visitors walking tours through the myriad tropical flowers, palm trees, sandalwood and other indigenous plants. Tours last about 45 minutes. The gardens are 1 mile off the Kamehameha Hwy.

Sleeping & Eating
Schrader's Windward Country Inn (☎ 239-5711, 800-735-5071; www.schradersinn.com; 47-039 Lihikai Dr; studio/2-bedroom units from $88/200; 🐕) Well off the tourist track, this low-rise seaside place is at the end of a congested residential neighborhood, but once you step onto the lanai all you see are bay views. Schrader's has long catered to military families from Kane'ohe's Marine Corps base, but it's expanding its appeal by offering a variety of complimentary services, including cruises, kayaking and free Wednesday dinners.

Aloha Chef (cnr Hwys 83 & 830; meals $8-11; ⏰ 10am-6pm) Share some aloha at this little plate-lunch haven that's run by a Hawaiian family. Meals range from traditional Hawaiian fare to tangy island-raised shrimp with pineapple and sweet-and-sour sauce. This is a fun spot – there's even music some nights at the outdoor stage. Look for the bright pink shrimp shack at the *makai* (oceanward) side of the road where the two highways meet.

WAIAHOLE & WAIKANE

The quintessential farming towns of Waiahole and Waikane abound with orchid nurseries, and small family-run farms of taro patches and groves of coconuts, banana and papaya trees. You'll see many of these homegrown operations right along the main road, but if you want an even closer look at the bountiful fields take the inland drive up Waiahole Valley Rd, the road that starts at the side of the Waiahole Poi Factory.

Not everything in these parts is as peaceful as the taro patches. Large tracts of Waikane Valley were taken over by the military during WWII for training and target practice, a use that continued until the 1960s. The government now claims the land has so much live ordnance it can't be returned to the families it was leased from, a source of ongoing contention with local residents who are upset that much of the inner valley remains off-limits.

Eating

Ono-Loa (☎ 239-5117; cnr Kamehameha Hwy & Waiahole Valley Rd; dishes $1-3, plate lunch $8.50; 10:30am-2pm Mon-Wed & Sat, 10am-3pm Sun) Located inside the historic Waiahole Poi Factory, this Hawaiian take-out eatery is the real deal. You can get huge plate lunches with *laulau* (a bundle of pork, chicken or fish wrapped in taro and ti leaves and steamed), *haupia* (coconut pudding) and all the trimmings or order à la carte. True local flavor.

KUALOA

In ancient times Kualoa (which means 'long ancestral background') was once one of the most sacred places on O'ahu. When a chief stood on Kualoa Point, passing canoes lowered their sails in respect. The children of chiefs were brought here to be raised, and it may have been a place of refuge where *kapu* (taboo) breakers and fallen warriors could seek reprieve from the law. Because of its rich significance to Hawaiians, Kualoa Regional Park is listed in the National Register of Historic Places.

Sights & Activities

KUALOA REGIONAL PARK

They just don't get much better than this 153-acre county **beach park** (Kamehameha Hwy; sunrise-sunset; 55), which has magnificent scenery, a white-sand beach, plenty of room to roam and camping to boot. The mountains looming precipitously across the road are called, appropriately enough, Pali-ku, meaning 'vertical cliff.' When the mist settles, it looks like a scene from a Chinese watercolor painting.

The long, thin beach here fronts shallow waters with safe swimming and is backed by open grassy lawns with a few palm trees and inviting picnic tables. There are rest rooms, showers and a lifeguard.

Ponds

Birders will want to stroll south along the beach to **'Apua Pond**, a 3-acre brackish salt marsh on Kualoa Point that's a nesting area for the endangered *ae'o* (Hawaiian stilt). If you walk down the beach beyond 'Apua Pond, you'll see a bit of **Moli'i Fishpond**, its rock walls covered with mangrove, milo and pickleweed.

Mokoli'i Island

That eye-catching island you see off Kualoa Regional Park is called **Mokoli'i**. In Hawaiian legend, Mokoli'i is said to be the tail of a nasty lizard or a dog – depending on who's telling the story – that was slain by a god and thrown into the ocean. Following the immigration of Chinese laborers to Hawaii, this cone-shaped island also came to be called Papale Pake, Hawaiian for 'Chinese hat' – although most everyone today refers to it as 'Chinaman's Hat.'

KUALOA RANCH

The horses grazing on the green slopes across the road from Kualoa Regional Park belong to **Kualoa Ranch** (☎ 237-7321; www.kualoa.com; 57-091 Kamehameha Hwy; 55), O'ahu's largest cattle ranch. The scenic 4000-acre ranch may well look familiar, as it's been the setting for scores of movies, including *Jurassic Park* and *Mighty Joe Young*, and TV shows from *Hawaii 5-0* to the current hit *Lost*.

Much of the activities are packaged for Japanese tourists who are shuttled in from Waikiki. But you might still want to see where Hurley built his *Lost* golf course, Godzilla left his footprints and the *Jurassic Park* kids hid from dinosaurs on a fun jeep tour of the movie-set sites (one hour, $15). You can also take off on your own for an ATV (All-Terrain Vehicle) ride (one hour,

$47). Forget the ranch's horseback trail rides, which are geared for inexperienced packaged tourists and are largely a yawn; Happy Trails Hawaii (p203) rides on the North Shore is the place to go if you want a horse with some giddy-up.

Back in 1850 Kamehameha III leased 625 acres of this land to a missionary doctor who became one of the king's advisers. Dr Judd planted the land with sugarcane, built flumes to transport it and imported Chinese laborers to work the fields. You can still see the stone stack **ruins** of the island's first sugar mill and a bit of its crumbling walls half a mile north of the beach park alongside the road.

Sleeping & Eating

Kualoa Regional Park (Kamehameha Hwy) Set your tent up and spend the night on this lovely beach where royalty once slept. Camping is allowed from Friday to Tuesday night, with a permit from the county; see p229 for details.

Aunty Pat's Paniolo Cafe (☎ 237-7321; 57-091 Kamehameha Hwy; dishes $5-7; ◷ 9am-3pm) Located in Kualoa Ranch's welcome center, this simple eatery has decent salads, sandwiches and plate lunches.

Shopping

Tropical Farms (☎ 237-1960; 49-227 Kamehameha Hwy; ◷ 9:30am-5pm) Just south of Kualoa Regional Park, this is a great place to buy gifts for friends back home. Everything is homegrown Hawaiian, from the family running it to the island-made products they sell. Pick up a bag of Waialua coffee from the North Shore, passion-fruit marmalade or yummy dark-chocolate macadamia nuts that put the more-commercial brands to shame. Surrounding the main shop are several stalls selling Hawaiian handicrafts, and if you've ever wondered what sugarcane, coffee and pineapple plants look like as they grow, you'll find them in the garden out front.

KA'A'AWA
pop 1325
In the Ka'a'awa area, the road tightly hugs the coast and the *pali* moves right on in, with barely enough space to squeeze a few houses between the base of the cliffs and the highway.

Swanzy Beach Park, a narrow neighborhood beach used mainly by fishers, has a grassy lawn fronted by a shore wall. Across the road from the park is a convenience store, a plate-lunch place, a gas station and a postage stamp–sized post office – pretty much the center of town, such as it is.

Information
Ka'a'awa Post Office (☎ 800-275-8777; 51-480 Kamehameha Hwy; ◷ 8am-noon & 1-3:45pm Mon-Fri, 9:30-11:30am Sat)

Sights
A natural rock formation resembling a lion sits on a cliff behind the Crouching Lion Inn, just north of Ka'a'awa center. Called the **Crouching Lion**, the formation bears a striking resemblance to an African lion, a creature Hawaiians had never heard of before Western contact. Not surprisingly, they saw something else in the image. According to legend, the rock is a demigod from Tahiti who was cemented to the mountain during a jealous struggle between Pele, the volcano goddess, and her sister Hi'iaka. When he tried to free himself by pulling into a crouching position, the demigod was turned to stone.

To find the image, pull into the Crouching Lion Inn parking lot, just north of the 27-mile marker. Stand at the restaurant sign with your back to the ocean and look straight up to the left of the coconut tree. You will see the figure on a cliff in the background.

Eating
Crouching Lion Inn (☎ 237-8511; 51-666 Kamehameha Hwy; lunch $6-12, dinner $15-33; ◷ 11am-3pm & 5-9pm) This restaurant attracts the lion's share of day-trippers to these parts. Lunch is mainly sandwiches and salads, while dinner offers decent versions of steak and seafood. The ocean views are great but be prepared for a tour bus in the picture, or better yet come in the evening when the buses are gone, the lanai tiki torches are lit and the sunset unfolds.

KAHANA VALLEY
A repository of ancient Hawaiian sites, Kahana is a unique preserve. In old Hawaii the islands were divided into *ahupua'a* – pie-shaped land divisions reaching from the mountains to the sea, providing everything

---

SURF & SAND STANDOUTS

When you're ready to hit the beach, you'll find many of the island's finest strands along the eastern side of O'ahu from Sandy Beach, at the southeastern tip of the island, to Turtle Bay, where windward O'ahu meets the North Shore.

Kailua Beach (p177) No matter what your interest, this beach has it all. It's as pretty as they come, and also scores as the island's top windsurfing destination and its best place for ocean kayaking. Even for novices it's easy, and you can rent equipment and get lessons for both sports right on the beach.

Kualoa Beach (p186) Arguably O'ahu's most scenic beach, Kualoa is backed by precipitous green mountains and overlooks an ancient fishpond. It's a good beach for kids, too, with shallow waters and safe swimming.

Lanikai Beach (p177) Home to millionaires but accessible to all, this beach boasts the softest powdery white sand on O'ahu and perhaps even the planet. Go see for yourself what brings Michelle Pfeiffer and Harrison Ford to the neighborhood.

Malaekahana Beach (p192) Not only does this lovely beach have good year-round swimming, but it's also popular with families because of its wide range of water activities.

Sandy Beach (p168) It's long, glorious and – you bet – sandy! Sandy Beach also boasts the most

challenging shorebreak on O'ahu, making it the top beach for advanced bodysurfers. In addition, there's good board surfing when the swells are big.

Kaihalulu Beach (p196) Looking for seclusion? You'll find it at this remote gem near the northern tip of O'ahu. It's a great place for beachcombing, long walks and basking in the sun. It can also be a fun diving spot when the seas are calm.

Kuilima Cove (p196) Want to swim with turtles? This pretty little cove fronting the Turtle Bay Resort is a favorite spot for these awesome creatures and you can rent snorkels right at the hotel's beach hut.

Moku Nui Beach (p177) It's worth a little effort to get to this hidden hideaway on an island off Lanikai Beach. Pack a picnic, rent a kayak at Kailua Beach and paddle out to your own little slice of paradise.

Waimanalo Bay Beach (p170) From this gorgeous beach all you see is endless sand, a sea of creamy turquoise waters and local kids hitting the surf. It's a scene right off one of those period postcards from 1930s' Hawaii. Bring a board and join 'em.

---

the Hawaiians needed for subsistence. Kahana Valley, 4 miles long and 2 miles wide, is the only publicly owned *ahupua'a* remaining on O'ahu.

Kahana Valley was once thickly planted with wetland taro, which thrived in this rainy valley. Archaeologists have identified the overgrown remnants of more than 130 agricultural terraces and irrigation canals, as well as the remains of a heiau, fishing shrines and numerous house sites.

In the early 20th century the area was planted with sugarcane, which was hauled north to the Kahuku Mill via a small railroad. During WWII the upper part of Kahana Valley was taken over by the military and used to train soldiers in jungle warfare. In 1965 the state bought Kahana Valley from the Robinson family of Kaua'i (owners of the island of Ni'ihau) in order to preserve it from development.

About 30 Hawaiian families currently live in the lower valley. The upper valley remains undeveloped and is mostly used by local hunters who come here on weekends to hunt feral pigs.

While many of Kahana's archaeological sites are deep in the valley and inaccessible, Kahana's most impressive site, **Huilua Fishpond** on Kahana Bay, is readily visible from the main road and can be visited simply by going down to the beach. Should you be up for a dip, the beach provides safe swimming, with a gently sloping sandy bottom.

Ahupua'a 'o Kahana State Park

The signposted entrance to **Ahupua'a 'O Kahana State Park** (☎ 237-7766; Kamehameha Hwy; ⏰ 8am-4pm Mon-Fri; 🚌 55) is a mile north of the Crouching Lion Inn.

When the state purchased Kahana, it also acquired tenants, many of whom had lived in the valley for a long time. Rather than evict a struggling rural population, the state agreed to let the residents stay on the land, hoping to eventually incorporate the families into a 'living park,' with the residents acting as interpretive guides. The 'living park' concept has inched forward ever so slowly, but there's now a simple orientation center near the park entrance and tours are being provided to local organizations.

Although there are no tours for individual travelers, you can pick up a trail map at the orientation center and walk through the valley on your own.

Hiking

The most accessible of the Ahupua'a 'O Kahana State Park trails is the 1.2-mile **Kapa'ele'ele Ko'a and Keaniani Kilo Trail**, which begins at the orientation center. It goes along the old railroad route, passes a fishing shrine called Kapa'ele'ele Koa and leads to Keaniani Kilo, a lookout used in ancient times for spotting schools of fish in the bay. The trail then goes down to the bay and follows the highway back to the park entrance.

If you want to get into the rain forest, there's the **Nakoa Trail**, which makes a 2.5-mile loop through tropical vegetation. The trail, named from the koa trees along the way, makes a couple of stream crossings and passes a swimming hole en route. However, the start of the Nakoa Trail is 1.3 miles inland from the visitor center on a rough dirt road, so the total walking distance equals 5 miles. Keep in mind that the trails can be slippery when wet – with an annual rainfall of 75in on the coast and triple that in the mountains, this is the wettest side of O'ahu.

PUNALU'U

pop 885

This scattered little seaside community doesn't draw much attention from tourists. Nevertheless, it has a couple of low-key places to stay and a decent beach. **Punalu'u Beach Park** has a long, narrow beach that offers fairly good swimming, as the offshore reef protects the shallow inshore waters in all but stormy weather. Be cautious near the mouth of the Waiono Stream and in the channel leading out from it, as currents are strong when the stream is flowing quickly or when the surf is high.

Sleeping

Punalu'u Guesthouse (☎ 946-0591; 53-504 Kamehameha Hwy; per person $25) In the center of Punalu'u, this little guesthouse is managed by Hostelling International Honolulu. Because there are only three rooms and it's a cozy situation, the hostel prescreens potential guests, so most people come here after

a stay at the HI hostel in Honolulu. The house has a communal kitchen and guests often eat together at dinnertime.

Pat's at Punalu'u (☎ 293-2624; 53-567 Kamehameha Hwy; 🏊) This 136-unit condominium is largely residential and a bit neglected, but on the plus side, it's on the water with all the rooms facing the ocean. There's no front desk; instead privately owned rentals are handled by realtors, some of whom post their listings on the condo bulletin board.

Paul Comeau Condo Rentals (☎ 293-2624, 800-467-6215; fax 293-0618; PO Box 589, Ka'a'awa, HI 96730; studio $100, 3-bedroom unit $235) Handles a number of units at Pat's at Punalu'u; all have a three-day minimum stay.

Eating

Maliko's (☎ 237-8474; 53-146 Kamehameha Hwy; mains $6-15; 🕙 11am-9pm Mon-Sat, to 8pm Sun) Pure honky-tonk, with sports TV, poker machines and an electric organ player, this is Punalu'u's one and only restaurant. The cook changes as often as the restaurant name, so no bets on the food, but sandwiches and shrimp dinners are the time-honored standards. It's a third of a mile north of the 25-mile marker.

Shopping

Kim Taylor Reece Gallery (☎ 293-2000; 53-866 Kamehameha Hwy; 🕙 noon-5pm Thu-Sat) Kim's classic sepia photographs of hula dancers in motion are among the most widely recognized art images in Hawaii. This classy gallery, on the inland side of the road between Punalu'u and Hau'ula, is well worth a stop even if it's just to browse.

HAU'ULA

pop 3650

This small coastal town sits against a scenic backdrop of hills and majestic Norfolk pines. Aside from a couple of gas pumps, a general store and a 7-Eleven store, the main landmark in town is the stone ruins of **Lanakila Church** (c 1853), perched on a hill next to the newer Hau'ula Congregational Church. Across the road is **Hau'ula Beach Park**, which is not particularly appealing for swimming but it does occasionally get waves big enough for local kids to ride. In the hills above town is the **Kaipapa'u Forest Reserve**, offering good hiking with ocean vistas.

Hiking

The **Division of Forestry & Wildlife** (☎ 587-0166) maintains two trails in the Kaipapa'u Forest Reserve. Both trails share the same access point and both head into beautiful hills in the lower Ko'olau Range. The Hau'ula Loop Trail is the better maintained of the two.

The signposted trailhead for both hikes is at a bend in Hau'ula Homestead Rd, about a quarter of a mile up from Kamehameha Hwy. Hau'ula Homestead Rd is located right in town, at the northern end of Hau'ula Beach Park. Follow the paved access road inland, past the hunter/hiker check-in station that marks the start of the forest reserve.

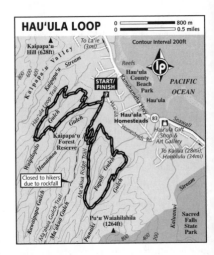

HAU'ULA LOOP TRAIL

The Hau'ula Loop Trail is a scenic 2.5-mile hike that makes a couple of gulch crossings and climbs along a ridge with broad views of the forested interior, the ocean and the town of Hau'ula. This trail takes about 1½ hours to hike, passes through a wide variety of native vegetation and offers the chance to see some of Hawaii's forest birds.

The Hau'ula Loop Trail forks off to the right immediately after the road enters the forest reserve, rising quickly through a forest of ohia and hala (screw pine) trees, as well as sweet-smelling guava and bizarre octopus trees, with their spreading tentacle-like branches of pink to reddish flowers. Birds fly about and ocean vistas open up as the trail climbs through shaggy ironwood trees, then splits into a loop about half a mile in.

By going left, the trail remains easier to follow and more clearly laid out. Under ironwoods and towering Norfolk pines, the trail switchbacks up and over a ridge into Waipilopilo Gulch, passing rare endemic flora, such as *a'ali'i* plants with red seed pods, *akia* shrubs and *lama* (Hawaiian persimmon). Ocean breezes and forest shade are a relief from the humidity. The trail crosses a streambed and muddily climbs out of the gulch to empty out atop of another ridge with fine overlooks of Kaipapa'u Valley.

Instead of heading uphill left on a hunting trail-of-use, turn right. As the footpath rolls up and down along the ridge, there are even more spectacular views into the valley. Eventually the trail descends back into ironwood

trees, Norfolk pines and Hawaiian ferns, all displaying infinite shades of green. The trail crosses a streambed, then ascends again and levels out into a wide forest path with views of Hau'ula, beaches and offshore islets. Even the roar of the surf reaches up here. Contouring around the ridge, which drops off steeply, tree roots emerge underfoot as the trail starts descending. Keep a sharp eye out for any obscure turnings in the switchbacks. Turn left at the loop trail junction to reach the trailhead and the paved road.

MA'AKUA RIDGE TRAIL

If you're up for a second hike, the more challenging Ma'akua Ridge Trail, which begins on the left about half a mile after entering the forest reserve, makes a 2.5-mile loop that climbs in and out of a couple of gullies and follows the narrow Ma'akua Ridge. Much of the trail is open and dry but there are sections that close in, including some thickets of acacia trees that create tunnel effects. There are fine ridge-top views of the coast and Hau'ula along the way. The hike takes about two hours.

Shopping

Hau'ula Gift Shop & Art Gallery (☎ 293-5145; 54-042 Kamehameha Hwy) Look for the bright pink building with the Ching Tong Leong Store sign, which houses this local shop selling all sorts of crafts and kitschy souvenirs, including Hawaii-made pottery, wind chimes and watercolor paintings.

LA'IE

pop 4600

This seaside community has long attracted those looking for a safe haven. In old Hawaii it was the site of an ancient *pu'uhonua* – a place where *kapu* breakers and fallen warriors could seek refuge. In more recent times it's become the center for the Mormon community in Hawaii.

The first Mormon missionaries to Hawaii arrived in 1850. After an attempt to establish a 'City of Joseph' on the island of Lana'i failed amid a land scandal, the Mormons turned to La'ie. In 1865 they purchased 6000 acres of land here, settled in and slowly expanded their influence.

In 1919 the Mormons constructed a **temple**, a smaller version of the one in Salt Lake City, at the foot of the Ko'olau Range. This stately temple, gleaming white at the end of a wide promenade, is like nothing else on the windward coast. Although there's a visitor center where enthusiastic guides will tell you about Mormonism, tourists are not allowed to enter the temple itself.

Nearby is the Hawaii branch of Brigham Young University (BYU), with scholarship programs that recruit students from islands throughout the Pacific. Many of those students help pay for their living expenses by working as guides at the Polynesian Cultural Center (see below).

Information

All of the following are clustered together in the La'ie Shopping Center, half a mile north of the Polynesian Cultural Center:

Bank of Hawaii (☎ 293-9238; 55-510 Kamehameha Hwy) Has a 24-hour ATM.

La'ie Post Office (☎ 293-0337; 55-510 Kamehameha Hwy; ☽ 9am-3:30pm Mon-Fri, 9:30-11:30am Sat)

La'ie Washerette (☎ 293-2821; 55-510 Kamehameha Hwy; ☽ 6am-9pm Mon-Sat) Coin laundromat.

Sights

POLYNESIAN CULTURAL CENTER

Join the crowds visiting the seven Polynesian 'villages' at the **Polynesian Cultural Center** (☎ 293-3333, 800-367-7060; www.polynesia.com; Kamehameha Hwy; adult/child 5-11yr $36/25, with evening show $50/34; ☽ noon-9pm Mon-Sat; ☐ 55). Called PCC by locals, this 'nonprofit' organization belonging to the Mormon Church draws nearly one million tourists a year, making it the most visited paid attraction in Hawaii.

The 42-acre park centers around seven re-created theme villages representing Samoa, New Zealand, Fiji, Tahiti, Tonga, the Marquesas and Hawaii. Each village has authentic-looking huts and ceremonial houses, many elaborately built with twisted sennit ropes and hand-carved posts, and containing examples of coconut weavings, tapa cloth and other handicrafts. BYU students of Polynesian descent dressed in native garb demonstrate dances, games, poi (fermented taro) pounding and the like. The interpreters are amiable and you could easily spend a few hours wandering around chatting or getting familiar with a craft or two.

The admission price also includes boat rides on the waterway winding through the park; the Pageant of the Long Canoes, a sort of trumped-up floating talent show; and van tours of the Mormon temple grounds and BYU campus. At 7:30pm there's a Polynesian song and dance show that can be fun – partly authentic, partly Hollywood-style and much like an enthusiastic college production, with elaborate sets and costumes.

Although PCC has many interesting features, it's also very touristy and hard to recommend at the steep admission price.

Activities

The 1.5 miles of beach fronting the town of La'ie between Malaekahana State Recreation Area and La'ie Point offer opportunities for surfers, bodysurfers and windsurfers. **Pounders Beach**, half a mile south of the main entrance to PCC, is an excellent bodysurfing

---

DETOUR: LA'IE POINT LOOKOUT

Crashing surf, a natural bridge and a slice of Hawaiian folk history are in store at the La'ie Point lookout. It also offers a fine view of the mountains looming to the south. The nearshore island with the hole in it is Kukuiho'olua, otherwise known as Puka Rock. In Hawaiian legend it's said to be part of a giant lizard that was chopped into pieces by a demigod to stop its deadly attack on O'ahu.

To get there from Kamehameha Hwy head toward the ocean onto Anemoku St, opposite the La'ie Shopping Center, then after 0.2 miles turn right on Naupaka St and go straight to the end.

beach, but the shorebreak, as the name of the beach implies, can be brutal. Summer swimming is generally good, though there's a strong winter current. The area around the old landing is usually the calmest.

Hukilau Surf Shop (☎ 293-9229; 55-730 Kamehameha Hwy; rental per day snorkel set $5, surfboard $25, boogie board $10; ☉ 10am-6pm Mon-Sat) rents all sorts of watersports gear and can give you the lowdown on all the best places for action that day.

Sleeping

La'ie Inn (☎ 293-9282, 800-526-4562; www.laieinn .com; 55-109 Laniloa St; r incl breakfast $89-99; ☒ ☒) Right at the gate of Polynesian Cultural Center, this two-story motel surrounds a courtyard swimming pool and offers 49 comfortable rooms. Each has a lanai, TV and mini-refrigerator.

Eating

Hukilau Cafe (☎ 293-8616; 55-662 Wahinepe'e St; dishes $3-7; ☉ 7am-2pm Tue-Fri, to noon Sat) This friendly little joint, off the Kamehameha Hwy on the north side of town, is one of those hidden secrets locals like to keep to themselves. The food is unassuming but right on, the portions huge and the prices modest. Sweet bread French toast, an unbeatable teriyaki beef plate lunch and good ol' *loco moco* are favorites.

La'ie Chop Suey (☎ 293-8022; 55-510 Kamehameha Hwy; dishes $6-9; ☉ 10am-8:45pm Mon-Sat) For decent Chinese fare, along with some local dishes like pot roast pork, stop by this little family-run eatery in the La'ie Shopping Center.

Foodland supermarket (☎ 293-4443; ☉ 6am-10pm) This supermarket joins several fast-food eateries at the La'ie Shopping Center. It stocks everything a Foodland store typically carries, except alcohol.

MALAEKAHANA STATE RECREATION AREA

With its glorious beach and offshore island, this place offers a variety of watery delights that will suit any beachgoer.

Sights & Activities
MALAEKAHANA BEACH

Malaekahana Beach is a beautiful strand that stretches between Makahoa Point to the north and Kalanai Point to the south.

The long, narrow, sandy beach is backed by ironwood trees. Swimming is generally good year-round, although there are occasionally strong currents in winter. This popular family beach can also be good for many other water activities, including bodysurfing, board surfing and windsurfing.

Kalanai Point, the main section of the state park, less than a mile north of La'ie, has picnic tables, barbecue grills, rest rooms and showers.

MOKU'AUIA (GOAT ISLAND)

This state bird sanctuary just offshore from Malaekahana Beach has a sandy cove with good swimming and snorkeling. It's possible to wade over to the island – best when the tide is low and the water's calm, but be careful of the shallow coral and spiny sea urchins.

You can also snorkel across to Goat Island and off its beaches. Beware of a rip current that's sometimes present off the windward end of the island where the water is deeper. Before going out, be sure to ask the lifeguard about water conditions and the advisability of crossing.

Sleeping

Malaekahana State Recreation Area has the best campground at this end of the windward coast. You can pitch a tent for free in the park's main Kalanai Point section if you have a state park permit (p230).

You can also rent a yurt or tent camp for a fee in the Makahoa Point section of the park, which has a separate entrance off Kamehameha Hwy, three-quarters of a mile north of the main park entrance. **Friends of Malaekahana** (☎ 293-1736; www.alternative-hawaii .com/fom; tent site per person $5, 2-6 person yurt $40-60), a local nonprofit group dedicated to cultural preservation, maintains this end of the park, offering 24-hour security and hot showers. Unlike other O'ahu campgrounds, this place allows camping seven nights of the week. Reservations are strongly recommended and there's a two-night minimum stay.

KAHUKU
pop 2100

Kahuku is a former sugar town, its roads lined with wooden cane houses. The town once radiated out from the Kahuku Plantation mill, which produced sugar from 1890 to 1971. A relatively small operation, it was unable to keep up with the increasingly mechanized competition of Hawaii's bigger mills. When the mill shut down, Kahuku's economy skidded into a slump that still lingers today.

Most of the mill has been knocked down, but the remnants of the smokestack and the old iron gears can be seen behind the post office, which occupies the mill's former offices. The rest of the mill's grounds has been turned into a small shopping center containing the town's bank, gas station and grocery store.

Today locals are still looking to the land, or more accurately the marsh, for their livelihoods. Shrimp ponds at the north side of Kahuku now supply O'ahu's restaurants, and shrimp trucks that cook up and sell the tasty treats are thick along the road.

And while making a living can be a challenge, Kahuku folks are a proud lot, their modest houses neat as a pin, their yards filled with gardens. You can get a sense of their spirit by catching one of the high school football games. Everyone in town turns out to cheer on the Red Raiders, which is not only the best high school football team in all Hawaii but is ranked in the top 10 nationally.

Information

First Hawaiian Bank (☎ 293-9271; 56-565 Kamehameha Hwy)

Kahuku Post Office (☎ 800-275-8777; 56-565 Kamehameha Hwy; ⊙ 8:30am-4:30pm Mon-Fri, to 11:30am Sat)

Activities

BIRD-WATCHING

This 164-acre **James Campbell National Wildlife Refuge** (☎ 637-6330; www.fws.gov/pacificislands/wnwr/ojamesnwr.html) encompasses a rare freshwater wetland that provides a habitat for Hawaii's four endangered waterbirds – the Hawaiian coot, the Hawaiian stilt, the Hawaiian duck and the Hawaiian moorhen.

From mid-February through July, during stilt nesting season, the refuge is off-limits to all visitors. From August 1 to February 15 you can join birders on staff-led tours from 4pm to 5:30pm every Thursday and

3:30pm to 5pm on Saturday. Tours are free, but reservations are required. The refuge is signposted 2 miles north of Kahuku's town center.

You're also assured of seeing birds – Hawaiian stilts, Hawaiian ducks and white egrets at the very least – grabbing themselves a free meal at the **roadside shrimp ponds** right alongside Kamehameha Hwy.

GOLF

If you're up for a quick round of golf, take a break at **Kahuku Golf Course** (☎ 293-5842; South Golf Course Rd, Kahuku; per 9 holes $10; ⊙ 7am-5pm), a casual seaside 9-hole, par 35 course. Be forewarned: on windy days it can be a real challenge. This is a walking-only course, but pull carts ($4) and golf clubs ($12) are available for rent.

Sleeping & Eating

For a real treat don't leave town without trying Kahuku's homegrown shrimp. You'll find nearly a dozen shrimp trucks and roadside shacks between Kahuku and the Turtle Bay Hilton on the North Shore.

Romy's Kahuku Prawns (☎ 232-2202; 56-781 Kamehameha Hwy; meals $11; ⊙ 11am-7pm) You can't get fresher than this – these buggers get pulled right out of the pond adjacent to this bright red roadside shrimp shack. Order them sweet and spicy, or with butter and garlic, take them to the picnic tables and enjoy your feast.

The only hotel in the area is the Turtle Bay Resort, just beyond the north end of Kahuku. For more information on the resort and the neighboring Turtle Bay Condos, see p198. Turtle Bay Resort also has a couple of restaurants.

Shopping

Only Show in Town (☎ 293-1295; 56-901 Kamehameha Hwy; ⊙ 11am-5pm) You just have to stop here – Hawaiian kitsch at its finest and cool collectibles, including classic posters, hula dolls and aloha shirts. The shop, occupying an old plantation grocery store, is one mile north of Kahuku center.

Also check out Island Roots Carvings next door, which has interesting carvings in wood, shell and bone.

North Shore

The very name North Shore conjures up images of surfers barreling their way across impossible waves. When winter's north swells bring in 30ft monsters, this is the place of legends. Sunset Beach, the Banzai Pipeline and Waimea Bay are among the most celebrated surf spots in the entire world, hosting top competitions and providing footage for scores of surfing films, like Bruce Brown's 1964 surf classic *Endless Summer*.

Surf mania prevails everywhere on the North Shore, from restaurants serving up omelettes with names like 'Wipe Out' to roadside signs warning 'Caution, Surfer Crossing.' When the surf's up, half the North Shore population can be found on the beach, and the convoys of cars crawling up from Honolulu to watch surfers jockey the waves are so thick the traffic jams up on the highway.

Still, surfing is only part of the allure. The North Shore's sparkling beaches appeal to sun worshippers year-round, and in summer provide splendid swimming and snorkeling conditions. Hale'iwa, the North Shore's gateway and only sizable town, is a charmer with cute shops and tasty restaurants.

And if you're beginning to think that the North Shore is a pretty well-beaten path, that's only half true. The western Mokule'ia side is so barren it's used for the beach scenes of the castaway island in the TV show *Lost*.

Hot tip: if you want to avoid the traffic, simply head to the North Shore on a weekday and let those islanders tied to a Honolulu office all week have the roads on the weekend.

HIGHLIGHTS

- Watching kamikaze surfers tackle incredible winter waves at **Sunset Beach** (p198)
- Exploring the remnants of ancient Hawaii at **Waimea Valley Audubon Center** (p202)
- Sampling the bounty of rural O'ahu at **North Shore Country Market** (p199)
- Taking the plunge as a tandem skydiver at **Dillingham Airfield** (p208)
- Treating yourself to O'ahu's favorite shave ice in **Hale'iwa** (p203)

History

Early Polynesian settlers were drawn to the North Shore by the region's rich fishing grounds, cooling trade winds and moderate rain. The areas around Mokule'ia, Hale'iwa and Waimea all once had sizable Hawaiian settlements, and abandoned taro patches still remain in their upland valleys.

By the early 20th century the O'ahu Railway & Land Company had extended the railroad from Honolulu to the North Shore, and the first beachgoers began to arrive from the city. Hotels and private beach houses sprang up to accommodate the tourists, but when the railroad stopped running in the 1940s the hotels shut down for good. Sections of abandoned track are still found along many of the beaches.

Waikiki surfers started taking on North Shore waves in the late '50s; big-time surf competitions followed. In 1963 the Beach Boys' hit song *Surfin' USA* rolled through a list of the best surf breaks in the country, and names like Sunset Beach suddenly became part of the country's vernacular.

Getting There & Away

If coming via the windward coast, take Hwy 61 from Honolulu to Kane'ohe, then proceed northwest along Hwy 83 all the way up the windward coast. Once you get north of Kahuku you're on the North Shore. One of the first places you'll encounter is Kawela, home of the Turtle Bay Resort. The Kamehameha Hwy (Hwy 83), the two-lane coastal road that runs along the North Shore, connects the beaches and villages between the Turtle Bay Resort and Hale'iwa.

If you're starting in Waikiki, the quickest route to the North Shore is to take the H1 Fwy west and then exit north onto the H2 Fwy to Wahiawa, where you can continue north via the Kamehameha Hwy.

Bus 52 is the main route serving the North Shore. It runs twice hourly from the Ala Moana Center in Honolulu and makes numerous stops, including Hale'iwa, Waimea and Sunset Beach before terminating at Turtle Bay. Bus 52 bypasses Waialua, but local bus 76 connects Hale'iwa and Waialua. All points west of Waialua or inland of the Kamehameha Hwy are beyond the bus routes and can only be reached with your own transportation.

KAWELA

pop 410

O'ahu's northernmost point, where the windward coast meets the North Shore, is the site of the 880-acre Turtle Bay Resort,

---

KING OF THE WAVES

If there's one name that every surfer hitting the waves here knows, it's unquestionably the Duke's. Born on O'ahu in 1890, Duke Paoa Kahanamoku so revived the ancient Hawaiian art of surfing that he earned the title 'father of modern surfing.'

A full-blooded Hawaiian, he was as much at home in the water as he was on land. Between 1912 and 1932, Duke won six Olympic medals, including three gold medals for swimming.

But it was surfing, not swimming, that was his greatest passion. Duke was an ardent traveler who spread the sport of surfing far and wide, traveling with his board along the west and east coasts of the Americas, and to Europe and Australia.

One of Duke's swimming companions, Johnny Weissmuller, a fellow Olympian best known as celluloid's first *Tarzan*, convinced Duke to come to Hollywood. With his athleticism, good looks and warm personality, Duke easily picked up parts in a score of movies, yet he made his greatest splash just weeks after moving to California in 1925. While surfing off Corona del Mar he became a national hero when he used his surfboard to rescue the passengers of a yacht that had capsized in heavy seas. Battling stormy conditions, Duke managed to paddle back and forth between the yacht and the shore repeatedly, saving the lives of eight people.

After six years on the silver screen, Duke followed his heart back to the islands. From 1932 to 1960, Duke was elected sheriff of Honolulu for 13 consecutive terms. He loved meeting people and often mingled with visiting tourists, offering impromptu surf lessons and spreading good cheer. Duke Kahanamoku so greatly symbolized Hawaii that to millions of people he was also known as the 'Hawaii Ambassador,' an honorary title he held his entire adult life. He died in 1968 at the age of 77.

NORTH SHORE

NORTH SHORE

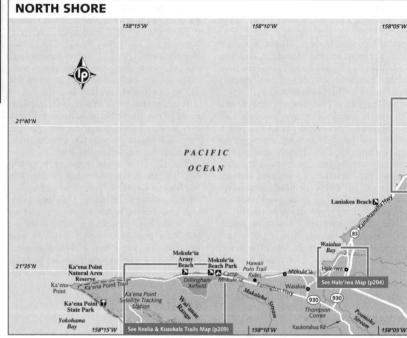

with its generous dose of sun and sand activities. Bus 55 goes into the resort. As you continue on the road toward Sunset Beach you'll pass a couple of roadside fruit stands where someone will gladly take out a machete, lop off the top of a coconut and hand you one of the most refreshing drinks on the planet. Welcome to the North Shore.

Sights & Activities
KUILIMA COVE
One look at this gem and it's easy to see why the first resort hotel built outside Waikiki sits in the background. Also known as Bay View Beach, this deep little cove fronting a white-sand beach and protected by a reef is one of the area's best swimming spots. Lots of tropical fish frequent the cove, it has a few coral patches and it's favored by turtles, all of which make it a treat for snorkelers. For the best snorkeling stick to the right side of the cove. While the beach is mostly used by resort guests, like all beaches on the island it's public and open to all – so whether or not you're staying at the resort, don't miss it.

The beach concession stand rents snorkel sets and boogie boards for $12 a day and floats for $10.

To snag one of the free beach access parking spaces, just tell the attendant at the gatehouse that you're here to use the beach.

BEACH HIKES
Turtle Bay Resort has several miles of oceanfront hikes offering a good variety of scenery.

Kaihalulu Beach Trail
This hike goes in an easterly direction from the resort to reach Kaihalulu Beach, a beautiful, curved white-sand beach backed by ironwoods. Although a shoreline lava shelf and rocky bottom make the beach poor for swimming, it's a fun place for beachcombing and you can walk east a mile to Kahuku Point and then another half-mile along the beach. Local fishers cast thrownets from the shore and pole fish from Kahuku Point.

To get to the trail, turn into the Turtle Bay Resort and just before the guard booth

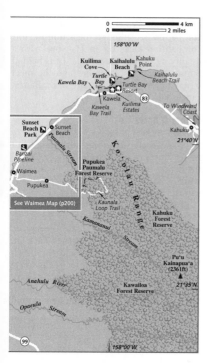

turn right into an unmarked parking lot, where there are free spaces for beachgoers. It's a five-minute walk out to the beach; just walk east on the footpath that begins at the field adjacent to the parking lot. Alternatively, you could begin the hike at Kuilima Cove by walking east along the shore.

Kawela Bay Trail

For good swimming and to visit an awesome thicket of banyan trees, walk west 1.5 miles on the shoreline trail that runs from the resort to Kawela Bay. The hike begins behind the resort's tennis courts and skirts Turtle Bay, which takes its name from the green sea turtles that swim into the bay to feed on algae. In winter you can sometimes see whales cavorting offshore to the north. After walking about 15 minutes you'll reach the western point of Turtle Bay, which is known as Protection Point for the WWII bunker there. Once you've walked around the point you're at Kawela Bay. Continue your hike to the middle of the bay, where you'll find the best conditions for

swimming and snorkeling. Once you've dried off, walk inland toward the highway to find a dense pack of banyan trees, profuse with side branches and hanging aerial roots. This is where the cast of *Lost* heads when they want to shoot in a banyan forest, including the scene where Walt huddled inside a vertical fence-like cluster of tree trunks as a polar bear tried to paw at him.

GOLF

Turtle Bay Golf (☎ 293-8574; 57-049 Kuilima Dr; Fazio/Palmer course $155/165; ⏱ 6:30am-6:30pm) features two top-rate par 72 18-hole courses abounding in water views. The more challenging is the Palmer Course, which was designed by golf pro Arnold Palmer and is the site of the PGA Championship Tour. The Fazio Course, designed by George Fazio, has generous fairways, deep bunkers and is host of the LPGA Tour's Hawaiian Open. There are handsome discounts for twilight play and for hotel guests.

HORSEBACK RIDING

The salt breeze blowing in your face, the sound of the surf – there's nothing that quite matches a horseback ride on the beach. Turtle Bay Resort's **trail rides** (☎ 293-8811; 57-091 Kamehameha Hwy; 45min ride adult/child 7-12yr $45/30) leave several times a day from 8:30am to 1:30pm, skirting the beach and taking in some tropical forest as well. It's best to call ahead for reservations.

TENNIS

Turtle Bay Tennis (☎ 293-8811; 57-091 Kamehameha Hwy; per person per day $12; ⏱ 8am-6pm) has 10 Plexipave courts and a pro shop that provides lessons and equipment hire. Four courts are lit for night play.

Sleeping

Kuilima Estates (☎ Turtle Bay Condos 293-2800, 888-266-3690; www.turtlebaycondos.com; 57-101 Kuilima Dr; studio/1-/2-/3-bedroom apt from $100/110/180/240; ❄ ≈) There's no need to pay lofty resort prices to be in this area. Kuilima Estates, a modern condominium complex on the grounds fronting the Turtle Bay Resort, has comfortable, fully equipped units, each with a kitchen, washer/dryer, TV, phone and lanai. Turtle Bay Condos, which books the units, has its office at the Kahuku Sugar Mill shopping center in Kahuku.

Turtle Bay Resort (☎ 293-6000, 800-203-3650; www .turtlebayresort.com; 57-091 Kamehameha Hwy; r from $430; ❌ 🖳 🖳) On Kuilima Point between Turtle Bay and Kuilima Cove, this is the only hotel on the North Shore. Covering more than 800 acres, the resort is self-contained with a few restaurants, two golf courses, a spa and a slew of activities. Each of the 485 rooms has a lanai with an ocean view as well as all the expected first-class amenities. The only drawback is the sky-high prices, which have nearly doubled in recent years.

Eating

Lei Lei's Bar & Grill (☎ 293-8811; Turtle Bay Resort, 57-091 Kamehameha Hwy; mains $6-24; ❨ 7am-10pm) Overlooks the resort's golf course. The eclectic menu includes oyster shooters, sandwiches, prime rib and Japanese-accented dishes, such as seafood scampi with udon noodles. Decent breakfast fare, too.

Macky's Cooked Shrimp (Kamehameha Hwy; meals $11; ❨ 9am-7pm) On the highway, a third of a mile west of the Turtle Bay Resort entrance, this roadside operation mixes up all sorts of scrumptious Kahuku shrimp plates from spicy hot to the local favorite coconut shrimp. All come with rice and salad.

21 Degrees North (☎ 293-8811; Turtle Bay Resort, 57-091 Kamehameha Hwy; mains $28-40; ❨ 6-10pm Tue-Sat) Windows and spectacular ocean views galore are the highlights at this fine-dining resort restaurant that played host to TV's short-lived drama *North Shore*. The surf 'n' turf menu is spiced up with island flavors and local delights like Kona lobster.

Bayclub (☎ 293-8811; Turtle Bay Resort, 57-091 Kamehameha Hwy; dishes $7-16; ❨ noon-8:30pm) The resort's lobby-side Bayclub serves up sandwiches, salads and tropical drinks. The food is not particularly memorable, but the splendid ocean views certainly are.

Entertainment

Hang Ten Bar (☎ 293-8811; Turtle Bay Resort, 57-091 Kamehameha Hwy; ❨ 11am-9pm) You'll find a lot more than frosty mai tais at this poolside bar, which brings in performers from the Polynesian Cultural Center for a free show every Wednesday and Friday at 5:30pm.

SUNSET BEACH

This is definitely the place to stop and worship the sun, the sunset and the surf. Sunset Beach is most famous as the home of the Triple Crown, the king of all surfing competitions. Although the action for this competition kicks off in Hale'iwa with a qualifying round, the middle leg is held at Sunset Beach in November and the meet wraps up at 'Ehukai Beach Park's Banzai Pipeline in December.

Sights & Activities
SUNSET BEACH PARK

At O'ahu's classic winter surf spot, with monstrous waves and challenging breaks, all the action isn't in the water. This dazzling white-sand beach is also the place for chic sun worshippers to see and be seen.

Because of the tremendous pounding of the surf in winter, the slope of the beach becomes steeper as the season goes on. In summer, as the sand washes back in, the shoreline smooths out and the beach broadens dramatically. Winter swells create powerful rips but even when the waves have quieted down in summer, there's still an along-shore current that swimmers should know about.

The beach has rest rooms, showers and a lifeguard tower. If the beachside parking is full, you can find parking in the lot across the street.

BACKYARDS

A smokin' surf break off Sunset Point at the northern end of the beach, Backyards draws top windsurfers. There's a shallow reef and strong currents to contend with, but Backyards has the island's biggest waves for sailing.

BEFORE JUMPING IN...

With the exception of Hale'iwa Beach Park, North Shore beaches are notorious for treacherous winter swimming conditions. There are powerful and dangerous currents along the entire shore. If the water doesn't look as calm as a lake, it's probably not safe for swimming or snorkeling.

During summer surf conditions along the whole North Shore can mellow right out. Shark's Cove in Waimea then becomes a prime snorkeling and diving spot, and Waimea Bay, internationally famous for its winter surf, turns into a popular swimming and snorkeling beach.

WAHINE WAVE RIDERS

Wahine (girls, women) started hitting the waves long before *Blue Crush* (2002) featured young female surfers ripping along the North Shore's hottest surf. But true to that movie, shot on the North Shore, more women are taking up surfing every day. And there's no reason to just watch them – even if you've never ridden a wave before, you're in the right place to jump on board.

Here are some starting points:

- **Women's Surf Style Magazine** (WSSM; www.womenssurfstyle.com) is dedicated to the everyday, noncompetition female surfer. It comes out four times a year and can be picked up free at surf hangouts around O'ahu.

- A good book to curl up with is *Girl in the Curl: A Century of Women in Surfing* by Andrea Gabbard, which gives long overdue recognition to the role of *wahine* surfers, including a poignant tribute to the late Rell Sunn of Makaha, O'ahu's undisputed surf queen.

- The female surf instructors at **Girls Who Surf** (www.girlswhosurf.com) specialize in getting *wahine* up on a board.

- Or learn to surf at **April Grover's Surf School** (☎ 561-7142; www.aprilsurf.com), where pro surfer April Grover, one of the stars of MTV's *Surf Girls,* gives lessons.

- Call for the day's surf report at 971-CHIC (971-2442).

See p56 for more on *wahine* surfers.

'EHUKAI BEACH PARK

Ancient Hawaiians named 'Ehukai (meaning 'sea spray') for its powerful breaking surf. People flock to 'Ehukai Beach Park to watch the pros surf the world-famous **Banzai Pipeline** – or in local lingo, just Pipeline or the Pipe. A death-defying wave to ride, the Pipe breaks over a shallow coral reef. The Pipeline takes its name from the near-perfect glassy tubes that are formed when huge westerly swells hit the reef, exploding into a forward curl as they break.

Boogie boarders and bodysurfers also brave a hazardous current to ride the waves. Water conditions mellow out in summer, when it's good for swimming, but even then there can occasionally be strong currents.

The entrance to 'Ehukai Beach Park is opposite Sunset Beach Elementary School. The beach has a lifeguard, rest rooms and showers.

Festivals & Events

Women's Pipeline Championship Held during the first two weeks of March, the best of *wahine* (women) surfers ride the waves at the Banzai Pipeline off 'Ehukai Beach Park.

O'Neill World Cup of Surfing The second leg of the Triple Crown of Surfing takes place in late November and early December at Sunset Beach.

Rip Curl Pro Pipeline Masters The final leg of the Triple Crown of Surfing is in early to mid-December at Banzai Pipeline, with the world's top pros vying for a $275,000 purse.

Eating

Ted's Bakery (☎ 638-8207; 59-024 Kamehameha Hwy; items $1-7; ⏰ 7am-4pm) A sweet-tooth mecca opposite Sunset Beach, Ted's is island-famous for its chocolate *haupia* (coconut) pie, but also does a fine job whipping up all sorts of pastries and deli delights.

Sunset Pizza (☎ 638-7660; 59-176 Kamehameha Hwy; pizza $11.50-19; ⏰ 8am-9pm) Opposite Sunset Beach Park, this take-out place popular with the surf crowd has $5 meatball subs, $3 pizza slices and whole pizzas made to order. There are some awning-shaded outdoor tables where you can enjoy a quick eat.

North Shore Country Market (Sunset Beach Elementary School, Kamehameha Hwy; ⏰ 8am-2pm Sat) Buy locally grown organic produce direct from farmers as well as fresh-baked goods and handicrafts at this weekly market. It's a good place to get in touch with O'ahu's rural community.

WAIMEA

This laid-back village spreads out along the shore, with virtually everyone on or near the beach 24/7. The beaches here are like community centers, where people meet up, hang out and hit the waves. The area's crowning glory is beautiful Waimea Bay,

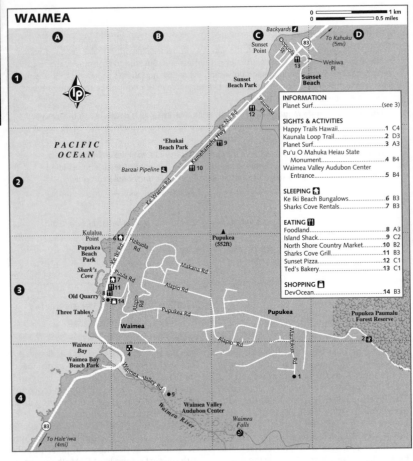

WAIMEA

INFORMATION
Planet Surf....................................(see 3)

SIGHTS & ACTIVITIES
Happy Trails Hawaii...........................1 C4
Kaunala Loop Trail............................2 D3
Planet Surf..3 A3
Pu'u O Mahuka Heiau State
    Monument....................................4 B4
Waimea Valley Audubon Center
    Entrance.....................................5 B4

SLEEPING
Ke Iki Beach Bungalows......................6 B3
Sharks Cove Rentals..........................7 B3

EATING
Foodland..8 A3
Island Shack.....................................9 C2
North Shore Country Market...............10 B2
Sharks Cove Grill.............................11 B3
Sunset Pizza...................................12 C1
Ted's Bakery...................................13 C1

SHOPPING
DevOcean.......................................14 B3

a deeply inset bay with turquoise waters
and a wide white-sand beach almost 1500ft
long. Ancient Hawaiians believed its waters were sacred, and only royalty were
allowed to take their long-boards out to
surf Waimea's huge waves.

And what surf there is! Waimea Bay
holds the record for the highest waves ever
ridden in international competition. Winter's huge north swells bring out throngs
of spectators who crowd to watch surfers
perform near-suicidal feats on waves of up
to 35ft.

What do you do when the surf's not up?
Well, just inland of the bay the National
Audubon Society preserves a vast unspoiled
tract of Waimea Valley, ideal for nature
lovers of all types. And if it's summer, some

of the best snorkeling and diving on O'ahu
is found off Pupukea Beach Park.

History
Waimea Valley was once heavily settled,
the lowlands terraced in taro, the valley
walls dotted with house sites and the ridges
topped with heiau (stone temples). Just
about every crop grown in Hawaii thrived
in this valley, including a rare pink taro
favored by the ali'i (royalty).

Waimea River, now blocked at the beach
by a sandbar, originally emptied into the
bay and served as a passage for canoes
traveling to villages upstream.

In 1779, when the crew of one of Captain
Cook's ships became the first Westerners to
sail into Waimea Bay, an entry in the ship's

log noted that the valley was uncommonly beautiful and picturesque. However, contact with the West did nothing to preserve that beauty. Logging and the clearing of land to build plantations deforested the hills above the valley, resulting in a devastating flood to Waimea in 1894. So much mud washed through the valley that it permanently altered the shape of Waimea's shore, after which residents abandoned the valley and resettled elsewhere.

Information
The Foodland supermarket has an ATM. To check your email, go across the street to **Planet Surf** (☎ 638-5060; 59-051 Pupukea Rd; per hr $3; ☺ 9:30am-7:30pm).

Sights
WAIMEA BAY BEACH PARK
It may be a beauty but it's certainly a moody one. Waimea Bay changes dramatically with the seasons: it can be tranquil and flat as a lake in summer, then savage with incredible surf and the island's meanest rip currents in winter.

Winter is prime time for surfers. On winter's calmer days boogie boarders are out in force, but even then sets come in hard and people get pounded. Winter water activities at this beach are not for novices. Usually the only time it's calm enough for swimming and snorkeling is from June to September.

This is the most popular North Shore beach, so parking is often tight. Don't park along the highway, even if you see others doing so; police are notorious for towing away dozens of cars at once, particularly when surf competitions are taking place. Facilities include showers, rest rooms and picnic tables, and a lifeguard is on duty daily.

PUPUKEA BEACH PARK
Pupukea Beach Park is a long beach along the highway that includes Three Tables to the south, Shark's Cove to the north and Old Quarry in between. Pupukea, meaning 'white shell,' is a very scenic beach, with deep blue waters, a varied coastline, and a mix of lava and white sand. The waters off Pupukea Beach are protected as a marine-life conservation district.

The large boulders on the end of Kulalua Point, which marks the northernmost end

---

SURFSPEAK
Don't know the difference between a stick and a tube? Surfers everywhere have their own lingo. Hit the waves in Hawaii and you're likely to hear some of these terms:

brah or cuz – friend, surfing buddy

da kine – a great wave, top quality (in many contexts beyond surfing, too)

goofy-footing – surfing with the right foot forward

keiki waves – small, gentle waves good for kids

macked – to get clobbered by a huge wave, as if by a Mack truck

ne'e nalu – traditional Hawaiian term for board surfing

pau – quitting time

snake – steal; as in 'that dude's snaking my wave'

stick – local slang for a surfboard

---

of the beach, are said to be followers of Pele, the Hawaiian volcano goddess. To acknowledge their loyalty, Pele gave her followers immortality by turning them to stone.

There are showers and rest rooms in front of Old Quarry. The entrance to the beach is opposite an old gas station; bus 52 stops out front.

Three Tables
Three Tables gets its name from the flat ledges rising above the water. In summer when the waters are calm, Three Tables is good for snorkeling and diving. It is possible to see some action by snorkeling around the tables, but the best coral and fish, as well as some small caves, lava tubes and arches, are in deeper water further out. However, this is a summer-only spot. In winter dangerous rip currents flow between the beach and the tables. Watch for sharp rocks and coral; diving gloves are recommended.

Old Quarry
A fascinating array of jagged rock formations and tide pools are exposed at low tide at the Old Quarry section of the park. The rocks and tide pools are tempting to explore, but be careful – they're razor sharp, and if you slip, it's easy to get a deep cut.

Shark's Cove
Shark's Cove is beautiful both above and below the water's surface. The naming of the

cove was done in jest – sharks aren't a particular problem. In summer, when the seas are calm, Shark's Cove has super snorkeling conditions, as well as O'ahu's most popular cavern dive. A fair number of beginning divers take lessons here, while the underwater caves will thrill advanced divers.

To get to the caves, swim out of the cove and around to the right. Some of the caves are very deep and labyrinthine, and there have been a number of drownings, so divers should only venture into them with a local expert.

WAIMEA VALLEY AUDUBON CENTER
Beautiful plants and rare archaeological sites are featured at this National Audubon Society-run park (☎ 638-9199; 59-864 Kamehameha Hwy; adult/child 4-12yr $8/3; ☼ 9:30am-5:30pm; ☒ 52) across from Waimea Bay Beach Park. The park's main path leads up the Waimea Valley to a 60ft waterfall, where you can change into a swimsuit and take a cool dip. The 0.8-mile path to the waterfall is a gem, flanked by extensive naturalized gardens that are arranged by theme, including sections of fragrant ginger, native food plants and medicinal species. In all, the park nurtures some 6000 plant species, including many that are rare and endangered. Along the walk you'll also pass ancient stone platforms and terraces, and replicas of thatched buildings similar to those used by the early Hawaiians. Stop and play some of the traditional Hawaiian games laid out for visitors and soak up the beauty of this rare preserve.

PU'U O MAHUKA HEIAU STATE MONUMENT
A stellar view of the coast and a stroll around the grounds of O'ahu's largest temple reward those who venture up to this national historical landmark, perched on a bluff above Waimea. The temple's stacked stone construction is attributed to the legendary *menehune*, elflike people who are said to have completed their work in just one night. Pu'u O Mahuka means 'hill of escape,' and it was a *luakini* heiau, where human sacrifices took place.

The terraced stone walls are a couple of feet high, although most of the heiau is now overgrown. Collectively, the three adjoining enclosures that form the main body of the heiau are more than 550ft in length. This was a dramatic site for a temple, and it's

well worth the drive for the commanding view, especially at sunset.

To get there, turn up Pupukea Rd at the Foodland supermarket. The heiau turnoff is half a mile up, and from there it's 0.7 mile in to the site.

Activities
WATER SPORTS
Waimea's beaches offer excellent swimming, snorkeling, diving, surfing and boogie boarding at various times throughout the year.

If it has to do with water, you can get it at **Planet Surf** (☎ 638-5060; 59-051 Pupukea Rd; ☼ 9:30am-7:30pm) opposite Old Quarry Beach. The daily rental rate is $20 for surfboards, $10 for boogie boards and $12 for snorkel sets. It also sells T-shirts, sarongs, board shorts – you get the idea.

HIKING
Little-known **Kaunala Loop Trail** sits quietly above Waimea Valley, a good place to mix an easy valley walk with a moderate ridge climb for sweeping views of Waimea Bay. After seeing the beauty of the bay from viewpoints high atop this trail, it's easy to see why Hawaiian royalty considered it sacred.

To get to the trailhead, turn up Pupukea Rd at the Foodland supermarket and continue for 2.5 miles, where the road ends at a Boy Scout camp. Park in the camp parking

---

DETOUR: SUNBATHING TURTLES
Awesome green sea turtles *(honu)*, which can weigh upwards of 200lb, like to haul up on the sand to bask in the sun. Like other beachgoers they have their favorite spots. To see these majestic creatures up close, stop at Laniakea Beach, a little strand of sand along the Kamehameha Hwy midway between the 3- and 4-mile markers and immediately south of Pohaku Loa Way. Turtles hang out right on the beach here. Loud noises and abrupt movements startle them, so approach slowly and keep a safe distance. Incidentally, the turtles are not permanent O'ahu residents – about once every four years they return to their ancestral nesting grounds in the remote French Frigate Shoals, 500 miles east of O'ahu, where they mate and nest.

lot and follow the Na Ala Hele signs to the trailhead. This 4.5-mile hike averages about two hours. This trail is officially open to the public only on weekends and state holidays. Hunting is also allowed in this area, so hikers should wear bright colors and avoid wandering off the trail.

HORSEBACK RIDING

Two miles up from Foodland, **Happy Trails Hawaii** (☎ 638-7433; Maulukua Rd; 1½/2hr ride $49/69; ⊙ 9am-5pm) offers the real deal. The horses take to the mountainsides, over open pasture, past orchards, offering panoramic views in all directions. The rides begin with an orientation and instruction, so even if you've never been in a saddle before, you'll be up to speed before heading out. Reservations are essential.

Sleeping

In addition to the places listed here, the bulletin board at Foodland has 'roommates wanted' notices and the occasional vacation-rental listing.

Ke Iki Beach Bungalows (☎ 638-8229; www.keiki beach.com; 59-579 Ke Iki Rd; streetside 1-bedroom units $120-150, beachside 1-bedroom units $170-200, beachside 2-bedroom units $195-230) This hideaway retreat fronts a beautiful white-sand beach just north of Pupukea Beach Park. The 11 units are comfortably furnished with tropical decor of floral prints and rattan chairs that fit the setting like a glove. Each unit has a full kitchen, TV and phone, and guests have access to a barbecue, picnic tables and hammocks lazily strung between coconut trees. The location is an absolute gem – the beachside units are right on the sand, the others just a minute's walk from the water.

Sharks Cove Rentals (☎ 779-8535, 888-883-0001; www.sharkscoverentals.com; 59-672 Kamehameha Hwy; r $60-85) Friendly hosts and clean affordable rooms right across the street from Pupukea Beach Park make a winning combination. The place consists of three adjacent houses, one of which has double rooms with bunk beds, so two people can share a room for just $30 each. The more expensive rooms are spacious with two queen beds, TV and the like. All guests have access to a kitchen and a living room where you can share a beer and travel tips with fellow travelers. And Foodland is within easy walking distance.

Eating

Island Shack (☎ 638-9500; 59-254 Kamehameha Hwy; mains $7-15; ⊙ 11am-9:30pm; **V**) It's reggae all day long at this fun fish shack, in the open with a gravel floor and serving *ono* (delicious) grilled fish topped with ginger and onions. There are several good vegetarian offerings too, plus steak and chicken dishes. The giant wooden tiki figure along the highway marks the spot at the north side of Waimea.

Sharks Cove Grill (☎ 638-8300; Kamehameha Hwy; dishes $5-8; ⊙ 8:30am-7pm) This aqua-blue trailer parked along the highway about 100 yards north of Foodland has good burgers, fresh fish sandwiches and plate lunches. A couple of tables are set up so you can enjoy your North Shore grinds while watching the beach action across the road.

Foodland (☎ 638-8081; 59-720 Kamehameha Hwy; ⊙ 6am-11pm) This modern supermarket opposite Pupukea Beach Park sells hot fried chicken at its deli, perfect for a beachside picnic.

Shopping

DevOcean (☎ 638-5391; 59-059 Pupukea Rd; ⊙ 7:30am-5:30pm) You can feel your hair growing dreadlocks and tie-dye Ts wrapping themselves around your body as you step into this hippie-cum–New Age hangout. Crystal pendants, feng shui treasures and cosmic clothing are for sale; henna tattoos are available; and *lomilomi* massage is offered at the side. It's an eatery, too – sit for a spell with kava served in a coconut bowl, a cup of organic coffee or a soy-milk smoothie.

HALE'IWA
pop 2225

The only sizable town on the North Shore, Hale'iwa caters to the multitude of day-trippers making the circle-island ride. Sizable is a relative term – the commercial strip with its tempting restaurants, water-sports centers and fun shops is just one road, Kamehameha Hwy, which doubles as Hale'iwa's Main St. Though that's the heart of Hale'iwa, its soul is on the coast, where glorious beaches and mighty surf provide an ocean full of activities. The folks in this town are as colorful as the shops, a multiethnic mix of families who've lived here for generations and more recently arrived surfers and artists. For day-tripping, if you're beginning your North

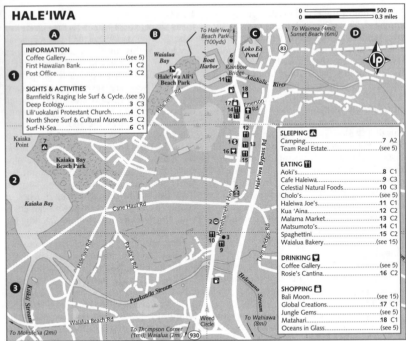

HALE'IWA

INFORMATION
Coffee Gallery.............................(see 5)
First Hawaiian Bank...........................1 C2
Post Office..2 C2

SIGHTS & ACTIVITIES
Barnfield's Raging Isle Surf & Cycle..(see 5)
Deep Ecology.....................................3 C3
Lili'uokalani Protestant Church.........4 C1
North Shore Surf & Cultural Museum.5 C2
Surf-N-Sea..6 C1

SLEEPING 🛏
Camping...7 A2
Team Real Estate...........................(see 5)

EATING 🍽
Aoki's..8 C1
Cafe Haleiwa......................................9 C3
Celestial Natural Foods...................10 C3
Cholo's...(see 5)
Haleiwa Joe's..................................11 C1
Kua 'Aina...12 C2
Malama Market................................13 C2
Matsumoto's.....................................14 C1
Spaghettini.......................................15 C2
Waialua Bakery..............................(see 15)

DRINKING 🍺
Coffee Gallery................................(see 5)
Rosie's Cantina...............................16 C2

SHOPPING 🛍
Bali Moon.......................................(see 15)
Global Creations............................17 C1
Jungle Gems...................................(see 5)
Matahari..18 C1
Oceans in Glass..............................(see 5)

Shore travels in Hale'iwa, the town is *the* place to stop for breakfast or lunch, and if you're ending them here you can't do better than unwinding over a sunset dinner.

Information

Coffee Gallery (☎ 637-5355; North Shore Marketplace, 66-250 Kamehameha Hwy; per 10min $1; ☼ 7am-8pm) Internet access is available at this café.
First Hawaiian Bank (☎ 637-5034; 66-135 Kamehameha Hwy) Just north of the Hale'iwa Shopping Plaza.
Post Office (☎ 637-1711; 66-437 Kamehameha Hwy; ☼ 8am-4pm Mon-Fri, 9am-noon Sat) At the south side of town.

Sights

HALE'IWA ALI'I BEACH PARK

Surfing is king at Hale'iwa Ali'i Beach Park. This attractive park with its generous sandy beach is the site of several surfing tournaments in winter, when north swells can bring waves as high as 20ft.

When waves are less than 5ft, young kids bring out their boards. Waves 6ft or higher bring strong currents, making conditions more suited to experienced surfers.

The 20-acre beach park has rest rooms, showers, picnic tables and lifeguards. The shallow areas on the southern side of the beach are generally the calmest places to swim.

The park's knotty-pine beachfront community building may look familiar. It served as the lifeguard headquarters in the TV show *Baywatch Hawaii*, which used this beach park as its main setting when the show was filmed in Hawaii from 1999 to its demise in 2001.

HALE'IWA BEACH PARK

On the northern side of Waialua Bay, this park is protected by a shallow shoal and breakwater so the water is usually calm, and a good choice for swimming. There's little wave action, except for the occasional north swells that ripple into the bay.

Although the beach isn't as pretty as Hale'iwa's other strands, this 13-acre park has a broad range of facilities, as well as basketball and volleyball courts, an exercise area and a softball field. It also offers a good view of Ka'ena Point.

KAIAKA BAY BEACH PARK

The 53-acre Kaiaka Bay Beach Park is on Kaiaka Bay, about a mile west of town. This is a good place for a picnic, as there are shady ironwood trees, but the in-town beaches are better choices for swimming. Two streams empty into Kaiaka Bay, muddying up the beach after heavy rainstorms. Kaiaka has rest rooms, picnic tables, showers, drinking water and campsites.

NORTH SHORE SURF & CULTURAL MUSEUM

To get a sense of just how integral surfing is to the area's character, visit this funky little **museum** (☎ 637-8888; 66-250 Kamehameha Hwy; admission by donation; ۞ 11am-5:30pm Wed-Mon) in the North Shore Marketplace. The museum collection includes vintage surfboards, period photos and surfing videos. There's also a display of lost jewelry and old bottles found in the water by surfers, and much of what you see in that selection can be purchased. Since it's run by volunteers, the hours can be a bit flexible – and all bets are off when the surf's up!

LILI'UOKALANI PROTESTANT CHURCH

Hale'iwa's historic **church** (☎ 637-9364; 66-090 Kamehameha Hwy) takes its name from Queen Lili'uokalani, who spent summers on the shores of the Anahulu River and attended services here. The church dates back to 1832, and as late as the 1940s services were held entirely in Hawaiian.

The church's unique seven-dial clock, donated by Queen Lili'uokalani in 1892, is unlike any you've ever seen. It shows the hour, day, month and year, as well as the phases of the moon, with the queen's 12-letter name replacing the numerals on the clock face. The church is open only when the caretaker is in; usually in the morning.

Activities

A landmark operation, **Surf-N-Sea** (☎ 637-9887; www.surfnsea.com; 62-595 Kamehameha Hwy; 2hr beginner surfing lesson $75, 1-day surfboard/boogie-board hire $24/20; ۞ 9am-7pm) rents surfboards and boogie boards and offers surfing lessons for all levels. Its $200 half-day surf safari outing takes surfers out to three 'secret' surf spots. It also sells new and used surfboards, and handles just about anything else that has to do with the water.

Deep Ecology (☎ 637-7946, 800-578-3992; www.deepecology1.com; 66-456 Kamehameha Hwy; 2-tank dive $119; ۞ 9am-5pm Mon-Sat, to 4pm Sun) offers personalized dives geared to each diver's interest and experience level. You can get a good sense of its ecological bent in the shop, where you'll find displays on its turtle rescue involvement and an eco photo gallery.

Barnfield's Raging Isle Surf & Cycle (☎ 637-7707; www.ragingisle.com; North Shore Marketplace, 66-250 Kamehameha Hwy; bike rental per day $40-60; ۞ 10am-6:30pm) rents quality mountain and road bikes, and can give you the lowdown on the best routes in the area.

Festivals & Events

The kickoff leg of the world's premier surfing event, the **OP Pro Hawaii** , the Triple Crown of Surfing, is held at Hale'iwa Ali'i Beach Park in mid-November.

Sleeping

Hale'iwa has no hotels or guesthouses, but there are several privately owned vacation rentals that can be booked through agents.

Team Real Estate (☎ 637-3507, 800-982-8602; www.teamrealestate.com; North Shore Marketplace; 66-250 Kamehameha Hwy; 1-bedroom apt $100-135, 2-bedroom apt $165) This place handles a couple dozen vacation rentals on the North Shore, including several one- and two-bedroom apartments in

---

COOL FLAVORS

For many people, the circle-island drive isn't complete without lining up for shave ice at **Matsumoto's** (☎ 637-4827; 66-087 Kamehameha Hwy; shave ice $1.30-2.25; ۞ 9am-6pm) tin-roofed general store.

Hawaiian shave ice is drenched with sweet syrup like the snow cones found on the US mainland, but it's much better, because the ice is shaved more finely. Most popular are the tropical flavors like *liliko'i* (passion fruit), mango and piña colada. Or go completely local and add on ice cream and sweetened adzuki beans. Whatever your choice, the entire concoction begins dripping into a sticky mess the second you get it, so don't dawdle.

Although the crowds are at Matsumoto's, nearby **Aoki's** (66-117 Kamehameha Hwy) has equally delicious shave ice and none of the queues.

Hale'iwa. Small groups: ask about Hale Kai, a spacious three-bedroom beach house that sleeps up to six people for $300 nightly.

SandSea Vacation Homes (☎ 637-2568, 800-442-6901; www.sandsea.com; beachfront houses $175-750) This outfit specializes in renting beachfront homes along the North Shore. It has about 20 properties in all, ranging from places that can accommodate just two people to those that can sleep up to 20.

Hale'iwa's only camping option is at Kaiaka Bay Beach Park, where the county allows camping on Friday to Tuesday nights. For details on obtaining a permit, see p230.

Eating

Cafe Haleiwa (☎ 637-5516; 66-460 Kamehameha Hwy; breakfast $4-7, lunch $6-10; ☼ 7am-2pm) An unpretentious joint with formica tables and walls plastered with surf memorabilia, Cafe Haleiwa is a popular haunt for both local surfers and day-trippers. The food is good, prices cheap and servings generous. Breakfast offers egg dishes and unbeatable blueberry pancakes. Lunch is predominantly sandwiches and burritos.

Kua 'Aina (☎ 637-6067; 66-160 Kamehameha Hwy; sandwiches $4-8; ☼ 11am-8pm) This North Shore landmark has moved up the road to bigger digs, but still enjoys its well-deserved reputation for grilling up the island's best burgers. Good fish sandwiches and fries, too.

Cholo's (☎ 637-3059; North Shore Marketplace; 66-250 Kamehameha Hwy; combination plates $8-17; ☼ 10am-9pm) Solid home-style Mexican food is what attracts such a big crowd of locals and tourists alike. If you've never tried a fresh 'ahi taco or a grilled 'ahi burrito, here's your chance

to get one done to perfection. It serves good fajitas and chimichangas as well.

Spaghettini (☎ 637-0104, 66-200 Kamehameha Hwy; pizza slices $2.50-3, pizza $10-$16; ☼ 11am-8pm) Don't be fooled by its unassuming looks, this place serves up the best pizza in all O'ahu. For a quick, delicious lunch try a veggie slice loaded with spinach, olives and garlic. Forget the pasta – pizza is the real prize.

Waialua Bakery (☎ 637-9079; 66-200 Kamehameha Hwy; snacks $1-7; ☼ 11am-8pm) Tucked in the shopping center behind Spaghettini, head here for fresh cookies and sandwiches on homemade bread.

Celestial Natural Foods (☎ 637-6729; 66-443 Kamehameha Hwy; ☼ 9am-6pm Mon-Sat, to 5pm Sun) Carries everything from name-brand health foods to local organic produce, and has a vegetarian deli as well.

Malama Market (☎ 637-4520; 66-190 Kamehameha Hwy; ☼ 7am-9pm) Up for a picnic? Grab yourself a couple pieces of the hot chicken breast ($1.50) from the deli of this modern supermarket and head for the beach.

Drinking

Coffee Gallery (☎ 637-5355; North Shore Marketplace, 66-250 Kamehameha Hwy; ☼ 7am-8pm) The aromatic scent of roasting coffee beans will lead you to this mellow café, which has all sorts of good java as well as delicious smoothies and fresh juices.

Rosie's Cantina (☎ 637-3538; Hale'iwa Shopping Plaza, 66-165 Kamehameha Hwy; ☼ 7am-9pm Sun-Thu, to 10pm Fri & Sat) Come here to savor the fruit-flavored margaritas and the Mexican beer. If it happens to be Thursday night, you can toss them back for just $2.50 each.

THE AUTHOR'S CHOICE

Hale'iwa Joe's (☎ 637-8005; 66-001 Kamehameha Hwy; appetizers $5-12, lunch mains $7-16, dinner mains $14-28; ☼ 11:30am-9:30pm Sun-Thu, to 10:30pm Fri & Sat) Hands down the finest restaurant on the North Shore, Hale'iwa Joe's boasts innovative seafood with a breezy bayview setting to match. While you can't go wrong ordering anything with fish, which literally comes right off the boats in the adjacent harbor, the menu doesn't stop there. If someone in your party wants a juicy char-grilled steak, this is the top spot for that, too. Start with the fishmonger soup, a hearty seafood stew full of fish, tomatoes and local seasonings. At lunch the grilled fish sandwich dusted with a Cajun seasoning makes a great follow up, while at dinner the tempura-like coconut shrimp is a favorite. If you want to spice things up you'll have options aplenty – the fish of the day alone comes in half a dozen preparations, from the customary macadamia nut–encrusted to a savory cilantro ginger version. Or just munch away on the small plates menu, with crispy 'ahi spring rolls, spicy peel-and-eat fire shrimp and smaller versions of some of the luscious main dishes. And be sure to save room for the Paradise Pie!

Shopping

Hale'iwa boasts an ever-increasing collection of homespun shops that range from the trendy to the quirky.

Oceans in Glass (☎ 637-3366; North Shore Marketplace, 66-250 Kamehameha Hwy) If you like handblown glass, step inside to watch the artisans create cool tropical fish, turtles and dolphins that squeak 'take me home.'

Jungle Gems (☎ 637-6609, North Shore Marketplace, 66-250 Kamehameha Hwy) Gemstones, elaborate beadwork and delicate silver pendants with Hawaiian petroglyph designs are featured here.

Bali Moon (☎ 637-0012; 66-200 Kamehameha Hwy) Handsome furniture and woodwork from Asia are on display, but it's the luscious fabrics that really entice: traditional Indonesian sarongs, colorful cotton blouses and India silks.

Matahari (☎ 637-8515; 66-082 Kamehameha Hwy) A good place for lightweight beach stuff, from straw bags and T-shirts to halter tops and Brazilian bikinis.

Global Creations (☎ 637-1505; 66-079 Kamehameha Hwy) Last-minute shoppers will find an eclectic collection of paintings, jewelry and Hawaiian trinkets here.

WAIALUA
pop 3760

A former plantation town a mile southwest of Hale'iwa, Waialua began to collect dust when the Waialua Sugar Mill shut down in 1996, ending sugar operations on O'ahu. Low rent and an abundance of space at the old mill has since attracted a vibrant collection of young entrepreneurs and New Agers, morphing the place into one happening scene. Best of all, the revitalization is developing in a way that retains Waialua's down-home community character. The sugar mill, smack in the center of town, is once again the thriving heart of the community, with an increasing number of interesting shops to poke about. Still, don't expect a lot of bustle – it's a measure of just how small this town is that folks buy their vegetables at the liquor store.

Information

All of the following are near each other in the town center opposite the mill.

Post Office (☎ 800-275-8777; 67-079 Nauahi St)

Waialua Federal Credit Union (☎ 637-5980; 67-075 auahi St; ◷ 8:30am-4pm Mon-Fri)

Waialua Public Library (☎ 637-8286; 67-068 Kealohanui St; ◷ 9am-6pm Tue-Thu, to 5pm Fri, to 2pm Sat)

Activities

Jasmine Yoga (☎ 561-9639; www.jasmineyoga.com; 67-174 Farrington Hwy; drop-ins $11) welcomes visitors to join in on 75-minute Vinyasa and Astanga yoga classes in an airy, serene space at the Weinberg Community Center. Yoga classes are held from Monday to Saturday at various times; contact the center for the schedule.

Sleeping

Tree of Life Retreat (☎ 637-9363; nowandzenphotography@mac.com; 68-007 Aweoweo St; dm $40, r $65-110) A koi pond and a sitting Buddha welcome guests to this little New Age B&B opposite the beach in Waialua. Accommodations here are simple but comfortable, ranging from a three-bed dorm room to a private suite with its own bathroom and king bed. Guests are welcome to join owner Darrell Wilson in a guided meditation session, use the house kitchen, and borrow bikes and beach gear. Listed rates include breakfast.

Eating

Sugar Mill Cafe (☎ 637-4509; 67-292 Goodale Ave; dishes $3-7; ◷ 10am-8pm Mon-Sat) Join the locals at this humble family-run eatery next to the feed store in the town center. The menu centers around burgers and Hawaiian-style plate lunches

Ka'ala Cafe (☎ 637-2005; 66-216 Farrington Hwy; items $4-7; ◷ 10am-4pm) The town's other eatery attracts the New Age crowd with hummus plates, split-pea soup and organic salads. Finish off a healthy eat with a Waialua papaya and banana smoothie that's as much a dessert as a drink.

Brown Bottle (☎ 637-6728; 67-292 Goodale Ave; ◷ 7am-10:30pm) For the freshest tomatoes and asparagus you've ever seen, stop at this liquor store owned by a farmer.

Shopping

Waialua's old sugar mill is once again brimming with life, this time with small shops creating everything from surfboards to soap and salad dressing. It's a cool place to poke around. Most of the surfboard operations are not open to the public and truth be told there's not much to see, since the boards these days are made from precut poly-urethane foam, sprayed in a sterile room several at a time with layer after layer of glassy resins. One place you might be able to peek in, however, is at the boardmaking operation adjacent to the soap factory.

Hawaiian Bath & Body (☎ 637-8400; Old Sugar Mill, 67-106 Kealohanui St; ☺ 9am-5pm) Step into this fragrant shop to watch the soapmakers create handcut bars of soap in fragrances like ginger lemongrass. Body oils made from *kukui* nuts are sold here, too.

Island X Hawaii (☎ 637-2624; Old Sugar Mill, 67-106 Kealohanui St; ☺ 9am-3:30pm Mon-Fri, 8:30am-noon Sat) In part a clothing store selling reasonably priced sarongs and aloha shirts, this rambling old warehouse also offers Waialua-made soda (try the pineapple flavor), Waialua coffee grown in the hills above town and local papaya seed dressing.

MOKULE'IA
pop 1825

Mokule'ia is the least-traveled stretch of the entire island, and the further west you go from Waialua the more it feels like the boonies. It's mostly people looking for their thrills in the skies that come this way, going just as far as Dillingham Airport. Mokule'ia's beaches typically draw just a handful of locals and at many spots it may well be just you, a wind-whipped coast and the occasional fisher.

Orientation

The Farrington Hwy (Hwy 930) runs west from Thompson Corner to Dillingham Airfield and Mokule'ia Beach. Both this road and the road along the Leeward Coast are called Farrington Hwy, but they don't connect, as each side reaches a dead end about 2.5 miles short of Ka'ena Point.

Sights
MOKULE'IA BEACH PARK

Opposite Dillingham Airfield, Mokule'ia Beach Park has a large, open grassy area with picnic tables, rest rooms and showers. The beach is sandy, but it has a lava shelf along much of its shoreline, resulting in mediocre swimming conditions. It does, however, have fairly consistent winds, making for reliable windsurfing, particularly in spring and fall. In winter there are dangerous currents.

MOKULE'IA ARMY BEACH

This beach, opposite the western end of Dillingham Airfield, is the widest stretch of sand on the Mokule'ia shore. Once reserved exclusively for military personnel, the beach is now open to the public, but the army no longer maintains it and there are no beach facilities. The beach is unprotected, and there are very strong rip currents, especially during winter high surf.

ARMY BEACH TO KA'ENA POINT

From Army Beach, you can drive another 1.5 miles down the road, passing still more white-sand beaches with aquamarine water before the paved road ends at a locked gate.

The terrain is scrubland reaching up to the base of the Wai'anae Range, and the shoreline is wild and windswept. The area is not only desolate, but can also be a bit trashed, and this is certainly not a must-do drive.

From the road's end, it is possible to walk 2.5 miles to Ka'ena Point, but it's a more attractive walk from the other side of the point (see p227).

Activities
SKYDIVING & GLIDER RIDES

Just past Mokule'ia Beach Park, **Dillingham Airfield** (68-760 Farrington Hwy) is the jumping-off point for skydiving and glider rides.

If you fancy sailing with the wind, **Mr Bill's Original Glider Rides** (☎ 677-3404) and **Soar Hawaii** (☎ 637-3147) both offer a variety of glider rides, from short introductory flights for around $35 to longer $100 jaunts. If you've never been in a glider before, it's an amazing sensation, totally free of mechanical sounds. The engineless glider is towed by an airplane and then released to slowly glide back to earth, providing a bird's-eye view of the North Shore the entire time.

Skydive Hawaii (☎ 637-9700; www.hawaiiskydiving .com; jumps $225; ☺ 8am-3pm) has tandem jumps, attaching you to the hips and shoulders of an instructor so you can jump from a plane at 13,000ft, freefall for a minute and finish off with 10 to 15 minutes of canopy ride. The whole process, including some basic instruction, takes about 1½ hours. Participants must be at least 18 years of age and weigh less than 200 pounds. Arrangements can also be made for experienced skydivers to make solo jumps. Planes take off daily, weather permitting. A real rush!

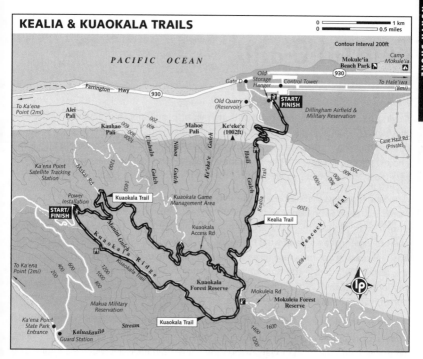

KEALIA & KUAOKALA TRAILS

HORSEBACK RIDING

You just knew those polo fields were harboring some beauts, didn't you? **Hawaii Polo Trail Rides** (☎ 220-5153; 68-411 Farrington Hwy; 1½hr rides $75-85; ☼ 1pm, 3pm & sunset Tue, Thu & Sat) lets you take a thoroughbred polo horse along the beach and around its 100-acre ranch, either in a group or on your own. It also caters to special requests, such as full-moon rides and *ku'uipo* (sweetheart) dalliances.

HIKING

The five-mile **Kealia Trail** ascends from Dillingham Airfield up a cliff-face and through a forest of ironwoods and *kukui* trees. The snaking trail switchbacks its way up the cliff, offering ocean views along the way, but the real prize is its connection to the **Kuaokala Trail**, which brings hikers to a justly celebrated viewpoint over Makua Valley and the Wai'anae Range. The Kealia Trail is best for those wishing to avoid the hassle of securing a permit and driving up the Wai'anae Coast just to hike the Kuaokala Trail, a 5.5-mile loop trail accessible from the Ka'ena Point Satellite Tracking Station.

The trailhead to Kealia Trail begins in the back of the airfield; head west 2 miles past the main airfield entrance and just before the airfield ends, take the road marked Gate D and follow it inland 0.4 miles. Just before the air control tower parking lot, there's an access road on the right. Walk around the old storage hanger to begin the trail. Give yourself about three hours to walk the Kealia Trail and back, and another three hours if you add on the Kuaokala loop.

Sleeping

Camp Mokule'ia (☎ 637-6241; www.campmokuleia .com; 68-729 Farrington Hwy; campsites per person $10, r from $65, cottages from $85; ☼) If you're looking to really escape the tourist scene, this Episcopal-run camp has a remote location smack on the beach and welcomes travelers to stay whenever there isn't a church conference going on. Set up a tent or rent a room in the lodge, hang by the pool, or take out one of the camp's kayaks ($15). Kitchen facilities are for groups only, but there are barbecue grills for all. The camp is opposite Dillingham Airfield.

Central O'ahu

Driving up O'ahu's spiny heartland with its mix of plantations and untamed wilderness, the highway cuts across red earth carpeted with green strips of pineapples – a scene so striking it makes Christo's environmental art look like kids' stuff. And towering above the endless pineapple rows, the island's highest peak, 4046ft Mount Ka'ala, pokes its head out of a mossy swamp that's so wet and overgrown it's accessible only to birds.

Most people just make a beeline through stolid Central O'ahu on their way to the sexier North Shore. Yet in an odd way, that's a big piece of what makes this quintessentially local district interesting, as there's no region of the island that is less affected by tourism. If you want to experience a slice of what O'ahu used to be like, slow down and take a closer look. The real character of this place reveals itself to those who take the time to scratch beneath the surface. Take a side trip through the plantation village of Kunia, go play a round with the locals at O'ahu's first public golf course or stop to dine on spicy grinds at the oldest Korean eatery in Hawaii.

And in at least one way, this is unquestionably the coolest place in all O'ahu. The Central O'ahu region forms a saddle between the Wai'anae Range on the west and the Ko'olau Range on the east, and the town of Wahiawa, on the highest terrain, is a few degrees cooler than all those coastal towns that ring the island.

HIGHLIGHTS

- Soaking up history at the **royal birthstones** (p213), where queens gave birth to future kings
- Inhaling the loamy fragrances at **Wahiawa Botanical Garden** (p213)
- Picnicking on a cool lake at **Wahiawa Freshwater State Recreation Area** (p214)
- Enjoying a drive through the island's picturesque **pineapple country** (opposite)
- Finding your way through the **'world's largest maze'** (p214)

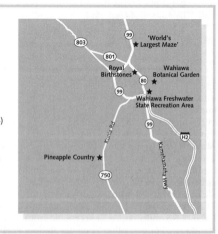

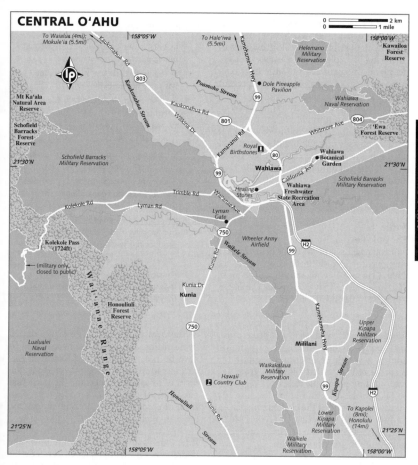

Getting There & Away

Three routes lead north from Honolulu to Wahiawa, the town smack in the middle of O'ahu. The H2 Fwy is the fastest route, whereas Kunia Rd (Hwy 750), the furthest west, is the most scenic. The least interesting option is the Kamehameha Hwy (Hwy 99), which catches local traffic as it runs through Mililani, a nondescript residential community.

From Wahiawa two routes, Hwy 803 (Kaukonahua Rd) and Hwy 99, lead through pineapple country to the North Shore. Hwy 803 is a slightly shorter route to Mokule'ia, and both routes are about the same distance to Hale'iwa. The two roads are equally picturesque, and if you're not circling the island, you might as well go up one and down the other.

KUNIA ROAD (HIGHWAY 750)

Kunia Rd adds a few miles to the drive through Central O'ahu, but if you have the time it's well worth it. Follow H1 from Honolulu to the Kunia/Hwy 750 exit, 3 miles west of where H1 and H2 divide.

As you drive up Hwy 750, the first mile climbs through creeping suburbia, followed by vast plantation lands. The road runs along the foothills of the Wai'anae Range and the countryside remains solidly agricultural all the way to Schofield Barracks Military Reservation. Two miles into the drive, you'll come to a strip of cornfields planted by seed companies. Three generations of corn are grown here each year, making it possible to develop hybrids of corn seed at triple the rate it takes on the mainland. Incidentally, the little bags covering each ear of corn are there to prevent cross-pollination.

And from there the earth is given over to the most scenic pineapple fields in the entire state of Hawaii. To take in the view, stop at the Hawaii Country Club golf course, just up the highway on the right, which sports a panorama of Honolulu all the way to Diamond Head. The view unfolds right in the parking lot, though it gets even better if you stop and play a round.

Kunia

The little town of Kunia, in the midst of the pineapple fields, is home to the field-workers employed by Del Monte. If you want to see what a current-day plantation village looks like, turn west off Hwy 750 onto Kunia Dr, about 5.5 miles north of H1.

Rows of gray-green wooden houses with corrugated tin roofs stand on low stilts. Residents take pride in their little yards, with bougainvillea and birds of paradise adding a splash of brightness despite the wash of red dust that blows in from the surrounding pineapple fields.

Take to the hills and enjoy the fine city view with a round at the challenging par 72, 18-hole **Hawaii Country Club** (☎ 621-5654; 94-1211 Kunia Rd; 18 holes $53; ⏱ 7am-6pm) golf course, the oldest public greens on O'ahu.

Kolekole Pass

This 1724ft pass occupies the gap in the Wai'anae Range that Japanese fighter planes flew through on their way to bomb Pearl Harbor. Film buffs may recognize the landscape, as the historic flight was re-created here 30 years later for the classic war film *Tora! Tora! Tora!*

Kolekole Pass, on military property above Schofield Barracks, can be visited as long as the base isn't on military alert. Access is through Lyman Gate on Hwy 750, 0.7 miles south of Hwy 750's intersection with Hwy 99. Follow Lyman Rd for 5.25 miles, passing a military golf course and bayonet assault course, to reach the pass.

A five-minute walk from the parking area leads to the top of the pass and a fine view

---

JUICY TIDBITS

- In 1901 James Dole planted O'ahu's first pineapple patch in Wahiawa.
- Dole's original 12-acre Wahiawa plot has since grown to 8000 acres.
- Each acre of a pineapple field supports about 6500 plants.
- The commercial variety grown in Hawaii is smooth cayenne.
- It takes nearly two years for a pineapple plant to reach maturity.
- Each plant produces just two pineapples, one in its second year and one in its third year.
- Pineapples are harvested year-round, but the long, sunny days of summer produce the sweetest fruit.
- The average pineapple weighs 5lb.
- Pineapples are unique among fruits in that they don't continue to ripen after they're picked.

---

of the Wai'anae Coast. The large, ribbed stone sitting atop the ridge here is said to have been a woman named Kolekole. According to Hawaiian legend, she took the form of this stone to become the perpetual guardian of the pass, keeping intruders from the coast from entering the sacred lands of Wahiawa.

Note the series of ridges on the stone's side. One drains down from the bowl-like depression on the top. Shaped perfectly for a guillotine, the depression has given rise to a more recent 'legend' that Kolekole served as a sacrificial stone for the beheading of defeated warriors. The fact that military bases flank the pass has no doubt had a little influence on forming this tale.

Just west of the pass the road continues through the Lualualei Naval Reservation down to the Wai'anae Coast, but you can't take it. The reservation is a storage site for nuclear weapons, and there's no public access through that side.

WAHIAWA
pop 16,250

Wahiawa – the very name means 'place of noise.' As if being chockablock with fast-food restaurants and pawn shops isn't enough,

Hawaii's largest army base, Schofield Barracks, sits on the town's southern edge. On the surface this is certainly a place you can pass through without pause. But this town actually has several different faces and the one you see on the commercial strip belies the others. Detour just a mile south of the center over to the reservoir and it's utterly serene; go a mile north of town and you're on land so sacred it was once the birthplace of kings. Never been in a tropical forest? Well that's just a mile to the west of the town center. If you've got the time to explore, Wahiawa will surprise you with some unexpected scenes.

Information

Bank of Hawaii (☎ 622-1651; 634 California Ave)
Post Office (☎ 800-275-8777; 115 Lehua St)

Sights

WAHIAWA BOTANICAL GARDEN

If you're venturing out of the concrete of Waikiki for the first time, this **botanical garden** (☎ 621-7321; 1396 California Ave; admission free; ☾ 9am-4pm), a mile east of Kamehameha Hwy (Hwy 80), is a wonderful place to stop and immerse yourself in a tropical forest. What started out in the 1920s as a site for forestry experiments by the Hawaii Sugar Planters' Association has blossomed into a 27-acre park with shady paths, grand old trees and a wooded ravine.

Interesting 80-year-old exotics, such as cinnamon, chicle and allspice, are grouped in one area, while palms, ginger and other Hawaiian natives are in other sections. The trees are identified by markers, the air is thick with birdsong and a small fortune has been spent sprucing the trails up.

Don't miss the tree ferns at the left side of the visitor center. Known as *hapu'u*, these huge ferns reach 20ft heights and form the understory of Hawaii's wetter forest areas. Ancient Hawaiians used the silky 'wool' at the base of the fronds as a surgical dressing, and until the late 19th century it was harvested commercially as a filling for mattresses.

DOLE PINEAPPLE PAVILION

This busy **complex** (☎ 621-8408; 64-1550 Kamehameha Hwy (Hwy 99); admission free; ☾ 9am-5:30pm) surrounded by miles of working pineapple

---

A DIVINE NAVEL

O'ahu's central uplands were once the domain of royalty, the area so sacred that commoners were forbidden to even pass through. Kukaniloko, just north of Wahiawa, took on unique importance. As the central point on the island, Kukaniloko symbolized the human *piko* (navel) and it was at this sacred spot that divine spirits welcomed chiefly offspring into the world.

Consequently it was of great importance that a female chief reach the site in time for childbirth. And there was a very strict regimen to be followed once she arrived. A certain number of chiefs had to be present to witness the birth, and the woman needed to lean properly against the stones while giving birth for her child to be blessed by the gods. If all went according to plan, that child would be taken to a nearby temple and welcomed into the world as an *ali'i* (member of royalty). Those born at Kukaniloko were of such a high lineage that chiefs from other islands would seek to enhance their prestige by marrying a Kukaniloko-born royal.

Some of the royal birthstones where Hawaii's queens gave birth to kings can still be seen at this site, which is now all but hidden in the midst of a pineapple field. These stones date back to the 12th century and were in use until the time of Kamehameha I, who rushed up to Kukaniloko for the birth of his son Liholiho in 1797.

Among the most sacred cultural treasures on O'ahu, these stones are one of only two documented birthstone sites in Hawaii (the other is on Kaua'i). Many of the petroglyphs you'll see on the stones are of recent origin, but the eroded circular patterns are original.

To get to the site from town, go three-quarters of a mile north on Kamehameha Hwy (Hwy 80) from its intersection with California Ave. Turn left onto the red dirt road directly opposite Whitmore Ave. The stones, marked with a state monument sign, are a quarter of a mile down the road, through a pineapple field, among a stand of eucalyptus and coconut trees. If it's been raining, be aware that the red clay can cake onto car tires, and once back on the paved road, the car may slide as if you're driving on ice.

fields consists of a crowded gift shop, gardens, a train ride and an expansive hibiscus hedge maze. The gift shop is essentially a tourist trap catering to a tour-bus crowd and selling pineapples that you could buy cheaper at home. The real fun is outdoors.

Maze
If you feel like getting lost, you can wander through the **'world's largest maze'** (adult/child $5/3), a claim confirmed by *Guinness World Records* (and sorry, there's no helpful Lonely Planet map for this one, so you're on your own). The maze covers nearly 2 acres and contains 1.7 miles of pathways. The goal is to find six different stations and things get quite challenging as there's no cheese (or pineapple) waiting at the end of the correct path to lure you. Most people take 15 to 30 minutes to get through – if you can make it in less than six minutes you've got yourself a new record!

Train Tour
If you're traveling with kids, consider hoppin' on the antique **steam train** (adult/child $7.50/5.50) that makes a 2-mile, 20-minute jaunt around the grounds with narration en route. The train departs every half-hour.

HEALING STONES
Among the more odd sights to be labeled with a visitors bureau marker are the 'Healing Stones' caged inside a small marble 'temple' next to the Methodist church

on California Ave, half a mile west of its intersection with Kamehameha Hwy.

The main stone is thought to be the gravestone of a powerful Hawaiian chief. Although the chief's original burial place was in a field a mile away, the stone was moved long ago to a graveyard at this site. In the 1920s people thought the stone had healing powers, and thousands made pilgrimages to it before interest waned. The housing development and church came later, taking over the graveyard and leaving the stones sitting on the sidewalk.

A local group with roots in India that sees a spiritual connection between Hawaiian and Indian beliefs now visits the temple, so you may see flowers or elephant statues placed around the stones.

Activities
The state maintains public freshwater fishing at the 300-acre Wahiawa Reservoir, which includes the **Wahiawa Freshwater State Recreation Area** (Walker St; 7am-6:45pm). The waters are stocked with largemouth and smallmouth bass, bluegill sunfish, channel catfish, puntat (Chinese catfish), tilapia and carp. Fishing is allowed year-round but you'll need a license ($10), which can be picked up in town at **Wahiawa Sporting Goods** (621-6091; 571 California Ave; usually 10am-6pm Mon-Fri, but closed some days).

Eating
Don't be deterred by the thick run of generic fast-food chains on Kamehameha Hwy, the main drag in downtown Wahiawa – this town has some worthy homespun eateries shuffled into the deck.

Shige's Saimin Stand (621-3621; 70 Kukui St; saimin $3.50-6; 10am-10pm Mon-Thu, to midnight Fri & Sat) Sit at the counter of this unpretentious Japanese eatery and slurp authentic homemade noodles that have few rivals this side of Tokyo. Ross Shigeoka, the owner, chef and server, makes the noodles fresh daily. To get there, go west on California Ave from Kamehameha Hwy and take the first right onto Kukui St.

Seoul Inn (621-9090; 410 California Ave; mains $5-8; 9:30am-8:30pm) This simple place lays claim to being Hawaii's oldest Korean eatery, so you can bet it has the recipes down pat. If you really want to see what warms a Korean heart, try the stir-fry kimchee.

DETOUR: WAHIAWA FRESHWATER STATE RECREATION AREA

Grab some picnic grub in town and head over to this lovely freshwater reservoir, where you can sit on a knoll surrounded by the scent of eucalyptus trees and enjoy a view of Lake Wilson. Despite being just beyond Wahiawa center, this place has an unspoiled countryside feel and the picnic tables are oh so inviting.

To get there, turn east off Kamehameha Hwy (Hwy 80) onto Avocado St at the south end of town and after 0.1 miles turn right onto Walker St. Continue 0.2 miles, turn right into the park entrance and go another 0.1 miles to the lakeside parking lot above the boat ramp.

THE AUTHOR'S CHOICE

Jimmy's Lakeside Bakery Cafe (☎ 621-6800; 1718 Wilikina Dr; sandwiches $6-8, mains $10-18; ⏰ 9am-8pm Mon-Thu, to 9pm Fri, 11am-9pm Sat, 11am-8pm Sun) The challenge is finding an empty parking space along the busy highway out front, but once you step into this gem there's an amazing transformation. The back of the café looks out onto a serene lake and the counter looks onto heavenly homemade cakes. The chef, a graduate of the prestigious Culinary Institute of America, wears his whites proudly and takes his cooking seriously. Jimmy's Dip, thin-sliced prime rib on a warm garlic hoagie, makes a memorable lunch, the pizzas are pure gourmet, and after 4pm the menu adds shrimp scampi and other pasta delights. Hawaiian music plays in the background. This place alone is worth the drive from Honolulu. If you're looking for a souvenir that brings home the taste of the islands, stock up on the white-chocolate, macadamia-nut cookies that Jimmy sells by the bag.

Maui Mike's (☎ 622-5900; 96 S Kamehameha Hwy; meals $5-7; ⏰ 11am-8:30pm Mon-Sat) Fire-roasted chicken is all Mike does but he does it right, using only fresh, all-natural birds that have never seen the inside of a freezer. A half-chicken served with fries makes a solid picnic lunch, and if you don't want to take it out, you can chow down at a couple of picnic tables right inside.

Molly's Smokehouse (☎ 621-4858; 23 S Kamehameha Hwy; meals $9-18; ⏰ 11am-9pm) Southern comfort comes to Wahaiwa with ex-Texan Molly Walker adding soul food, like collard greens and black-eye peas to her barbecue ribs and fried chicken menu. On the west side of the road, it's set back a bit and easy to miss, so keep an eye out for the Jack in the Box – Molly's is in the building next door.

Getting There & Away

To go through town and visit the botanical garden, healing stones and royal birthstones, take the Kamehameha Hwy (which is Hwy 80 as it goes through town, although it's Hwy 99 before and after Wahiawa). To make the bypass around Wahiawa, stick with Hwy 99.

Although exploring many of Central O'ahu's sights is practical only for those with their own transportation, you can get from Honolulu to Wahiawa (and onward to Hale'iwa) via bus 52.

Leeward O'ahu

The dry western side of the island encompasses two of the most diverse areas on O'ahu. At its southern end lies boomtown Kapolei, a planned community created in 1992 to shift O'ahu's future growth to the undeveloped southwestern region. Boasting some 35,000 new homes, Kapolei is slated to mushroom into an urban center second only to Honolulu in size. Its current population of 84,000 is expected to more than double by the year 2025.

At the southwest end of Kapolei lies the manicured Ko Olina Resort, a former coastal desert turned into an oasis, with lovely beaches, a luxury hotel and championship golf greens.

Just beyond lies the Wai'anae Coast, a stronghold of Hawaiian culture with a proud history of resisting change from the outside. When Kamehameha the Great invaded O'ahu in 1795, this area became a refuge for resisters, and when Christian missionaries arrived in O'ahu 25 years later Wai'anae folks shut them out by blocking the Kolekole Pass that connected Wai'anae to the rest of the island. Even today Wai'anae stands apart, with the largest native Hawaiian population on O'ahu and a deep sense of connection to the land. There are no tour buses, trinket shops or convoys of sightseers on this coast – actually, few tourists venture further than the 'Ewa area. What they're missing is a glimpse of a time-honored Hawaii that's found in few other places.

Nearly the entire coast is lined with white-sand beaches, mostly sleepers until you reach the surfer's haven of Makaha Beach. Fittingly, Wai'anae has the best preserved Hawaiian temple in O'ahu and the beautiful windswept Ka'ena Point, a repository of Hawaiian legends and native flora and fauna.

HIGHLIGHTS

- Hitting the beach at **Makaha** (p223), where surfing is awesome in winter, diving in summer
- Meditating on the spirit of old Hawaii at **Kane'aki Heiau** (p224)
- Hiking around remote **Ka'ena Point** (p227), the westernmost tip of O'ahu
- Enjoying a day at the beach with the celeb crowd at **Ko Olina Resort** (p218)
- Watching Jerome turn a koa log into a well-strung ukulele at **Valley Made Ukuleles** (p222)

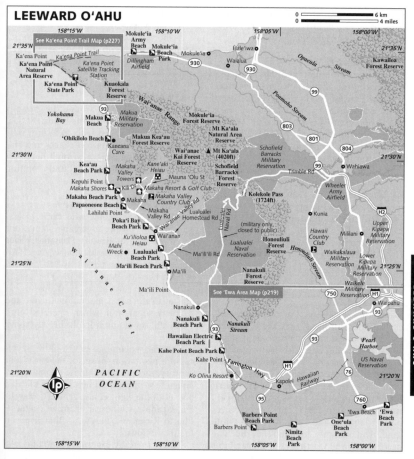

'EWA AREA

The southwestern side of O'ahu is a district in transition. Once solidly agricultural, its sugarcane fields were turned into housing lots after the region's last sugar mill shut down in 1995. With the closing of the Barbers Point Naval Air Station, which was demilitarized in 1999, another vast tract of land became available for civilian use, attracting businesses and jobs once based in Honolulu.

The 'Ewa area may be rapidly changing, but there are interesting sites dedicated to the region's past. In Waipahu, the Hawaii's Plantation Village complex showcases the multicultural heritage of those who came to work the sugar plantations. 'Ewa, the village southwest of Waipahu, also has its roots in sugar, and its main attraction – the restored Hawaiian Railway – takes visitors back in time with antique trains.

The area's other attractions are designed around water – the splashy thrills of the Hawaiian Waters Adventure Park and the quiet beaches at Ko Olina Resort.

Other beaches in this area are mostly used by local residents and military personnel. The best of the lot is 'Ewa Beach, a decent span of white sand, of which 5 acres is a county beach park and the rest set aside for the military. One'ula Beach and Nimitz Beach are predominantly rocky, with marginal swimming conditions, while Barbers Point Beach, just south of the industrial park, is outright unappealing.

Getting There & Away

H1 connects Honolulu and the 'Ewa area, terminating at Kapolei, where it merges with the Farrington Hwy (Hwy 93). To get to the Marketplace at Kapolei by car, take exit 2 off H1; to get to Hawaiian Waters Adventure Park, take exit 1. The road to Ko Olina Resort is off the southern side of the Farrington Hwy.

Bus 40 runs from the Ala Moana Center in Honolulu twice an hour, making stops in Kapolei at both Hawaiian Waters Adventure Park and the shopping center. The bus ride between Honolulu and Kapolei is about 1¼ hours. There's no bus into the Ko Olina Resort – the bus stops along the Farrington Hwy, and from there it's a mile walk to the nearest beach.

SIGHTS
Ko Olina Resort

When this coastal tract at the southwestern tip of O'ahu was earmarked to become Hawaii's newest resort development, it was lacking the one signature feature of upscale Hawaii resorts. It had no beach. But no problem: the investors struck a deal with the state to change that. In return for providing public access, the developers were allowed to carve out four picture-perfect lagoons and haul in tons of white sand. And a mighty good job they did. The beaches are well worth a visit, the facilities are excellent and the resort's other attractions make for fine diversions. Whether you're up for a round on a championship course, top-notch dining or *lomilomi* massage in a classy spa, this is one indulgent newcomer.

KO OLINA LAGOONS

The four sculptured lagoons at Ko Olina Resort all have inviting white-sand beaches. The largest lagoon, which borders the JW Marriott Ihilani Resort & Spa, is more than 200m across; the other three are about half that size. The lagoons are constructed with small islets at their mouths, a design that creates channels for water circulation. Swimmers should be aware of the seaward currents going out through the middle

channels; signs posted at each lagoon detail water-safety issues.

A shoreline path connects the four lagoons, making for an enjoyable stroll. Each lagoon has rest rooms, showers and parking spaces for about 20 cars.

SALTWATER POOLS

For a cool stroll, walk around the grounds of the JW Marriott Ihilani Resort & Spa, which are landscaped with free-form saltwater pools harboring reef sharks and Hawaiian stingrays, creatures you'll never get this close to elsewhere without donning dive gear.

Hawaii's Plantation Village

The lives of the people who came to Hawaii to work on the sugarcane plantations are showcased at **Hawaii's Plantation Village** (☎ 677-0110; www.hawaiiplantationvillage.org; 94-695 Waipahu St, Waipahu; adult/child 4-11yr $13/5; ☿ tours on the hr 10am-2pm Mon-Sat; 🚍 42). The setting is particularly evocative, as Waipahu was one of O'ahu's last plantation towns, and its rusty sugar mill, which operated until 1995, still looms on a knoll directly above this site.

The place encompasses 30 buildings typical of a plantation village of the early 20th century, including a Chinese cookhouse, a Japanese shrine and authentically replicated homes of the eight ethnic groups – Hawaiian, Japanese, Chinese, Korean, Portuguese, Puerto Rican and Filipino – that lived on the plantations.

To get there by car from Honolulu, take the H1 to exit 7, turn left onto Paiwa St, then right onto Waipahu St, continue past the sugar mill and turn left into the complex.

Hawaiian Railway

Railroad buffs won't want to miss this one. From 1890 until 1947 the O'ahu Railway & Land Company (OR&L) carried sugarcane and passengers along narrow-gauge tracks from Honolulu around the coast all the way to Kahuku. After WWII the increasing use of automobiles saw passenger numbers plummet and the rail service was abandoned. But thanks to the historically minded **Hawaiian Railway Society** (☎ 681-5461; www.hawaiianrailway .com; 91-1001 Renton Rd, 'Ewa; adult/child 2-12yr $10/7; ☿ 90min rides 1pm & 3pm Sun; 🚍 42), the trains again run for fun along 6.5 miles of restored

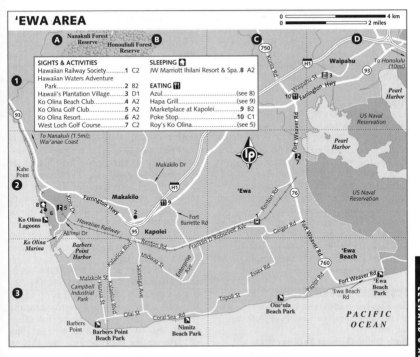

'EWA AREA

SIGHTS & ACTIVITIES		SLEEPING	
Hawaiian Railway Society..........**1** C2		JW Marriott Ihilani Resort & Spa..**8** A2	
Hawaiian Waters Adventure			
Park..........**2** B2		**EATING**	
Hawaii's Plantation Village.......**3** D1		Azul.........(see 8)	
Ko Olina Beach Club..........**4** A2		Hapa Grill..........(see 9)	
Ko Olina Golf Club..........**5** A2		Marketplace at Kapolei..........**9** B2	
Ko Olina Resort..........**6** A2		Poke Stop..........**10** C1	
West Loch Golf Course..........**7** C2		Roy's Ko Olina..........(see 5)	

track between 'Ewa and Nanakuli. A 1944 Whitcomb diesel locomotive pulls four cars of similar vintage. Displayed in the yard you'll find the coal engine that pulled the first OR&L train in 1889.

To get there, take exit 5A off the H1, drive south 2.5 miles on Fort Weaver Rd and turn right at the 7-Eleven onto Renton Rd.

ACTIVITIES
Hawaiian Waters Adventure Park
If the kids prefer their water thrills on slides, this multimillion-dollar water theme **park** (☎ 674-9283; www.hawaiianwaters.com; 400 Farrington Hwy, Kapolei; adult/child 3-11yr $35/25; ⏰ 10:30am-3:30pm Mon, Thu & Fri, to 4pm Sat & Sun), covering more than 25 acres, is the place. Main attractions include Hurricane Bay, a wave pool the size of a football field that generates 3ft waves for bodysurfing; and Kapolei Kooler, an 800ft artificial river geared for inner-tube rides.

Other attractions include Cliffhanger, a seven-story speed slide; Waterworld, the 20,000-sq-ft, multilevel, multiactivity pool; Keiki Kove, with water slides designed for young children; a teen activity pool with rope ladders; and an adults-only swimming pool with a swim-up bar.

Snorkeling
Snorkelers will find a fair number of tropical fish along the rock walls that form each of the four Ko Olina Lagoons. Your best bet is to start in the largest lagoon – not only does it have more space to explore, but sea turtles tend to favor this lagoon. Snorkel sets can be rented right at the beach from **Ko Olina Beach Club** (snorkel set per hr/day $8/15; ⏰ 8:30am-5pm).

Golf
Ko Olina Golf Club (☎ 676-5300; www.koolinagolf .com; 92-1220 Ali'inui Dr; 18 holes $160; ⏰ 6:30am-7pm), recognized by *Golf Digest* as one of the top 75 resort courses in the US, has hosted both the LPGA Tour and senior PGA Tour. With its multitiered greens and water features on eight holes, this Ted Robinson–designed course is nothing short of spectacular. Swing by in the afternoon for a $90 twilight rate.

LEEWARD O'AHU

Lots of ocean views, water features and a challenging layout highlight **West Loch Golf Course** (☎ 675-6076; 91-1126 Okupe St, 'Ewa Beach; per 18 holes $42; ⏱ 6am-6pm), a municipally run 18-hole, par-71 course. You won't need a high credit limit to play this one.

Hiking

The **Nature Conservancy** (☎ 587-6220; nature.org \hawaii) leads monthly hikes to two trails in the Honouliuli Forest Reserve on the slopes of the Wai'anae Range north of Kapolei. Palikea Ridge Trail is the easier of the two hikes, while the Kalua'a Loop Trail is considered intermediate. Honouliuli Preserve is home to nearly 70 rare and endangered plant and animal species. The land once belonged to Hawaiian royalty and was named Honouliuli – meaning dark harbor – for the dark, fertile lands that stretch from the waters of Pearl Harbor to the summit of the Wai'anae Range.

FESTIVALS & EVENTS

Hawaiian Ladies Open (www.lpga.com) This LPGA golf tournament takes place in mid-February at Ko Olina Golf Club.

World Billfish Challenge Ko Olina (☎ 879-1050; www.wbchawaii.com) This deep-sea fishing tournament takes place over three days in mid-August at the Ko Olina Marina in Leeward O'ahu.

SLEEPING

JW Marriott Ihilani Resort & Spa (☎ 679-0079, 800-626-4446; www.marriotthotels.com; Ko Olina Resort, 92-1001 Olani St; r from $370, with ocean view from $475; ⏹ 🖳 🖭) With its gorgeous beachside setting,

luxurious rooms and indulgent spa, it's little wonder this getaway resort attracts a celebrity crowd. Hollywood even filmed the resort scenes of the surfer-girl movie *Blue Crush* here. The grounds include six tennis courts and a championship golf course. Packages that include spa treatments and golf are available.

EATING

Azul (☎ 679-3166; JW Marriott Ihilani Resort & Spa, Ko Olina Resort; mains $30-46; ⏱ 6-9pm Tue-Sat) Moonlight dining on the terrace here makes for one romantic night out. The resort's signature dinner restaurant, Azul shines with innovative Mediterranean fare spiced with Hawaiian accents. How does Kona lobster with truffle risotto sound? The best deal is the daily prix-fixe menu of five courses for $60 – call to make reservations and see what's on the menu.

Roy's Ko Olina (☎ 676-7697; 92-1220 Ali'inui Dr, Ko Olina Resort; lunch $10-15, dinner $25-40; ⏱ 11am-2pm & 5:30-9:30pm) A golfer's dream scene, this clubhouse restaurant overlooking the greens dispenses with the usual club sandwiches and takes it gourmet, with the likes of kiawe-grilled filet mignon, rock shrimp spring rolls and dynamite sushi.

Hapa Grill (☎ 674-8400; Marketplace at Kapolei, 91-590 Farrington Hwy, Kapolei; mains $5-15; ⏱ 8am-9pm Sun & Mon, to 10pm Tue-Sat; 🖝) Families love this smart diner-style restaurant with sassy island favorites. The banana cream Belgian waffle will keep the kids smiling all day. Creative salads, stir-fries and pasta dishes shore up the rest of the menu.

THE AUTHOR'S CHOICE

Poke Stop (☎ 676-8100; Waipahu Town Center, 94-050 Farrington Hwy; mains $4-13; ⏱ 8am-7pm Mon-Sat, to 5pm Sun) So why would a renowned chef who's worked alongside such masters as Hawaii's Adam Wong and New Orleans' Emeril Lagasse (yep, that 'BAM!' guy on US TV's cooking channel) run off to start a take-out restaurant in Waipahu? Maybe he needed a break from the high-pressure scene, or perhaps he just wanted to do it his way. Whatever his inspiration, you've got to take advantage of this one. Elmer Guzman commands the neatest little kitchen on this coast, mixing up gourmet food on par with what you'll find at the island's finest restaurants. Poke is the specialty and here it's as good as it gets. Although the *'ahi* (yellowfin tuna) versions are sensational, Guzman doesn't stop there – he makes a spicy Korean crab poke that will turn on tastebuds you didn't even know you had. The sashimi and sushi are also knockouts, made from fish that were swimming in the sea earlier in the day. Or order hot dishes made to order, such as blackened fresh catch or the garlic white shrimp. Organic green salads and free-trade coffees are available, too. You can pack a meal for a feast at the beach, but there are also a couple of tables outside the shop if you can't wait!

The **Marketplace at Kapolei** (91-590 Farrington Hwy, Kapolei) also has a 24-hour Safeway supermarket and a bevy of other restaurants serving pizza, Thai and Chinese fare.

WAI'ANAE COAST

In 1793 English captain George Vancouver became the first Westerner to drop anchor on the Wai'anae Coast, and found only a few scattered fishing huts. Just two years later Kamehameha the Great invaded the island, and the population density along the remote Wai'anae Coast swelled with O'ahuans forced to flee their homes elsewhere on the island. This arid, isolated western extreme of O'ahu became their permanent refuge.

Today the people living along the Wai'anae Coast still have their own identity, not only as native Hawaiians but as Wai'anae Hawaiians. Everyone in Hawaii who listens to the music of the late, great Israel Kamakawiwo'ole, the former lead singer of the Ni'ihau Sons of Makaha, knows he was raised on the Wai'anae Coast. The place he was from was such an integral part of who he was – not just his music, or the lyrics, but his whole essence reflected the spirit of his homeland.

There's plenty of aloha here – *plenty* – if you travel gently, but it's equally true that some residents are wary of outsiders, so this is a particularly good place to stay attuned to the mood of people.

The Wai'anae Coast, with its long stretches of white-sand beaches, offers good swimming in summer and challenging surfing opportunities in winter. Although the towns themselves are ordinary in appearance, the cliffs and valleys cutting into the Wai'anae Range form an attractive backdrop. The two-lane Farrington Hwy runs the length of the coast through the heart of each town. At the road's end, there's an undeveloped mile-long beach and a fine nature hike out to scenic Ka'ena Point.

Getting There & Away

Exploring by car couldn't be easier: just follow the Farrington Highway (Hwy 93) up the coast, with beaches on one side, the mountains on the other.

For those traveling by bus, buses C and 40 connect Honolulu with the Wai'anae Coast, stopping in every town as far north as Makaha. If you're going to Makaha Beach Park, the express bus C is the more direct option, because it stays along the coast. Bus 40 goes up Makaha Valley Rd to the golf courses and then comes down Kili Dr to the beach. From the Ala Moana Center in Honolulu, the buses run a few times an hour and take about 1⅓ hours to reach Nanakuli, 1¾ hours to Wai'anae and two hours to Makaha Beach Park. No buses run beyond Makaha; that area can only be explored by those with their own transportation.

KAHE POINT BEACHES

Despite its name, **Kahe Point Beach Park** does not have a beach, just the rocky cliffs of Kahe Point that are favored by fishers. What it does offer is a fine view of the sandy beaches that lie ahead to the north, as well as running water, picnic tables and rest rooms. The park is easy to find as it's opposite the region's electric power plant with its towering smokestacks.

Hawaiian Electric Beach Park, the sandy beach north of Kahe Point, is more commonly known as Tracks, the name given to it by beachgoers who used to go there by train before WWII. In summer this is a calm place to swim, and in winter it's frequented by surfers. To get there, take the first turnoff after the power plant and drive over the abandoned railroad tracks.

NANAKULI
pop 10,814

Nanakuli is the first town you'll encounter on the Wai'anae Coast. The site of a Hawaiian Homesteads settlement, Nanakuli has one of the largest native Hawaiian populations on O'ahu. The town's commercial strip runs along the *mauka* (inland) side of Farrington Hwy, with supermarkets, a bank and a few fast-food places.

Nanakuli Beach Park is a broad, sandy beach park that lines the town, offering swimming, snorkeling and diving during the calmer summer season. In winter high surf can create rip currents and dangerous shorebreaks. As an in-town community park, it has a playground, sports fields and beach facilities. To get to the beach park, turn *makai* (oceanward) at the traffic lights on Nanakuli Ave.

Valley Made Ukuleles (☎ 620-5358; 87-110 Nanaikeola St; ☺ 9am-5pm Mon-Fri) is a shop homespun with aloha run by Jerome Werner, a third-generation ukulele maker and a full-blooded Hawaiian. Jerome makes his koa ukuleles on-site and if you're interested to see whether you can play, he can give you an introductory lesson that'll answer the question. To find the shop, turn off Farrington Hwy at the market, Nanakuli Super.

MA'ILI BEACH PARK
The long, grassy roadside Ma'ili Beach Park fronts almost the entire village of Ma'ili with its endless stretch of glistening white sands. Like other places on the Wai'anae Coast, the water conditions are often treacherous in winter but usually calm enough for swimming in summer. The park has a lifeguard station, a playground, beach facilities and a few castrated coconut palms that provide limited, but safe, shade.

WAI'ANAE
pop 10,525
The largest town on the Wai'anae Coast, not only has the lion's share of the coast's infrastructure, restaurants and the like, but also has the region's finest in-town beach park and a large protected boat harbor.

Information
First Hawaiian Bank (☎ 696-7041; 86-020 Farrington Hwy) Just south of the post office.
Post Office (☎ 800-275-8777; 86-014 Farrington Hwy; ☺ 8am-4:15pm Mon-Fri, 9am-noon Sat) On the corner at Lualualei Homestead Rd.
Wai'anae Comprehensive Health Center (☎ 696-7081; 86-260 Farrington Hwy; ☺ emergency room 24hr) The coast's hospital, on the corner at Maili'ili Rd.

Sights & Activities
POKA'I BAY BEACH PARK
This beach is a real beauty. Protected by both Kane'ilio Point and a long breakwater, it has calm year-round swimming. Waves seldom break inside the bay, and the sandy beach slopes gently, making it a popular spot for families with children.

Snorkeling is fair by the breakwater, where fish gather around the rocks. The bay is also used by local canoe clubs, and you can watch them rowing if you happen by in the late afternoon. There are showers, rest rooms and picnic tables, and a lifeguard is on duty daily.

HAWAIIAN HOME LANDS

In 1920, under the sponsorship of Prince Jonah Kuhio Kalaniana'ole, the Territory of Hawaii's congressional delegate, the US Congress passed the Hawaiian Homes Commission Act. The act set aside almost 200,000 acres of land for homesteading by native Hawaiians, who were by this time the most landless ethnic group in Hawaii. Despite this apparently generous gift, the land was but a small fraction of the crown lands that were taken from the Hawaiian kingdom when the USA annexed the islands in 1898.

Under the legislation, people of at least 50% Hawaiian ancestry were eligible for 99-year leases at $1 a year. Originally, most of the leases were for 40-acre parcels of agricultural land, although more recently residential lots as small as a quarter of an acre have been allocated.

Hawaii's prime land, already in the hands of the sugar barons, was excluded from the act. Much of what was designated for homesteading was on far more barren turf. Still, many Hawaiians were able to make a go of it. Presently, there are about 7400 native Hawaiian families living on about 32,000 acres of homestead lands.

As with many projects intended to help native Hawaiians, administration of the Hawaiian Home Lands has been controversial. Much of the land has not been allocated to native Hawaiians but has been leased out to big business, ostensibly as a means of creating an income for the program's administration.

In addition, the federal, state and county governments have, with little or no compensation, taken large tracts of Hawaiian Home Lands for their own use. The Lualualei Naval Reservation, which sits above Nanakuli, constitutes one-fifth of all homestead lands on O'ahu, despite the fact that more than 8000 O'ahuans of native Hawaiian descent remain on the waiting list – some for as long as 30 years. Along the Wai'anae Coast you can expect to see homeless families encamped along the beach, waiting for their name to come up and unable to pay sky-high O'ahu rents.

To get to the beach park, turn *makai* (oceanward) onto Lualualei Homestead Rd, off Farrington Hwy at the traffic light immediately north of the Wai'anae post office.

SNORKELING CRUISE

For a snorkel tour to remember, hop on board with **Wild Side Specialty Tours** (☎ 306-7273; www.wildsidehawaii.com; Slip A-11, Wai'anae Boat Harbor; cruises $95; ☺ morning cruise 7-11am). This well-managed outfit, with a marine biologist aboard, offers a four-hour catamaran cruise with snorkeling time in waters frequented by spinner dolphins and sea turtles. In winter you might even see whales. Also on offer: three-hour sunset cruises minus the snorkeling but with dinner included. It only takes a maximum of 16 passengers, so advance reservations are essential.

Eating

Surfah Smoodeez (☎ 478-9088; 85-979 Farrington Hwy; smoothies $4-5.25; ☺ 10:30am-7pm Mon-Fri, to 5:30pm Sat) Come here for smoothies named Shorebreak and Wipeout loaded with fresh tropical fruits, like papaya, mango and pineapple. Naturally sweet and oh so delicious. It's just south of the highway's intersection with Wai'anae Valley Rd.

Tacos & More (☎ 697-8800; 85-993 Farrington Hwy; mains $5-10; ☺ 10am-8pm Mon-Fri, 2-8pm Sat; **V**) Real Mexican and real friendly, this spicy little family-run place a stone's throw from Surfah Smoodeez serves up a full range of south-of-the-border delights with your choice of shredded meats or vegetarian. Don't know your machacas from your flautas? Just ask!

Hannara Restaurant (☎ 696-6137; 86-078 Farrington Hwy; mains $3-7; ☺ 6am-8pm Mon-Sat, to 3pm Sun) Rub shoulders with the Wai'anae crowd at this bustling place featuring a long menu of local grinds, ranging from macadamia-nut pancakes to *kalua* pig plates and Korean fare. If you're coming from the south, it's immediately before the Seventh Day Adventist Church.

MAKAHA
pop 7750

Makaha means 'ferocious,' and in days past the valley was notorious for the bandits who waited along the cliffs to ambush passing travelers. Today Makaha is best known for its world-class surfing and fine beaches.

DETOUR: KU'ILIOLOA HEIAU

Start at the Poka'i Bay Beach Park parking lot, walk straight across the lawn with the outrigger canoes at your right and take the path 200yd out to Kane'ilio Point. Here's your reward: Ku'ilioloa Heiau, a terraced stone platform temple, and spectacular coastal views all the way to Makaha in the north. At the foot of the heiau, if the waves aren't crashing strongly, you'll find little tidepools harboring miniature marine life that can be explored.

It also has some hidden secrets, including O'ahu's best-restored heiau.

Sights
MAKAHA BEACH PARK

Makaha Beach is broad, sandy and crescent-shaped, with some of the most daunting winter surf in the islands. Experienced surfers and bodysurfers both take to the waves here.

In the early 1950s Makaha hosted Hawaii's first international surfing competition. Although the biggest surfing events have since shifted to the North Shore, Makaha Beach is still favored by longboarders. When the surf's not up, Makaha is a popular beach for swimming. When the surf is up, rip currents and a strong shorebreak make swimming hazardous.

In summer the slope of the beach is relatively flat, while in winter it has a steeper drop due to the turbulent wave action. As much as half of the sand temporarily washes away during winter erosion, but even then Makaha is still an impressive beach.

The beach has showers and rest rooms, and lifeguards are on duty daily.

PAPAONEONE BEACH

Everybody heads to Makaha Beach Park, while this smaller beauty just a mile to the south sees barely a soul. It's a good spot for bodysurfing, with a decent shorebreak. Protected by Lahilahi Point to the south, Papaoneone Beach seldom has rip currents unless the surf is very big, but if you've got kids with you be cautious because the sandy bottom has a quick and steep drop-off. Access to the beach is immediately north of the Makaha Beach Cabanas condominiums.

LEEWARD O'AHU

A GLIMPSE OF THE PAST

Simply no other place on O'ahu comes close to **Kane'aki Heiau** (☎ 695-8174; Mauna Olu Estates; admission free; ❇ 10am-2pm Tue-Sun) in providing a glimpse into pre-Western contact Hawaiian culture. Restored to its original splendor and set at the base of verdant hills, the temple looks much like it did centuries ago. Because it's on restricted land, very few tourists make it up this way, and that adds a quiet, untouched element to it all. It's an awesome sight to walk around and well worth working a visit into your schedule.

Built in the center of Makaha Valley, midway between the valley's wet, forested uplands and its dry, coastal lowlands, the heiau dates back to 1545 and was originally dedicated to Lono, the god of agriculture. As with many Hawaiian temples, over time it went through transformations in both its physical structure and use. In its final phase it was rededicated as a *luakini* (dedicated to Ku, the god of war) temple, and it's thought that Kamehameha the Great used Kane'aki Heiau as a place of worship after he conquered O'ahu. The heiau remained in use until his death in 1819.

The social and religious upheaval introduced by Kamehameha's successors resulted in the abandonment of Kane'aki Heiau – and all other Hawaiian temples as well. Although many of Hawaii's more accessible coastal heiau were dismantled and their stones used to build cattle fences and other structures, Kane'aki Heiau, protected by its remoteness, survived largely intact.

Constructed of stacked basalt rocks, Kane'aki Heiau has two terraced platforms and six enclosed courtyards. Its restoration, undertaken by the esteemed Bishop Museum, took years to complete. The heiau was authentically reconstructed using ohia logs handhewn with adzes and thatch made from native *pili* grass gathered on the Big Island. Two prayer towers, a taboo house, a drum house, an altar and several god images were built by Hawaiian craftspeople using traditional techniques and materials.

To get to the heiau, take Kili Dr to the Makaha Valley Towers condominium complex and turn right onto Huipu Dr. A half-mile down, make a left onto Mauna Olu St, which leads a mile into Mauna Olu Estates and up to Kane'aki Heiau. The guard at the Mauna Olu Estates gatehouse lets visitors enter to see the heiau only during the listed hours. You might want to call the gatehouse in advance to inquire, as they can be a bit inconsistent in providing access, especially in wet weather. You'll need to show your rental-vehicle contract and driver's license at the gatehouse, so be sure to bring them.

MAKAHA VALLEY

For a little loop drive, turn inland from the Farrington Hwy onto Kili Dr opposite Makaha Beach Park. The road skirts up along scalloped cliffs into Makaha Valley. If you can, stop to visit **Kane'aki Heiau** (see the boxed text, above) – Hawaii's most authentically restored temple.

And here's a colorful perk: an estimated 3000 wild peacocks live in Makaha Valley. They can be spotted, or at least heard, throughout the upper valley, and if you visit the heiau, it's not unusual to see some of them performing their courting rituals in the field adjacent to the parking lot.

Activities
WATER SPORTS

Snorkeling is good off Makaha Beach Park during the calmer summer months. Makaha Caves, out where the waves break furthest offshore, is a popular leeward diving spot,

featuring underwater caverns, arches and tunnels at depths of 30ft to 50ft. You can rent snorkel sets or a complete set of dive gear from **Ocean Concepts** (☎ 696-7200; www.ocean concepts.com; 85-371 Farrington Hwy; snorkel/dive gear per day $14/50; ❇ 8am-3pm). Ocean Concepts can also take you out to the *Mahi*, a 165ft naval vessel that was sunk off Makaha to create an artificial reef with spectacular corals.

Paradise Isle (☎ 695-8866; Makaha Marketplace, 84-1170 Farrington Hwy; boogie board/surfboard/longboard hire per 6hr $12/20/25; ❇ 8am-8pm), just south of Makaha Beach Park, is the place to buy or rent boards of all shapes and sizes. It also rents snorkel sets ($10) and sells fishing supplies, beachwear etc. If it has to do with the water, it's got it.

GOLF

Makaha Resort & Golf Club (☎ 695-7519; 84-626 Makaha Valley Rd; 18 holes $85; ❇ 6am-6pm), with the Wai'anae Range at its back and the ocean at its foot, is one beautiful championship course. The slope of the land creates some interesting optical illusions, such as sloping down when it appears to rise up – how's that for a challenge?

Makaha Valley Country Club (☎ 695-7111; 84-627 Makaha Valley Rd; 18 holes $80; ☺ 7am-5:30pm Mon-Fri, 6:30am-6:30pm Sat & Sun) is a great local. The par 72 course can be tough in spots, but it offers great views of the Wai'anae Range and the coast. The price drops to $55 on weekdays if you have a US driver's license.

Sleeping

Makaha Resort & Golf Club (☎ 695-9544; www.makaharesort.net; 84-626 Makaha Valley Rd; r from $205, 1-bedroom unit $325; ⊠ ⚫) Perched above the golf course with a panoramic view clear down to the ocean, this small hillside resort makes for an unbeatable golfing getaway. The hotel itself is quiet and mellow, almost like an overgrown boutique hotel. If you want room to move, the one-bedroom units are huge with a separate living room and two bathrooms. Ask about the best available rates, which can cut prices as much as 50%.

Makaha Shores (☎ 696-8415; www.hawaiiwest.com; Suite 201, Hawaii Hatfield Realty, 85-833 Farrington Hwy; studio/1-bedroom unit per week from $500/600; ⚫) With a prize location right on the northern end of Makaha Beach and a bird's-eye

view of wave action right from your lanai, these condos are a surfer's dream. Lots of snowbirds return here each winter, so book well in advance during high season. Hawaii Hatfield Realty also handles similarly priced units in Makaha Valley Towers, the high-rise complex that's tucked into the valley.

Eating

Makaha Valley Country Club (☎ 695-7111; 84-627 Makaha Valley Rd; mains $5-10; ☺ 7am-2pm Mon-Fri, 6am-3pm Sat & Sun) Overlooking the golf course, this is a favorite breakfast and lunch spot with a varied menu that includes sandwiches and plate lunches. Until 10:30am, you can get banana pancakes, omelettes and similar fare.

Kaiona Restaurant (☎ 695-9544; Makaha Resort & Golf Club, 84-626 Makaha Valley Rd; mains $8-28; ☺ 7am-2pm & 5:30-9pm) This is the place for dinner in Makaha, with a decent surf 'n' turf menu and a good view to go along with it. If you have a big appetite, swing by on a Friday or Saturday night when there's a $26 prime rib and seafood buffet.

Entertainment

Pumana Lounge (☎ 695-9544; Makaha Resort & Golf Club, 84-626 Makaha Valley Rd) This open-air lounge at Makaha Resort & Golf Club features live Hawaiian entertainment from 7pm to 10pm Friday and Saturday. It's a nice place to stop for a drink and *pupu* (snacks) anytime.

MAKAHA TO KA'ENA POINT

Farrington Hwy continues north to Ka'ena Point, but this area is solely for those with their own transportation. There are no buses beyond Makaha – nor gas stations, restaurants or towns.

Kea'au Beach Park

This beach park is a long, open, grassy strip that borders a rocky shore. It has rest rooms, showers, drinking water and picnic tables, making it a good place to unpack that picnic lunch. A sandy beach begins at the very northern end of the park, although a rough reef, sharp drop and high seasonal surf make swimming uninviting.

North along the coast you'll see lava cliffs, white-sand beaches and patches of kiawe, while on the inland side you'll glimpse a run of little valleys.

SLIPPING AWAY

Early Hawaiians believed that when people went into a deep sleep or lost consciousness, their souls would wander. Souls that wandered too far were drawn west to Ka'ena Point. If they were lucky, they were met there by their 'aumakua (ancestral spirit helper), who led their soul back to their body. If not, their soul would be forced to leap from Ka'ena Point into the endless night, never to return.

On clear days the island of Kaua'i is visible from Ka'ena Point. According to legend, it was from Ka'ena Point that the demigod Maui attempted to cast a huge hook into Kaua'i in order to pull it closer to O'ahu and join the two islands. But the line broke and Kaua'i slipped away, with just a small piece of it remaining near O'ahu. Today this splintered rock, off the end of Ka'ena Point, is known as Pohaku O Kaua'i.

LEEWARD O'AHU

Kaneana Cave

About 2 miles north of Kea'au Beach Park, this massive cave on the inland side of the road was once underwater. Its impressive size is the result of wave action that wore away loose rock around an earthquake crack. Over the millennia, the cavern expanded as the ocean slowly receded. It's a somewhat uncanny place – strong gusts of wind blow near the cave, while just down the road it's windless.

Hawaiian *kahuna* (priests) once performed rituals inside the cave's inner chamber. Older Hawaiians consider it a sacred place and won't enter the cave for fear that it's haunted by the spirits of deceased chiefs. From the collection of broken beer bottles and graffiti inside, it's obvious not everyone shares their sentiments.

Ohikilolo Beach

From Ohikilolo Beach, which is below Kaneana Cave, you can see Ka'ena Point to the north. Ohikilolo Beach is sometimes called Barking Sands – the sand is said to make a woofing sound when it's very dry and is walked upon. Don't consider more than strolling on this one – the beach is too rocky and the current too nasty for swimming.

Makua Valley

Scenic Makua Valley opens up wide and grassy, backed by a fan of sharply fluted mountains. It serves as the ammunition field of the Makua Military Reservation. The seaside road opposite the southern end of the reservation leads to a little graveyard that's shaded by yellow-flowered be-still trees. This site is all that remains of the Makua Valley community that was forced to evacuate during WWII when the US military took over the entire valley for bombing practice. War games still take place in the valley, which is fenced off with barbed wire and signs that warn of stray explosives.

Makua Beach

The white-sand beach opposite the Makua Military Reservation was a canoe landing in days past. A movie set was built on the beach for the 1966 movie *Hawaii,* based on James Michener's classic novel and starring Julie Andrews and Max von Sydow, but no trace of the set remains.

KA'ENA POINT STATE PARK

Running along both sides of the western-most point of O'ahu, Ka'ena Point State Park is an undeveloped 853-acre coastal strip.

Until the mid-1940s the O'ahu Railway ran up here from Honolulu and continued around the point, carrying passengers on to Hale'iwa on the North Shore. The gorgeous, mile-long sandy beach on the southern side of the point is Yokohama Bay, named for the large numbers of Japanese fishers who came here during the railroad days.

Rest rooms, showers and a lifeguard station are at the southern end of the park. It's best to bring food and drinks with you, though occasionally a lunch wagon parks here selling beef stew and smoothies.

RARE TREASURE

In addition to being a state park, Ka'ena Point is designated as a natural area reserve because of its unique ecosystem. The extensive dry, windswept coastal dunes that rise above the point are the habitat of many rare native plants. The endangered *ka'ena akoko* growing on the talus slopes is found nowhere else in the world. In winter you can identify it by its pale green leaves, while in summer it's leafless.

Other plants growing here include beach *naupaka,* a native shrub with white flowers that look like they have been torn in half; *pa'u-o-hi'iaka,* a vine with blue flowers; and beach morning glory, sometimes found entwined with *kaunaoa,* a parasitic vine that looks like orange fishing line.

Seabirds seen at Ka'ena Point include shearwaters, boobies and the common noddy – a dark-brown bird with a grayish crown. You can often see schools of spinner dolphins off the beach, and in winter humpback whale sightings are not unusual.

Dirt bikes and 4WD vehicles once created a great deal of disturbance in the dunes, but after Ka'ena Point became a natural area reserve in 1983, vehicles were restricted and the situation improved. The reserve is once again a nesting site for the rare Laysan albatross, and Hawaii's endangered monk seals occasionally bask in the sun here.

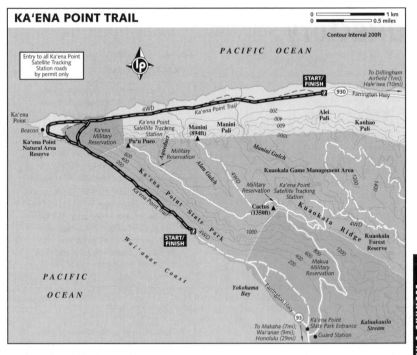

KA'ENA POINT TRAIL

Incidentally, those domes sitting above the park that resemble giant white golf balls belong to the Air Force's Ka'ena Point Satellite Tracking Station.

Activities
KA'ENA POINT TRAIL
A coastal trail runs from Yokohama Bay to Ka'ena Point, and around the point to the North Shore, utilizing the old railroad bed. Most hikers take the trail, which begins from the end of the paved road at Yokohama Bay, as far as the point (2.5 miles one way) and then come back the same way; it takes about three to four hours roundtrip. This easy-to-follow hike offers fine views the entire way, with the ocean on one side and the lofty cliffs of the Wai'anae Range on the other. Along the trail there are tide pools, sea arches and a couple of lazy blowholes that occasionally come to life on high-surf days.

The trail is exposed and lacks shade (Ka'ena means 'the heat'), so take sunscreen and plenty of water. Be cautious near the shoreline, as there are strong currents, and the waves can reach extreme heights. In fact, winter waves at Ka'ena Point are the highest in Hawaii, sometimes towering in excess of 50ft.

Don't leave anything valuable in your car. Telltale mounds of shattered windshield glass litter the road's-end parking area used by most hikers. Parking closer to the rest rooms or leaving your doors unlocked can decrease the odds of having your car windows smashed.

WATER SPORTS
Winter brings huge, pounding waves into Yokohama Bay, making it a popular surfing and bodysurfing spot. It is, however, best left to the experts, because of the submerged rocks, strong rip currents and dangerous shorebreak. Swimming is pretty much limited to summer, and even then only during calm conditions. When the water's flat, it's possible to snorkel; the best spot with the easiest access is at the southern side of the park.

Directory

CONTENTS

PRACTICALITIES

- O'ahu's two daily newspapers are the *Honolulu Advertiser* and *Honolulu Star-Bulletin*. For the best scoop on the entertainment scene, read the free *Honolulu Weekly*.

- Free tourist magazines like *Spotlight's O'ahu Gold* and *This Week O'ahu* are packed with useful visitor information.

- All the major US TV networks are represented, as well as cable channels offering tourist information. For local flavor, the Channel 2 evening news ends with slack key guitar music by Keola and Kapono Beamer and clips of people waving the *shaka* (Hawaiian hand greeting) sign.

- O'ahu has about 35 AM and FM radio stations. Radio station Da KINE (105.1FM) plays classic Hawaiian music.

- If you're buying videos to take home, be aware Hawaii uses the NTSC system, the same as in the rest of the USA, which is incompatible with the PAL system used in Europe and Australia.

- Plug in to Hawaii's 110/120V, 60 cycles current using a flat, two-pronged plug, as elsewhere in the USA.

- As on the US mainland, distances are measured in feet, yards and miles; weights in ounces, pounds and tons.

ACCOMMODATIONS

O'ahu offers a wide variety of accommodations in every price range from simple hostels to luxury resorts. Although most places have the same rates year-round, some have high-season rates in effect from mid-December to mid-April. When demand peaks, including at Christmas and during special events like the Honolulu Marathon (p235), lodgings book up well in advance. During the off-season finding a choice room is easier and on-line discounts plentiful. Many hotel websites offer handsome on-line rates that aren't available over the phone and doing a little surfing on other travel websites can turn up even better deals. The following are good places to look, especially for last-minute deals:

CheapTickets (www.travelocity.com)
Expedia.com (www.expedia.com)
Orbitz (www.orbitz.com)

Reviews in this book indicate rates for single occupancy (s), double (d) or simply the room (r) when the price is the same for one or two people – which is the norm on O'ahu. A double room in our budget category usually costs $90 or less, midrange doubles cost $90 to $235 and top-end rooms start at $235. Unless otherwise noted, breakfast is *not* included, bathrooms are private and all lodging is open year-round. Rates don't include Hawaii's steep 11.41% room tax.

A reservation guarantees your room, but most reservations require a deposit and there may be restrictions on getting a refund if you change your mind. Some places may issue only a partial refund, and in some cases you may forfeit your entire deposit, so check the cancellation policy carefully.

B&Bs

Although elsewhere the term often conjures up images of Victorian inns, on O'ahu B&Bs are typically rooms in private homes. B&Bs on the island operate under antiquated local regulations that make it difficult to establish new businesses and limit most B&Bs already in operation to renting only two guest rooms. As a result, there's often a pleasant tropical-underground feel to them; for example, most cannot display signs and are not legally permitted to offer a hot breakfast.

B&Bs discourage unannounced drop-ins and, for that reason, they do not appear on maps in this book. Because hosts are often out during the day, same-day reservations are hard to get; especially in winter, when most B&Bs book full weeks in advance. B&B rates range from around $60 for a basic room to $200 for luxurious seaside digs. Many require a minimum stay of a few days.

The majority of O'ahu's B&Bs are in the Kailua area. This book includes B&Bs that can be booked directly, but there are others that can be booked only through B&B reservation services. The following are reputable agencies:

Affordable Paradise (☎ 261-1693; www.affordable -paradise.com; 332 Kuukama St, Kailua, HI 96734; rentals $55-535) Books the widest range of properties in the Kailua area, with something for every taste and budget.

All Islands Bed & Breakfast (☎ 263-2342, 800-542-0344; www.all-islands.com; 708 Kanaha St, Kailua, HI 96734; rentals $75-200) A decent selection of rooms, apartments and cottages.

Bed & Breakfast Hawaii (☎ 822-7771, 800-733-1632; www.bandb-hawaii.com; PO Box 449, Kapa'a, HI 96746)

Pat's Kailua Beach Properties (☎ 261-1653; www .patskailua.com; 204 S Kalaheo Ave, Kailua, HI 96734; rentals $80-500) Properties on or near the beach, ranging from small studios that can sleep two people to large beachfront houses with four bedrooms.

Camping

Camping is allowed at several O'ahu parks. There are, however, no full-service private campgrounds of the Kampgrounds Of America (KOA) type that are popular on the US mainland. Although O'ahu's campgrounds are fairly well spread around the island, none of them are in Waikiki or the central Honolulu area.

All county and state campgrounds on O'ahu are closed on Wednesday and Thursday nights, ostensibly for maintenance, but also to prevent permanent encampments by the homeless.

Campgrounds are at their busiest on weekends, particularly three-day holiday weekends, and throughout the summer, as those are the times O'ahu residents are most apt to camp.

Although thousands of visitors use these campsites each year without incident, rip-offs are not unknown, especially at roadside campgrounds, so keep an eye on your belongings. Because of turf issues and an undercurrent of resentment by some residents against outsiders, camping along the Wai'anae Coast is not recommended for nonresidents.

COUNTY PARKS

Camping at county beach parks is free with a permit, which can be picked up at the **Department of Parks & Recreation** (☎ 523-4525; www.co.honolulu.hi.us/parks/permits.htm; 650 S King St, Honolulu; ☺ 7:45am-4pm Mon-Fri) in the Honolulu Municipal Building on the corner of King and Alapa'i Sts. Camping permits are also available from satellite city halls at the **Ala Moana Center** (☎ 973-2600; 1450 Ala Moana Blvd, Honolulu; ☺ 9am-5pm Mon-Fri, 8am-4pm Sat) and in **Kailua** (☎ 261-8575; Keolu Shopping Center, 1090 Keolu Dr; ☺ 8am-4pm Mon-Fri).

Camping is allowed from 8am Friday to 8am Wednesday, except at Bellows Field

---

BOOK ACCOMMODATION ON-LINE

For more accommodation reviews and recommendations by Lonely Planet authors, check out the on-line booking service at www.lonelyplanet.com. You'll find the true, insider lowdown on the best places to stay. Reviews are thorough and independent. Best of all, you can book on-line.

Beach Park, which is open only on weekends. For information on camping at the county's Ho'omaluhia Botanical Garden, see p184.

STATE PARKS

To camp at a state park, you'll need to purchase a permit, which costs $5 per night per site. Camping is limited to five nights per month in each park. Another camping permit for the same park will not be issued until 30 days have elapsed.

Permit applications can be made no more than 30 days before the first camping date. As permits are issued on a first-come, first-served basis, it's best to apply as soon as possible; if you have a change of plans, be sure to cancel so that other campers get a chance to use the space.

Applications may be made by phone, mail or in person to the **Division of State Parks** (☎ 587-0300; www.state.hi.us/dlnr/dsp; Room 131, 1151 Punchbowl St, PO Box 621, Honolulu, HI 96809; ☒ 8am-3:30pm Mon-Fri).

Hostels

There are two **Hostelling International** (HI; www.hiusa.org) hostels in O'ahu: Hostelling International Waikiki in the center of Waikiki and Hostelling International Honolulu near the University of Hawai'i. Both are clean and well managed by the same native Hawaiian family.

In addition to the HI hostels, there are a few private businesses providing hostel-like dorm accommodations around Waikiki. These private hostels are very fluid and unpredictable – a change in management can see a shabby operation become newly respectable, or a good place quickly become uninviting. They occupy older apartment buildings; some have a cluster of units, while others have taken over a whole complex. The private hostels cater to backpackers and draw a fairly international crowd, but don't expect pristine digs. Some are mere crash pads that won't compare favorably to the back seat of your car.

Hotels

Over 90% of O'ahu's 40,000 hotel rooms are in Waikiki. Unlike the other Hawaiian Islands where resort hotels are in multiple destinations, only a handful of O'ahu's hotels are outside the Waikiki and Honolulu area.

In many hotels, the rooms and amenities are the same, with only the views varying. Generally, the higher the floor, the higher the price, and an ocean view will commonly bump up the bill by 50% to 100%. If you're paying extra for a view, you might want to ask to see the room first, since Waikiki doesn't have any truth-in-labeling laws governing when a hotel can call a room 'ocean view.' Although some 'ocean views' are the real thing, others are mere glimpses of the water as seen through a series of high-rise buildings.

Always ask about deals. If you plan on renting a car, it may pay to ask about car and room promotions. A few of the larger chains, such as Ohana and Outrigger, often throw in a free rental car and some hotels actually have room/car packages for less than the 'standard' room rate!

Rental Accommodations

Most tourist accommodations in the Waikiki area are in hotels, not condominiums, so the sort of lease-free monthly condo rentals that are readily found in tourist locales elsewhere in Hawaii are not so easily found here.

Most condos are filled with long-term residents, but you can look in the classified sections of Honolulu's two daily newspapers to see what's available. Keep in mind that Honolulu is one of the most expensive housing markets in the USA, and the vacation-rental listings can be meager, especially in winter when demand is at its peak.

ACTIVITIES

As long as it doesn't involve snow, you can probably do it on O'ahu. The sheer number of outdoor activities offered is almost as endless as the horizon. If you're an old pro, you'll find great conditions for anything to do with the water. And if you want to try something for the first time, no problem – on O'ahu you don't have to be an aficionado to participate. Most water-sports stores and activity centers offer lessons for beginners. So go ahead, grab a sailboard or hop in a kayak and head off to an uninhabited island; swim in protected coves; bodysurf the breaking waves; or don a snorkel and watch the underwater world unfold beneath you. Novices can even learn to scuba dive, and those already certified will find a variety of solid dives from coral-encrusted shipwrecks to underwater caverns.

As for surfing, that quintessential Hawaiian pastime that reaches its greatest heights on O'ahu, visitors can hang ten and watch world-class athletes strut their stuff during competitions, or find their sea legs with the help of a buff instructor.

Don't want to get wet? Sunset catamaran cruises and winter whale-watching offer a fine perspective of the water world while keeping your sandals dry. On land, O'ahu's golf courses are in a class unto themselves, offering challenging greens in stunning settings. Tennis is also a draw and most resorts have their own courts, but public courts are plentiful as well.

O'ahu's hiking is exceptional, with conditions ranging from parched desertlike trails skirting the coast to muddy rain forest paths in the heart of the island. Opt for rigorous hikes that require an early start or hour-long loops that fit into a day of sightseeing. Mountain biking is available along some trails as well. Or if you prefer to travel in the saddle, you can choose from horseback trails along the beach and in the mountains.

That covers water and land but there's also plenty of action in the air over O'ahu. Tandem skydiving is hot on the North Shore and there are glider rides for those who prefer the view without the freefall.

For further details, see O'ahu Outdoors (p50) and the destination chapters.

BUSINESS HOURS

Unless there are variances of more than a half-hour in either direction, the following are standard opening hours for entries in this book:

Banks 8:30am to 4pm Monday to Friday; some banks open to 6pm Friday and 9am to 1pm Saturday.
Bars & Clubs To midnight daily; some clubs open to 2am Thursday to Saturday.
Businesses 8:30am to 4:30pm Monday to Friday; some post offices open 9am to noon Saturday.
Shops 9am to 5pm Monday to Saturday, some also open noon to 5pm Sunday; major shopping areas and malls keep extended hours.

CHILDREN

Families with children will find lots to do on O'ahu. In addition to beaches, swimming pools and a range of water sports, there are lots of other outdoor activities and cool sightseeing attractions for kids of all ages.

Successful travel with young children requires planning and effort. Try not to overdo things; even for adults, packing too much into the time available can cause problems. Include children in the trip planning, because if they've helped to work out where you will be going, they will be much more interested when they get there. When the going gets tough, bust out the chocolate macadamia nuts or stop for shave ice. Consult Lonely Planet's *Travel with Children,* which is packed full of valuable tips and interesting anecdotal stories. Also, see the Honolulu for Children (p95) and Waikiki for Children (p125) sections of this book.

Children are welcome at hotels throughout O'ahu, and those under 17 often stay for free when sharing a room with their parents and using existing bedding. Cots and roll-away beds are usually available (for an additional fee) at hotels and resorts, but it's wise to ask ahead.

Hawaiians love kids, and children are a normal part of the scenery here. Many restaurants have children's menus with significantly lower prices. Let's face it, cheese sandwiches and chicken wings take less preparation than seared 'ahi (yellowfin tuna). High chairs are usually available, but it pays to inquire ahead of time.

Most car-hire companies lease child-safety seats, but they don't always have them on hand; reserve in advance if you can.

If you're traveling with infants and come up short, **Baby's Away** (☎ 800-496-6386; www.babysaway.com) rents cribs, strollers, playpens, high chairs and more. You can find babysitters through your hotel concierge, or contact **Aloha Nannies** (☎ 394-5434; www.alohanannies.com). Larger resort hotels, like the Hilton Hawaiian Village in Waikiki, often have extensive children's programs and day camps, letting parents slip away for a day.

CLIMATE CHARTS

O'ahu's climate is typically warm and sunny. It's unusually pleasant for the tropics, as near-constant trade winds prevail throughout the year. Although there can be spells of stormy weather, particularly in winter (mid-December through March), much of the time the rain falls as short daytime showers accompanied by rainbows.

DIRECTORY

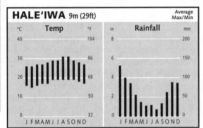

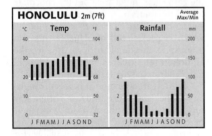

In Honolulu the average daily maximum temperature is 84°F and the minimum is 70°F. Average temperatures are only about 7°F different between summer and winter, and extremes are virtually unknown. The highest temperature on record in Honolulu is 94°F.

Rainfall varies greatly with elevation, even within short distances. Waikiki has an average annual rainfall of only 25in, whereas the Lyon Arboretum in the upper Manoa Valley, on the northern side of Honolulu, averages 158in. Midafternoon humidity averages 56%. Average water temperatures in Waikiki are 77°F in March, 82°F in August.

The **National Weather Service** provides recorded weather forecasts for all **O'ahu** (☎ 973-4381) and a **marine forecast** (☎ 973-4382) with detailed water conditions. You can also find current weather information on-line at www.prh.noaa.gov/hnl.

See also the When to Go (p13) section near the front of this book.

CUSTOMS

Each visitor is allowed to bring 1L of liquor and 200 cigarettes duty-free into the USA, but you must be at least 21 years old to possess the former and 18 years old to possess the latter. In addition, each traveler is permitted to bring up to $100 worth of gift merchandise into the US without incurring any duty.

Most fresh fruits and plants are restricted from entry into Hawaii to protect the islands' fragile ecosystem. Because Hawaii is a rabies-free state, the pet quarantine laws here are very strict and bringing Pooch on a short vacation is probably impractical. For more information, contact the **Hawaii Department of Agriculture** (☎ 483-7151; www.hawaiiag.org).

DANGERS & ANNOYANCES

As a traveler you're often fairly vulnerable and when you do lose things it can be a real hassle. The most important things to guard are your passport, tickets and money. It's best to always carry these next to your skin or in a sturdy pouch on your belt.

Although Hawaii is generally a safe place, tourism is its biggest industry by far and, as such, officials want to ensure that visitors remain safe and happy. Concern about visitors' negative experiences in Hawaii has led state officials to establish the **Visitor Aloha Society of Hawaii** (VASH; ☎ 926-8274; www.visitoralohasocietyofhawaii.org; Waikiki Shopping Plaza, Ste 403-3, 2250 Kalakaua Ave; ☺ office 8:30am-5pm Mon-Fri, with longer on-call hr), an organization providing aid to visitors who are victims of accidents or crimes while vacationing on the islands.

For information on issues relating to health, see the Health chapter (p253).

Earthquakes

There is a great deal of seismic activity in the Hawaiian Islands, although most of it takes place on the island of Hawai'i (the Big Island), well to the southeast of O'ahu. Should you be in an area where an earthquake occurs, there are several precautions you can take to minimize the risk of injury. If you're indoors, take cover under a desk or table and stay clear of windows and anything that's in danger of falling, such as mirrors and bookcases. If you're outdoors, get into an open area away from buildings, trees and power lines. If you're in a car driving, pull over to the side of the road away from overpasses and power lines and stay inside the car until the shaking stops.

Scams

The main scams directed toward visitors in O'ahu involve fake activity-operator booths and timeshare booths. If you see a sign that is touting car rentals for $5 a day, you've probably found one.

Theft & Violence

Petty theft is one crime that ranks high on O'ahu. Watch your belongings and never leave anything unattended on a beach. Most accommodations have a place where you can store your valuables.

It is important to be aware that Hawaii is notorious for rip-offs from parked rental cars. The people who break into these cars are good at what they do; they can pop a trunk or pull out a lock assembly in seconds to get to the loot inside. What's more, they do it not only when you've left your car in a secluded area to go for a long hike, but also in crowded parking lots where you'd expect safety in numbers.

It's certainly best not to leave anything of value in your car any time you walk away from it. If for some reason you feel you must, at least pack things well out of sight *before* pulling up to the place where you're going to leave the car. Many locals keep their cars unlocked at all times to avoid paying for broken windows.

Other than rip-offs, most hassles encountered by visitors are from drunks. While Waikiki Beach is well patrolled by the police, you should be tuned in to the vibes on other beaches at night and in places where young men hang out to drink.

For the most part, O'ahu is a safe place. Honolulu has a lower violent crime rate than most other US cities, but like any city, crime does occur and reasonable precautions are advisable. Be aware there are some pockets of resentment against tourists as well as off-islanders moving in. This is particularly true on the Wai'anae Coast.

If you're unlucky enough to have something stolen, immediately report it to the nearest police station. If your credit cards or

---

HEY, THAT LOOKS FAMILIAR

You may notice that Hawaii's state flag has a Union Jack in the top left corner. But, no, Hawaii was never part of the UK. Kamehameha the Great simply thought the Union Jack would add an element of regal splendor, so he took the liberty to add it to Hawaii's first flag.

---

traveler's checks have been taken, notify your bank or the relevant company without delay.

Tsunami

Tsunami, or tidal waves, are not common in Hawaii but when they do hit they can be severe.

Tsunami are generated by earthquakes or other natural disasters. The largest tsunami known to have hit Hawaii was in 1946, the result of an earthquake in the Aleutian Islands (Alaska). Waves reached a height of 55.8ft, entire villages were washed away and 159 people died. Since that time, Hawaii has installed a modern tsunami warning system, which is aired through yellow speakers mounted on telephone poles. They're tested on the first working day of each month at 11:45am for about one minute.

If you're in a low-lying coastal area when a tsunami approaches, the main rule is to immediately head for higher ground. Tsunami inundation maps in the front section of O'ahu phone books show susceptible areas and safety zones.

For ocean safety information, see p57.

DISABLED TRAVELERS

Overall, O'ahu is an accommodating destination for travelers with disabilities, and Waikiki is considered one of the more accessible destinations in the USA. Many of the larger hotels have elevators, TTY-capable phones, wheelchair-accessible rooms and other features to smooth the way – and as more hotels renovate their facilities, accessibility just keeps improving.

General access is getting much better, too. The Waikiki beachfront, for instance, has been extensively renovated with curb cuts and lots of low-profile ramps throughout.

The **Department of Parks and Recreation** (☎ 692-5750; www.co.honolulu.hi.us/parks/programs /beach/index.htm) provides all-terrain wheelchairs that allow disabled visitors to wheel onto the sand at many O'ahu beaches, including Ala Moana Beach Park, Hanauma Bay Nature Preserve, Sans Souci Beach, Kailua Beach Park, Kualoa Regional Park and Poka'i Bay Beach Park. These wheelchairs are free of charge, but call ahead to make arrangements.

The state **Disability & Communication Access Board** (☎ 586-8121; www.hawaii.gov/health/dcab) provides travel tips on-line for physically

DIRECTORY

disabled people. Topics include transportation and travel, arrival at the airport, medical equipment and supplies, and support services. If you have a disability parking placard from home, bring it with you, because Hawaii recognizes valid placards issued by other states and countries; the card must be hung from the car's rearview mirror whenever the vehicle is parked in a designated handicapped-parking space.

In terms of getting around on O'ahu, all of the island's modern fleet of public buses are accessible to people with disabilities and will 'kneel' if you are unable to use steps or need to have the bus doorway lowered. Just let the driver know you need to use the lift or ramp.

Access Aloha Travel (☎ 545-1143, 800-480-1143; www.accessalohatravel.com), an established local business, is a great resource for wheelchair-accessible accommodations, sightseeing tours and equipment rental. The company also has wheelchair-accessible vans for hire.

Hawaiian Rent All (☎ 949-3961; 1946 S Beretania St, Honolulu) rents wheelchairs and walkers. **HandiCabs of the Pacific** (☎ 524-3866; www.handicabs.com) offers a wheelchair-accessible taxi and tour service.

Those with a physical disability may want to get in touch with their national support organization before leaving home. In the USA, the **Society for Accessible Travel and Hospitality** (SATH; ☎ 212-447-7284; www.sath.org; Suite 610, 347 Fifth Ave, New York, NY 10016) publishes a quarterly magazine and has various information sheets on travel for the disabled.

Seeing-eye and guide dogs are not subject to the same quarantine requirements as other pets, provided they meet certain requirements; contact the **Animal Quarantine Station** (☎ 483-7171) for details well in advance of your planned arrival in Hawaii.

For a list of services available to disabled passengers by airlines, go to www.everybody.co.uk/airindex.htm.

DISCOUNT CARDS

A multitude of glossy tourist magazines are distributed freely wherever tourists can be found on O'ahu. Replete with discount coupons for activities and restaurants, they're well worth perusing, perhaps while you're waiting for your baggage by the airport carousel. The phone book also has a surprising number of coupons for activities of interest to visitors. Although Hawaii doesn't offer a lot of student discounts, if you have a student card, bring it along anyway, as it may occasionally win you a discount at museums and other sights.

If you're a card-carrying member of the **American Automobile Association** (AAA; www.aaa-hawaii.com), you'll find handsome discounts on car rentals, hotels and many sightseeing attractions. And these discounts can be substantial; all of Waikiki's Outrigger hotels, for instance, take 20% off regular rates for AAA members.

Since Hawaii is a popular destination for retirees, lots of senior discounts are available and the applicable age has been creeping lower as well. The nonprofit American Association of Retired Persons (AARP) is a good source for travel bargains, and its members will find generous car rental and accommodations discounts on O'ahu. For information on joining this advocacy group for Americans 50 years of age and older, contact **AARP** (☎ 888-687-2277; www.aarp.org; Membership Center, 3200 E Carson St, Lakewood, CA 90712).

The mainland Go Visitor Cards company now has a **Go Oahu Card** (www.gooahucard.com) that offers admission to museums and sightseeing tours, but it's pricey at $159 for a three-day card or $269 for a seven-day card, and most people will do better off on their own.

EMBASSIES & CONSULATES
US Embassies & Consulates

US embassies abroad include the following:

Australia (☎ 61-2-6214-5600; 21 Moonah Pl, Yarralumla, Canberra, ACT 2600)

Canada (☎ 613-238-5335; 490 Sussex Dr, Ottawa, Ontario K1N 1G8)

France (☎ 33-1-43-12-22-22; 2 Ave Gabriel, 75008 Paris)

Germany (☎ 030-2385-174; Neustädtische Kirchstrasse 4-5, 10117 Berlin)

Ireland (☎ 353-1-668-8777; 42 Elgin Rd, Ballsbridge, Dublin 4)

Italy (☎ 39-06-46741; Via Veneto 119/A, 00187 Rome)

Japan (☎ 81-3-3224-5000; 10-5, Akasaka 1-chome, Minato-ku, Tokyo)

Netherlands (☎ 31-70-310-2209; Lange Voorhout 102, 2514 EJ The Hague)

New Zealand (☎ 64-4-462-6000; 29 Fitzherbert Tce, PO Box 1190, Thorndon, Wellington)

UK (☎ 44-20-7499-9000; 24/31 Grosvenor Sq, London W1A 1AE)

Embassies & Consulates in O'ahu

Consulates located in Honolulu include the following:

Australia (☎ 524-5050; 1000 Bishop St)
Germany (☎ 946-3819; 252 Paoa Pl)
Italy (☎ 531-2277; Suite 201, 735 Bishop St)
Japan (☎ 543-3111; 1742 Nu'uanu Ave)
Netherlands (☎ 531-6897; Suite 702, 745 Fort St Mall)
New Zealand (☎ 547-5117; Suite 414, 900 Richards St)
Philippines (☎ 595-6316; 2433 Pali Hwy)

FESTIVALS & EVENTS

With its diverse cultural heritage and good year-round weather, O'ahu has a variety of holidays, festivals and sporting events. For events that are in a specific part of the island, see the destination chapters. As event schedules and venues can change from year to year, it's best to check activity schedules in local papers or on-line at the **Hawaii Visitors and Convention Bureau** (http://calendar.goha waii.com).

JANUARY

New Year's Eve Firecrackers are set off through the night to welcome the first day of the year and everyone says *Hau'oli Makahiki Hou* (Happy New Year). The best place to be is on the beach in Waikiki at midnight, when a grand fireworks display lights up the night sky.

MARCH

Prince Kuhio Day This state holiday on March 26 honors Prince Jonah Kuhio Kalaniana'ole, Hawaii's first delegate to the US Congress, with festivities around O'ahu.

MAY

May Day In Hawaii, May Day is Lei Day (May 1) and everybody on O'ahu dons a lei. Lei-making competitions take place at various locations around the island. One of the main sites is Waikiki's Kapi'olani Park, where a lei queen is crowned.

JUNE

King Kamehameha Day A state holiday, King Kamehameha Day is celebrated on or near June 11. The statue of Kamehameha opposite 'Iolani Palace is ceremoniously draped with lei and there's a parade from downtown Honolulu to Kapi'olani Beach Park, where there are hula shows, music and crafts.

Gay Pride Weekend (www.thecenterhawaii.org) Experience the diversity of aloha during this event in late June, with the crowning of queens, a beach party at Ala Moana Beach Park, a parade from Magic Island to Kapi'olani Beach Park, drag revues and dancing till your head spins.

JULY

Independence Day July 4 is a public holiday, celebrated in O'ahu with fireworks at Ala Moana Beach Park and a parade to Kapi'olani Park.

AUGUST

Obon Observed in July and August at locations around the island, this event is marked by Japanese *bon odori* (dances) to honor deceased ancestors.

SEPTEMBER

Aloha Festivals Week (www.alohafestivals.com) A celebration of all things Hawaiian, held in mid-September, with cultural events, contests, street fairs, canoe races, Hawaiian music at various venues, and huge block parties in both Waikiki and downtown Honolulu.

OCTOBER

Hawaii International Film Festival (www.hiff.org) Featuring over 100 films from Pacific Rim and Asian nations, movies are shown throughout O'ahu for around 10 days in late October, with the schedule listed in local newspapers.

NOVEMBER

Triple Crown of Surfing (www.triplecrownofsurfing .com) Consisting of three professional competitions that draw the world's top surfers to O'ahu's North Shore, the events begin in November and run through December, with the exact dates and locations depending on when and where the surf's up. The event attracts throngs of both locals and visitors – bring your binoculars!

DECEMBER

Bodhi Day The Buddhist Day of Enlightenment is celebrated on December 8 with ceremonies at Buddhist temples.

Honolulu Marathon (www.honolulumarathon.org) In terms of the number of runners, this is the third-largest marathon in the USA. It's run on the second Sunday of the month along a 26-mile course from the Aloha Tower in Honolulu to Kapi'olani Park in Waikiki.

Christmas Festivals and craft fairs are held around O'ahu throughout the month. Kids will love the lighting of the giant Christmas tree at Honolulu's city hall, complete with Santa Claus in board shorts.

OFFICIAL O'AHU

O'ahu's nickname is 'The Gathering Place.' The island's official color is yellow-orange, which is the same color as the delicate blossoms of the native *'ilima,* O'ahu's official flower. *'Ilima,* a ground cover, grows wild on the island.

DIRECTORY

FOOD

Reviews in the Eating section for each destination are broken down into three price categories: budget (for meals costing $10 or less), midrange (where most main dishes cost $10 to $20) and top end (where most dinner mains cost more than $20). These price estimates do not include taxes, tips or beverages.

For information about Hawaiian specialties and delicacies, see the Food & Drink chapter (p63).

GAY & LESBIAN TRAVELERS

Hawaii is a popular vacation spot for gays and lesbians. The state has strong minority protections and a constitutional guarantee of privacy that extends to sexual behavior between consenting adults.

Still, gay Hawaii is not an in-your-face kind of place; public hand-holding and other outward signs of affection between gays are not commonplace. One exception is during Gay Pride Weekend, at the end of June, which includes a festival and splashy beach party at Ala Moana Beach Park and a parade from Magic Island to Kapi'olani Beach Park in Waikiki.

In terms of nightlife, the main gay club scene on O'ahu is unquestionably centered in Waikiki (p149).

The following sources can help gay and lesbian visitors to become oriented to the island. The volunteer-run **Gay & Lesbian Community Center** (☎ 951-7000; www.thecenterhawaii.org; PO Box 22718, Honolulu, HI 96823) is a good source of local information. The center has support groups, movie nights, a community newspaper and a library. The monthly **Odyssey** (www.odysseyhawaii.com) magazine, free at gay-friendly businesses throughout Hawaii, covers O'ahu's gay scene. The best website for general information on gay issues is **Gay Hawaii.com** (www.gayhawaii.com); it also has links to a variety of gay and lesbian sites that cover topics from travel and entertainment to politics.

Pacific Ocean Holidays (☎ 923-2400, 800-735-6599; www.gayhawaiivacations.com; PO Box 88245, Honolulu, HI 96830) arranges package vacations for gays and lesbians.

HOLIDAYS

It's good to make advance reservations around the Christmas and New Year's holidays, as these are the busiest times of the year for hotels and car-rental agencies. When a public holiday falls on the weekend, it is often celebrated on the nearest Friday or Monday instead. These weekends can also be busy, as people from other Hawaiian Islands often take advantage of the break to visit O'ahu. Also see Festivals & Events (p235).

New Year's Day January 1
Martin Luther King Jr Day Third Monday in January
Presidents' Day Third Monday in February
Good Friday March/April
Prince Kuhio Day March 26
Memorial Day Last Monday in May
King Kamehameha Day June 11
Independence Day July 4
Admission Day Third Friday in August
Labor Day First Monday in September
Columbus Day Second Monday in October
Election Day Second Tuesday in November
Veterans Day November 11
Thanksgiving Fourth Thursday in November
Christmas Day December 25

INSURANCE

It's best to purchase travel insurance as early as possible. If you buy it the week before you fly, you might find, for instance, that you're not covered for delays to your flight caused by a strike that may have been in force before you took out the insurance. Worldwide coverage to travelers from over 44 countries is available on-line at www.lonelyplanet.com/travel_services.

For information on car and health insurance, see p251 and p253 respectively.

INTERNET ACCESS

If you bring a laptop from outside the USA, you'll need a universal AC and plug adapter. Also, your PC card modem may not work once you leave your home country – but you won't know until you try. The safest option? Buy a reputable 'global' modem before leaving home. Ensure that you have at least a US RJ-11 telephone adapter that works with your modem. For more technical help, visit www.teleadapt.com.

Major Internet service providers, such as **America Online** (AOL; www.aol.com) and **Microsoft Network** (MSN; www.msn.com), have local dial-in nodes on O'ahu. If you usually access your e-mail through your office or school, you will find it easier to open a free account with a service such as **Yahoo!** (www.yahoo.com)

or **Hotmail** (www.hotmail.com). You can then access your mail on any Internet-connected machine.

On O'ahu cybercafés offer inexpensive on-line Internet access and are particularly abundant in Waikiki and around the University of Hawai'i; for locations, see the Information section of the destination sections in this book. When accommodations provide Internet access for those traveling without laptops, this is noted in this book with 💻.

Even if your hotel room does not have a modem port on its phone, you can plug into the main line as long as you remember to set your machine to dial for an outside line first. Some midrange and top-end hotels are installing wi-fi access for guests, so for the latest inquire when booking. In addition there are plans underway to provide free wi-fi access throughout Waikiki – the beach area along Kalakaua Ave, from Seaside to Kapahulu Ave, is already up and running.

LEGAL MATTERS

Anyone arrested in Hawaii has the right to have the representation of a lawyer, from the time of their arrest to their trial, and if a person cannot afford a lawyer, the state will provide one for free. If you want to hire a lawyer, the **Hawaii State Bar Association** (☎ 537-9140) can make referrals; foreign visitors may want to call their consulate for advice.

It's illegal to have open containers of alcohol in motor vehicles, and drinking in public parks or on the beaches is also forbidden. Drunk driving is a serious offence and you can incur stiff fines, jail time and other penalties. In Hawaii, anyone caught driving with an alcohol blood level of 0.08% or greater is guilty of driving 'under the influence' and will have their driver's license taken away on the spot.

As in most places, the possession of marijuana and nonprescription narcotics is illegal

in Hawaii. Be aware that US Customs has a zero-tolerance policy for drugs; federal authorities have been known to seize boats after finding even minute quantities of marijuana on board. Tobacco smoking is prohibited in enclosed public places, including restaurants and hotel lobbies.

For consumer issues, Hawaii's **Department of Commerce & Consumer Affairs** (☎ 587-1234) provides information on your rights regarding refunds and exchanges, time-share contracts, car rentals and similar topics.

MAPS

The ubiquitous free tourist magazines contain simple island maps, but if you're going to be renting a car and doing any exploring at all it's worth picking up a good road map, especially for navigating around Honolulu.

The American Automobile Association (AAA) puts out a reliable road map of Honolulu and O'ahu that you can pick up from your local affiliate before leaving home. If you're not an AAA member, you can buy a similar road map published by Rand McNally in convenience stores throughout O'ahu for a few dollars.

The 200-plus-page *Bryan's Sectional Maps O'ahu* atlas, which maps out and indexes every street on the island, is the most comprehensive and reliable mapping source of the island, though it's more detailed than most visitors will need. It can be purchased at bookstores throughout O'ahu.

The United States Geological Survey (USGS) publishes topographical maps of O'ahu, both as full-island and detailed sectional maps. Despite the precise geographic detail, the practical use of these maps is limited for casual visitors due to their unwieldy size and infrequent updates. Maps can be ordered from the **USGS** (☎ 888-275-8747; www .usgs.gov; Map & Book Sales, Denver Federal Center, Denver, CO 80225). In Honolulu, USGS maps, nautical charts and other specialty maps can be purchased at the **Pacific Map Center** (☎ 545-3600; Ste 206A, 560 N Nimitz Hwy, Honolulu).

Divers and snorkelers will want to take a look at **Franko's Maps** (www.frankosmaps .com), which produces a laminated, waterproof map of O'ahu showing snorkeling and diving spots. The map can be readily purchased at dive stores and water-sports rental stores.

THE LEGAL AGE FOR...	
Drinking	21
Driving	16
Sex	16
Voting	18

MONEY

The US dollar is the only currency that is used in Hawaii. The dollar (commonly called 'a buck') is divided into 100 cents. Coins come in denominations of one cent (penny), five cents (nickel), 10 cents (dime), 25 cents (quarter) and the rare 50-cent piece (half dollar). Notes (also called 'bills') come in one-, five-, 10-, 20-, 50- and 100-dollar denominations. There is also a one-dollar coin that the government has tried unsuccessfully to bring into mass circulation and a two-dollar note that is out of favor but still occasionally seen.

There are nearly 150 banks located throughout O'ahu, so it is never a problem finding one in the major towns. The Bank of Hawaii, Hawaii's largest bank, has a branch at the airport and another one in central Waikiki. Elsewhere around O'ahu, banks can easily be found in central areas and in shopping centers.

See the Quick Reference on the inside front cover for exchange rates, and Getting Started (p13) for information on costs.

ATMs

Automated teller machines (ATMs) are a convenient way of obtaining cash from a bank account within the USA or abroad. Plus, using an ATM card eliminates the necessity of carrying around a bundle of traveler's checks. But watch out for ATM surcharges; most banks charge around $1.50 per withdrawal, so it's best to withdraw in larger amounts.

Major banks, such as the **Bank of Hawaii** (www.boh.com) and **First Hawaiian Bank** (www.fhb .com), have extensive ATM networks throughout O'ahu that will give cash advances on major credit cards (MasterCard, Visa, American Express, Discover and JCB) and allow cash withdrawals with affiliated ATM cards. Most ATMs in Hawaii accept bank cards from both the Plus and Cirrus systems, the two largest ATM networks in the USA.

In addition to traditional bank locations, you can also find ATMs at most grocery stores, in mall-style shopping centers and in many convenience stores.

Cash

If you're carrying foreign currency, it can be exchanged for US dollars at larger banks, such as the ubiquitous Bank of Hawaii, or at the exchange booths at Honolulu International Airport.

Credit Cards

Major credit cards are widely accepted throughout Hawaii, including at car rental agencies and most hotels, restaurants, gas stations, stores and larger grocery stores. Most recreational and tourist activities can also be paid for by credit card.

The most commonly accepted cards in Hawaii are Visa, MasterCard and American Express, although JCB, Discover and Diners Club cards are also accepted by a fair number of businesses. Note, however, that some B&B establishments and condominiums, particularly those handled through rental agencies, do not accept credit cards, so it is best to inquire in advance.

If you lose your credit cards or they are stolen, you should contact the company immediately. Toll free reporting numbers include **American Express** (☎ 800-992-3404), **MasterCard** (☎ 800-826-2181) and **Visa** (☎ 800-336-8472).

Taxes

The price you see is not always the price you pay. Hawaii has a 4.17% state sales tax that is tacked onto virtually everything, including all meals, groceries, car rentals and accommodations. An additional 7.24% room tax brings the total tax added to accommodation bills to 11.41%. Another tax targeted at visitors is a $3-a-day 'road use' tax imposed upon all car rentals.

Tipping

Tipping practices in Hawaii are the same as in the rest of the USA. In restaurants, good waiters are tipped at least 15%, while dissatisfied customers make their ire known by leaving 10%. There has to be real cause for not tipping at all. Taxi drivers and hairstylists are typically tipped about 10% and hotel bellhops $1 to $2 per bag, depending on the weight.

Traveler's Checks

The main benefit of traveler's checks is that they provide protection from theft and loss. Large companies, such as American Express and Thomas Cook, generally offer efficient replacement policies. Keeping a record of the check numbers and those you have used is vital when it comes to replacing lost checks, so you should keep this information separate from the checks themselves.

Foreign visitors who carry traveler's checks will find it much easier if the checks are in US dollars. Restaurants, hotels and most stores accept US dollar traveler's checks as if they're cash, so if that's what you're carrying, odds are you'll never have to use a bank or pay an exchange fee.

For refunds on lost or stolen traveler's checks, call **American Express** (☎ 800-992-3404) or **Thomas Cook** (☎ 800-287-7362).

PHOTOGRAPHY

O'ahu is a great place for photography. There's an abundance of interesting subjects, from the architecture in downtown Honolulu to landscapes, hula dancers and beach scenes.

Because of the sunny climate, a few precautions should be taken. Most important, don't leave your camera in direct sun any longer than necessary. A locked car can heat up like an oven in just a few minutes.

Sand and water are intense reflectors, and in bright light they'll often leave foreground subjects shadowy. You can try compensating by adjusting your f-stop (aperture) or attaching a polarizing filter, or both, but the most effective technique is to take photos in the gentler light of early morning and late afternoon.

For a very complete short course on photographic ins and outs, dos and don'ts, consult Lonely Planet's *Travel Photography*.

Both print and slide film are readily available on O'ahu. Disposable underwater cameras costing about $10 are sold everywhere and deliver surprisingly good snaps. If you're going to be in Hawaii for any length of time, consider having your film developed here, because the high temperature and humidity of the tropics greatly accelerate the deterioration of exposed film. The sooner it's developed, the better the results.

Longs Drugs (Upper Level, Ala Moana Center) is one of the cheapest places for both purchasing film and having it developed. There are also numerous places in Waikiki that do one-hour photo processing.

With the implementation of high-powered X-ray at many airports, don't pack film into checked luggage or carry-on bags. Instead carry your film in a zip-lock plastic bag to

show separately to airport security officials (known as a hand check). Remember to finish off the roll in your camera and take it out, too, or those photos may end up foggy. And last but not least, don't even think about taking snaps of military installations.

POST

By world standards, the US Postal Service is both reliable and inexpensive. There are 35 post offices on O'ahu. The main Honolulu **post office** (⏰ 7:30am-8:30pm Mon-Fri, 8am-4:30pm Sat) is not in central Honolulu, but next to the airport at 3600 Aolele St, opposite the inter-island terminal. You can get detailed 24-hour postal information, including the business hours for every post office in Hawaii, by dialing toll-free ☎ 800-275-8777.

Postal Rates

Postage rates for 1st-class mail within the USA are 39¢ for letters up to 1oz (24¢ for each additional ounce) and 24¢ for postcards. First-class mail between Hawaii and the mainland is sent by air and usually takes three to four days.

International airmail rates for letters up to 1oz are 63¢ to Canada or Mexico and 84¢ to other countries. Postcards cost 55¢ to Canada or Mexico and 75¢ to other countries.

Receiving Mail

All general delivery mail sent to you in Honolulu must be picked up at Honolulu's main post office, next to the airport. Mail sent general delivery to the Waikiki post office or other Honolulu branches will go to the main post office or be returned to sender.

To receive mail in Honolulu, have it addressed to you as follows:

Your name
c/o General Delivery, Main Post Office
3600 Aolele St, Honolulu, HI 96820-3600

It's also possible to have general delivery mail sent to you in Kailua. To do so, have it addressed to you as follows:

Your name
c/o General Delivery, Kailua Post Office
335 Hahani St, Kailua, HI 96734-9998

DIRECTORY

For general delivery service, domestic mail will usually be held for 10 days, international mail for 30 days. You'll need to present photo identification to collect your mail.

SHOPPING

Honolulu is a large, cosmopolitan city with scores of sophisticated stores selling designer clothing, jewelry and the like. Most of the more fashionable shops are either in Waikiki or have branches there.

There are many fine craftspeople in O'ahu and choice handicrafts are easily found around the island. Some of the most prized items are native-wood bowls, often made of beautifully grained Hawaiian hardwoods, such as koa and milo. Hawaiian bowls are not decorated or ornate, but are shaped to bring out the natural beauty of the wood. The thinner and lighter the bowl, the finer the artistry and greater the value. Many of O'ahu's talented potters are influenced by Japanese styles and aesthetics; good raku work, in particular, abounds in island galleries and gift shops.

Hawaii's island-style clothing is colorful and light, often with prints of tropical flowers. The aloha shirt is a Hawaii creation, the product of Ellery Chun, a Honolulu tailor who created the original in 1931. It was influenced by two things: the baggy checkered shirts worn by plantation workers and the then-popular children's shirts made from colorful kimonos. Aloha shirts have been the island dress for men ever since. Today the classiest aloha shirts are those made of lightweight cotton with subdued colors (like those of reverse fabric prints).

For local-made jewelry, the premium product in Hawaii is the delicate Ni'ihau shell lei. These necklaces, made from tiny seashells that wash up on the island of Ni'ihau, are one of the most prized Hawaiiana souvenirs. Ni'ihauans painstakingly string the tiny shells into finely handcrafted spiral strands with intricate patterns. Ni'ihau shell lei don't come cheap – the best pieces cost thousands of dollars and are sold at top-end jewelry stores around Honolulu. Even if you're not buying, it's fun to go and admire them.

The standard edible souvenir is macadamia nuts, either plain or covered in chocolate. But there are a large number of food products made in Hawaii, such as macadamia nut butters, liliko'i (passion fruit) preserves and mango chutney, that all make convenient, compact gift items.

Another popular food item is Hawaiian-grown coffee. O'ahu has recently begun harvesting its own crop – Waialua coffee. It's yet to gain the gourmet cachet of Kona coffee, but the latest harvest is well worth sampling. Another O'ahu-grown souvenir, pineapples, are not a great choice in the gift department – not only are they heavy and bulky, but they're likely to be just as cheap back home.

SOLO TRAVELERS

Travel, including solo travel, is generally safe and easy on O'ahu. In tourist meccas like Waikiki, you're unlikely to encounter problems and it's easy to meet and pair up with fellow travelers. However, solo travelers, especially women, need to exercise vigilance when traveling in secluded areas after dark. Everyone should avoid hiking, cycling long distances or camping alone, especially in unfamiliar places. For more safety advice, see Dangers & Annoyances (p232).

TELEPHONE & FAX

Always dial '1' before toll-free (800, 888 etc) and domestic long-distance numbers. Some toll-free numbers may only work within the state or from the US mainland, while others may work from Canada, too. But you'll only know if it works by making the call.

All phone numbers within the USA consist of a three-digit area code followed by a seven-digit number. All of the Hawaiian Islands share the same area code (808). The

---

TELEPHONE AREA CODE

The telephone area code for all of Hawaii is 808. The area code is not used when making calls on the same island, but it must be added to all Hawaiian phone numbers when calling from outside the state or from one Hawaiian island to another.

Because the area code is not dialed when making a local call, the phone numbers in this book do not include the area code. Just remember if you're dialing from home before arriving in O'ahu to add 808 to the local number.

area code is not used when making calls from one O'ahu number to another.

Pay phones can readily be found in public places, such as shopping centers and beach parks. Local calls cost 50¢ at pay phones. Any call made from one point on O'ahu to any other point on O'ahu is a local call.

Calls from O'ahu to the other Hawaiian Islands are long distance. To dial direct from one Hawaiian island to another from a pay phone, or to call the US mainland, costs 25¢ per minute with a four-minute minimum.

Most hotels add a service charge of $1 for each local call made from a room phone and most also have hefty surcharges for long-distance calls. Public phones, which can be found in most hotel lobbies, are cheaper. You can pump in coins, use a phonecard or make collect calls from pay phones. You can make toll-free calls from pay phones without inserting any money.

To access directory assistance for O'ahu phone numbers dial ☎ 1-411, and for phone numbers elsewhere in Hawaii dial ☎ 1-808-555-1212.

Fax
Faxes can be sent and received through the front desks of most hotels. There are also business centers that offer reasonably priced fax services, such as Kinko's, which has several branches in Honolulu, all listed in the O'ahu phone book.

International Calls
To make an international call direct from Hawaii, dial ☎ 011 + country code + area code + number. (An exception is to Canada, where you dial ☎ 1 + area code + number.) For international operator assistance, dial ☎ 0. The operator can provide specific rate information and tell you which time periods are the cheapest for calling.

If you're calling Hawaii from abroad, the international country code for the USA is '1,' and all calls to Hawaii are then followed by the area code 808 and the seven-digit local number.

Cell Phones
The USA uses a variety of cell-phone systems, 99% of which are incompatible with the GSM 900/1800 standard used throughout Europe and Asia. Check with your cellular

service provider before departure about using your phone in Hawaii. Verizon has the most extensive cellular network on the islands, but AT&T, Cingular and Sprint also have decent coverage. Cellular coverage is quite good on most of O'ahu, but because of the high central mountains it can be spotty in remote areas and on hiking trails.

Phonecards
Numerous and ever-changing brands of prepaid phone cards are available from convenience stores, supermarkets and pharmacies. Compare the fine print, as rates vary widely. Otherwise, pick up a phonecard at the post office, where the rates are reasonable and straightforward and there's no expiration date.

TIME
When it's noon in Honolulu, the time in other parts of the world is as follows: 1pm in Anchorage, Alaska; 2pm in Los Angeles, California; 5pm in New York, New York; 10pm in London, England; 11pm in Paris, France; 7am the next day in Tokyo, Japan; 8am the next day in Sydney and Melbourne, Australia; and 10am the next day in Auckland, New Zealand. For more about other time zones and their relation to Hawaii, see the World Time Zones map (pp272-3).

Hawaii does not observe daylight saving time. Therefore, the time difference is one hour greater during those months when other countries observe daylight saving.

And then there's 'Hawaiian Time,' which is either a slow-down-the-clock pace or a euphemism for being late.

Hawaii has about 11 hours of daylight in midwinter and almost 13½ hours in midsummer. In midwinter, the sun rises at about 7am and sets at about 6pm. In midsummer, it rises before 6am and sets after 7pm.

TOILETS
Relatively speaking, it's not hard to go in O'ahu. Public toilets are free and easy to find – at least in comparison to the US mainland. Virtually every beach park has toilet facilities (also referred to as rest rooms), as do larger shopping centers and most hotel lobbies. Fast-food restaurants are another possibility, though they're generally intended for customers only.

TOURIST INFORMATION

By far the best place to pick up information is at Honolulu International Airport when you arrive. In the arrival lounge you'll find staffed information desks, and while you're waiting for your bags to appear on the carousel you can leaf through rack after rack of tourist brochures and magazines, covering everything from accommodations to activities.

For information before you go, the Hawaii Visitors and Convention Bureau (HVCB) will mail you a glossy magazine containing general Hawaii-wide tourist information.

Local Tourist Offices

Hawaii Visitors & Convention Bureau (☎ 923-1811, 800-464-2924; www.gohawaii.com; Ste 801, Waikiki Business Plaza, 2270 Kalakaua Ave, Waikiki, HI 96815)
O'ahu Visitors Bureau (☎ 524-0722, 877-525-6248; www.visit-oahu.com; Ste 1520, 733 Bishop St, Honolulu, HI 96813)

Tourist Offices Abroad

HVCB representatives abroad include the following:
Australia (☎ 02-9286-8951; www.hawaiitourism.com.au; PO Box Q1348, Sydney, NSW 1230)
Germany (☎ 89-23-66-21-97; Hawaii Tourism Europe, Sonnestr 9, D-80331 Munich)
UK (☎ 207-202-6384; 36 Southwark Bridge Rd, London SE1 9EU)

TOURS

Because Honolulu has such a good public bus system, extensive self-touring, even without a rental car, is an option. However, waiting for buses and walking between the bus stops and the sights does take time, so you can undoubtedly pack much more into a day by joining an organized tour.

Conventional sightseeing tours by van or bus are offered by **Polynesian Adventure Tours** (☎ 833-3000; www.polyad.com) and **Roberts Hawaii** (☎ 539-9400, 800-831-5541; www.robertshawaii.com).

These companies offer several different tours. Polynesian Adventure Tours, for example, has a half-day tour that includes the main downtown Honolulu sights, Punchbowl Crater and the USS *Arizona* Memorial at Pearl Harbor. It also has another half-day tour of southeast O'ahu that takes in Diamond Head, Hanauma Bay, Sandy Beach, Nu'uanu Pali Lookout, Queen

Emma Summer Palace and Tantalus. Each of these tours costs $25 for adults and $18 for children.

The mainstay for the tour companies, however, are full-day (roughly 8am to 5:30pm) Circle Island tours that average $55 for adults and $30 for children. A typical tour starts out with a visit to Diamond Head Crater and a drive past the southeast O'ahu sights; goes up the Windward Coast, taking in the Byodo-In temple in Kane'ohe; circles back along the North Shore, stopping at Sunset Beach and Waimea Bay; and then drives past the pineapple fields of central O'ahu on the return to Waikiki.

If you want to visit another Hawaiian island but only have a day or two to spare, it might be worth looking into 'overnighters,' which are handy mini-package tours to the Neighbor Islands that include roundtrip airfare, car rental and hotel accommodations. Rates depend on the accommodations you select, with a one-night package typically starting at $265 per person, based on double occupancy. You can add additional days for a reasonable fee. The largest tour company specializing in overnighters is Roberts Hawaii.

If you're 55 or older, **Elderhostel** (www.elderhostel.com) offers organized tours that delve into the islands' unique history, culture and environment.

See p247 for more information.

VISAS

The conditions for entering Hawaii are the same as those for entering any other state in the USA.

Since the establishment of the Department of Homeland Security following the events of September 11, 2001, immigration now falls under the purview of the **Bureau of Citizenship & Immigration Service** (BCIS; www.bcis.gov).

Getting into the US can be a bureaucratic nightmare, depending on your country of origin. To make matters worse, the rules are rapidly changing. For up-to-date information about visas and immigration, check with the **US State Department** (http://unitedstatesvisas.gov/visiting.html).

Most foreign visitors to the USA need a visa. However, there is a Visa Waiver Program through which citizens of certain countries may enter the USA for stays of

90 days or less without first obtaining a US visa. This list is subject to continual re-examination and bureaucratic rejigging. Currently these countries include: Andorra, Australia, Austria, Belgium, Brunei, Denmark, Finland, France, Germany, Iceland, Ireland, Italy, Japan, Liechtenstein, Luxembourg, Monaco, the Netherlands, New Zealand, Norway, Portugal, San Marino, Singapore, Slovenia, Spain, Sweden, Switzerland and the UK. Under this program you must have a return ticket (or onward ticket to any foreign destination) that is nonrefundable in the USA. Note that you will not be allowed to extend your stay beyond 90 days.

Because the **Department of Homeland Security** (DHS; www.dhs.gov) is continually modifying its requirements, even those with visa waivers may be subject to enrolment in the US-Visit program. This program may require that visa recipients have a machine-readable passport and/or a digital scan of their fingerprints. Contact the DHS for current requirements.

Regardless, your passport should be valid for at least six months longer than your intended stay, and you'll need to submit a recent photo (50.8mm x 50.8mm) with the visa application. Documents of financial stability and/or guarantees from a US resident are sometimes required, particularly for those from developing countries. Visa applicants may be required to 'demonstrate binding obligations' that will ensure their return back home. Because of this requirement, those who are planning to travel through other countries before arriving in the USA are generally better off applying for their US visa while they are still in their home country rather than while they are on the road.

The validity period for a US visitor visa depends on your home country. The actual length of time you'll be allowed to stay in the USA is determined by the BCIS at the port of entry. If you want to stay in the USA longer than the date stamped on your passport, go to the Honolulu office of the **Citizenship & Immigration Service** (☎ 532-3721; 595 Ala Moana Blvd, Honolulu) before the stamped date to apply for an extension.

WOMEN TRAVELERS

Women travelers are no more likely to encounter problems in O'ahu than elsewhere in the USA. The usual precautions apply when it comes to potentially dangerous situations, such as hitchhiking and walking alone in remote areas at night.

If you're camping, opt for secure, well-used camping areas over isolated locales. Many county parks and their campgrounds are notorious for late-night beer binges and some are also known for long-term squatting, particularly on the Wai'anae Coast, all of which may be unpleasant for solo travelers.

If you are the victim of an assault, call the **police** (☎ 911). Women who have been abused or sexually assaulted can also call the **Sex Abuse Treatment Center's 24-hour hotline** (☎ 524-7273).

WORK

US citizens can pursue employment in Hawaii as they would in any other state. Foreign visitors who are in the USA on tourist visas are not legally allowed to take up employment.

Much of the economy is tied to the service industry, with wages hovering close to the minimum wage. For newcomers, the most common work is waiting on tables in Waikiki, and if you're young and energetic there are plenty of job possibilities in restaurants and clubs. Folks with language, scuba or similar skills might investigate employment with the resorts.

If you're hoping to find more serious 'professional' employment, you should note that Hawaii is considered a tight labor market, with a lack of diversified industries and a relatively immobile labor force. Professional jobs that do open up are generally filled by established Hawaii residents. The biggest exceptions to this rule are for teachers and nurses, both of which are in short supply.

Also check the **Honolulu Advertiser's** (www .honoluluadvertiser.com) classified job ads and continue surfing at www.jobshawaii.com. For more information on employment in Hawaii, contact the **State Department of Labor & Industrial Relations** (☎ 586-8700; www .hawaii.gov/labor; 830 Punchbowl St, Honolulu, HI 96813), which can be a good resource.

Transportation

GETTING THERE & AWAY

The vast majority of travelers to O'ahu arrive by air. Honolulu is a major Pacific hub and an intermediate stop on many flights between the US mainland and Asia, Australia, New Zealand and the South Pacific. Flights, tours and rail tickets can be booked on-line at www.lonelyplanet.com/travel_services.

ENTERING THE COUNTRY

A passport is required for all foreign citizens except Canadians, who only need to show proof of residence. Residents of most other countries need a tourist visa. It's always advisable to confirm this information since it changes constantly. See p242 for details.

THINGS CHANGE...

The information in this chapter is particularly vulnerable to change. Check directly with the airline or a travel agent to make sure you understand how a fare (and ticket you may buy) works and be aware of the security requirements for international travel. Shop carefully. The details given in this chapter should be regarded as pointers and are not a substitute for your own careful, up-to-date research.

All visitors, including Americans, should keep in mind that US airlines require passengers to present a photo ID as part of the airline check-in procedure.

AIR

US domestic and international airfares vary tremendously depending on the season, general tourism trends to the islands and how much flexibility the ticket allows for flight changes and refunds. There's a lot of competition, and at any given time any one of the airlines could have the cheapest fare.

Airports & Airlines

All flights to O'ahu arrive at **Honolulu International Airport** (HNL; ☎ 836-6413; www.honoluluairport.com), a modern and relatively visitor-friendly facility with all the usual amenities from currency-exchange booths to shops and eateries. You'll find a visitor information booth, car-rental counters and hotel/condo courtesy phones in the baggage claim area. The free **Wiki Wiki Shuttle** (⏱ 6am-10:30pm) connects the more distant parts of the airport and links the main terminals with the inter-island terminals.

Airlines flying into Honolulu include the following:

Air Canada (AC; ☎ 888-247-2262; www.aircanada.ca)
Air New Zealand (NZ; ☎ 800-262-1234; www.airnz.co.nz)
Air Pacific (FJ; ☎ 800-227-4446; www.airpacific.com)
Alaska Airlines (AS; ☎ 800-252-7522; www.alaskaair.com)
All Nippon Airways (ANA; ☎ 800-235-9262; www.anaskyweb.com)
Aloha Airlines (AQ; ☎ 800-367-5250; www.alohaairlines.com)
American Airlines (AA; ☎ 800-223-5436; www.aa.com)
China Airlines (CL; ☎ 800-227-5118; www.china-airlines.com)
Continental Airlines (CO; ☎ 800-523-3273; www.continental.com)
Delta (DL; ☎ 800-221-1212; www.delta.com)
Hawaiian Airlines (HA; ☎ 800-367-5320; www.hawaiianair.com)
Japan Airlines (JL; ☎ 800-525-3663; www.japanair.com)
Korean Airlines (KE; ☎ 800-438-5000; www.koreanair.com)

Northwest-KLM (NWA; ☎ 800-225-2525; www.nwa
.com)
Philippine Airlines (PR; ☎ 800-435-9725; www.philip
pineair.com)
Qantas Airways (QF; ☎ 800-227-4500; www.quantas
usa.com)
United Airlines (UA; ☎ 800-241-6522; www.ual.com)
US Airways (US; ☎ 800-428-4322; www.usairways.com)

Tickets

Airfares are constantly in flux and vary with
the season you travel and the day of the week
you fly, but in the end nothing determines
fares more than business. When things are
slow, regardless of the season, airlines will
drop their fares to fill the empty seats.

With so many airlines flying into Hawaii,
competition is fierce and good deals plentiful. Check both the airline websites and
travel websites – the best deal could be on
either one. Good places to start searching
are www.travelocity.com, www.expedia.com
or www.orbitz.com.

Once in Hawaii, you'll find discounted
fares to virtually any place around the Pacific. Larger travel agencies that specialize
in discount tickets include **Non-Stop Travel**
(Map pp84-5; ☎ 593-0700, 800-551-1226; www.nonstop
hawaii.com; 1350 S King St, Honolulu) and **Panda Travel**
(Map pp114-15; ☎ 734-1961, 888-726-3288; www.panda
online.com; 1017 Kapahulu Ave, Honolulu).

Round-the-world tickets (RTW) allow
you to fly on the combined routes of two or
more airlines and can be a good deal if you're
coming from a great distance and want to
visit other parts of the world in addition to
Hawaii. There's an almost endless variety
of possible destination and airline combinations and because of Honolulu's central
Pacific location, it can be included on most
RTW tickets. **British Airways** (☎ 800-247-9297;
www.ba.com) and **Qantas Airways** (☎ 800-227-4500;
www.qantas.com.au) pair up to offer some of
the most interesting RTW plans, which are
called oneworld Explorer.

Circle Pacific tickets are essentially
a takeoff on RTW tickets, but instead of
requiring you to continue moving in one
general direction, they allow you to keep
traveling in the same circular direction. Because you start and end at a city that borders
the Pacific, these tickets are most practical
for travelers who live in or near the Pacific region. Contact **Air New Zealand** (☎ 800-
262-1234; www.airnz.co.nz) or **Continental Airlines**

(☎ 800-523-3273; www.continental.com), whose program is called Circle Micronesia. Continental's flights originate in Los Angeles, San
Francisco and Honolulu.

Australia

Hawaiian Airlines flies nonstop between
Sydney and Honolulu. Qantas flies to Honolulu from Sydney and Melbourne (via Sydney, but without changing planes). Fares
vary with the season but typically begin
around A$1100 from Sydney and A$1250
from Melbourne.

Canada

Air Canada offers direct flights to Honolulu
from Vancouver and from other Canadian
cities via Vancouver. The cheapest round-
trip fares to Honolulu are around C$800
from Vancouver, C$1000 from Calgary or
Edmonton and C$1400 from Toronto.

Japan

Japan Airlines flies to Honolulu from Tokyo,
Osaka, Nagoya and Fukuoka. Round-trip
fares vary a bit with the departing city and the
season but, except at busier holiday periods,
they're generally around ¥50,000.

The American carriers Continental Airlines and Northwest Airlines also both have
flights to Honolulu from Tokyo and Osaka,
with ticket prices that are competitive with
those of Japan Airlines.

All Nippon Airways (ANA) also flies to
Honolulu, departing from Sapporo and Ku-
mamoto, with fares from around ¥70,000.

Micronesia

Continental Airlines has nonstop flights from
Guam to Honolulu with round-trip fares
from US$1000. Some tickets from Guam
allow stops en route at the Micronesian
islands of Chuuk, Pohnpei, Kosrae and Ma-
juro before reaching Honolulu – a nice way to
see some of the world's most remote islands.

New Zealand

Air New Zealand flies from Auckland to
Honolulu for about NZ$1600 return, with
the possibility of en route stopovers in Fiji.

South Pacific Islands

Hawaiian Airlines flies to Honolulu from Tahiti and American Samoa. From American
Samoa a round-trip fare starts at US$600.

From Tahiti to Honolulu round-trip fares are around US$800.

For travel from Fiji, Air New Zealand offers a round-trip ticket for about NZ$1450. Air New Zealand also flies to Honolulu from Tonga, the Cook Islands and Western Samoa, with round-trip tickets at around NZ$900 from Western Samoa and NZ$1100 from Tonga and the Cook Islands.

UK & Continental Europe

The most common route to Hawaii from Europe is west via New York, Chicago or Los Angeles. If you're interested in heading east with stops in Asia, it may be cheaper to get a RTW ticket instead of returning the same way.

The lowest return fares with Northwest-KLM from London, Paris and Frankfurt to Honolulu are usually around €1000. United Airlines, American Airlines, Delta and Continental Airlines have similarly priced service to Honolulu from European cities.

London is arguably the world's headquarters for bucket shops specializing in discount tickets, which are well advertised. Two good, reliable agents for cheap tickets in the UK:

STA Travel (☎ 020-7240 9844; www.statravel.co.uk; 33 Bedford St, Covent Garden, London)

Trailfinders (☎ 020-7628 7628; www.trailfinders.co.uk; 1 Threadneedle St, London)

US Mainland

Competition among airlines flying to Honolulu from the major mainland cities is intense. Typically, the lowest round-trip fares from the US mainland to Honolulu are about US$700 from the east coast and US$400 from the west coast. American Airlines, Continental Airlines, Delta, Northwest-KLM and United Airlines fly to Honolulu from both the east and west coasts. In addition, Hawaiian Airlines and Aloha Airlines both fly to Honolulu from several west coast cities and from Las Vegas.

Then there's Air Tech's Space-Available FlightPass, which certainly can be the cheapest way to fly between the west coast and Hawaii. **Air Tech** (☎ 212-219-7000; www.airtech.com) offers super deals by selling standby seats at $159 one way. If you provide them with a three-day travel window, they'll get you a seat at a nice price. Currently, Air Tech flies to Honolulu from San Francisco and Los Angeles.

The nonstop flight time to Hawaii is about 5½ hours from the west coast and 11 hours from the east coast.

See also Tours, opposite, for some cheap flights if you're short of time.

Hawaii

Frequent flight service between Honolulu and the other Hawaiian islands is available on Hawaii's two main inter-island carriers, **Hawaiian Airlines** (☎ 800-367-5320, on O'ahu ☎ 838-1555; www.hawaiianair.com) and **Aloha Airlines** (☎ 800-367-5250, on O'ahu ☎ 484-1111; www.alohaairlines.com). These are not puddle hoppers; both airlines fly comfortable wide-body jets and boast good safety records.

From Honolulu the airlines fly about once hourly to Kahului (on Maui), Kona and Hilo (both on the Big Island) and Lihu'e (on Kaua'i). Fares range from around $100 to $130 one way, depending on which flight you catch and how full it is. Round-trip fares are double the one-way fares. The earlier you book the more likely you are to find a cheaper fare. It's usually best to buy your tickets on the airline websites, which sometimes post Internet-only deals and other promotions.

AGRICULTURAL INSPECTION

All luggage and carry-on bags leaving Hawaii for the US mainland are checked by an agricultural inspector using an X-ray machine. You cannot take out gardenia, jade vine or roses, even in lei, although most other fresh flowers and foliage are permitted. You can bring home pineapples and coconuts, but most other fresh fruits and vegetables are banned. Other things not allowed to enter mainland states include plants in soil, fresh coffee berries (roasted beans are OK), cactus and sugarcane.

However, seeds, fruits and plants that have been certified and labeled for export aren't a problem. For more information call the **Plant Protection and Quarantine Office** (☎ 861-8490).

GETTING ORIENTED

Almost all visitors to O'ahu land at Honolulu International Airport, the only commercial airport on the island. The airport is on the western outskirts of the Honolulu district, 9 miles west of Waikiki.

The H1 Fwy, the main south-shore freeway, is the key to getting around the island. The H1 connects with Hwy 72, which runs around the southeast coast; with the H3 Fwy and the Pali (61) and Likelike (63) Hwys, which go to the windward coast; with Hwy 93, which leads up the leeward Wai'anae coast; and with H2 and Hwys 99 and 750, which run through the center of the island on the way to the North Shore.

Incidentally, H1 is a US *interstate* freeway – an amusing designation for a road on an island state in the middle of the Pacific.

Directions on O'ahu are often given by using landmarks. If someone tells you to 'go 'Ewa' (an area west of Honolulu) or 'go Diamond Head' (east of Waikiki), it simply means to head in that direction. Two other commonly used directional terms that you can expect to hear are *mauka*, meaning inland side, and *makai*, meaning ocean side.

SEA

In recent years, a growing number of cruise ships have begun offering tours that include Hawaii. Many of these trips are referred to as 'repositioning tours,' since they typically visit Hawaii during April, May, September and October on ships that are otherwise used in Alaska during the summer months, and in the Caribbean during the winter months.

Most cruises last 10 to 14 days and have fares that start at around $150 per day per person, based on double occupancy – though discounts and promotions can bring that price down to around $100 a day. Airfare to and from the departure point costs extra.

Most Hawaiian cruises not only include stopovers in Honolulu but also go on to visit the Hawaiian islands of Maui, Kaua'i and the Big Island. Cruise lines sailing to Honolulu include the following:

Holland America Cruise Line (☎ 877-724-5425; www.hollandamerica.com) Typically departs for Honolulu from San Diego, Seattle or Vancouver.

Princess Cruises (☎ 800-568-3262; www.princess .com) Offers the most cruises; operates between Honolulu and Tahiti.

Royal Caribbean Cruise Line (☎ 800-327-6700) Has departures for Honolulu from San Diego, Los Angeles, Ensenada, Mexico and Vancouver.

You can also get to Hawaii by private yacht. If you don't have one of your own, and you're hoping to get on a crew, start poking around the ports in early spring. Experienced crew should try www.boatcrew.net, a well-organized website with a database of boats leaving from various mainland ports.

TOURS

For those with limited time, package tours can sometimes be the cheapest way to go, covering airfare, accommodations and in some cases car rental. If you're going to Hawaii on a short getaway, packages may cost little more than what the airfare alone would normally cost. Although costs vary, one-week tours with airfare and no-frills hotel accommodations usually start around $550 from the US west coast or $900 from the east coast, based on double occupancy. **Pleasant Holidays** (☎ 800-742-9244; www.pleasantholidays.com) has departures from various US mainland points. **Sun Trips** (☎ 800-786-8747; www.suntrips.com) offers packages from Oakland, California.

GETTING AROUND

O'ahu is an easy island to get around, whether you're traveling by public bus or private car.

Compared with mainland urban centers, O'ahu's traffic is generally manageable, although in Honolulu it can get jammed during rush hour – weekdays from 7am to 9am and 3pm to 6pm. Expect heavy traffic in both directions on the H1 Fwy during this time, as well as on the Pali and Likelike Hwys headed toward Honolulu in the morning and away from Honolulu in the late afternoon. If you're going to the airport during rush hour, give yourself plenty of extra time.

BICYCLE

For the intrepid traveler, it's possible to cycle your way around O'ahu, but there's a lot of traffic to contend with, especially in the greater Honolulu area. Hawaii has been slow to adopt cycle-friendly policies – a few new road projects now include bicycle lanes, but such lanes are still relatively rare.

In Waikiki, the best main roads for cyclists are the one-way streets of canalside Ala Wai Blvd and beachside Kalakaua Ave, both of which have minimal cross-traffic.

The State Department of Transportation publishes a free *Bike O'ahu* map with possible routes, divided into those for novice cyclists, those for experienced cyclists and routes that are not cycle-friendly. You can pick up the map at the **Hawaii Visitors & Convention Bureau** (Map pp114-15; ☎ 923-1811; www.go hawaii.com; 8th fl, Waikiki Business Plaza, 2270 Kalakaua Ave, Waikiki; ☺ 8am-4:30pm Mon-Fri) in Waikiki and at bike rental shops around O'ahu; you can also peruse the map on-line at www.state .hi.us/dot/highways/bike/oahu.

One good way to get into the countryside without peddling through Honolulu traffic is to take the bus beyond the city limits. Public buses are now equipped with racks that can carry two bicycles. To use the bike rack, first tell the bus driver you will be loading your bike, secure your bicycle onto the fold-down rack, hop on board and pay the regular fare. There's no additional fee for bringing your bike along.

Road Rules

When cycling on O'ahu, there are a couple of rules of the road to keep in mind. Any bicycle used from 30 minutes after sunset until 30 minutes before sunrise must have a headlight facing forward, and at least one red reflector mounted on the rear. Cyclists are not allowed to ride on sidewalks within a business district, such as Waikiki or downtown Honolulu. Cyclists using a roadway have all the rights and duties applicable to motor-vehicle drivers, and must travel on the right side of the road, stop at red lights etc. The state of Hawaii does not require cyclists over the age of 15 to wear helmets, but they are recommended.

Hire

The following places rent bicycles. Prices typically range from $15 to $25 a day, with discounts by the week. The Waikiki shops are convenient, but if you're renting for any length of time, consider the Bike Shop in Honolulu, which has top-notch gear.

Bike Shop Honolulu (Map pp84-5; ☎ 596-0588; 1149 S King St); Kailua (Map p176; ☎ 261-1553; 270 Kuulei Rd)
Blue Sky Rentals (Map pp114-15; ☎ 947-0101; 1920 Ala Moana Blvd, Waikiki)
Coconut Cruisers (☎ 924-1644; 2301 Kalakaua Ave, Waikiki) At the side of the Royal Hawaiian Shopping Center.
Go Nuts Hawaii (☎ 926-3367; 159 Kaiulani Ave, Waikiki)

BUS

O'ahu's excellent public bus system, called **TheBus** (www.thebus.org), is extensive and easy to use. TheBus has about 80 routes, which collectively cover most of O'ahu. You can take TheBus to watch windsurfers at Kailua or surfers at Sunset Beach, visit Chinatown or the Bishop Museum, snorkel at Hanauma Bay or hike Diamond Head. TheBus is also useful for short hops around Honolulu's neighborhoods.

Some of the island's prime viewpoints are beyond reach, however. For instance, TheBus doesn't stop at the Nu'uanu Pali Lookout, go up to the Tantalus green belt or run as far as Ka'ena Point on the Wai'anae coast.

Buses stop only at marked bus stops. Each bus route can have a few different destinations; the destination is written on the front of the bus next to the number. Buses generally keep the same number when inbound and outbound. For instance, bus 8 can take you either into the heart of Waikiki or away from it toward Ala Moana, so take note of both the number and the written destination before you jump on. If in doubt, ask the bus driver – they're used to disoriented visitors, and most drivers are patient and helpful.

The fleet is modern and accessible to the disabled. And all have bike racks that cyclists can use for free. One caveat: be prepared for the frigid airconditioning. A bus in Honolulu is probably the coldest place on O'ahu, regardless of the season.

Although TheBus is convenient enough, this isn't Tokyo – if you set your watch by the bus here, you'll come up with Hawaiian Time. In addition to not getting hung up on schedules, buses can sometimes bottleneck, with one packed bus after another passing right by crowded bus stops. Waiting for the bus anywhere between Ala Moana and Waikiki on a Saturday night can be a particularly memorable experience.

TRANSPORTATION

Still, TheBus usually gets you where you want to go, and as long as you don't try to cut your travel time too close or schedule too much in one day, it's a great deal.

Costs

A one-way fare for all rides is $2 for adults and $1 for children aged six to 17. You can use either coins or $1 bills, but nothing larger; bus drivers don't give change. Children under the age of six ride for free.

Transfers, which have a two-hour time limit stamped on them, are given free when more than one bus is required to get to a destination. If needed, ask for one when you board.

The best deal for short-term visitors is the O'ahu Discovery Passport, which is valid for unlimited rides over four consecutive days, costs $20 and can be purchased at any of the ubiquitous ABC stores.

There's no weekly pass so if you want a pass for a longer period, you'll have to go with the monthly bus pass, valid for unlimited rides in a calendar month. It costs $40 and can be purchased at 7-Eleven convenience stores and Foodland and Star supermarkets. Keep in mind, though, that this is for a calendar month, not just any 30-day period, so if your two-week stay spreads into a second calendar month it may not work for you.

Seniors (65 years and older) and disabled people of any age can buy a $30 bus pass valid for unlimited rides during a one-year period. For more information on these passes, call ☎ 848-4444.

Routes

TheAla Moana Center is Honolulu's central transfer point. Buses 8, 19, 20 and 58 run between Waikiki and the Ala Moana Center; it's hardly worth checking timetables, as one of these buses comes by every few minutes throughout the day. From Ala Moana you can connect with a broad network of buses to points throughout the island.

Buses 2, 19 and 20 will take you between Waikiki and downtown Honolulu. There's usually a bus every 10 minutes or so.

Bus 4 runs between Waikiki and the University of Hawai'i every 10 minutes.

Schedules & Information

Bus schedules vary with the route; many operate from about 5am to 9pm, though some main routes, such as those that serve Waikiki, continue until around midnight.

TheBus has an excellent **information service** (☎ 848-5555; ☺ 5:30am-10pm). As long as you know where you are and where you want to go, the staff can tell you which bus to catch and when the next one will arrive. You can get printed timetables for individual routes free from any satellite city hall, including the one at the Ala Moana Center (p229). Timetables can also be found at the library in Waikiki.

When you pick up the timetables, be sure to grab one of the free schematic route maps, a brochure that maps out routes for the entire island and shows the corresponding bus numbers. These are handy if you're using the bus system a lot.

TRANSPORTATION

MAKE YOUR OWN TOUR

It's possible to make a nifty day excursion circling the island by bus, beginning at the Ala Moana Center. The No 52 Wahiawa-Circle Island bus goes clockwise up Hwy 99 to Hale'iwa and along the North Shore. At the Turtle Bay Resort, on the northern tip of O'ahu, it switches signs to No 55 and comes down the Windward coast to Kane'ohe and down the Pali Hwy, then west back to Ala Moana. The No 55 Kane'ohe-Circle Island bus does the same route in reverse.

The buses operate every 30 minutes from 5am to around 11pm. If you take the Circle Island route nonstop, it takes about four hours and costs just $2.

For a shorter excursion from Waikiki, you can make a loop around southeast O'ahu by taking bus 58 to Sea Life Park, in the Makapu'u area, and then bus 57 up to Kailua and back into Honolulu. As you'll need to change buses on this route, ask the driver for a transfer when you first board. Transfers have time limits and aren't meant to be used for stopovers, but you can usually grab a quick break at Ala Moana. If your transfer expires while you're exploring, you'll need to pay a new $2 fare when you reboard the bus.

CAR

If you really want to explore off the beaten path, a car is the way to go. The minimum age for visitors to drive in Hawaii is 18, though car-rental companies usually have higher age restrictions. If you're younger than age 25, you should call the car-rental agencies in advance to check their policies regarding restrictions and surcharges.

Automobile Associations

American Automobile Association (AAA; ☎ 593-2221; www.aaa-hawaii.com; 1130 Nimitz Hwy, Honolulu) can provide AAA or other affiliated automobile club members with information on motoring in Hawaii, including detailed Honolulu and Hawaii road maps. Members are also entitled to discounts on car rentals and some hotels and sightseeing attractions. It also provides members with emergency road service and towing; call ☎ 800-222-4357.

AAA has reciprocal agreements with automobile associations in other countries, but be sure to bring your membership card from your country of origin. For information on joining AAA on the mainland before arrival in Hawaii, call ☎ 800-564-6222.

Distances & Driving Times

Although actual times vary depending upon traffic conditions, the average driving times and distances from Waikiki to points of interest around O'ahu are as follows:

Destination	Miles	Time
Hale'iwa	29	50min
Hanauma Bay	11	25min
Honolulu Airport	9	20min
Ka'ena Point State Park	43	75min
Kailua	14	25min
La'ie	34	1hr
Makaha Beach	36	1hr
Nu'uanu Pali Lookout	11	20min
Sea Life Park	16	35min
Sunset Beach	37	65min
USS *Arizona* Memorial	12	30min
Waimea	34	1hr
Waipahu	16	30min

Driver's License

Visitors can legally drive in the state with a valid driver's license issued by a country that is party to the United Nations Conference on Road & Motor Transport – which covers virtually everyone. However, car-rental companies will generally accept valid foreign driver's licenses only if they are in English. Otherwise, most will require renters to present an international driver's license along with their home license. The national automobile association in your home country can provide one for a small fee.

Fuel & Spare Parts

Hawaii has the most expensive gasoline in the USA. Prices on average are about 25% higher in Hawaii than on the US mainland, and spare parts average around 20% more.

Hire

Car rentals are available at the airport and in Waikiki. With most companies the weekly rate works out significantly cheaper per day than the straight daily rate. The daily rate for a small car with unlimited mileage ranges from around $30 to $50, while weekly rates typically range from $150 to $200. You're usually required to keep the car for a minimum of five days to get the weekly rate.

Rates vary a bit from company to company, and also within each company, depending on the season, time of booking and current promotional fares. If you belong to an automobile club, a frequent-flyer program or a travel club, you'll often be eligible for some sort of discount with at least one of the rental agencies, so always ask.

One thing to note when renting a car is that rates for mid-sized cars are often only a few dollars more per week than small cars. Because some promotional discounts exclude the economy-sized cars, at times the lowest rate available may actually be for a larger car.

It's always best to make reservations in advance; with most companies there's no cancellation penalty if you change your mind. Walking up to the counter without a reservation will subject you to higher rates, and during busy periods it's not uncommon for all the cars to be rented out.

On daily rentals, most cars are rented on a 24-hour basis, so you could get two days' use by renting at midday and driving around all afternoon, then heading out to explore somewhere else the next morning before the car is due back. Most companies even allow an hour's grace period.

Rental rates generally include unlimited mileage, though if you drop off the car at a location that is different from where you picked it up, there's usually a drop-off fee of around $50.

Having a major credit card greatly simplifies the rental process. Without one, some agencies simply will not rent you a vehicle, while others will require prepayment by cash or traveler's check, as well as a deposit of around $300, pay stubs, proof of return airfare and more. If you intend to rent a car without a credit card, it's wise to make your plans well in advance.

Most car-rental agencies typically request the name and phone number of the place where you're staying. Be aware that many car-rental companies are loath to rent to people who list a camping ground as their address on the island, and a few specifically add 'No Camping Permitted' to their rental contracts.

The following international companies operate in Honolulu; their cars can be booked from offices around the world or on-line.

Alamo (☎ 800-327-9633; www.alamo.com)
Avis (☎ 800-831-8000; www.avis.com)
Budget (☎ 800-527-0700; www.budget.com)
Dollar (☎ 800-800-4000; www.dollarcar.com)
Hertz (☎ 800-654-3131; www.hertz.com)
National (☎ 800-227-7368; www.nationalcar.com)

Budget, National, Hertz, Avis and Dollar all have rental cars available at Honolulu International Airport. Alamo has its operations about a mile outside the airport, on the corner of Nimitz Hwy and Ohohia St.

All things being equal, try to rent from a company with its lot inside the airport – it's more convenient and, more importantly, on the way back to the airport all the highway signs lead to the in-airport car returns. Having to drive around looking for a car-rental agency lot outside the airport can cost you valuable time when you're trying to catch a flight.

In addition to their airport facilities, most of the international companies have multiple branch locations in Waikiki, many of them in the lobbies of larger hotels. When you make your reservation, keep in mind that the best rates sometimes aren't offered at the smaller branch offices, so even if you're already in Waikiki, it might be worth your while to catch a bus to the airport and pick your car up there, especially for longer rentals or if you're planning on keeping the car until you fly out of O'ahu.

Insurance

Car-rental companies in Hawaii have liability insurance that covers people and property you might damage while driving a rental vehicle. Damage to the rental vehicle itself is not covered, unless you accept the collision damage waiver (CDW) option offered by the rental agency. This added coverage is typically an additional $15 to $20 a day.

The CDW is not really insurance per se, but rather a guarantee that the rental company won't hold you liable for any damage to their car (though even then there are exceptions). If you decline the CDW, you will usually be held liable for any damages up to the full value of the car. If damage does occur and you find yourself in a dispute with the rental company, you can call the state **Department of Commerce & Consumer Affairs** (☎ 587-1234) for recorded information on your legal rights.

If you have collision coverage on your vehicle at home, it might cover damages to car rentals in Hawaii. Check with your insurance company before your trip.

Additionally, some credit cards, including many 'gold cards' issued by Visa and MasterCard, offer you reimbursement coverage for collision damages if you rent the car with their credit card and decline the CDW. Be aware, however, that most collision coverage provided by a credit card isn't valid for rentals of more than 15 days or for exotic models, SUVs, vans and 4WD vehicles.

Road Rules

As with the rest of the USA, driving is on the right-hand side of the road. Drivers at a red light can make a right turn after coming to a full stop and yielding to oncoming traffic, unless there's a sign at the intersection prohibiting the turn.

Locals will tell you there are three golden rules for driving on the islands: don't honk your horn unless it's absolutely required, don't follow too closely, and do let people pass whenever it's safe to do so. Any cool moves like this are acknowledged by waving the *shaka* (Hawaiian hand greeting) sign. To make the shaka sign, fold down your three middle fingers to your palm and extend your thumb and little finger. Then hold the hand out and shake it back and forth.

In Hawaii, drivers and front-seat passengers are required to wear seat belts. State law also requires the use of child safety seats for children aged three and younger, while four-year-olds must be either in a safety seat or secured by a seat belt. Most car-rental companies rent child-safety seats for around $5 a day, but they don't always have them on hand so it's advisable to reserve one in advance.

Speed limits are posted and enforced. If you are stopped for speeding, expect to get a ticket, as the police rarely just give warnings.

HITCHHIKING

Hitchhiking is never entirely safe in any country in the world, and Lonely Planet does not recommend it. Travelers who do decide to hitch should understand that they are taking a small but potentially life-threatening risk. Hitchhikers should size up each situation carefully before getting into cars, and women should be especially wary of hitching alone. People who nevertheless choose to hitch will be safer if they travel in pairs, let someone know where they are planning to go, keep their luggage light and with them at all times, and sit by a door.

MOPED

Mopeds are another transportation option, though perhaps they're a bit daunting for the uninitiated. You have to contend with Honolulu's heavy traffic, which presents a challenge to those who don't have much moped experience, and local car drivers loath them because of the many accidents or near-accidents they believe mopeds cause.

State law requires mopeds to be ridden by one person only and prohibits their use on sidewalks and on freeways. Mopeds must always be driven in single file and may not be driven at speeds in excess of 30mph. In Hawaii, all mopeds are limited to a maximum 2 horsepower, 50cc. To drive a moped, you must have a valid driver's license. Mopeds are available for around $40 a day at a couple of places in Waikiki (see p152).

TAXI

Taxis have meters and charge a flag-down fee of $2.75 to start with, and then $3 a mile. There's an extra charge of 50¢ for each suitcase or backpack.

Taxis are readily available at the airport and larger hotels but are otherwise generally hard to find. To phone for one, try **City Taxi** (☎ 524-2121), **TheCab** (☎ 422-2222) or **Charley's** (☎ 955-2211).

Carey Chauffeured Services (☎ 888-563-2888) offers chauffeur tours of the island that can take you anywhere you want to go; prices vary with the tour.

Health

O'ahu encompasses a range of terrains but none is especially severe. Because of the high level of hygiene, infectious diseases will not be a significant concern for most travelers, who will experience nothing worse than a mild sunburn. The greatest threats are actually drowning and car accidents, which can both be avoided by prudence.

BEFORE YOU GO

INSURANCE
The USA offers possibly the finest health care in the world. The problem is that, unless you have good insurance, it can be prohibitively expensive. It's essential to purchase travel health insurance if your regular policy doesn't cover you for medical expenses when you're abroad.

Bring any medications in their original containers, clearly labeled. A signed, dated letter from your physician that describes all medical conditions and medications, including generic names, is also a good idea.

Check **LonelyPlanet.com** (www.lonelyplanet.com /health/predeparture.htm) for more information on travel health insurance. Find out in advance if your insurance plan will make payments directly to providers or reimburse you later for overseas health expenditures.

RECOMMENDED VACCINATIONS
No special vaccines are required or recommended for travel to the USA. All travelers should be up-to-date on routine immunizations, listed on p254.

INTERNET RESOURCES
There is a wealth of travel health advice on the Internet. The World Health Organization publishes a superb book, called *International Travel and Health*, which is revised annually and is available on-line at no cost at www.who.int/ith. Another website of general interest is **MD Travel Health** (www.mdtravelhealth.com), which provides complete travel health recommendations for every country, updated daily, also at no cost.

It's usually a good idea to consult your government's travel health website before departure, if one is available.

Australia (www.smartraveller.gov.au)
Canada (www.hc-sc.gc.ca/english/index.html)
UK (www.dh.gov.uk/PolicyAndGuidance/HealthAdvice ForTravellers/fs/en)
USA (www.cdc.gov/travel)

MEDICAL CHECKLIST
- acetaminophen (eg Tylenol) or aspirin
- anti-inflammatory drugs (eg ibuprofen)
- antihistamines (for hay fever and allergic reactions)
- antibacterial ointment (eg Neosporin) for cuts and abrasions
- steroid cream or cortisone (for poison ivy and other allergic rashes)
- bandages, gauze, gauze rolls
- adhesive or paper tape
- scissors, safety pins, tweezers
- thermometer
- pocket knife
- insect repellent containing DEET for the skin
- insect spray containing permethrin for clothing, tents and bed nets
- sunblock

ON O'AHU

AVAILABILITY & COST OF HEALTH CARE
For immediate assistance, call ☎ 911. If you have a medical emergency, the best bet is to find the nearest hospital and go to its emergency room. If the problem isn't urgent, you can call a nearby hospital and ask for a referral to a local physician, which is usually much cheaper than a trip to the emergency

REQUIRED & RECOMMENDED VACCINATIONS

Vaccine	Recommended for	Dosage	Side effects
tetanus-diphtheria	all travelers who haven't had a booster within 10 years	one dose lasts 10 years	soreness at injection site
measles	travelers born after 1956 who've had only one measles vaccination	one dose	fever; rash; joint pains; allergic reactions
chicken pox	travelers who've never had chicken pox	two doses a month apart	fever; mild case of chicken pox
influenza	all travelers during flu season (Nov–Mar)	one dose	soreness at the injection site; fever

room. O'ahu has excellent medical facilities; people from islands throughout the Pacific come to Honolulu (p71) for treatment.

Pharmacies are abundantly supplied, but you may find that some medications that are available over the counter in your home country require a prescription in the USA, and, as always, if you don't have insurance to cover the cost of prescriptions, they can be shockingly expensive.

INFECTIOUS DISEASES

In addition to the more common ailments, there are several infectious diseases that are unknown or uncommon outside of the mainland. Most are acquired by mosquito or tick bites, or environmental exposure. Currently Hawaii is rabies-free.

Dengue Fever

Dengue is transmitted by aedes mosquitoes, which bite preferentially during the daytime and are usually found close to human habitations, often indoors. They breed primarily in artificial water containers, such as jars, barrels, metal drums, plastic containers and discarded tires. As a result, dengue is especially common in densely populated urban environments. In Hawaii the last outbreak of this mosquito-borne disease was in 2002. For updates, check with the **Hawaii State Department of Health** (www.state.hi.us/doh).

Dengue usually causes flu-like symptoms, including fever, muscle aches, joint pains, headaches, nausea and vomiting, often followed by a rash. There is no treatment for dengue fever, except to take analgesics such as acetaminophen/paracetamol (eg Tylenol) – do not take aspirin as it increases

the likelihood of hemorrhaging – and drink plenty of fluids. See a doctor to be diagnosed and monitored. Severe cases may require hospitalization for intravenous fluids and supportive care. There is no vaccine. The cornerstone of prevention is insect protection measures.

Giardiasis

This parasitic infection of the small intestine occurs throughout the world. Symptoms may include nausea, bloating, cramps and diarrhea, and may last for weeks. To protect yourself, you should avoid drinking directly from waterfalls, ponds, streams and rivers, which may be contaminated by animal or human feces. The infection can also be transmitted from person to person if proper hand washing is not done. Giardiasis is easily diagnosed by a stool test and readily treated with antibiotics.

HIV/AIDS

As with most parts of the world, HIV infection occurs throughout the USA. Never assume, on the basis of someone's background or appearance, that they're free of this or any other sexually transmitted disease. Use a condom for all sexual encounters.

Leptospirosis

Leptospirosis is acquired by exposure to water contaminated by the urine of infected animals, such as rats, mongooses and feral pigs. Outbreaks often occur at times of flooding, when sudden overflow may contaminate water sources downstream from animal habitats. Even an idyllic waterfall may, in fact, be infected with leptospirosis.

The initial symptoms, which resemble a mild flu, usually subside uneventfully in a few days, but a minority of cases are complicated by jaundice or meningitis. It can also cause hepatitis and renal failure, which might be fatal. Diagnosis is through blood tests and the disease is easily treated with doxycycline. There is no vaccine. You can minimize your risk by staying out of bodies of fresh water (eg waterfalls, pools, streams) that may be contaminated, especially if you have any open cuts or sores. Because hikers account for many of the cases of leptospirosis in Hawaii, the state posts warning signs at trailheads. If you're camping, water purification is essential.

West Nile Virus

These infections were unknown in the USA until a few years ago, but have now been reported in almost every state. Humans in Hawaii have not been affected so far, but the rising number of reported cases in California is cause for concern. The virus is transmitted by culex mosquitoes, which are active in late summer and early fall and generally bite after dusk. Most infections are mild or asymptomatic, but the virus may infect the central nervous system, leading to fever, headache, confusion, lethargy, coma and sometimes death. There is no treatment for West Nile virus.

For the latest update on the areas affected by West Nile, see the **US Geological Survey** (http://westnilemaps.usgs.gov).

ENVIRONMENTAL HAZARDS
Bites & Stings

There is no established wild snake population on the island.

Leeches are found in humid rain forest areas. They do not transmit any disease, but their bites are often intensely itchy for weeks afterwards and can easily become infected. Apply an iodine-based antiseptic to any leech bite to help prevent infection.

Bee and wasp stings mainly cause problems for people who are allergic to them. Anyone with a serious bee or wasp allergy should carry an injection of adrenaline for emergency treatment. For others pain is the main problem – apply ice to the sting and take painkillers.

Commonsense approaches to these concerns are the most effective: wear long sleeves and pants, hats and shoes (rather than sandals) to protect yourself.

MAMMAL BITES

Do not attempt to pet, handle or feed any animal, with the exception of domestic animals known to be free of any infectious disease. Most animal injuries are directly related to a person's attempt to touch or feed the animal.

Any bite or scratch by a mammal, including bats or feral pigs, goats etc, should be promptly and thoroughly cleansed with large amounts of soap and water, followed by application of an antiseptic, such as iodine or alcohol. It may be advisable to start an antibiotic, as wounds caused by animal bites and scratches often become infected.

MARINE ANIMALS

Marine spikes, such as those found on sea urchins, scorpion fish and Hawaiian lionfish, can cause severe local pain. If this occurs, immediately immerse the affected area in hot water (as high a temperature as can be tolerated). Keep topping up with hot water until the pain subsides and medical care can be reached. The same advice applies if you are stung by a cone shell.

Marine stings from jellyfish and Portuguese man-of-war (aka bluebottles, which have translucent, bluish, bladder-like floats) also occur. Even touching a bluebottle a few hours after it's washed up onshore can result in burning stings. Jellyfish are often seen eight to 10 days after a full moon when they float into shallow waters; the influx usually lasts for three days. If you are stung, first aid consists of washing the skin with vinegar to prevent further discharge of remaining stinging cells, followed by rapid transfer to a hospital; antivenins are widely available.

Despite extensive media coverage, the risk of shark attack in Hawaiian waters is no greater than in other countries with extensive coastlines. Avoid swimming in waters with runoff after heavy rainfall (eg around river mouths) and those areas frequented by commercial fishing operators. Do not swim if you are actively bleeding, as this attracts sharks. Check with lifeguards about local risks. Keep in mind that your chances of being hit by a falling coconut on the beach are greater than those of a shark attack, though!

MOSQUITO BITES

When traveling in areas where West Nile or other mosquito-borne illnesses have been reported, keep yourself covered and apply a good insect repellent, preferably one containing DEET, to exposed skin and clothing. In general, adults and children over 12 should use preparations containing 25% to 35% DEET, which usually lasts about six hours. Children between two and 12 years of age should use preparations containing no more than 10% DEET, applied sparingly, which will usually last about three hours. Neurologic toxicity has been reported from DEET, especially in children, but appears to be extremely uncommon and generally related to overuse. DEET-containing compounds should not be used on children under age two.

Insect repellents containing certain botanical products, including oil of eucalyptus and soybean oil, are effective but last only 1½ to two hours. Products based on citronella are not effective.

See the **Centers for Disease Control** (CDC; www .cdc.gov/ncidod/dvbid/westnile/qa/prevention.htm) for prevention information.

SPIDER BITES

Although there are many species of spiders in the USA, the only ones that cause significant human illness are the black widow, brown recluse and hobo spiders. It is a matter of debate which of these species are conclusively found in Hawaii. The black widow is black or brown in color, measuring about 15mm in body length, with a shiny top, fat body, and distinctive red or orange hourglass figure on its underside. It's found usually in woodpiles, sheds, harvested crops and outdoor toilets. The brown recluse spider is brown in color, usually 10mm in body length, with a dark violin-shaped mark on the top of the upper section of the body. It is active mostly at night, lives in dark sheltered areas such as under porches and in woodpiles, and typically bites when trapped. The symptoms of a hobo spider bite are similar to those of a brown recluse, but milder.

If bitten by a black widow, you should apply ice or cold packs and go immediately to the nearest emergency room. Complications of a black widow bite may include muscle spasms, breathing difficulties and high blood pressure. The bite of a brown recluse or hobo spider typically causes a large, inflamed wound, sometimes associated with fever and chills. If bitten, apply ice and see a physician.

Diving & Snorkeling Hazards

Divers, snorkelers and surfers should seek specialized advice before they travel to ensure their medical kit contains treatment for coral cuts and tropical ear infections, as well as for the standard problems. Divers should ensure their insurance covers them for decompression illness – get specialized dive insurance through an organization such as **Divers Alert Network** (DAN; www.divers alertnetwork.org). Have a dive medical before you leave your home country – there are certain medical conditions that are incompatible with diving that your dive operator may not always ask you about. On O'ahu, divers who get the bends are taken to the **UH Hyperbaric Treatment Center** (☎ 587-3425; 347 N Kuakini St, Honolulu).

See p57 for general advice on ocean safety.

Heat

Travelers should drink plenty of fluids and try to avoid strenuous exercise in high temperatures.

Dehydration is the main contributor to heat exhaustion. Symptoms include feeling weak, headache, irritability, nausea or vomiting, sweaty skin, a fast, weak pulse and a normal or slightly elevated body temperature. Treatment involves getting out of the heat and/or sun, fanning the victim and applying cool wet cloths to the skin, laying the victim flat with their legs raised and rehydrating with water containing one-quarter of a teaspoon of salt per liter. Recovery is usually rapid and it is common to feel weak for some days afterwards.

Heatstroke is a serious medical emergency. Symptoms come on suddenly and include weakness, nausea, a hot, dry body with a body temperature of over 106°F, dizziness, confusion, loss of coordination, fits, and eventually collapse and loss of consciousness. Seek medical help and commence cooling by getting the person out of the heat, removing their clothes, fanning them and applying cool, wet cloths or ice to their body, especially to the groin and armpits.

HEALTH

Language

CONTENTS

Hawaii has two official state languages: English and Hawaiian. Although English has long replaced Hawaiian as the dominant language, many Hawaiian words and phrases are commonly used in speech and in print.

Before the arrival of Christian missionaries in 1820, the Hawaiians had no written language. Knowledge was passed on through complex oral genealogies, stories, chants, songs and descriptive place names. The missionaries rendered the spoken language into the Roman alphabet and established the first presses, used to print religious materials.

Throughout the 19th century, as more and more foreigners settled in the islands, the everyday use of Hawaiian declined. In the 1890s, English was made the official language of government and education.

The push for statehood (1900–59) added to the decline of the Hawaiian language. Speaking Hawaiian was seen as a deterrent to American assimilation, thus adult native speakers were strongly discouraged from teaching their children Hawaiian at home.

This attitude remained until the early '70s when the Hawaiian community began to experience a cultural renaissance. A handful of young Hawaiians lobbied to establish Hawaiian language classes at the University of Hawai'i, and Hawaiian language immersion preschools followed in the '80s. These preschools are modeled after Maori *kohanga reo* (language nests); the primary method of language perpetuation is through speaking and hearing the language on a daily basis. In Hawaii's 'Aha Punana Leo preschools, all learning and communication takes place in the mother tongue – *ka 'olelo makuahine*.

Hawaiian has been revived from the point of extinction. Record numbers of students enroll in Hawaiian language classes in high schools and colleges, and immersion school graduates are raising a new generation of native speakers.

If you'd like to discover more about the Hawaiian language, get a copy of Lonely Planet's *South Pacific Phrasebook*.

PRONUNCIATION

Written Hawaiian has just thirteen letters: five vowels (**a, e, i, o, u**) and seven consonants (**h, k, l, m, n, p, w**). The letters **h, l, m** and **n** are pronounced much the same as in English. Usually every letter in Hawaiian words is pronounced. Each vowel has a different pronunciation depending on whether it is stressed or unstressed.

Consonants

p/k similar to English, but with less aspiration; **k** may be replaced with **t**

w after **i** and **e**, usually a soft English 'v;' thus the town of Hale'iwa is pronounced 'Haleiva,' After **u** or **o** it's often like English 'w,' thus Olowalu is pronounced as written. After **a** or at the beginning of a word it can be as English 'w' or 'v,' thus you'll hear both Hawai'i and Havai'i (The Big Island).

Unstressed vowels (without macron)

a as in 'ago'
e as in 'bet'
i as the 'y' in 'city'
o as in 'sole'
u as in 'rude'

Glottal Stops & Macrons

Written Hawaiian uses both glottal stops ('), called *'okina*, and macrons (a straight bar above a vowel, eg **ā**), called *kahako*. In modern print both are often omitted. In this guidebook, the macrons have been omitted, but glottal stops have been included, as they can be helpful in striving to pronounce common place names and words correctly.

The glottal stop indicates a break between two vowels, producing an effect similar to saying 'oh-oh' in English. For example, *'a'a*, a type of lava, is pronounced 'ah-ah,' and Ho'okena, a place name, is pronounced 'Ho-oh-kena.' A macron indicates that the vowel is stressed and has a long pronunciation.

LANGUAGE

Glottal stops and macrons not only affect pronunciation, but can give a word a completely different meaning. For example, *ai* (with no glottal) means 'sexual intercourse,' but *'ai* (with the glottal) means 'food.' Similarly, the word *ka'a* (with no macron over the second **a**) means 'to roll, turn or twist,' but *ka'ā* (with a macron over the second **a**) is a thread or line, used in fishing.

Compound Words

In the written form, many Hawaiian words are compound words s made up of several different words. For example, the word *humuhumunukunukuapua'a* can be broken down as follows: *humuhumu-nukunuku-a-pua'a* (literally, trigger fish snout of pig), meaning 'the fish with a snout like a pig.' The place name Waikiki is also a compound word: *wai-kiki* (literally, freshwater sprouting), referring to the freshwater swamps once found in the area. Some words are doubled to emphasize their meaning, much like in English. For example, *wiki* means 'quick,' while *wikiwiki* means 'very quick.'

Common Hawaiian Words

For more Hawaiian words, see the Glossary on p259.

aloha – love, hello, welcome, goodbye
hale – house
heiau – religious temple
kane – man
kapu – taboo, restricted
luau – traditional Hawaiian feast
mahalo – thank you
mahimahi – dolphin fish, popular in restaurants
mauka – a directional, toward the mountains
makai – a directional, toward the sea
'ono – delicious, tasty
pau – finished, completed
poi – staple food made from taro
ukulele – four-stringed musical instrument, used in modern Hawaiian music (literally, 'leaping flea,' because of the action of the fingers when playing)
wahine – woman

PIDGIN

Hawaii pidgin is a distinct language, spoken by over 500,000 people. It developed on sugar plantations where the *luna* (foreman) had to communicate with field laborers from many foreign countries. Early plantation pidgin used a very minimal and condensed form of English as the root language, to which elements from Cantonese, Hawaiian and Portuguese were added. It became the second language of first-generation immigrants and many Hawaiians.

As this English-based pidgin evolved, it took on its own grammatical structure and syntax. Many words were pronounced differently and combined in ways not found in English. Rather than a careless or broken form of English, it evolved into a separate language, called Hawaii Creole by linguists.

Today, there is ongoing controversy about the validity of pidgin, with opponents saying that it erodes standard English and becomes a barrier to social and educational advancement. Proponents argue that pidgin is a rich and vibrant language that should not be looked down upon or banned from schools, and that pidgin speakers are often unjustly seen as less intelligent.

In recent years much poetry and many award-winning plays and books have been written in pidgin by local authors who are passionate in their determination to keep pidgin alive in the community.

Common Pidgin Words & Phrases

brah – shortened form of *bradah* (brother); also used as 'hey you'
broke da mout – delicious, as in 'My auntie make *broke da mout kine* fish!'
buggahs – guys, as in '*Da buggahs* went to without me!'
bumbye – later on, as in 'We go movies *bumbye den* (then).'
bummahs – bummer; an expression of disappointment or regret
chicken skin – goose bumps
cockaroach – to steal, as in 'Who went *cockaroach* my *slippahs*?'
da kine – whatchamacallit; used whenever you can't think of the word you want
Fo' real? – Really? Are you kidding me?
funny kine – strange or different, as in 'He stay *acking* (acting) all *funny kine*.'
geev 'um – Go for it! Give it all you got!
Howzit? – Hi, how's it going? As in 'Eh, *howzit brah*?'
How you stay? – How are you doing these days?
kay den – 'OK then,' as in '*Kay den*, we go beach.'
laydahs – Later on. I'll see you later, as in, '*Kay den*, *laydahs*.'
no ack – (Literally, 'no act.') Stop showing off, cool it.
rubbah slippahs – (rubber) thongs, flip-flops
talk story – any kind of casual conversation
to da max – a suffix that adds emphasis to something, as in '*Da waves* was big *to da max*!'

Glossary

For definitions of food and drink terms, see p67.

adzuki bean – sweetened paste in Japanese desserts
ae'o – Hawaiian black-necked stilt
'ahi – yellowfin tuna
ahupua'a – traditional land division extending from the mountains to the sea
'aina – land
akamai – clever
aku – bonito (skipjack tuna)
akua – god, spirit, idol
'alae ke'oke'o – Hawaiian coot
'alae 'ula – Hawaiian moorhen
alaia – shorter, stand-up surfboard
ali'i – chief, royalty
aloha – traditional greeting meaning love, welcome, good-bye
aloha 'aina – love of the land
'amakihi – small, yellow-green native bird
'apapane – bright-red native Hawaiian honeycreeper
a'u – swordfish, marlin
'aumakua – protective deity; deified ancestor
awa – milkfish
'awa – kava, a native plant, *Piper methysticum*, used to make a mildly intoxicating drink

crack seed – Chinese preserved fruit; a salty, sweet or sour snack

'elepaio – brownish native bird with a white rump, found in the understory of native forests

goza – roll-up straw mat used at beaches and parks
grinds – food; *'ono kine grinds* is good food

hala – pandanus tree; the *lau* (leaves) are used in weaving mats and baskets
hale – house
hana – work; a bay, when used as a compound in place names
haole – Caucasian; literally, 'without breath'
hapa – portion or fragment; person of mixed blood
hau – indigenous hibiscus tree whose wood is used for making canoe outriggers
haupia – coconut pudding
Hawai'i nei – all the Hawaiian Islands taken as a group; indicates affection (ie 'beloved' or 'cherished' Hawai'i)
he'e nalu – surfing (literally, 'wave sliding')
heiau – ancient stone temple, a place of worship in Hawaii

Hina – Polynesian goddess (wife of *Ku,* one of the four main gods)
honu – turtle
hui – group, organization
hukilau – fishing with a seine or the feast that follows
hula – Hawaiian dance form
hula halau – hula school or troupe
hula kahiko – traditional (ancient) hula
humuhumunukunukuapua'a – triggerfish; Hawaii's state fish

'i'iwi – bright-orange Hawaiian honeycreeper
'iliahi – Hawaiian sandalwood
'ilima – native coastal ground cover with delicate yellow-orange flowers
imu – underground earthen oven used to cook *kalua* pig and other *luau* food

kahili – feathered standard, used as a symbol of royalty
kahuna – knowledgeable person in any field; commonly a priest or healer
kaiseki ryōri – Japanese multicourse chef's tasting menu
kaku – barracuda
kalo – plant whose rootstock is mashed to make *poi* (*taro* in English)
kalua – traditional method of baking in an underground pit
kama'aina – person born and raised in Hawaii; literally, 'child of the land'
kanaka – man, human being, person; also native Hawaiian
kane – man; also the name of one of four main Hawaiian gods
kapa – cloth made by pounding the inner bark of the paper mulberry tree (*tapa* in English)
kapu – taboo, part of strict ancient Hawaiian social and religious system
kaukau – food
kaukau wagon – lunch wagon
kauna'oa – thin, parasitic groundcover vine
kava – see *'awa*
keiki – child, offspring
ki – native plant whose leaves are used for wrapping food and making hula skirts (also *ti*)
kiawe – a relative of the mesquite tree whose branches have sharp thorns, and whose wood is used for grilling food
ki'i – image, statue (often of a deity)
kiko'o – longer, stand-up surfboard
kioe – small surfboard, belly board (2ft to 4ft long)
koa – native hardwood tree used in making furniture, bowls and canoes

kohola – whale
koi – brightly colored, ornamental Japanese carp
kokua – help, cooperation
kona – leeward side; a leeward wind
ko'olau – windward side
Ku – Polynesian god of many manifestations, including god of war, farming and fishing
kukui – candlenut tree and the official state tree; its oily nuts were once burned in lamps
kupuna – grandparent, elder

Laka – goddess of the *hula*
lanai – veranda
lau – leaf
lauhala – leaves of the *hala* plant used in weaving
laulau – a bundle made of pork or chicken and salted butterfish, wrapped in taro and *ti* leaves and steamed
lei – garland, usually of flowers, but also of leaves or shells
li hing mui – sweet-sour crack seed
liliko'i – passion fruit
limu – seaweed
loco moco – dish of rice topped with a hamburger, a fried egg and gravy
lolo – feeble-minded, crazy
lomilomi – traditional Hawaiian massage
Lono – Polynesian god of harvest, agriculture, fertility and peace
luakini – type of *heiau* (temple) dedicated to the war god Ku and used for human sacrifices
luau – traditional Hawaiian feast

mahalo – thank you
mahele – to divide; usually refers to Hawaii's 1848 land divisions
mahimahi – also called 'dolphin,' but actually a type of fish unrelated to the marine mammal
mai tai – alcoholic drink made from rum, grenadine, and lemon and pineapple juices
maile – native plant with twining habit and fragrant sap; often used to make *lei*
makahiki – traditional annual festival dedicated to the agricultural god Lono
makai – toward the sea
malama 'aina – to take care of the islands' natural resources
malihini – newcomer, visitor
malo – loincloth
mana – spiritual power
mano – shark
mauka – toward the mountains; inland
mele – song, chant
menehune – the 'little people' who built many of Hawaii's fishponds and *heiau* according to legend
milo – native shade tree with beautiful hardwood

naupaka – native shrub with delicate white flowers
Neighbor Islands – the term used to refer to the main Hawaiian Islands other than O'ahu
nene – native goose; Hawaii's state bird
nisei – second-generation Japanese immigrants
niu – coconut palm
noni – Indian mulberry; a small tree with yellow fruit used medicinally
nui – large, great, many, much; *aloha nui loa* means very much aloha

'ohana – family, extended family
ohia lehua – native Hawaiian tree with feathery, pom-pom-like flowers
olo – traditional longer, wooden surfboard
onaga – mild-tasting red snapper
ono – wahoo fish
'ono – delicious
'ono kine grinds – good food
'opah – moonfish
'opakapaka – blue snapper

pakalolo – marijuana; literally, 'crazy tobacco'
pali – cliff
paniolo – cowboy
papio – jack fish
pau – finished, no more
Pele – goddess of volcanoes
pho – Vietnamese soup of beef broth, noodles and fresh herbs
piko – navel, umbilical cord
pili – bunchgrass used for thatching houses
pipikaula – salted, dried beef served broiled; Hawaiian-style beef jerky
pohaku – rock
pohuehue – morning glory
poi – staple Hawaiian starch made of *taro*
poke – cubed raw fish mixed with shoyu, sesame oil, salt, chili pepper and other condiments
puka – hole; small shells that are made into necklaces
pupu – snack food, hors d'oeuvres
pu'u – hill, cinder cone
pu'uhonua – place of refuge

raku – style of Japanese pottery characterized by a rough, handmade appearance

saimin – Hawaiian version of Japanese noodle soup
sansei – third-generation Japanese immigrants
shaka – hand gesture used in Hawaii as a greeting or sign of local pride
shoyu – soy sauce
soba – buckwheat noodles

talk story – to strike up a conversation, make small talk

tapa – see *kapa*

taro – see *kalo*

teppanyaki – Japanese style of cooking with an iron grill

ti – see *ki*

tiki – see *ki'i*

uhu – parrotfish

uku – gray snapper

ukulele – stringed musical instrument common to Hawaiian music

wahine – woman

wikiwiki – hurry, quick

Behind the Scenes

THIS BOOK

The 3rd edition of *Honolulu, Waikiki & O'ahu* was written by Glenda Bendure and Ned Friary. They also wrote the 1st and 2nd editions, which were entitled *Oahu*. Jake Howard contributed the boxed text on surfing to the Outdoors chapter. The Language chapter was largely based on previous work by Nanette Naioma Napoleon for *Hawaii 7*, and the Health chapter was adapted from material written by Dr David Goldberg. This guidebook was commissioned in Lonely Planet's Oakland office, and produced by the following:

Commissioning Editor Emily K Wolman
Coordinating Editor Brooke Clark, Kyla Gillzan
Coordinating Cartographer Corey Hutchinson
Coordinating Layout Designer Palmer Higgs Pty Ltd (Simon Longstaff, Andrew Seymour)
Assisting Editors Lutie Clark, Thalia Kalkipsakis, Kristin Odijk
Cover Designer Wendy Wright
Color Designer Jessica Rose
Project Manager Chris Love, John Shippick
Managing Editor Melanie Dankel
Managing Cartographer Alison Lyall, Emma McNichol, Andrew Smith
Language Content Coordinator Quentin Frayne

Thanks to Carol Chandler, Erin Corrigan, Sally Darmody, Jennifer Garrett, Laura Jane, Katie Lynch, Kate McDonald, Nanette Naioma Napoleon, Raphael Richards & Celia Wood.

THANKS
NED FRIARY & GLENDA BENDURE

Mahalo to all those who aided us with our research and worked with us on this project. A special thanks to LP's Emily Wolman and Erin Corrigan for their support and inspiring suggestions. And a shout-out to Glenn Thering, who tramped the beaches, rode the waves and shared his favorite haunts with us. Thanks to Joan Lima for insights on the environmental challenges facing the island, to Lynelle Miyashiro of the Oahu Visitors Bureau for updates on island happenings, to Allen Tom from the Hawaiian Islands Humpback Whale National Marine Sanctuary, to Teruo Koike for his insights on all things Japanese, and to the helpful people at the Office of Hawaiian Affairs, Na Ala Hele and the Division of Forestry & Wildlife.

OUR READERS

Many thanks to the travelers who used the last edition and wrote to us with helpful hints, useful advice and interesting anecdotes:

Frederik Alme, Sebastien Ananian-Cooper, Kellie Avery, Kurt & Monique Bergwerff, Walter Chapko, Erin Culling, Kathy Fadigan, Corinne Florit, Ilima Hamasaki, Cecilia Han, Jo Ingle, Lindsay Jones, Tim Julou, Laura LaLonde, Roger Lyman, Sarah Maguire, Anja Maria, Gerrard Meneaud, Barrett Rabinow, Mark Schlagboehmer, James Sears, Jill Shaw, Glen Stevens, Jessica Viola

---

THE LONELY PLANET STORY

The story begins with a classic travel adventure: Tony and Maureen Wheeler's 1972 journey across Europe and Asia to Australia. There was no useful information about the overland trail then, so Tony and Maureen published the first Lonely Planet guidebook to meet a growing need.

From a kitchen table, Lonely Planet has grown to become the largest independent travel publisher in the world, with offices in Melbourne (Australia), Oakland (USA) and London (UK). Today Lonely Planet guidebooks cover the globe. There is an ever-growing list of books and information in a variety of media. Some things haven't changed. The main aim is still to make it possible for adventurous travelers to get out there – to explore and better understand the world.

At Lonely Planet we believe travelers can make a positive contribution to the countries they visit – if they respect their host communities and spend their money wisely. Every year 5% of company profit is donated to charities around the world.

SEND US YOUR FEEDBACK

We love to hear from travelers – your comments keep us on our toes and help make our books better. Our well-traveled team reads every word on what you loved or loathed about this book. Although we cannot reply individually to postal submissions, we always guarantee that your feedback goes straight to the appropriate authors, in time for the next edition. Each person who sends us information is thanked in the next edition – and the most useful submissions are rewarded with a free book.

To send us your updates – and find out about Lonely Planet events, newsletters and travel news – visit our award-winning website: **www.lonelyplanet.com/feedback**.

Note: We may edit, reproduce and incorporate your comments in Lonely Planet products such as guidebooks, websites and digital products, so let us know if you don't want your comments reproduced or your name acknowledged. For a copy of our privacy policy visit www.lonelyplanet.com/privacy.

Index

INDEX

INDEX

000 Map pages
000 Photograph pages

INDEX

| 12am | 1am | 2am | 3am | 4am | 5am | 6am | 7am | 8am | 9am | 10am | 11am | 12pm |

Mon / Sun

International Date Line

ARCTIC OCEAN

CHUKCHI SEA

Russia

Alaska (US)

3am

BEAUFORT SEA

Queen Elizabeth Is (Can)

Banks Is (Can)

Victoria Is (Can)

Ellesmere Is (Can)

BAFFIN BAY

9am Greenland (Denmark)

11am

GREENLAND SEA

NORWEGIAN SEA

4am

5am

Baffin Is (Can)

HUDSON BAY

Iceland

NORTH SEA

United Kingdom

Ireland

BERING SEA

2am

GULF OF ALASKA

Canada

6am

LABRADOR SEA

NORTH ATLANTIC OCEAN

8am

NORTH PACIFIC OCEAN

7am

8.30am

1am Midway Is (US)

United States

Bermuda (UK)

Azores (Port)

Portugal

Spain

Morocco

Hawaii (US)

Mexico

GULF OF MEXICO

The Bahamas

Cuba

Haiti

Canary Is (Sp)

Cape Verde

12pm

Mauritania

Mali

EQUATOR

Kiribati

Samoa

Guatemala

Nicaragua

CARIBBEAN SEA

Eastern Caribbean Islands

Senegal

Guinea

Burkina Faso

Liberia

Ghana

GULF OF GUINEA

2.30am

Tahiti

French Polynesia (Fr)

2am

Galapagos Is (Ecuador)

Panama

Colombia

Venezuela

Guyana

Suriname

Ecuador

Ascension (UK)

Tonga

12am

Cook Is (NZ)

1am

Pitcairn Is 3.30am (UK)

Easter Is (Chile)

Peru

7am

8am

Bolivia

Brazil

9am

SOUTH ATLANTIC OCEAN

New Zealand

12.45am Chatham Is (NZ)

SOUTH PACIFIC OCEAN

Paraguay

Chile

Uruguay

Argentina

Tristan da Cunha (UK)

Gough Is (UK)

Falkland Is (UK)

South Georgia & South Sandwich Is (UK)

Bouvet Is (Norway)

| 12am | 1am | 2am | 3am | 4am | 5am | 6am | 7am | 8am | 9am | 10am | 11am | 12pm |

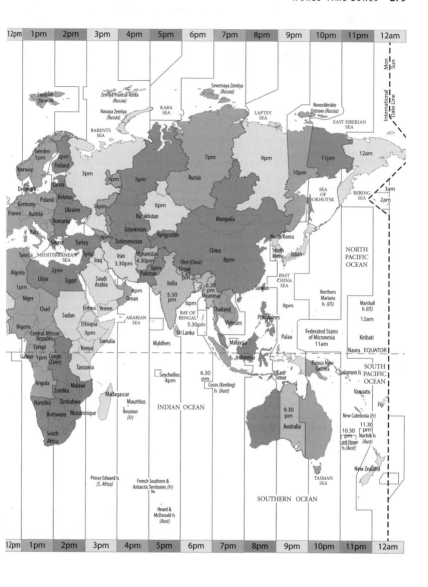

| 12pm | 1pm | 2pm | 3pm | 4pm | 5pm | 6pm | 7pm | 8pm | 9pm | 10pm | 11pm | 12am |

International Date Line

Mon
Sun

Svalbard (Norway)

Zemlya Frantsa-Iosifa (Russia)

Severnaya Zemlya (Russia)

KARA SEA

LAPTEV SEA

Novosibirskie Ostrovo (Russia)

EAST SIBERIAN SEA

Novaya Zemlya (Russia)

BARENTS SEA

Sweden 1pm
Finland 2pm

Norway

Denmark
Latvia
Germany Poland Belarus
France Austria Ukraine
Italy Romania
Greece Turkey
Tunisia MEDITERRANEAN SEA
Algeria Syria
Libya Iraq
Niger Egypt
Chad Saudi Arabia
Nigeria Sudan
Central African Republic Ethiopia
Congo
Gabon 1pm Congo (Zaire)
Angola Zambia Malawi
Namibia Zimbabwe
Botswana Mozambique
South Africa

3pm
4pm
5pm
6pm
Kazakhstan
Uzbekistan
4pm Turkmenistan Kyrgyzstan
Iran 3.30pm Afghanistan 4.30pm
Pakistan 5pm
Oman
Eritrea Yemen
ARABIAN SEA
Somalia
Kenya
Tanzania
3pm
Madagascar
Mauritius Reunion (Fr)

7pm
Russia
6pm
Mongolia
China 8pm
Tibet (China)
Nepal 5.45 pm
India
5.30 pm
6pm
Myanmar 6.30 pm
BAY OF BENGAL
Thailand
Sri Lanka 5.30pm
Maldives
Vietnam
Malaysia
Indonesia

9pm
10pm
11pm
12am
SEA OF OKHOTSK
North Korea
South Korea
Japan
EAST CHINA SEA
Taiwan
Philippines
Palau
East Timor

BERING SEA
3am
2am
NORTH PACIFIC OCEAN
Northern Mariana Is (US)
9pm
Federated States of Micronesia 11am
Marshall Is (US)
12am
Kiribati
Nauru EQUATOR
SOUTH PACIFIC OCEAN
Papua New Guinea
Solomon Is
Vanuatu
New Caledonia (Fr)
Fiji
11.30 pm
10.30 pm Norfolk Is (Aust)
Lord Howe Is (Aust)
New Zealand

Seychelles 4pm
Cocos (Keeling) Is (Aust) 6.30 pm
INDIAN OCEAN
Australia 9.30 pm
TASMAN SEA

Prince Edward Is (S. Africa)
French Southern & Antarctic Territories (Fr)
Heard & McDonald Is (Aust)
SOUTHERN OCEAN

| 12pm | 1pm | 2pm | 3pm | 4pm | 5pm | 6pm | 7pm | 8pm | 9pm | 10pm | 11pm | 12am |

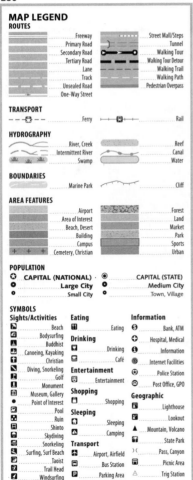

MAP LEGEND

ROUTES

- Freeway
- Primary Road
- Secondary Road
- Tertiary Road
- Lane
- Track
- Unsealed Road
- One-Way Street
- Street Mall/Steps
- Tunnel
- Walking Tour
- Walking Tour Detour
- Walking Trail
- Walking Path
- Pedestrian Overpass

TRANSPORT

- Ferry
- Rail

HYDROGRAPHY

- River, Creek
- Intermittent River
- Swamp
- Reef
- Canal
- Water

BOUNDARIES

- Marine Park
- Cliff

AREA FEATURES

- Airport
- Area of Interest
- Beach, Desert
- Building
- Campus
- Cemetery, Christian
- Forest
- Land
- Market
- Park
- Sports
- Urban

POPULATION

- CAPITAL (NATIONAL)
- Large City
- Small City
- CAPITAL (STATE)
- Medium City
- Town, Village

SYMBOLS

Sights/Activities
- Beach
- Bodysurfing
- Buddhist
- Canoeing, Kayaking
- Christian
- Diving, Snorkeling
- Golf
- Monument
- Museum, Gallery
- Point of Interest
- Pool
- Ruin
- Shinto
- Skydiving
- Snorkeling
- Surfing, Surf Beach
- Taoist
- Trail Head
- Windsurfing
- Zoo, Bird Sanctuary

Eating
- Eating

Drinking
- Drinking
- Café

Entertainment
- Entertainment

Shopping
- Shopping

Sleeping
- Sleeping
- Camping

Transport
- Airport, Airfield
- Bus Station
- Parking Area
- Gas Station

Information
- Bank, ATM
- Hospital, Medical
- Information
- Internet Facilities
- Police Station
- Post Office, GPO

Geographic
- Lighthouse
- Lookout
- Mountain, Volcano
- State Park
- Pass, Canyon
- Picnic Area
- Trig Station
- Waterfall

LONELY PLANET OFFICES

Australia
Head Office
Locked Bag 1, Footscray, Victoria 3011
☎ 03 8379 8000, fax 03 8379 8111
talk2us@lonelyplanet.com.au

USA
150 Linden St, Oakland, CA 94607
☎ 510 893 8555, toll free 800 275 8555
fax 510 893 8572
info@lonelyplanet.com

UK
72–82 Rosebery Ave,
Clerkenwell, London EC1R 4RW
☎ 020 7841 9000, fax 020 7841 9001
go@lonelyplanet.co.uk

Published by Lonely Planet Publications Pty Ltd
ABN 36 005 607 983

© Lonely Planet Publications Pty Ltd 2006

© photographers as indicated 2006

Cover photographs: Hula girl dashboard ornament, Photolibrary (front); Surfer on Waikiki Beach, Holger Leue/Lonely Planet Images (back). Many of the images in this guide are available for licensing from Lonely Planet Images: www.lonelyplanetimages.com.

Printed through Colorcraft Ltd, Hong Kong.
Printed in China